DOCUMENTARY HISTORY *of the* STATE OF MAINE

Containing

THE BAXTER MANUSCRIPTS

Volume IX

Edited by

James Phinney Baxter, A. M., Litt. D.

HERITAGE BOOKS
2019

HERITAGE BOOKS
AN IMPRINT OF HERITAGE BOOKS, INC.

Books, CDs, and more—Worldwide

For our listing of thousands of titles see our website
at
www.HeritageBooks.com

A Facsimile Reprint
Published 2019 by
HERITAGE BOOKS, INC.
Publishing Division
5810 Ruatan Street
Berwyn Heights, Md. 20740

Originally published Portland 1910

Cover illustration from
The Pine Tree Coast
by Samuel Adams Drake

— Publisher's Notice —
In reprints such as this, it is often not possible to remove blemishes from the original. We feel the contents of this book warrant its reissue despite these blemishes and hope you will agree and read it with pleasure.

International Standard Book Number
Paperbound: 978-0-7884-1483-1

PREFACE

THIS volume bring us to the period of the Revolutionary War, a period of much interest to students of our history. I trust that persons having knowledge of unpublished documents relating to the subject will call my attention to them, that I may publish them in the next volume should they prove of interest.

JAMES PHINNEY BAXTER.

61 DEERING STREET,
 January 12, 1910.

CHRONOLOGICAL TABLE OF CONTENTS

				PAGE
1766	June	19	A COUNCIL IN BOSTON	1
	June	20	Message, Fra Bernard	2
			Report of Committee on Petition of Henry Young Brown,	4
	June	23	Resolve, on Report on Pet^n of Henry Young Brown,	5
	June	24	Resolve,	6
	June	27	Supplies to Eastern Indians,	7
	Aug.	11	Fra^s Waldo to the Surveyor General,	8
	Aug.	18	A Council in Boston,	10
			John Cotton Esqre to Ter Powell, Enoch Freeman, Alex^r Ross & Stephen Longfellow Esqr .	11
	Oct.	2	Letter, Govr Wentworth to Govr Bernard,	11
	Dec.	8	" Enoch Freeman & Alex^r Ross to Hon. A. Oliver,	14
1767	Jan.	14	Petition of Inhab^{ts} of Broad Bay,	14
			" " " " Freetown,	16
			" " " " Muscongus & Medumcook,	17
			" " " " the Town of Andover,	18
	Jan.	28	" " S. Downe & M. Thornton,	20
			" " Nathan Jones & others,	21
	Jan.	30	Plan Accepted,	22
	Feb.	5	Resolve,	23
			Report on Petition of Capt. H. Y. Brown,	24
			Petition,	25
			" of Josiah Richardson, Agent,	26
	May	27	" " B. Mulliken & M. Bridges,	28
	May	30	Resolve,	29
	June	6	Message,	34
	June	11	"	30
			" Fra: Bernard,	30
	June	12	Resolve,	31
			Act of Incorporation,	32
	June	13	Order,	34
	June	17	Message,	38
	June	18	Letter, John Brown to Andrew Oliver,	39
			Pet^n of Inhabitants of Machias,	39
	June	25	Message,	41
			Report of Committee *in re* Township of Conway,	42

CHRONOLOGICAL TABLE

				PAGE
1767	Aug.	26	Letter, Gov. Wentworth to Gov. Bernard,	47
	Sept.	10	" " " " '	48
			" Gov. Bernard to Gov. Wentworth,	49
	Sept.	28	" " " Thos Goldthwait Esqr	52
	Sept.	29	" " " "	54
	Oct.	12	Petition of the Officers and Soldiers of Fort Pownall together with the Inhabitants,	56
	Oct.	21	Letter, from Dennys De Berdt,	58
	Dec.	30	Extracts from speech, Fra Bernard,	59
1768	Jan.		Petition of Josiah Richardson, Agent for the Petitioners,	59
	Jan.	4	Deposition of Simon Ayer,	60
	Jan.	19	Message, Fra Bernard,	61
			Petition of Henry Y. Brown,	62
			" " John Cox,	64
	Feb.	15	Resolve,	65
	Feb.	16	Message,	66
	Feb.	18	Extract from Message to the Governor,	66
			Bill for incorporating Phillipstown,	67
	Mar.	3	Resolve passed on the Petition of Abraham Anderson,	73
	May		Petition of Selectmen of Sanford,	68
	May	23	Deposition of Josiah Richardson,	70
			Petition of Inhabitants of Town of Windham,	70
	May	25	" " Inhabts of Sebascodegin Island,	74
	June	1	" " the Selectmen of Gorham,	77
			Memorial of James Small and others.	78
			Report of Committee on petition of Ichabod Jones,	80
	June	7	Vote on same,	80
	June	15	Report of Committee on Petition of H. Y. Brown,	82
			Petition of David Bean & others,	83
	July	12	Letter, Wm. Tyng, "Sheriff of Cumberland" to Gov. Bernard,	84
			Letter, Dudley Carlton to Col. Goldthwait,	84
	July	22	Earl of Stirling's Advertisement,	85
	Aug.	10	Earl of Stirling to Gov. Bernard,	87
	Aug.	30	Reply of Council to Stirling,	88
	Sept.	7	Report of Committee appointed to take into consideration the Earl of Stirling's Letter,	88
			Proclamation by Francis Bernard,	90
1770	Jan.	10	Petition of Town of York,	91
			" to Govr Hutchinson by Inhabitants of the Fifth Township,	92
			Petition of B. Mulliken & Moody Bridges, Agents,	94
	April	4	Vote on petition of Ichabod Jones & others,	95
	April	7	Resolve *in re* above petition,	97

			PAGE
1770	April	9 Resolve on petition of Benjamin Mulliken and Moody Bridges,	98
	April	14 Resolve *in re* petition of Inhabitants of Cape Elizabeth,	99
	April	24 Report on Petition of D. Phips & others,	99
		" " " " J. Fuller & others,	100
	April	26 Resolve *in re* Capt. Henry Young Brown,	101
		Report of Committee *in re* Capt. Henry Young Brown,	103
	Sept.	Lt. Govr's Speech,	103
		Petition of Joseph Frye,	106
	Oct.	" " H. Eggleston,	107
		" & Remonstrance of S. Livermore & others,	108
	Oct.	30 Resolve in favor of Joseph Frye,	110
	Nov.	2 " on the Petition of Hezekiah Egglestone,	110
	Nov.	6 " " " " " "	111
		Jonathan Longfellow's Memorial to Govr Hutchinson,	112
	Nov.	9 Memorial of Inhabitants of Mass. Bay to Govr Hutchinson,	114
		Petition of H. Y. Brown,	116
	Nov.	16 Trade with Indians,	117
	Dec.	Petition of Pondstown,	117
1771	April	Act relative to York Bridge,	119
		Act of Incorporation,	122
		" " "	124
		" " "	126
		Petition in behalf of George Town,	129
	May	30 Extract from Speech,	130
	June	11 Report on Petition of S. Livermore & others,	131
	June	19 Message,	132
	June	21 Committee appointed,	134
	June	24 Act of Incorporation,	135
	June	27 Resolve,	136
	Sept.	12 Report of Commissioners on Machias,	137
		Memorial of Arthur Savage,	143
	Nov.	27 Proceedings of the Council Regarding the Riot at Falmouth,	147
	Dec.	18 The Petition of the Proprietors of the Kennebec Purchase,	149
1772	Jan.	2 Thomas Scammell to Govr Hutchinson,	152
	Jan.	3 Govr Hutchinson to the Earl of Hillsborough,	155
	Jan.	13 Dr Franklin to Hon. Thos Cushing & Committee,	156
	Jan.	31 Govr Hutchinson to the Earl of Hillsborough,	158
		Petition of James Chase & others,	159
	April	22 Confirmation to Capt. Joshua Fuller,	161

CHRONOLOGICAL TABLE

				PAGE
1772	April	22	Confirmation to David Phips & others,	162
			Resolve, confirming Plan of Township to S. Livermore & others,	163
	April	23	Resolve Confirming Grant to Hon. James Otis & others,	164
	June		Petition of the Inhabitants of Boothbay,	166
	June	6	Letter, Benjⁿ Foster & others to Rev. James Lyon,	172
	June	8	Petition of Benjamin Foster and others,	173
			Answer of Rev. James Lyon,	174
	June	10	Memorial of J. Wyman & others,	175
			Saml March's Petition,	177
	June	17	Objection against the Petition,	179
	July	7	Act of Incorporation,	181
			Memorial of the Associated Ministers of York,	182
	July	9	Answer,	183
			An Act to encourage the Preaching of the Gospel,	185
	Nov.	13	Govr Hutchinson to the Earl of Dartmouth,	186
1773	Jan.		Petition of members of the Church of England,	188
	Mar.	8	" " Selectmen of Winthrop,	190
			" " Members of the Church of England,	191
	May	31	" " Selectmen of North Yarmouth,	194
			Deposition of Stephen Holt,	195
			Petition of James Miller and others,	196
	June	14	Act of Incorporation,	199
	June	15	" " "	200
			Petition of Noah Johnson & others,	202
	Oct.	23	Deposition of Benjⁿ Holt,	205
	Oct.	26	Govr Hutchinson to Lord Dartmouth,	206
1774	Jan.	8	Deposition of Capt. Joseph Baker and John Knox,	208
	Jan.	18	The Memorial of Samuel Freeman,	208
	Jan.	25	Petition of William Elder,	210
	Jan.	26	" " Timothy Walker,	212
			" " Inhab^{ts} of Freetown,	216
			" " Joseph Josselyn,	217
	Feb.	5	Resolve,	219
			Petition of Saml Whittemore & Amos Lawrence,	220
	Feb.	8	Henry Young Brown,	222
	Feb.	16	Account Allowed,	225
			Act of Incorporation,	226
			Petition of John Gardner & others,	229
			Report on the Petition of Seth Sweetsir & others,	230
	May	16	Petition of John Brown & others,	231
	June	3	Boothbay Petition,	233
	June	11	Resolve,	232
	June	15	" that petition in behalf of Town of Boothbay be granted,	234

OF CONTENTS xi

				PAGE
1774	June	20	Resolves passed by the Town of Buxton,	235
			Bond given by Dum^r Sewall and Jordan Parker,	236
1775	Mar.	6	Damariscotta Resolves, etc.,	237
	Mar.	29	Letter from J. Brown,	238
	April	6	" Silvester Gardiner to Dr. John McLeeline,	242
	April	26	" from the Selectmen of Falmouth,	242
	April	29	" from H. Mowatt,	243
			" of Samuel Thompson,	243
	May	3	" from Brunswick,	244
	May	5	Extracts from Letter of Hon. Enoch Freeman,	245
	May	6	Order *in re* Masts &c.,	246
			Letter from Dummer Sewall,	247
	May	10	" " Edwd Parry,	247
			" " "	249
			" Edwd Parry to the President of the Delegates of the Province of the Massachusetts Bay,	249
	May	14	Letter from Falmouth Comm^{ee} of Correspondence to the Provincial Congress,	250
	May	15	Letter from Col. Jedidiah Preble to The Comm^{ee} of Safety at Cambridge,	253
			Letter to the Eastern Indians,	254
	May	20	" of Committee to Gen'l Preble,	256
	May	22	" from Abiel Wood to the Comm^{ee} for the County of Lincoln,	258
	May	23	Letter from Mr. Dummer Sewall in behalf of the County Committee at Georgetown,	259
	May	27	Letter from Partridgefield to the Provincial Congress,	261
	May	29	Letter from William Shirreff, D. Q. M. G.,	262
	May	30	Agreement between Maj. William Sherriff D. Q. M. G. and Ephraim Perkins,	263
			Letter from William Shirreff,	264
			" " "	264
	June	3	" " Winslow to the Comm^{ee} for the County of Lincoln,	265
			Acct. of taking a sloop belonging to Arundel,	266
			Letter from the Committee of Waldoborough to the Committee at Pownalborough,	267
	June	7	Letter from Penobscot to the Provincial Congress,	268
			Petition of Edwd Parry,	269
	June	9	Letter from John Lane,	270
			" " Elihu Hewes,	271
			Deposition of Samuel Smith,	273
			Provincial Congress,	274
			Deposition of Eben^r Whittier,	274
			Report on Jones & Hicks,	275
	June	10	Letter from Elihu Hewes,	277

CHRONOLOGICAL TABLE

				PAGE
1775	June	14	Extract of a letter from Hon. Eonch Freeman,	278
	June	14	Account of the Capture of the King's Cutter at Machias,	280
			Letter from Jedidiah Preble & Enoch Freeman,	283
	June	17	"Letter from the Com^tee of Machias relative to fitting out an Arm'd Vessel — & Report thereon accepted,"	283
	June	23	Answer to Petition from Belfast, etc.,	284
			Receipt,	285
			Report on John Lane's Account,	286
			Resolve *in re* John Lane,	286
	June	26	" " Machias petition,	286
	June	28	Letter from Committee of Biddeford,	288
			Report on petition of Thos Donnell & others,	290
	July	8	Letter from Bowdoinham,	290
	July	19	Stephen Jones' conduct justified,	292
	July	22	Letter from Stephen Jones,	293
	July	24	" James Warren Esq.,	293
			J. A. to Mrs. Abigail Adams,	294
	July	25	Report,	295
	July	28	Address to the Continental Congress,	296
			" " " " "	297
			Representation of Bristol,	297
	July	29	Report on petition of D. Scott & others,	298
	Aug.	3	Order,	299
			Bond given by John Hobby and Obe Hubbs,	300
			Report on Examination of Edward Parry,	300
			Account,	302
	Sept.	5	Lord Dartmouth to Major Gen¹ Howe,	304
	Sept.	9	Letter from Joseph Simpson,	305
	Oct.		Accounts of Losses sustained at Falmouth,	305
			Letter from Committee of Safety at Machias,	310
	Oct.	20	Orders,	315
			Account of Loss & Damage sustained by Elisha Snow,	315
	Oct.	24	Memorial of Com^ee of Safety of N. Yarmouth & New Glocester,	316
			Letter from Jer^h Powell,	319
	Nov.		Report,	320
	Nov.	14	Letter to Gen¹ Frye,	321
	Dec.	21	Report *in re* Seaports	321
1776	Jan.	6	Letter from Haunce Robinson & Wm. Walton,	322
	Jan.	15	" " Stephen Parker to Gen. Washington,	322
	Jan.	16	Copy of Letter from Stephen Parker to Christopher Prince "Enclosed to Gen¹ Washington,"	324
	Jan.	18	Copy of Receipt,	326
	Jan.	19	Letter from James Lyon,	326

				PAGE
1776	Jan.	19	Letter to the Committee of Safety at Machias,	327
	Feb.	1	Ld George Germain to Maj^r Genl Howe,	328
			Loss at Majorbagwaduce,	331
	Feb.	3	Petition of Nathan Jones,	332
			Letter from William Cutter,	333
	Feb.	16	Report *in re* Petition of Nathan Jones,	323
			" on the letter of M. Lyon of Machias,	334
	Feb.	20	Deposition of Jeremiah Wardwell,	335
			Letter from Edwd Parry,	335
	Mar.	11	" " Selectmen for Sturbridge to Capt. Timothy Parker,	336
	Mar.	19	Letter from Timothy Pickering,	337
	Mar.	20	" " Major Daniel Ilsley,	338
	Mar.	28	" " the Committee of Brunswick,	339
	May	2	Report in respect to Powder,	340
	May	7	Extract from Letter of General Howe to Lord George Germain,	342
	May	11	Petition of Stephen Parker,	343
	May	13	Letter from "	346
	May	24	Complaint against Rev. Jacob Bailey,	349
	May	25	Letter from the Committee at Machias,	350
	May	27	" " Hon. Charles Chauncey,	352
	May	28	Bond of Rev. Jacob Bailey,	352
	May	29	Representatives at Watertown, York Co.,	354
	June	4	Letter from James Sullivan,	355
			" " Committees of Newbury, Haverhill, Bath, etc.,	356
	June	8	Report, ,	358
	June	9	Letter from the Committee of Machias	358
	June	19	" " Benj. Austin,	359
	June	20	" " William Loud,	360
	June	25	" " Hon. James Bowdoin,	361
	June	30	" " "	362
	Aug.	3	Subscriptions *in re* the Canada Expedition,	365
	Aug.	9	Letter from Timothy Langdon,	366
			" " Col. Jon: Mitchell,	366
	Aug.	16	" " Thomas Fletcher,	367
	Aug.	20	" " Major Danl Ilsley,	369
	Aug.	22	" " Thos Rice,	373
	Aug.	28	" " Francis Shaw,	374
	Sept.	3	" " James McCobb,	377
	Sept.	7	Report on Taxes,	378
			Letter from James Lyon,	379
	Oct.	4	Certificate, *in re* Major Daniel Ilsley,	385
	Oct.	11	Petition of Maj^r Danl Ilsley,	386
	Oct.	15	Extract of a letter,	387

CHRONOLOGICAL TABLE

				PAGE
1776	Oct.	19	Order, respecting the purchase of cloth for Troops, ...	388
	Oct.	23	Report, ...	388
	Oct.	28	Copy of record, Rev. Jacob Bailey's Case,	389
			Rev. Mr. Bailey's reasons for not reading the Declaration of Independence, ...	390
			Report of Selectmen of Town of Falmouth,	394
	Nov.	3	Letter, Jon^a Eddy to the Committee of the Township of Machias, . , ...	394
			Letter, Jon^a Eddy to Capt Stephen Smith,	395
	Nov.	12	" " " the Hon^{bl} Council & Assel^y at Boston, ...	396
	Nov.	13	Petition of the Committee for the County of Cumberland, ...	396
	Nov.	16	Letter from Charles Cushing, ...	397
	Nov.	27	" " William Tupper, ...	399
	Dec.	4	" " Roland Cushing, ...	399
			" " Noah Mo^{ton} Littlefield, . .	400
			" " Col. Jon^a Mitchell, ...	400
	Dec.	9	" " William Lithgow Junr, . .	401
	Dec.	23	" " Joseph Dimuck, ...	402
1777	Jan.	3	" " Col. Eben^r Francis, . . .	403
	Jan.	23	" " the Council to Gov. Nicholas Cook,	405
	Jan.	27	" " John Preble, ...	405
	Feb.	14	" " Selectmen & Comm^{ee} of Safety for Winslow, ...	407
	Feb.	16	Letter from Ezekiel Pattee, ...	409
	April	25	" " Tristram Jordan, ...	410
	May	21	" " Jon^a Lowder, ...	411
	May	22	" " Jonas Mason, ...	412
	May	27	" " Col. Josiah Brewer, . . .	413
	May	30	" " J. Allan, ...	414
	June	4	" " J. Allen (Allan), ...	418
	June	5	Report upon Mr. Hancock's letter and the Petition of the Com^{tee} of Machias, . . .	419
			Report of Committee appointed to consider papers relative to David Thatcher Esqr .	422
			Report of the Committee appointed to consider the Acco^{ts} of John Allen Esq., . . .	422
	June	6	Letter from Francis Shaw, ...	424
	June	7	" " Saml Jordan Esq., . . .	425
	June	12	" " Charles Chauncey Esq., . . .	426
	June	18	" " Col. J. Allan, ...	426
			" " George Stillman, ...	436
			" " Col. Moses Little, ...	437
	June	20	" to John Allan Esq., ...	437

OF CONTENTS XV

					PAGE
1777	June 25	"	from Jon^a Warner,	438
	July 4	"	"	Francis Shaw,	439
	July 13	"	"	Col. Alex^r Campbell,	440
	July 14	"	"	Meshech Weare,	442
	July 15	"	"	Francis Shaw,	443
	July 16	"	"	Meshech Weare,	443

DOCUMENTARY HISTORY

OF THE

STATE OF MAINE

At a Council held at the Council Chamber in Boston, on Thursday ye 19th June 1766 —
Present in Council His Excel{y} the Governor

Saml Danforth	James Russell	Isaac Royall
Thomas Flucker	Benja Lincoln	Nathll Ropes
John Erving Esq{rs}	John Bradbury	Wm Brattle
Royall Tyler Esq{rs}	Gam{l} Bradford	Samuel White
Thos Hubbard	Jer: Powell	Harr{n} Gray
James Pitts		

His Excellency acquainted the Board that the Establishment made in the present Session of the General Court, for Castle William, & Fort Pownall had been laid before him; by which Establishment the Garrisons of those two Fortresses are so reduced, that he apprehends them to be unsafe, while they are thus weakened and therefore cannot give his Consent thereto and desired the Advice of the Board on this Occasion —

The Board thereupon unanimously declared that their concurring the House in the said Reduction, was not because they really approved of it, but because they tho't it better to have smaller Garrisons at those places, than none at all, and thereupon unanimously —

Advised that his Excellency represent the true State of the Case in a Message to the House of Representatives and move them to reconsider the said Establishment, and place such respectable Garrisons, in those two Fortresses as shall be a sufficient Protection to them —

A true Copy from the Council Minute Book

Attest: A Oliver Sec^r

Message. June 20, 1766

Gentlemen of the House of Representatives.

Having had laid befor— me your Resolution for the Establishment of the Garrisons of his Majesty— Fortresses, Castle William and Fort Pownall, for the year ensuing, I have communicated to his Majesty's Council my reasons why I cannot consent to any Reduction of the Garrison of the former, nor so great a reduction of the Garrison of the latter, which I perswade my self have been deemed conclusive by them, and would be so by every one, who is really acquainted with the State of those Fortresses.

As you did not consult me, the Captain General, on a proposal tending so greatly to render those Fortresses, for the Security of which I am answerable, weak and insecure, I did not intend to trouble you with my Sentiments on this Occasion. But the Council having unaminously joined with me in concern at and disapprobation of this injudicious Measure, and having given their Advice that I should endeavour to divert it, by recommending to you a reconsideration of this Business, I cannot refuse complying with their request, and therefore do earnestly recommend to you, that you would fully and seriously reconsider this business before it is out of your Power to alter your late Resolutions.

I always have had, and have continually expressed a Desire

that the two royal Fortresses, which have been committed to the Government of this Province, should be continued to it; I have considered it as a Trust reflecting great honour on the Province, at no great expence; and I have always intended to use my little Influence to obtain the Continuance of this Trust, whenever any new regulations should require an interest for that Purpose.

But Gentlemen, this will be impracticable, if you will not make Provisions for sufficient Garrisons for those Fortresses; at least my Mouth must be shut, unless I can give it as my Opinion that you have made such Provision; which it will be impossible for me to do, if you make any reduction at Castle William, or a reduction greater than six or eight Privates at Fort Pownall.

If you are desirous of saving the Expence of these Garrisons, your best way will be to surrender the Forts directly rather than to give them up indirectly by withdrawing the Garrisons by piece-meal. The greatest Inconvenience of this purpose will be the uneasiness it will create among the People: for which reason I shall do all I can to prevent it; and I think so ought you.

If you will enable me to keep these Fortresses by renewing the present Establishment of the Castle, and reducing that of Fort Pownall no lower than I have before mentioned, I will use my utmost endeavours that they shall be continued to this Government. But if you will put it out of my Power to retain these Fortresses, I desire it may be remembered that neither I nor the Council have spared Pains to prevent this unadvisable Reduction taking effect, at this time.

I sent you at the same Time a Copy of the Minutes of the Advice of Council given to me upon this Occasion, which you will perceive to be unanimous in a full Council

Fra Bernard

Council Chamber, June 20th 1766

Report of Committee.

The Committee to whom was Reffered the petition of Capt Henry Young Brown having attended that Service and find that he purchased a Township of this Province in the year 1764 and that he Lay^d out the same according to order and presented a plan of the Same for acceptance & which was accepted and the Lands therein was Confirmed to him his heirs and assigns for Ever on the 7th of June 1764 he complying with the Conditions of the Grant which we find he hath done the Committee also find that he hath made Considerable Improvements and would have made much Greater had he not been disturbed by the Government of New hampshire who Clames almoste the whole of s^d Township by a Line they have Run from the N E Branch of Salmon falls River that Persons Claming under New hampshire have Lay^d out a Considerable part of s^d Land into Lotts and that the petitioner and two of his Settlers are now Sued – Actions of Ejectment which actions are now depending in the province of New hampshire for Land lying on the Eastwardly part of their Claim the Com^{tte} also find that the Line Run by the Committee from this province Last March from the head of the Main Branch of Salmon falls River Takes off Eight Thousand five hundred and forty four acres of the west Side of s^d Browns Township the Committee also find that the General Court Last Novr Ordered the petitioner to Go forward with his Settlement & Improvement in s^d Township and if any person Should attempt to Lay out any of the Lands in s^d Town or make any Settlement there the said petitioner Should warn them against it and give Information to this Court who Engag^d to Relive him in Such manner as Should be thought Best begg Leave to Report that the petitioner be and hereby is Directed to defend all actions that are or Shall be Brought against him for Lands he purchesed of this province to the Eastward of the afores^d Line Run by order of this Court Last March at the Expence of this province he being Directed to do his Endeavour to git all actions against him or those under him Continued untill a final Settlement of the Line between the province of New hampshire and the province of Main So called that the petitioner be directed to prosecute at the Expence of this province such person or persons that have or Shall enter on S^d Land under the Title of New hampshire to the Eastward of the Line Run Last March by order of this Court he the petitioner following the orders of this Court Relitive theretoo that he have Liberty to draw out of the province Tresury Twenty pounds for that use & purpose he to be accountable for the Same, And that there also be Granted unto the petitioner Eight thousand five hundred and forty four acres of Lands adjoyning to the Eastwardly part of his Township or to either of the two other Townships Lay^d out at or near pigwacket So Called one Lay^d out To Col^o Jos. Frye the other to the propriators of Rowley Cannedy he to Give Bonds to the province Tresurer to Settle the Same with Eighteen familyes in Six years from the Confirmation of a plan of s^d Land which he – to Return for acceptance in one year that s^d petitioner Give a full discharge from any farther demands on this Government for the afores^d Eight thousand five hundred and forty four acres taken off of the West Side of his Township by the above s^d Line Run by order of this Court

al which is humbly Submitted by

       Joseph Gerrish p^r order

Resolve.

On the Report of the Committee on the Pet^n of Henry Young Brown
In the House of Representatives June 23 1766
Resolved that there be granted to the Petitioner Eight thousand five hundred & forty four Acres of Land adjoyning

to the Eastwardly Part of his Township or to either of the two other Townships laid out at or near Pigwackett so called, one laid out to Coll° Joseph Fry, the other to the Town of Rowley Canada he giving Bond to the Province Treasurer to settle the same with Eighteen familys in six years from the Confirmation of a Plan of said Town which he is to return for Acceptance in one year And also giving a full Discharge from any further Demands on this Government for the Aforesaid Quantity of 8544 Acres taken off from his West Side of his Town by the Line run by order of this Court

  Sent up for Concurrence   T. Cushing Spk^r

In Council June 25th 1766 Read & Concur^d

           Jn° Cotton D Sec̃ry

  Consented to Fra Bernard

Resolve.

In the House of Representatives June 24 1766

On the further Consideration of the report of the Com^{tee} upon the Pet^n of Henry Young Brown

Resolved that the Pet^r be & hereby is directed to defend all Actions that are or shall be bro^t against him for Lands purchased of this Province to the Eastward of the Line run by Order of this Court last March, at the Expence of this Province; he being directed to do his Endeavor to get all Actions against him or those under him continued till the final Settlement of the Line run between the Province of New Hampshire & the Province of Main so called, and that the Pet^r be directed to prosecute, at the Expence of this Province, such Person or Persons as have or shall enter on said Land under the Title of New Hampshire to the Eastward of the Line run last March by Order of this Court; he following the Directions of this Court relative thereto. And that he have Liberty to draw out of the Treasury of the Province Twenty Pounds for that Purpose for which he is to be accountable

  Sent up for Concurrence   T. Cushing Spk^r
In Council June 25th 1766,   Read & Concurred
            Jn° Cotton D Secry
 Consented to   Fra Bernard

Supplies to Eastern Indians. 1766.

Anno Regni Regis Georgii Tertii Sexto

 An Act for reviving and Continuing an Act made in Fourth year of his present Majestys Reign entitled an Act for Allowing Necessary Supplies to the Eastern Indians and for regulating the Tread with them; and preventing Abusses therein

 Whereas An Act made in the Fourth Year of his present Majestys Reign intitled An Act for Continuing & Amending An Act for Allowing Necessary Supplies to the Eastern Indians and for Regulating the Tread with them and for preventing Abusses therein, has been found Usefull & Beneficial and is Now Expired

 Be it therefore Enacted by the Govenor, Council & House of Representatives, that the said Act, in all & every Article & Clause, Matter and thing, be and is hereby revived, and shall be in force untill ye Thirtieth of June which will be in the Year of our Lord One thousand seven hundred & sixty seven.

In the House of Representatives.
 June 27 1766   Read a first time
 June 27, 1766   Read a second Time
 Read a third time & passd to be engrossd
  Sent up for Concurrence

In Council June 28, 1766
  Read a first time
  Read a second time and passed a concurrence to be engrossed

A Oliver Sec^y

Fra^s Waldo to the Surveyor General

Falmouth 11th August 1766 —

Sir
  On the 7th Currant about 11 Clo. AM. in consequence of an Information, we the Collector and Comptroller of this Port went to the House of Enoch Ilsley Shopkeeper, & after Searching it, demanded the key of a Store belonging to him, but that not being granted we proceeded to spring the Lock of said Store, in presence of Alex^r Ross Esqr a Magistrate, who attended in obedience to a Writ of Assistance shewn him by the said Collector, thereupon seven hogsheads, & one small Tierce of Sugar, & part of a hogshead, & part of a Tierce ditto, three hogsheads of Rum & 2 Ullages of ditto, were Seized and marked (with the T) by us the Collector & Compt^r and a lock then put on the said Store. Hereupon it became our endeavour to procure a proper place to remove the Goods into, as likewise Trucks and Horses for halling them, but every person to whom we applied, either refused, or were so backward that we could not obtain either.
  The same Evening about 6, Clo. upon hearing that a rescue of the Goods was intended, we acquainted the aforementioned Magistrate thereof in writing, and requested his Support & assistance (he being the only one then in Town) thereupon he granted us his Warrant directed to the Sheriff and his Deputys requiring them to assist us, After enquiring for the Sheriff we found he was at a considerable distance

from the Town— by this time (7 Clo) numbers of people were assembled round the dwelling House of the said Ilsley in passing whom when in a quest of a Deputy Sheriff we Rec^d some small Insult from, and having found the Deputy Sheriff To' Noyes we committed the said Warrant to him, and enjoyned him to do the needful to prevent a rescue of the Goods. Night coming on and people assembling in great numbers we went to the Dwelling House of the Comptroller being in the neighbourhood of the said Ilsleys and soon experienced the violence of the Mob, the House being beset and pelted with Clubs & Stones by intermissions until 10, or ½ past 10 Clock when they dispersed it being said that in that time the aforementioned Goods were carried away by persons unknown and disguised— the Morning following about 9 Clock the Collector having visited the said Store accordingly found all the said Goods missing, and in presence of Benj^a Wait Esqr enquired of said Ilsley whether he knew by whom they were taken away, but his Answer was that he did not, he being sick and confined to his House— the aforementioned Deputy Sheriff declares that he was forcibly borne away by the Mob, his pockets Rifled and the Warrant taken away & he prevented from doing his duty.

Upon the best information we can git a considerable part of the Town were active in the said Rescue, and we conceive it becomes our duty to inform that we think ourselves unsafe at present, and that it is out of our power to carry the Laws of Trade into Execution without some other support than what we at present have.

We are very respectfully Sir
   Your most obed^t Humble Servants
      Fra^s Waldo Collec^t
      Ar. Savage Compt^r

Copy
   Exam^d p Jno Cotton D. Sec̃ry

At a Council held at the Council Chamber in Boston upon Monday the 18th day of August 1766.

Present

His Excellency Francis Bernard Esqr Governor —

James Bowdoin   Thos Flucker   Thos Hubbard Esqr
Royall Tyler Esqr Harrison Gray   Andrew Belcher
James Russell   James Pitts

His Excellency laid before the Board a Letter from the Surveyor General with a representation of some riotous proceedings in rescuing seven hogsheads & one Tierce and part of an hogshead & part of a tierce of Sugar, and three hogsheads & two Ullages of Rum from the officers of his Majesty's Customs in Falmouth in the County of Cumberland which they had Seized & marked as forfeited to his Majesty. The Council proceeded to Advise on the business and thereupon —

Advised that a Proclamation be issued with a Reward of Fifty pounds for discovering the offenders or any of them, wherein the Civil officers are called upon to support & maintain the officers of the Customs in the recovery of said Goods, and in all matters relative thereto in the due execution of their office, and also to use their utmost endeavours for discovering apprehending and bring to Justice the said offenders — And further—

Advised, That a Letter be wrote to Tere Powell, Enoch Freeman, Alex^r Ross & Stephen Longfellow Esqr Justices of the peace for the County of Cumberland directing them to meet and consult together, and do what is proper as soon as may be in this business, and make Return of their doings therein as soon as may be.

Copy Exam^d

p Jno Cotton D. Sec̃ry

John Cotton Esqre to Ter Powell, Enoch Freeman, Alex^r Ross & Stephen Longfellow Esqr

Boston August 18th 1766

Gentlemen

By Order of his Excellency the Governor with the Advice of the Council, I now send you a Proclamation this day issued which was occasioned by some late Riotous proceedings in the County of Cumberland, with directions that you do immediately upon Receipt thereof meet together, or as many of you as can conveniently, and consult upon the most vigirous measures for carrying the intention of the said Proclamation into Execution.

You are therefore to take such Measures as you shall think most requisite for the Recovery of the Goods which have been unlawfully taken out of the possession of the Custom House officers, and in supporting them in the due Execution of their office on this occasion, and also in suppressing any further Riotous proceedings and in apprehending and securing all offenders, and make Return of your proceedings in this enquiry as soon as may be, and of the names of any of the offenders that may be discovered to you.

Signed   Jno Cotton D Sec̃ry

A true Copy

Attest: Jno Cotton D. Sec̃ry

Letter, Govr Wentworth to Govr Bernard 2 Oct. 1766.

Sir

I have had the Honor to receive your Letter of the 10th September. The difficulty in procuring Copies has hitherto prevented my acknowledging it. Herewith is inclosed according to your Excellencys request Copys of the various plans & Records which together with the opinion of the

Council & Mr Bryent's Deposition forwarded the 10th Instant, have induced me to judge the Lands now in question are clearly within the bounds of this Province. I presume they will procure equal certainty where may be considered. As many of these papers apply immediately to the respective positions of your Excellencys Letter, I do not trouble you with further reasons thereon. Upon enquiry I am informed that the late Govr Wentworth always declined appointing any Committee to join in running this Line again or in any way to consider the propriety of it, supposing it a matter by no means either disputable after being determined and markt by Royal Authority and the unexceptionable practice of both Provinces thereon, for so many years: Or if any uncertainty cou'd possibly remain, that He cou'd in faithfulness to the Crown take any such Measure. Indeed Mr Wentworth did consent that Bryant shou'd attend the Committee of the Mass^a Bay to show them and renew the Marks on the Line he run, merely out of Civility & just respect to your Letters — but by no means giving or intending any Authority to him. Col° Wentworth went upon similar terms: but without any particular official knowledge of the intent of the Committee, or that his presence or absence was material to either Province. I therefore beg leave to observe that Col° Wentworth or Mr Bryent cannot be considered as a Committee for this Province, who have no right or power to appoint any — The property being Royal; Or for his Majesty, as the Governor never did or wou'd admit it to require or even bear a reconsideration from him, after the Line was so authentically surveyed, markd, recorded and acted upon so long and without Exception.

In compliance with your Excellency's desire I have hitherto defer'd any executive measures; but must very soon proceed to a positive preservation of the Kings property, nor suffer it to be taken by mere supposition, without his Command: This is not practicable against a subject; at least not acceded to. I find it the more necessary as Capt Brown and others have threatned the Grantees under the Crown with personal Arrests and to hurry them to Boston, for judicial process; that wou'd be ruinous, even if their property in the Land was preserved: Such poor Settlers you are sensible Sir, cannot bear the time & expence of distant Suits; I was very happy that your Excellency's desire confirmed my earnest inclination to prevent any violences or unnecessary interruption of the Borderers, and conclude that Capt Brown's precipitation is unknown to your Excellency whose ready benevolence I am convinced woud powerfully plead against such severity; especially during an enquiry, which might be hoped would determine the Case, without Calamity. Since this matter has been considered again, this Government appear determined to prosecute the Execution of the judgment in Council, that decrees the Cost to be equally paid by both Provinces. What the result may be is uncertain: perhaps the two miles observed / heretofore / to be by accident lost to this Province may be restored to them, if it is bro't before his Majesty in Council. I have omitted sending the paragraph in my Commission as it is verbatim, the same as in the 85th Instruction to the late Governor Wentworth, respecting the Line; However I will yet send it if it is tho't to any purpose.

I shall be obliged, if your Excellency wou'd inform me, when this matter is sent home, unless upon perusing the Copies &c It is intirely dismiss'd, which I am inclined to expect: That I may also transmit such Evidence as may expedite the affair.

I am with great esteem and respect Sir
Your most obedient humble Servant
J. Wentworth

Letter, Enoch Freeman & Alex^r Ross to Hon. A. Oliver

Falmouth Decr 8th 1766

Sir

Last Night we receiv'd Your Honour's Letter of 2nd Inst^t with a Proclamation relative to One Joseph Andrews (alias Saunders) committing a Murder on One Capt Dorria &c; we have made Enquiry, and find that one David Stickney arived here above a month ago from St Eustatia in the West Indies, that he brought with him three Passengers vizt One Man and two Boyes, Said Stickney Sail'd again for the West Indies about a week ago; it is reported that the man said he belonged to Boston, and presently after arival here, he & one of the Boyes, departed hence in a Sloop, but we have no Information where they went, the other Boy went in a Schooner, James Witridge Master bound to St Vincents in the West Indies -

If we can possibly find out the Murderer, his Excellency and Your Honour may depend on our Utmost Endeavours to have him Apprehended and Secured for Tryal —

We are Your Honour's Most hum^l Servants

Enoch Freeman
Alex^r Ross

Petition of Inhab^{ts} of Broad Bay. 1767.

Province of the Massachusets Bay

To his Excellency Francis Bernard Esqr Governour &c
The Honble his Majesty^s Council & House of Representatives in General Court Assembled Jany 14th 1767

The Petition of the Inhabitants of a Plantation Called Broad Bay in the County of Lincoln Humbly Sheweth

That Frankfort in the west side of Pownalborough in said County the Place where the Courts of General Sessions of the Peace & Inferiour Court of Common Pleas are now held

is Very near the Westren side of said County & Quite
Remote from by far the Greatest Part of the Inhabitants of
said County & that there are but a Very few Houses near
said Place in which People who have nesesary business at
said Courts can have Lodging and Entertainment so that a
Great Part of the People during their Nesesary attendance
on said Courts are much distressed for Nesesarys and are
Oblidged to lodge on a floor or in Barns or set all night by
the fire during their whole stay at said Courts — Wherefore
Your Petitioners humbly Pray Your Excellency & Honours
that said Courts may be Removed to the Eastren side of
Pownalborough aforesaid which is much nearer to the Center
of said County both as to land and Inhabitants and where
those who have Business at said Courts may be sufficiently
Provided for there being a sufficient Number of Houses there
in which to Entertain and lodge them and for the Reasons
aforesaid if Pownalborough should be Divided into two Distinct Towns agreable to a Petition as we understand now
before your Excellency & Honours for that Purpose we humbly Pray that what is now the Eastren side of Pownalborough
may be made the Shire Town of said County it being a Place
well Situated for the Court to be held at and your Petitioners as in Duty Bound Shall ever Pray &c,—

Johannes   David   John Martin Schoeffer   Char^s Leissner
Martin   Gottfried   Paul Ksihor   Johannes
Johannes   J   M   Jacob
Jacob   Johannes   Jacob   Jacob Ludwig
Gr   Jonathan Robbins   J Ludwig   Freidrich Winchenboch
J   Carll   G   S
M   David X Kubler   John X   Johannes
  (his mark)   (his mark)
John Jost Oberlach Martin   John Henry X P   Johannes
    (his mark)
M   Will   M   freidrich
Jacob   M   G   M
Jacob   Johannes   Wm Farnsworth   Ezra Pitcher Ju^r
George Storer   M Storer

Petition of the Inhab^{ts} of Freetown   1767.

Province of the Massachusetts Bay
 To His Excellency Francis Bernard Esqr Governour &c The hon^{ble} his Majesty^s Council the House of Representatives in General Court Assembled Jany 14th 1767

The Petition of the Inhabitants of a Plantation Called Freetown in the County of Lincoln Humbly Sheweth

That Frankfort in the West side of Pownalborough in said County the Place where the Court of General Sessions of the Peace and Inferiour Court of Common Pleas are now held is very near the Westren side of said County and Quite remote from by far the greatest part of the Inhabitants of said County and that there are but a very few Houses near said Place in which People who have Nesesary business at said Courts can have Lodging and Entertainment so that a Great Part of the People during their Nesesary attendance on said Courts are oblidged to lodge on a floor or in Barns or sit all Night by the fire during their whole stay at said Courts — Wherefore your Petitioners humbly Pray your Excellency & Honours that said Courts may be removed to the Estren side of Pownalborough aforesaid which is much nearer the Center of said County both as to land and Inhabitants and where those who have Business at said Courts may be sufficiently Provided for there being a sufficient Number of Houses there in which to Entertain and lodge them and for the Reasons aforesaid if Pownalborough should be Divided into two Distinct Towns agreeable to a Petition as we understand now before your Excellency & Honours for that Purpose we humbly Pray that what is now the Eastren side of Pownalborough may be made the Shire Town of said County it being a Place well situated for the Courts to be held at and your Petitioners as in duty bound shall ever Pray &c

| William X | William Clifford | Abner Day |
| John | lot Colby | Nicolus Canady |

John Leeman	Joseph Trask	**D**
Ebenezer Dow	Solomon	John Cuningham
Solomon G	Asel	William Cuningham
Solomon Trask	John gray	Solomon Laighton
Samuel Trask	Abel Colby	Benjamin Laighton
james Chase	Samuel Webber	Simeon Pearl
Solomon	Allen	David
Nathaniel Breed	James Richards	Samuel Trask Ju[r]
Joshua Cross	Joseph Richards	Benjamin Allbee
james	Joseph Brown	Thomas Trask
Jeremiah Dalton	Patrick Kenney	Daniel Webster
joseph	Webster	Ed Hatch

Petition of Inhab[ts] of Muscongus & Medumcook 1767.

Province of the Massachusets Bay

To his Excellency Francis Bernard Esq[r] Governour &c The Hon[ble] his Majesty[s] Council & House of Representatives in General Court Assembled Jan[y] 14th 1767

The Petition of the Inhabitants of the Plantations Called Muscongus & Madumcook in the County of Lincoln

Humbly Sheweth

That Frankfort in the West side of Pownalborough in said County the Place where the Courts of General Sessions of the Peace & Inferiour Court of Common Pleas are now held is very near the Westren side of said County & Quite Remote from by far the Greatest Part of the Inhabitants of said County & that there are but a very few Houses near said Place in which People who have nesesary Business at said Courts can have Lodging & Entertainment so that a Great Part of the People during their nesesary attendance on said Courts are much distressed for Nesesarys and are Oblidged to lodge on a floor or in Barns or sett all night by the fire during their whole Stay at said Courts Wherefore Your Petitioners humbly Pray Your Excellency & Honours that said Courts may be Removed to the Estren side of Pownalborough aforesaid which is much nearer the Center of said County both as to land & Inhabitants and where those who have Business at s^d Courts may be sufficiently Provided for there being a sufficient Number of Houses their in which to Entertain & lodge them & for the Reasons aforesaid if Pownalborough should be Divided into two Distinct Towns agreable to a Petition as we Understand now before Your Excellency & Honours for that Purpose we humbly Pray that what is now the Eastren side of Pownalborough may be made the Shire Town of said County it being a Place well situated for the Courts to be held at & Your Petitioners as in Duty Bound shall ever Pray &c

Cornelius Tomson	Samuel	Joshua
Joshua	Paul Jameson	Cornelius Bradford
Wadsworth	Joshua Bradford	Abiah Wadsworth
John	Robert	Elijah Cook
Richard	Asa	John Robinson
John	Jacob Grifen	Jesse Thomas
George Biggmore	Alexander Jameson	Jacob Grafon
John Grafton	John Bigmore	Samuel Condon
Ebenezer Morton J^r	William Elwell	Ebenezer Morton
John Brazer	William Elwell jun^r	Jacob Davis
Grafen Davis	William Davis	Ebn^r Davis
Zachariah Davis	Samuel Davis	

Province of the M Bay
    To His Excellency Francis Bernard Esqr Govern^r and Commander in Cheif of said Province, To the Honble His Majestys Council & House of Representatives in General Court Assembled Jany 28th 1767 —

The Petition of the Subscribers hereto, who are Freeholders and Inhabitants of the Town of Andover
humbly Sheweth —
That Agriculture having been the business your Petitioners and Their Children have been bred up to, and now stand in Nead of Land to Settle Their Children upon, and there being a number of Persons in their Neighbourhood in the same Situation Your said Petitioners and Neighbours would be glad of liberty to Exercise their Calling upon some part of the Wilderness Land in the County of York — And as there are three Townships already laid out at and near Pigwacket viz Fryestown, Browns town and another lately laid out to Benjamin Mulliken Esqr & Others, and a Considerable number of Families Settled in the first, some in the Second, and preparations making for Settling the third, It Occasions a great deal of Traveling betwen this part of the Province and those Townships; and as there is a Space between Phillips-Town and said Townships of fifty four Miles; in all which distance there is not a House for Travelers to Shelter Themselves in, be the weather ever so severe: Your Petitioners humbly apprehend That if a Settlement was made between the two Rivers called great Ossapee and Little Ossapee, (which is about mid-way between Phillipstown and the aforesaid Township,) it would Answer a very good Purpose; as there would be a place of Entertainment for Travelers to and from the said Pigwacket Townships, And People in the Proposed Settlement (It's Probable) might be Supply'd with bread from the aforesaid Townships while Subduing their own Lands, which would Enable Them to proceed more Expeditiously in the Settlement and the sooner have a place of Shelter for Travelers to the Pigwacket Townships of which they stand in great need — And as your Petitioners do not Expect to obtain a Township of Wilderness Land any other way than by purchase, They humbly Pray Your Excellency

and Hon^{rs} would please to Grant them a Township, with liberty to lay it out between the said great & little Ossapee Rivers, for such a Consideration, and under such Injunctions, as your Excellency & Hon^{rs} shall think, Those who Settle the Wilderness Land ought to be Subjected to, and as in duty bound will ever Pray

Nathan Chandler Joshua Chandler   Isaac Abbot Ju^r
John Abbot 5th David Chandler   Thomas Russell
Stephen Abbot   Ephraim Abbot   Joshua Lovejoy
Jonathan Abbot 1th Nathan Chandler J^r John Dane
John Patten   Eliakim Darling   Zebadiah Shattuck
John Wardwell   John Holt J^r James Griffen
Joshua holt   David Holt   Samuel Osgood
Joseph Holt   John Willson   Isaac Blunt
Nehemiah Abbot J^r George Abbot Junr William Dane
Samuel Fiealds   Isaac Chandler   Asa Abbot
Benjamin Walker Darius Abbot

Indorsed   Petition of Nathan Chandler & others — Feb 23 1767

Coll Ward   Cap Dix   Coll Bagley
referrd to May Sess^n

June 18 revived & Com^d to Mr Sayward Cap Thayer Coll Cushing to ascertain the Value of the Land & enquire whether it belongs to the province to report next Session May 17 1768 —

Petition of S. Downe & M. Thornton. 1767.

To His Excellency Francis Bernard Esqr Capt Generall & Governor in & over His Majestys Province of the Massachusetts Bay — The Honble His Majestys Council & the Honble House of Representatives in Generall Court Assembled

The petition of Samuel Downe & Mathew Thornton in behalf of the Grantees of the six Townships in the Territorys of Sagadahoc Granted to David March &c Humbly Shews

That your petitioners presented a Memorial to your Excellency & Honors in June last praying that a further time may be granted to them for Obtaining His Majestys Approbation for the reasons Mentioned in said Memorial —

Upon which the Hon[ble] House Agreed to the further Term of Eighteen months, which was consented too by the Hon[ble] Board — But by reason of the Six Lower Townships (who had never petitioned nor had been at any expence towards geting his Majesties approbation) being Joined with them by the Com[tee] to whom it was refered, the said Grant of Eighteen months was not consented to by His Excellency, they therefore pray they may have a further time allowed them, Seperate from the Lower Six Townships.

Sam[l] Downe
Mathew Thornton

January 28th 1767 —

Petition of Nathan Jones & others. 1767.

Province of the Massachusetts Bay

To His Excellency Francis Bernard Esq, Governor and Commander in Chief The Hon[ble] His Majestys Council & Representatives of said Province in General Court Assembled at Boston January 28th 1767 —

The Memorial of Nathan Jones Francis Shaw and Robert Gould, in behalf of themselves and others Grantees of a Township N. Three, in the Territory of Saggadehock, East of Union River — Humbly Sheweth

That whereas by a Grant of their said Township made in February 1763, it was provided that in case his Majesty should not in eighteen Months next coming approve of said Grants they should be null and void, and whereas upon

Application made to your Excellency at the expiration of said Term — Your Excellency and Honors were pleased to allow a farther Time of Eighteen Months from the third of November 1764 which Time is now expired without our having been able as yet to obtain his Majestys Approbation.

Your Memorialists beg leave further to represent to your Excellency and Honors that they have exerted themselves so greatly in carrying on the Settlement that they have at one Time been upwards of Six thousand Pounds Str^g in advance, and the Settlement is now in so flourishing a state as to contain about Forty Dwelling Houses, Seven Mills and other Buildings and about three or four hundred Inhabitants. And having Lately received a Letter from Our Agent in England, signifying the great encouragement he has received from the Ministry whereby he assures us of his hopes for success on our behalf in his further Applications to the Board of Trade and others concerned in American Affairs — They therefore humbly pray that they may have a further Time allowed them for obtaining his Majestys Approbation —

Francis Shaw
Robt Gould

Plan Accepted. 1767

In the House of Representatives Jan^{ry} 30th 1767

This Plan of a Township of Land of the Contents of Six Miles and three Quarters of a Mile Square, granted to Captain William Raymond and others who served in the Expedition against Canada in 1690, their legal Representatives or Assigns, and by them laid out in the County of Cumberland adjoining to great Sebago Pond, and adjoining to New-Boston, bounded as follows, Viz^t Beginning at the Northwesterly Corner Bounds of the Township of Windham, and extending by the Needle due Northeast seven and an half Miles, on the

Head Line of said Windham, and New Boston; thence extending on a due Northwest Course seven and an half Miles; thence from the first mentioned Bounds extending up the Northeast Side of the Great Pond of Sebago, as the Pond doth run, till a North east Line shall terminate at Head of Seven Miles and an half on the northeast Side Line, was presented for acceptance.

Accordingly, Resolved, That it be, and hereby is accepted, and the Land therein contained be confirmed unto them, their Heirs and Assigns for ever, they complying with the Conditions of the original Grant; Saving only that they settle seventy five Families instead of Thirty Families.

Provided the same doth not exceed the Quantity of seven and an half Miles square, with a Neck of Land and Island adjacent, delineated on said Plan, including Allowance for Ponds therein contained, nor interfere with any former Grant.

 Sent up for Concurrence Thomas Cushing Spk^r

In Council Jany 30th 1767 Read & Concurred
           Jno Cotton D Sec̃ry

 Consented to Fra Bernard

Resolve

In the House of Representatives Feb. 5th 1767.

Resolved that the prayer of this petition be granted, & that the petitioner above named, for the reasons mentioned in s^d petition be further allowed the term of Eighteen Months, from this Day, to obtain his Majesty's approbation of the within mentioned Grant

 Sent up for Concurrence Thomas Cushing Spk^r

In Council Feby 5th 1767 — Read & Conc^d
           Jno Cotton D Sec̃ry

 Consented to Fra Bernard

Report on Petition of Capt. H. Y. Brown.

The Com^{ttee} on the Petition of Capt Henry-Young Brown haveing Considered the Same Report that in the year AD 1764 ye Petitioner had a Grant of a Township of the Contents of Six mile Square to be laid out on Saco River above Col^o frys Town which was accordingly lay^d out & a plan thereof returned & accepted ; That in the year (1765) he ye Petitioner Informed the General Court, that part of s^d Township was Claimed by newhampshire ; That s^d Court Incouraged him to Go forward with his Settlements & Improvements ; and if he met with any Difficultys they would be ready to Give him releiff ; That in ye year (1766) he Set forth his Difficultys ; and the Court appointed ye Honble John Bradbury Esqr James Gowing Esqr & m^r Sayward, a Com^{ttee} to run out the line according to ye Claim of this Province ; That they run as far as Saco River with a line which took off 8544 acres of the Petitioners Town ; That ye Court thought Best not to be at any Expence in Defending and agreed with ye Petitioner to Discharge the Government from any Demands for s^d lands or Expence ; That the Court then ordered the Petitioner to prossecute all Such persons as Should Enter on ye lands, to ye East of ye s^d line run as affores^d at ye Expence of the Province as also to Defend all actions Brought against him at ye Goverments Expence —

That in march (1767) a Committee was appointed to prepare ye Papers to send to Dennis Debert Esqr who was appointed to Get a Settlement of ye province line ; or alteration of s^d line as run by Bryant and orders to have it run agreeable to Settlement ; after the Committee had prepared the papers the whole matter was refferred to ye next Setting of ye Court and that there hath not been any thing Determined upon it Sence —

That upon a Tryall at ye Superior Court in New hampshire last may for thirty five acres of land lying on ye line they

Call ye Province line it appear^d that m^r Bryant run ye line in 1740/1; and after a full hearing the Court & Jury both Declared the land was in Newhampshire; and Gave Judgment for ye lands Sued for & Cost.

That it appears the Petitioner hath already rec^d out of the Publick Treasury by warrant from ye Govr & Council at Sundry Times

The sum of one hundred & fifty three pounds Ten shillings pursuant to his Ac^{ots} of Disbursements & Expences } £153 : 10—

That ye Petitioners Ac^{ot} now Exhibeted amounts to ye Sum of one hundred & one pound nine Shillings & Eleven pence more to Ball^{ce} } 101 : 9 : 11

and further the Committee Beg leave to report that ye Petitioner was to Give the Province as a Valluable Consideration for Said Township the Sum of Two hundred pounds which said sum hath not been paid or any part thereof

       Jo^s Williams p order

Petition. 1767.

Province of the Massachusetts Bay

 To his Excellency Francis Bernard Esqr Governor & Commander in Chief in and over said Province &c and the Honourable his Majestys Council & House of Representatives in General Court Assembled May 1767

 The Petition of the Proprietors of the New Township lying at the head of the Town of Berwick adjoyning on the Eastern side of Salmon Fall River in the County of York —
    Humbly Shews —

 That the Great & General Court of this Province in the year 1733 did Grant a Township of Land of Six miles Square

To Sixty Three Proprietors Bounded Southerly on the head of the Town of Berwick Westerly by Salmon Falls River Northerly partly by said River & Ponds and party by Province Lands Easterly by Province Lands —

By Reason of the Frequent wars & the Danger of the Indian Enemie the Settlement of said Township has been Retarded Till since the Ruduction of Canada to the Crown of Greate Britain Since which your Petitioners have Settled a Minister in said Township in Gospel order, and have now more than Forty Families Settled there, and Many more will Soon Settle there and your Petitioners Humbly apprehend that the Incorporating said Plantation into a Town that the Settlers that may have the Priviledge of Others Town in this Province will Greatly Promote the Settlement & Growth of said new township

Wherefore your Petitioners Humbly pray your Excellency & Honours that the said new township or Plantation may be Incorporated into a Town that the Inhabitants thereof may Do Duty & Receive the Priviledges of Other Towns in this Province and your Petitionrs in Duty bound shall pray &c

Benj[a] Chadbourn in behalf of said Proprietors

The Committee to whom is Refer[d] the within Petition have Considered the same & beg leave to Report the Petitioners have Liberty to bring in a bill for the purposes mentiond in this Petition

       Jonathan Sayward pr order

Petition of Josiah Richardson, Agent. 1767.

Province of the Massachusetts Bay

 To his Exelencey Frainces Barnard Esq[r] Captain Genarail and Commander in Cheife in and over his Majest_ Province of the Massachusetts Bay in New England and Vice Admiral of the same and to the Honorable his majestys Counsill and to the Honorable The House of Representatives in the Grate And Generail Court Assembled at Boston on the 27th day of may anaqe Domini 1767 —

Josiah Richardson of Sudbury in the County of Middlesex Esqr and agent for a Number of Petitioners whose Anchestors ware in the Expodition to Canada in the year 1690 —

Humbley Reminds your Exclency and Honours that In the yeare 1737 a number of Men whose Names Are hereunto Anexed Prefered a Petition to this Honourable Court for to have a Grant of Land for a Township to be Layed out in the unapropriated Lands within the said Province as maney oathers for the same Merit before had had town shipp Granted to them and this Honorable Did then Sostain the s^d petition and then ordered the s^d petitioners to mak out and prove their Claims that their Anchesters ware in the s^d Expodition, and Come and they Should be heared with which order of Court the said Petitioner fully Comployed with and at a Grat Coust proved their Clams Sence which by A Number of memorials to this honorable Court the said Petition has ben Revived but the said Petitioners have not as yet had aney Grant of Land made to them on that Accompt and by Reason of the wars and of the Townhouse being burnt the same petition has not of Late ben moved to this Honourabel Court but sence this Honorable Court in theire Grat Wisdom and Justice was Pleased on the 24 Day of June A D 1765 to make a Grant of a Township of Land to Capt William Raymond and Company for the same merit which your Memorlis now plead and now your memorlis in behalfe of himselfe and Compney Humbley pray youre Exelency and Honours would take the primises under your Wise and Just Consideration and mak us A Grant of Land for a Township As you Was plesed to Do to the s^d William Raymond and

Companey And youre memorilis in the Behalfe of himselfe and Companey Shall Ever Pray

Josiah Richardson Agent for said Petitioners

Petition of B. Mulliken & M. Bridges   1767.

To His Excellency Francis Bernard Esqr Govr and Commander in Chief of his Majesty's Province of the Massachusetts Bay in New England to the Honble the Council & House of Representatives in General Court assembled May 27th 1767

The Petition of Benjamin Mulliken & Moody Bridges agents for the proprietors of a Township granted to Benjamin Mulliken Esqr and others June 25 1765. humbly sheweth

That the pond called long Pond contained in the plot of said Township occupys a much larger space than it describes by said plot. That the course of said Pond is different from the Representation thereof dividing the Land in such a Form as will greatly discomode the settlement of said Township — That that part thereof that lies East of said pond would serve the Province to accomodate another Township, and that a Strip of the Province Land between s^d Township and Saco River with the addition of another Strip at the Southend of s^d Township would accomodate said proprietors and would leave the Province Land in a much more regular form than it is now in.

That a number of the Proprietors of said Township are in arrears of the Taxes levyed on them in the concerns of a former Township called Rowley Canada.

That the Council in Law of your petitioners adviseth that the Laws of the Province respecting the regulation of Townships are not sufficient to enable said proprietors to make Sale of said delinquent Rights in said Township granted to Benjamin Mulliken and others to defrey the Charges of said Township called Rowley Canada of which s^d Proprietors are Owsted.

Wherefore your Petitioners humbly entreat your Excellency & Honors to Grant to said proprietors an equivalent for that part of said Township that lies East of said pond in the unappropriated Lands of the Government on the Westerly side thereof contiguous to Saco River & adjoining to said Township as afores^d — and that it would please your Excellency & Honors to enable said proprietors to make Sale of said delinquent Rights in said Township granted to Benj^a Mulliken & others to defrey their arrears of said former Township called Rowley Canada together with the Charges that have arisen on their Rights in the other Township aforesaid. And your Petitioners as in duty bound shall ever pray.—

Benj^a Mulliken
Moody Bridges

Resolve 1767.

In the House of Representatives May 30 1767

Whereas there was a Plan taken of several Townships by John Brown Esqr Surveyor, by Order of a Committee of this Court in 1763 viz of Narragansett No 1 Pearson town N° 7 with the Lines of Biddeford Scarborough & Falmouth as run by said Comittee which Plan is mislaid or lost

Resolved that the Secretary be directed to write to the said John Brown Esqr to take an exact Plan of said Townships & runing said Lines of said Biddeford Scarborough & Falmouth from his field Book or Journal to make Oath to the same that it is a true plan & return said Plan into the Secretarys Office as soon as may be

Sent up for Concurrence   Tho Cushing Spk^r

In Council 2^d June 1767   Read and Concurred

A Oliver Sec^y

Consented to   Fra Bernard

Message. "June 11, 1767."

Gentlemen

I never understood that the charges contained in the Earl of Shelburne's Letter were particularly intended against this Province as there have been no Complaints of this kind made from hence that I know of. There has been but one instance of Murther of Indians happened within my time; and in that the Government exerted itself to the utmost to discover and punish the offenders and to give satisfaction to the Indians; in the latter of which we had all desired Success.

The Justice and tenderness which this Government has exercised towards the Indians which have been intermixed with the People is, I believe, very well known: such instances as have happened within my time have been faithfully represented, and the Province has had full Credit for them. But still great care remains to be taken of the Eastern Indians who are not the objects of domestic regulations. And this cannot be done without restraining the Hunting & Trading of the English in their Country, which have been & ever will be the Causes of frequent Offence given to Indians in those parts. Injuries of this kind are much better prevented than redressd. I therefore depend that you will carry into present execution the assurances you give me at the close of your address, by continuing the present Act for restraining private trading with the Indians and hunting in their Country which will otherwise expire with the present Session, or by bringing in another Bill for the same purposes.—

Message. June 11, 1767.

Gentlemen of the Council and Gentlemen of the House of
      Representatives

Last Winter I received a Letter from the Earl of Sherburne, signifying his Majesty's commands that Care be taken that a due Obedience be paid to his Majesty's royal proclamation for restraining the Indian trade & preventing incroachments upon the Indian Country. I have reserved the communication of this untill the subject matter should come before you in the course of business; which it does now by the time for renewing the Indian trade-act coming on. I have more than once represented to his Majesty's Ministers that it is not in my power to carry the proclamation into execution, without the aid of the general Court; and that so far as It has hitherto been obeyed, has been effected by means of the aforementioned Act. I now desire that you will take the whole of the said Letter into consideration, & provide for what is required thereby, either by the same Act or by another, as you shall see Cause.

Fra: Bernard

Council Chamber June 11, 1767.

Resolve

In the House of Representatives June 12 1767

Resolved that that part of the Township granted to Benj[a] Mulliken Esq[r] and others June 25th 1765 lying on the Easterly side and northerly end of the pond called Long pond containing Eight thousand, six hundred & forty five Acres, bounded as followeth; Begining at a stone set into the ground at the northeasterly corner of said Township, thence South 25 degrees East nine Miles to a Stone set into the ground, thence West 25 degrees South seven hundred & forty pole to said pond; thence northerly by s[d] pond to a Stake & stones standing by a Brook at the head of said pond; thence north 25 degrees West six hundred & sixty pole to a stake & stones standing in the northerly line of s[d] Township thence East 25 degrees North one hundred & sixty pole to the first bound, be exchanged for an equivalent of Land lying on the westerly side, provided there be a sufficiency of Land belonging to the Province on that side, otherwise that the deficiency be made up in Lands at the Southerly end of said Township adjoining thereto, and that a plan thereof taken by Surveyor & Chainmen on oath be returned to this Court within twelve Months from this date for Confirmation.

And that the petitioners notify the delinquent Proprietors mentioned in their petition by inserting the substance of that Clause in one of the Boston News papers three weeks successively that they shew cause if any they have on the first Tuesday of the next Session of this Court why the prayer thereof should not be granted.—

 Sent up for Concurrence   T. Cushing Spk^r
In Council June 12th 1767   Read & Concurred
            A Oliver Sec^y
   Consented to   Fra Bernard
   A true Copy   Exam^d p Jno Cotton D: Secry

Act of Incorporation. 1767.

Anno Regni Regis Georgii Tertii Septimo.

An Act for erecting the new Plantation called Lebanon lying at the Head of the Town of Berwick adjoining on the Eastern Side of Salmon Falls River in the County of York, into a Town by the name of

Whereas the erecting the Plantation called Lebanon into a Town will greatly contribute to the Growth thereof and remedy many Inconveniences to which the Inhabitants and Proprietors may be otherwise subject:

Be it enacted by the Governor, Council and House of Representatives That the Plantation aforesaid **A** bounded as follows vizt Southerly on the Head of the said Town of Berwick; Westerly by Salmon Falls River; Northerly partly by said River, and Ponds, and partly by Province Lands; & Easterly by Province Lands; be and hereby is erected into a Town by the Name of   and that the Inhabitants thereof be and hereby are invested with all the Powers, Privileges and Immunities, which the Inhabitants of the Towns within this Province do enjoy.

And be it further enacted, That Benjamin Chadburne Esqr be and hereby is empowered to issue his Warrant directed to some principal Inhabitant in said Town, requiring him to warn the Inhabitants of said Town to meet at such Time and Place as shall be therein set forth, to chuse all such Officers as are or shall be required by Law to manage the affairs of the said Town.

In the House of Representatives
   Read a first time June 9 1767
   Read a second time June 10, 1767
   Read a third time June 11, 1767 & passed to be Engrossed
      Sent up for Concurrence   T. Cushing Spk^r

   In Council 11 June 1767   Read a first time
   12 June 1767   Read a second Time & passd a Concurrence with the amendment
      Sent down for Concurrence   A Oliver Sec^y

In the House of Representatives June 12 1767
      Read & Concurred   T. Cushing Spk^r

Bounded as followeth begining at Salmon fall river in the North Bounds of the Township of Berwick & to Run Northeast & by East with that Line 6 mile 200 Rods then N W & by N: Six miles & 36 Rod with the Province Land, then S W & by W with the unappropriated Lands of ye Government & a Grant made to Jon^a Bagly Esqr to the River afores^d then with the s^d River to the Bounds first mentioned.

Order.

June 13th 1767

Ordered that his Excellency the Governour be Desired, to forward, Duplicates, of his last Letters, to the Officers, at Port Royall, by a Shallop, or some other fit vessel, with oars, that they may not fail of his Commands

And Give Order that the ffrigate Province Galley, do Convoy & Cover the vessels that may be Improved to Transport the great Artillery above the ffort. And also to Lie before the ffort, & Assist in Taking it, If the Councill of War shall Determine to Attempt it.

Sent up for Concurrence   John Burrill Speak^r

Message.

June 6th 1767

May it please your Excellency

Your Excellency's Message to both Houses of the 11th Instant, together with His Majesty's Royal Proclamation for restraining the Indian Trade and preventing Incroachments upon the Indian Country; as also the Earl of Shelburn's Letter signifying his Majesty's Commands, that a due Obedience be paid to the said Proclamation, we have most attentively considered — And are convinced that neither were founded upon any Complaints against this province by his Majesty's Superintendents for Indian Affairs: Nor will any one presume to say that the most **A** provoked Violences and Murthers which have been lately committed on the Indians under the Protection of his Majesty, were done by this Government,

or that any one Settlement hath been made by us without proper Authority, and beyond the Limits prescribed by his

Majesty's Royal Proclamation of One Thousand seven Hundred and Sixty-three; or that we have made Settlements beyond the utmost Boundaries of any Province in America, in Consequence of which the greatest Discontents among the Indians have arisen, which may endanger the Peace of his Majesty's Provinces, and the Safety of his Subjects: We say May it please your Excellency, it is impossible that these Complaints were made against us, because they are without even a colour **B** and therefore that said Letter was a circular one, and would have been sent to your Excellency had there not been an Indian, or any Indian Land in the Province. **B**

It is with Pleasure, that we remind your Excellency, and inform the World, that greater Care was taken of the Indians by our pious Ancestors during the old Charter, and by this Government under the new even to this Day than is ordered or recommended either by the Proclamation or the Letter aforesaid — But about three Years after the Arrival of our Forefathers vizt Anno Domini 1633, they made a Law in these Words that no Person shall henceforth buy Land of any Indian without License first had and obtained of the General Court, and if any offended herein such Land so bought shall be forfeited — And least the Indians should be defrauded in their Trade, in the same Year they made a Law that no Person should trade with the Indians for any sort of Peltry &c, excepting only such as are authorized by the General Court under the Penalty of One Hundred Pounds for every offence — And so tender was their Regard for them upon other accounts that there were Indian Instructors provided; the Bible which they were perfect Strangers to translated into Indian, as well as other Books the Means of Instruction, English and Indian Ministers provided for them, the Gospel preached to them, Churches gathered, some of which continue even unto this Day: By Law severe Penalties were to be inflicted upon any that should sell them strong

Drink — By Law the Justices of every Shire were bound to give it in special Charge to the Grand Jury to inquire and present the Breaches of said Laws, Provision was therein made, that when any Damage should be done the Indians in their Fields tho' unfenced should be made good by the Town where the Land lay — Provision was likewise made for their being incorporated into Townships, they to be vested with all the Priviledges of other Towns. They were empowered from among themselves to appoint Indian Justices to hear and determine small Causes that might arise among the Indians — This was the Care the Government took of the Indians under the old charter; and this very much indeared the English to them. The Indians had a perfect Confidence in the Government, looked upon them as their civil and spiritual Fathers, and went to them in all their Difficulties as Children to a Father.

May it please your Excellency, These are a few of the many Instances of the Care our Forefathers took of the Indians — Nor hath the Scene been changed at any Time since. There is now a standing Law of this Province made in the Reign of King William and Queen Mary declaring every Deed of Bargain and Sale, Lease, Release &c, of any Lands, Tenements, or Hereditaments within this Province as well for Term of years as for ever procured or obtained from any Indian by any Person at any Time since the year 1633 the year the above mentioned Law was made, without License first had and obtained, or that shall hereafter be made or procured without the License and Approbation of the Great and General Court or Assembly of this Province for the Same shall be deemed and adjudged in the Law to be null and void and of none Effect. The same Care hath been and is now taken of them in every other Instance, there are Laws now subsisting, prohibiting the English selling strong Drink, or trading with them, to prevent their being drunk by the one and cheated by the other: there are Churches and Congregations of Indians in this Province to whom the Gospel is preached, ministers Ordained over them, the Sacraments administred to them, Schoolmasters provided for the Instruction of their Children, decent respectable Houses for publick Worship erected, and all without the least Expence to them: There are Districts and Parishes in the Province wherein the English & Indians unitedly enjoy the same Privileges; and in one of our Towns they unite in voting for Representatives.

With Respect to the Eastern Indians — By the Instigation of the French, perhaps as inhuman as themselves: How much and how many Cruelties have our People met with from them; how much human Blood have they spilt; how much Treasure have they obliged us to expend — Yet when they desired Peace, did the Government ever refuse them: And in the Year 1726 when a Peace was concluded by the then Lieutenant Governor Dummer, whose Memory is precious to them and us, there were Truck Houses erected, by a Law of the Government, both in the Eastern and Western Frontiers, and the Trade in them was put under the wisest and most equitable Regulations, in Favour of the Indians: At ye Truck house Things are sold as cheap even at this day to the Indians as they could purchase them singly at Boston: There is not one Tract of Land in the eastern Country enjoyed by the English, but what was purchased of the Indians Sachems y^r deeds acknowledged and recorded — And when There has been any Trespasses by any of the English upon the Indians there hath been the utmost Care taken by the General Assembly of setting, if not, by the Governor and Council to bring the Offenders to condign Punishment.

Nor, may it please your Excellency hath the Government omitted anything that can be suggested from the Principles of Humanity and Justice, from the year 1633, to this Day for the Interest of the Indians in their several Dispersions throughout the whole Province: The Conduct of the Government towards them we glory in, we make our Boast of as unrivalled — And we perswade our selves, that your Excellency as the Head of the Province, and its Father hath or will make these Representations to his Majesty's Ministers —

Upon the Principles of Christianity, upon the Rules of good Policy, Justice and Equity We have ever acted towards them, sensible that the Violations of these Principles will be attended with fatal Consequences; and that if a due Obedience had been paid to his Majesty's Royal Proclamation, and a due Attention given to proper Restraints on the Conduct of the Indian Traders, those Evils that took Place in some of the Southern Governments might have effectually been avoided.—

It is with the highest Satisfaction that we reflect upon the Government's Conduct relative to the Indians, all free and spontaneous on our Part, especially as it in Substance so exactly corresponds with his Majesty's Sentiments — And we do assure your Excellency, that being animated by the same Principles, we shall do every thing that Duty to the King, and the Rules of good Policy, of Justice and Equity to the Indians can require.

Message June 17, 1767.

Gentlemen &c

Least my Reasons for dissenting to the Resolve for an Establishment for Fort Pownall should be Mistaken I think it proper to ascertain them; they are first, because the Pay appointed for the Officers is insufficient for their Support: —

2. Because the Number of Men appointed is too small for the Defence of so respectable a Fortress. At the same Time

I must recommend to You to make Provision for a Garrison, suitable to the Fort.

Fra Bernard

Council Chamber June 17. 1767

Gentlemen &c

I Consent to the Resolve for the Establishment for Castle William; I dissent to the Resolve for the Establishment for Fort Pownall.

Fra Bernard

Letter, John Brown to Andrew Oliver. 1767.

Newbury June 18th 1767

Hon^d S^r

Agreeable to a Resolve of the Great & Genl Court I herewith Return a Plan of the Towns & Lines therein mentioned and am well assured they are truly described as I had the same Chainmen for the whole Survey, who were on Oath I was put to some Trouble in Collecting my Minutes & Reducing my Plan, as I had but One Sheet of Paper Suitable, Hope it will answer the purpose designed. And am with Sincere Regards to His Excel^y & the whole Court Their & Your most Obedient Hum^l Servt

John Brown

Province of the Massachusetts Bay

To his Excellency Francis Bernard Esqr Captain General and Governor in Cheif the Honble the Council and House of Representatives of the Province aforesaid in General Court assembled at Boston June 1767

The Subscribers Inhabitants of a place called Machias
Humbly Shew

That they with their Families according to the Kings Proclamation went upon and took possession of a Tract of Land called Machias bounding as follows vizt beginning at a dry

Rock at a place called the Eastern Bay near the House of Mr Samuel Holmes and extending North ten Miles, then West eight Miles then South to the Sea which Lands after proper Allowance for Water and Heaths will make only the contents of a Township six Miles Square; and they have made considerable Improvements thereon apprehending the same to be Crown lands But so it is may it please your Excellency and Honours the said Tract of land falleth within the belongs to this Province

Now may it please your Excellency and Honours as it was thrô the Ignorance of your petitioners they thinking the Lands belonged to the Crown, and as they have been at great Cost and pains in clearing and making Improvements on the Tract of Land aforesaid; if they should be dispossessed thereof it would be a means of ruining them and their Families.

Your petitioners would also represent to this Honble Court that they are about Seventy four in Number, and are without the common priviledges other People within this Province enjoy, having no Gospel Minister, School Master or any officers whatsoever, which is absolutely necessary for the Peace and good Order of any People; and as they are willing and desirous to pay their proportion of the Province expence as they become able.

Your petitioners therefore humbly pray your Excellency and Honours would be pleased to take the premises into your wise serious and Compassionate consideration and make them a Grant of the said Tract of land; which will prevent the ruin of so many Families; And also Incorporate them into a Town or otherwise invest them with Authority sufficient to chuse Town Officers, or otherwise relieve them as you in your known Wisdom and goodness shall think best

And as in duty bound shall ever pray &c

   Ichabod Jones for himself and as Attorney & Agent for the Under mentioned persons

Stephen Jones	Jonathan Longfellow	David Libby
Thomas Buck	George Libby jun^r	Thos Buck jun^r
Joseph Dubuisont	Benj^a Foster jun^r	Joseph Sevey
Sarah X Libby (her mark)	George Libby	Timoth. Libby
Saml Kenny	Abiel Sprague	Elijah Bent
Stephen Munson	John Stone	Ebenezer Libby
Sarah Fogg	Nathl Young	Willm X Kelly (his mark)
Joshua Webster	Solomon Meserve	Joseph Holmes
Samuel Rich	Ichabod Jones	Gideon Obrion
Jonath Woodrigh	Wesbruk Berre	Obadiah Hill
Samuel Holmes	Eleazer X Bryant (his mark)	Samuel Davis Bryant
Amos Boynton	George Sevey	Joseph X Getchell (his mark)
Samuel Lebbee	Nathan Longfellow	Jacob Lebbee
John Manchestere	John Underwood	Archelaus Hammond
Joseph Munson	Daniel Stone	John Stone
Daniel Stone in behalf of Sol^o Stone		Reuben Libby
John Crocker	Stephen Parker	James Eliott
Benjamin Corbet	Fannater Obrian	Joel Booney
Jacob Foster	John Wieland	Nathl Davis
Abiel Sprague	Job Burnum	Thaddeus Trafton
Moris Obrion	John X Berre (his mark)	James Dyer
Jeremiah Jenks	Samuel Burnem	Daniel Longfellow
Isaac Larrabee		

Message. June 25, 1767.

A Message from the Board to the honorable House of Representatives

    Gentlemen of the House of Representatives

The Board have concurred the vote of the honorable house relative to the establishment for Castle William & Pownal:

and thô it has been for some time practised to make establishments in this connected manner, yet as there is no necessary connection between s^d Castle & fort, it is proper in the nature of the thing that the establishments for them, and also that all matters whatever acted upon by the General Court, that are in their nature seperate & distinct, should be by seperate & distinct Acts, in order that each Branch of the legislature might act with the utmost Freedom: otherwise they might be necessitated to consent to a thing they utterly disapprove, for the sake of another that merits their approbation, and to which the public good demands their assent.

The Board apprehend the establishment aforesaid, with regard to the form of it was a meer transcript from the establishment of the last year; and that the honorable house had no design by it to infringe on the right of the Board to judge of every matter, that comes before them, upon its own circumstances: and they assure themselves the honorable house will never act upon principles, which they themselves would undoubtedly and very justly censure in the other Branches of the legislature.

In Council 25, June 1767 — Ordered That James Bowdoin, Harrison Gray, James Russell, Samuel White & James Pitts Esq^{rs} be a Committee to wait on the Honble House with the foregoing Message.

May it please your Excellency

On your Excellency's laying before his Majesty's Council the Representations of the Inhabitants & proprietors of the Township of Conway in this Province, that they are prevented from complying with the conditions on which his Majesty was pleased to grant the said Township to them, by the Incroachments & vexations of sundry settlers under pretence of a Grant from the Province of the Massachusetts

Bay, and that they pray your Excellency's protection and assistance.

We were appointed a Committee to furnish your Excellency with a state of the Controversy in the said Township; In pursuance whereof we beg leave to Report that the said Township of Conway was granted by the late Governor in the year 1765; that it is bounded on one side upon the Northerly boundary line between this Province and the old Province of Main now belonging to the Province of the Massachusetts Bay; and that the Justice or injustice of the Complaint made to your Excell^y depends solely on this; Whether the said Line was run where it ought to be?

In order to throw light on this Question we further Report to your Excellency that a controversy had long subsisted with the Province of the Massachusetts Bay concerning the Boundary lines between the two Provinces. That in the year 1737 his late Majesty was pleased by a Commission under the Great Seal to appoint five of the Council from each of the Colonies & Provinces of New York, New Jersey, Nova Scotia & Rhode Island to settle the controversey. The Commissioners met at Hampton on the first day of August 1737 and proceeded to the Business, and after several Adjournments the parties having been fully heard & their pleas, Evidences & allegations fully considered, the Commissioners entered up their Judgment the latter part of which being all that relates to the present dispute and runs in the following words vizt

"And as to the Northern Boundary between the said " Provinces the Court Resolves and determines that the dividing Line shall pass up thro' the mouth of Piscataqua Harbour and up the middle of the River into the River of Newichewanock (part of which is now called Salmon falls) and thro' the middle of the same to the furthest head thereof, and from thence north two degrees westerly until

One hundred and twenty miles be finished from the Mouth of Piscataqua Harbour aforesaid or until it meets with his Majesty's other Governments, and that the dividing Line shall part the Isles of Shoals & run thro' the middle of the Harbour between the Islands to the Sea on the Southerly side, and that the South Westerly part of the s^d Islands shall be in and be accounted part of ye Province of New Hampshire, and that the northerly part thereof shall be in and be accounted part of the Province of the Massachusetts bay and be held & enjoyed by the said Provinces respectively and in the same manner as they now do and have heretofore held and enjoyed the same, and the Court do further judge that the Cost and Charges arising by taking out the Commission, as also for the Commissioners and their Officers vizt the Two Clerks, Surveyor and Waiters for their Travelling Expences & attendance in the Execution of the same be equally born by the said "Provinces."

Both Parties Appealed from the Judgment of the Commissioners to his Majesty in his Privy Council, and the Province of the Massachusetts Bay in their Bill of Exceptions object to the line in Question for this Reason, that it should run North Westward, and not North two degrees Westerly, but they offer not any Exceptions to that part of the River which the Commissioners had considered as the furthermost Head thereof.

This part of the Determination concerning the Line in Question after a rehearing of the partys on the Appeal, was affirmed & a final Judgment given between the two Provinces by the King in Council in the year 1741 & Governor Belcher then Governor of both Provinces received a Copy of the Commissioners Plan and the Kings Instructions to cause the Lines to be run according to the said final Judgment on pain of his Majesty's highest displeasure and a Removal from his Government. Whereupon Governor Belcher came into the Province & ordered the Lines to be run according to the said Instructions, the Northerly line now brought into Question was run by Walter Bryent Esqr an experienced Surveyor of Lands in the Woods who was appointed thereto and Sworn by Governor Belcher to the due and faithful discharge of the Trust and proper Chainmen were also duly Sworn to the faithful discharge of their trust in the marking s^d Line.

Accordingly Mr Bryent went up with them to Newichewanock River and ascended that Branch of it described in the Commissioners Plan until he came to the large ponds at the furthermost head thereof, from thence he began to mark the Line in Question, and proceeded therein as far as at that time he durst on Acco^t of the Indians — This Survey Governor Belcher returned to the proper Office at home where it now lays upon Record.

These are all the principal Facts relative to the running this Line, but the Settlers under the Massachusetts Bay now say that Bryent did not take the main Branch of the River; We have just grounds to assert the very contrary, that he did take the main Branch of the River, and we shoud now offer to your Excellency our Reasons for this Assertion, but that is wholly foreign to the matter under consideration, which is briefly this, not whether Bryent ascended the main Branch, but whether he ascended the Branch markt as the main River in the Commissioners Plan sent to Governor Belcher as part of his Instructions, & that he did so, will appear on compairing his Return and Survey with the said Plan, and is a fact that is indisputed by either party.

Thus after a formal and final Decision of this Boundary of the Provinces by a Judgment of the Commissioners affirmed by the King in Council and in Acquiescence therein on both sides for twenty six years the dispute is now revived the Kings Jurisdiction in this Province is incroached upon, and the Line that was fixed by such high Authority is set aside by one party who in contempt of the Kings final Judgment have boldly made Grants on this side of the Line on no better pretence than that the Commissioners mistook the main Branch of the River when if there was any Reason to suppose such a mistake it ought and it undoubtedly woud have been offered in Argument either before the Commissioners or on the Appeal before the King in Council, but surely it is now too late to offer it, even if it was Fact which in Truth it is not.

And we must further observe to your Excell[y] that if either of the partys have Reason to object to Bryent's Line it must be this Province for there is reason to think that by accident not having upon the spot the Plan sent Governor Belcher he begun the Line one mile to the Westward of the place which the Commissioners had called the head of the River, whereby this Province lost the Breadth of one Mile upon the whole length of their Line. Yet this mistake tho' soon discovered the Province had acquiesced under to avoid litigating a matter anew that had been the subject of so much uneasiness.

We would further remark to your Excell[y] that the Judgment of the Commissioners directs that all the charges of taking out the Commission &c shall be equally born by both Provinces.

This part of the Judgment was also affirmed by the King in Council, but the Province of the Massachusetts Bay refusing to do their duty therein, this Province badly able as they were at that time to bear so great a Charge yet chearfully paid the whole in hopes that with Time and due reflections their Neighbours woud come to a better mind, and reimburse it, but this has not as yet happen'd, and the Province remains as yet unpaid.

Upon the whole matter it appears to us that the Line in question was justly run and not ex Parte by New Hampshire, but that Bryent was ordered & appointed thereto by the authority of Governor Belcher in the capacity of Governor of both Provinces and in obedience to the Instructions he had received for that purpose & without the Advice or concurrence of either the Council or Assembly of this Province, and it appears to us that Bryent ascended the River laid out as the Main River on the Commissioners plan & that his Survey was returned by Govr Belcher to the proper Office at home where it now layes upon Record.

Province of New Hampshire August 12th 1767 — Theodore Atkinson, Peter Livius, Daniel Pierce George Jaffrey /Committee/

Letter, Gov. Wentworth to Gov. Bernard 26 Aug. 1767

Sir

The Grantees of sundry Tracts of Land near the Northeast Limits of this Province have complained to me, that they are obstructed in their Settlement, and prevented from complying with the terms of their respective patents, as granted by the late Governor of this Province, by Capt Brown and his Associates, also by Claimants in the Right of Col^o Frye; who alledge that they have Grants of the said Lands from the Province of the Massachusetts Bay. I have examined the Plan annexed to the Royal Instruction to Governor Belcher (then Governor of both Provinces) Recorded and upon file in the Secretary's Office; I have also interrogated Walter Bryant Esqr the Surveyor, who Surveyed and marked this Line, by order of Govr Belcher, not ex parte, but as Commander in chief of both Provinces: from the fullest consideration of these, and many other irrefragable Evidences I am convinced that the said Lands are clearly within the Bounds of this Province, in which I am confirmed by the plainest Expressions of my Commission. I therefore beg leave to represent to your Excellency that I must preserve his Majesty's Rights committed to my Care, & protect the Subjects of this Province, in the enjoyment of their Property.

It will not avail to trespass on your time by discussing this affair, which at last might be vain, as I can do no other than adhere to the directions prescribed in the Royal Commission.

It is with great reluctance that I am obliged to trouble you upon this Matter which perhaps may be adjusted by a consideration of facts.

I am very respectfully Your Excellency's most Obedient and most devoted humble Servant

J Wentworth

Portsmouth 26th Augt 1767 —

Letter, Gov. Wentworth to Gov. Bernard

Sir

I have before me your Letter of 31st August; And herewith inclose you, the opinion of his Majesty's Council upon the question of the Province Line; wherein you'll readily see, there is not left the least doubt or even the most distant probability that the sd Line was not run by proper and legal Order. The inclosed Deposition of Mr Bryant also urges the Truth & skilfulness of the Survey — Or at least, that if there has been any Error it was to the prejudice of his Majesty's Rights & Revenue in the Province of New Hampshire.

New Hampsh. 10 Sepr 1767

I am with great truth & esteem

Sir your most obedt & most devoted Servt

J Wentworth

Letter, Gov. Bernard to Gov. Wentworth

Boston Sep^t 10th 1767

Sir

I communicated your Letter of Augt 26th to the Council, as I advised you in my last I should do and the same was referred to a Committee upon whose Report the Council advised me to return your Excellency the following Answer.

Your Excellency mentions you have examined the Plan annexed to the Royal instruction to Governor Belcher Recorded & upon file in your Secretary's Office, also interrogated Mr Bryant who Surveyed & marked this Line; and that from there and many other irrefragable evidences you are convinced that the Lands you refer to are clearly within the bounds of the Province of New Hampshire: in which you are Confirmed by the plainest expression of your Commission."

As I am desirous of an amicable adjustment of the Line & to prevent all occasions of contention between the borderers, I am to request that you would be pleased to furnish me with a Copy of the plan & instruction afores^d; Mr Bryants declaration and the other evidences your Excellency refers to, together with such part of your Commission as relates to this matter; and I will lay them before the Assembly who may thereby be enabled to judge of the facts which have induced your Excellency to adopt the sentiments you profess, and you shall be furnished with copies of any papers in the affair you shall want from hence; Extracts from which, containing the substance of said papers are below communicated to your Excellency. In this we shall both of us be possessed of the facts: by a consideration of which this matter (as you observe) may perhaps be adjusted. In the mean time I would acquaint you that the General Assembly here being informed that Mr Bryant had made a mistake in running the Line between the two Provinces; taking his

departure from the head of the Northeast branch of Newich-
awanock or Salmon fall River instead of the main River:
they divers times appointed Committees to be joined by a
Committee on the part of New Hampshire and desired me to
write to the late Governor Wentworth that such Committee
might be appointed, in order to the just Settlement of the
Line. I wrote to him several times accordingly, but no such
Committee was appointed till the last year; when Col° John
Wentworth with Walter Bryant Esqr (the Surveyor who run
the Line) were appointed by him. This Committee with
ours proceeded last November and viewed the main River
and the Northeast Branch aforesaid.— I will now mention
to you the substance of the several Reports of our Committees, and of the evidence that has been taken on our part
relative to said River and Branch.

January 1764 Benjamin Lincoln, Samuel Livermore and
Joseph Frye Esq^{rs} having in Oct° 1763 viewed said River
and Branch report "That from the view we had on the spot
the quantity of water flowing from said River contains two
parts in three more than what run from said branch."
"We beg leave further to offer it as our opinion that the
place from whence the Surveyor took his departure as the
head of Newichwannock or Salmon fall River, when this
Line was run in the year 1741 is not and we think cannot
be understood to be the place intended by the order of his
late Majesty in Council for settling that line."

1766 Decem^r Jonathan Bagley Esqr from another Committee reports, that he with ten others, of which number
were Col° John Wentworth and Walter Bryant Esq^{rs} the
Surveyor (the Committee appointed by Governor Wentworth) proceeded in Novem^r 1766 to the forementioned
River and branch, and after viewing both of them several
times the whole party were called together Sunday Novr 23^d
to judge how large a hole would vent the water that run in

that branch: and after measuring the wedth and depth the party judged the whole water that then run in said Branch would run through a hole as big as a Barrel;" then they took their departure the main River or main branch again in order to view that: which accordingly they did the next day and "it appeared that it was more than three times as large as the northeast branch that Mr Bryant run in 1741, and yielded more than three times as much water."

1767. January 7th James Warren jun^r Gilbert Warren and James Hasty declare, "that in the month of November last / 1766 / they were employed by Jon^a Bagley Esqr and others a Committee appointed by the General Court of Massachusetts Bay and John Wentworth & Walter Bryant Esq^{rs} a Committee appointed by Governor Wentworth, Governor of the Province of New Hampshire in order to view Salmon fall River and the Rivulets running into it and the branches thereof. In pursuance of which the deponents went with said Committees up said Salmon fall River until they came to the place where the Northeastly branch or Brook united with the main River, and they viewed the same" &c and after several views of both, the result is "that it appeared to them that the main River is about three times as large and yielded about three times the quantity of water that the Northeasterly branch did."

The said Gilbert Warren and James Hasty add "That they are well acquainted with the Southwesterly Branch of Salmon fall River which vents into the main River about three miles and an half above the place where the Northeasterly Branch unites with the said main River, and are of opinion that the said Southwesterly branch is near or quite as large and issues near or quite as much water as the Northeasterly Branch."

1767 June 22^d Walter Bryant Esqr the Surveyor who run the Line in 1741 among other questions was asked the following vizt Are you fully satisfied that the Westward Branch [by w^{ch} 'tis supposed the main River was intended] is much bigger than the Eastward Branch which you went up "? his answer is, "I am fully persuaded that the Westw^d branch is much the biggest for several miles up said Branch from where they come together.

This is the Substance of the Report & evidence on our part relative to Newichwannock or Salmon fall River and the Norther Branch of it: which has influenced me and the Assembly to apprehend Mr Bryant made a mistake in running the Line in 1741; and I have here communicated it to you that you might consider it in connection with the Evidence already before you; and that from a view of the whole you might be able to form a Judgment whether a mistake has been made or not.

And in order that I may form a Judgment myself from a view of the whole Evidence & circumstances relative to this matter, I request the favor you would send me a Copy of the Plan, instruction & other papers & evidence mentioned above: the charge of which I shall order to be paid.

    I am &c

           Fra. Bernard

Letter, Gov. Bernard to Thos Goldthwait Esqr

       Jamaica Farm Sep^t 28th 1767

Sir

I communicated your Letter to the Council and upon full deliberation they advised that I should Order you to Augment the Garrison with 8 men, if you shall still think it necessary. I send you a Copy of the Minute which must be your direction. You have two objects in view the repressing the insolence of the Indians & relieving the fears of the people: and if either of these shall require this inforcement, you must raise it. For it is expedient to guard not only against real danger, but against the ill consequences of the apprehension of it; especially so detrimental as the unsettling that Country would be. And as these 8 men make but a small addition, I have thought of a method to double the Service with the same pay; inlist 16 men at half pay & half duty and let them relieve one another every week, the whole being paraded at the time of relieving and let them engage all to repair to the Castle upon a certain Signal. You will judge of the practicability of this: but at all Events let the men enlisted be cloathed as Soldiers; it is in my Opinion a very material Circumstance I hope you attend to it.

We have very unpleasing accounts of the frequent exposure of the Fort. It is said that it is allways in the hands of the Indians when they come to Trade in any number. I am sensible that so small a Garrison as you have now must occasion a great relaxation of discipline; as there are not Men enough to exercise it upon. But you must keep up the forms of Discipline as well as you can. Let the Drumer beat all the usual beats, the reveille, the relief of Guard, the retreat and the tattoo. After the beating the latter, let the Keyes of the Gates be brought to you, and remain with you till the Reveille is beat next Morning. As for the danger arising from the trading, it will not be removed but by setting the Truck house out of the Fort which it seems to me must be done.

I must desire you would do your best to quiet Peoples minds, that they mayn't think of deserting their Settlements; which would be a great disgrace as well as a detriment to the Province. If the People are convinced that it is the smalness of the Garrison which has encouraged the Indians to insult and plunder them (as indeed it has been fully proved before the Council, that it is the chief or sole cause of it) they should petition the General Court & pray that they would allow for a larger Garrison. In such case they will have my Opinion on their side whether it will weigh more or less: I always expected that this reduction would have these Effects.

I have sent you six Barrells of Powder for the use of the Fort, understanding that you have none but what belongs to the Truck Trade. I will write upon the subject of the Indians in a separate Letter that you may communicate it to them with more ease

I am Sir &c
Fra Bernard

P. S. In regard to the Bridge, Platform & Outworks of the Fort, you must do what is necessary for their repair, as you propose, in the most frugal manner.—

Letter, Gov. Bernard to Thos Goldthwait Esq.

Boston Septem^r 29th 1767 —

Sir

I have received your Letter informing me of the Indians insulting & plundering the English Settlers. I know not whether my astonishment or resentment at these hostilities was the greater: and I should have immediately set about punishing the Authors of them, if you had not in the same Letter informed me that the Chiefs of the Tribe had apologized for the Acts of their people and promised to make satisfaction. I am upon that account willing to leave this to a Treaty; but expect that they satisfy not only the people for what they have lost, but the King's Government also for what his dignity has suffered by this insult upon his subjects.

I had intended upon this occasion to have set out for Fort Pownall myself: but am obliged to wait here for particular

Orders which I expect every day to receive from the King. I must therefore leave this negociation to you: and if the Chiefs with whom you have talked are sincere, I hope there will be no great difficulty in it. I must therefore desire that you will call them together as soon after you receive this as may be, and endeavour to reduce what we are to expect and they to undertake to as great a certainty as can be.

Tell them that the Reduction of the Garrison which is supposed to have encouraged this insolence, was made by the confidence we had in their professions of friendship, and they should not have rendered our considering them as our friends a reason for treating us as Enemies. You have now an Order to augment the Garrison if you think fit, & tell them, that if nothing but Soldiers can keep them in order, they shall have Soldiers enough and higher up the River than they are at present. There is now at Halifax a Regiment quite unemployed; and I can have from thence at an hours warning 2 or 300 Men to send up to Passidoukeag if it shall be necessary. If Phillip is among them, tell them I insist upon their delivering him up as a public disturber of the peace. For whilst they harbour such a Villain their Enemy as well as ours, they cannot expect that their professions can gain credit with us. For if they are really our friends, they should show the same resentment against a Man who endeavours to make a Breach between us, which we do. If you can lay hold of that fellow send him to me in Irons; and I will take care that he shant disturb Penobscot again.

Tell them not to deceive themselves with idle stories about a War between England & France. There never was a more cordial intercourse between the two Kings than there is at present: there is nothing for them to quarrel about. But if there should be a variance, N America will not be affected by it: for the French know well they can never get a footing in Canada again. So that if the Indians will fight on the side of France, they must do it by themselves.

As to the satisfaction to be made to the Sufferers by these plunderers, if it is not made when this Letter arrives, I desire you will immediately demand it. And if they cannot pay directly let the damages be liquidated & allowed by the Indians, and let them give their note for the mony payable as soon as can be. And dont be put off with a pretence that they dont know who did the mischief: they must know it, and if they wont discover & deliver up particulars, they must answer for it in the whole. But if they are sincere & are really poor (for I understand their pretended priest has plundered them unmercifully) I would have them allowed all reasonable time for their payments, they giving Security as afores^d

As for the satisfaction to be made to the Government, you will consider what is due to it's honour and dignity, which has been violated upon this occasion. Tell them in general that I am really & truly their friend, and I desire that they would not oblige me to appear as their Enemy.—

I am Sir &c

Fra. Bernard

Petition. Oct. 12, 1767

To His Excellency Francis Bernard Esqr Governor & Commander in Chief of the Province of the Massachusetts Bay &c &c The Honble His Majesty's Council, And the Honble House of Representatives.

The Petition of the Officers and Soldiers of Fort Pownall together with the Inhabitants in the new settlements adjacent thereto, humbly sheweth, That whereas we your Petitioners sometime past had the great advantage and satisfaction of attending upon divine Service at Fort Pownall, while Mr William Crawford was continued Chaplain to that Garrison, and also had his assistance as a Physician & surgeon, which has been a great Benefit to us who are placed at so great a distance from other help; we would humbly represent, that we your humble Petitioners, have endeavour'd to give what Encouragement we could to cause Mr Crawford to tarry amongst us But we are new settlers and most of us have but little to help ourselves with & as most of us who do not now belong to the Garrison, have been disbanded from it, & but very bare handed, so that if he has no assistance but w^t we at present can afford him, he must unavoidably leave us, which will be very hard as there is no Preacher, nor Doctor within fifty Miles of this Place And as he has always done his Duty faithfully and to acceptance; If this Hon'ble Court will see fit to continue him, it will be esteem'd a Great favor done to your Petitioners, And your Petitioners As in Duty Bound will ever pray

 Penobscot River October 12, 1767.

Tho Goldthwait	Jedidiah Preble Ju^r	Jeremiah Veasey
William Wescutt	Jon^a Lowder Junr	Sam^ll Cousens
Josh^a Treat	William Pratt	Joseph Lowel
Lunchlan McLean	William Oliver	Asa Harriman
Thomas Cooper	Sebaen Colwell	Moses Crags
Lach^or McDonald	Joseph Viles	Mathew X (his mark) Toben
Samuel low	Robert McFerlend	Jonathan Buck Junr
William Thomson	Willem Berreck	Jonathan Harrod
Reuben Petcher	William Maycock Junr	Kenneth McKenzie
Stephen Littlefield	Paul Bouden	Daniel X Warren
Joshua M	Tim X (his mark) Pratt	Samuel Crarge
Gustavus Swan	John Peirce	Charls Curtis
James Martin	John X (his mark) Bouden	Joshua Eayr
Joshua X (his mark) Grindle	Daniel Lancaster	Jac^o Clayford

Isaac Clewly	Samuel Wilson	John H^his M̄S Morton	Smith
Jeremiah Thompson	Eph^m X^his Stimson	Donold X^mark	Godill
Zethem French	Hatr Collson^mark	James Clements	
Josiah Collson	Joseph X^his Page	Ichabod Collson	
Timothy Clements	Pierce Hurley^mark		

Letter, from Dennys De Berdt

London 21ᵗ of octʳ 1767

Sir

I have the Honour of your Letter from the House, and with regard to the affair of the Fishery: I had made application for removing your grievances before I rec^d this your Letter from the House, and as I have heard no complaints this Season I flatter myself the Effort was not fruitless —

I was well apprised how happily you were releived from the late difficulties of a paper currency and the contentment the sensible part of your Province experience in having a solid Medium to have ever recommended [a change from a] solid Coin to a precarious [and doubtful paper] currency and whenever the matter is under consideration, [I hope you may repeat] the precautions in your Letter —

The Limits of the Colonies whenever any disputes arise about them are always refer'd to the Board of Trade and the Lords of Trade according to the evidence produced report the same to the King & Council: so that I can do nothing in the Matter as Agent of the Province untill my appointment under the Seal of the Province is register'd at that Board: which would also give me additional weight in every other application.

I am with the highest Esteem yours and the House's devoted Humble Servant

Dennys De Berdt

Extracts from Speech   Dec. 30, 1767.

" Gentlemen of the Council, and Gentlemen of the House of Representatives."

" I have also to communicate a Letter which I have received from his Excellency Govr Wentworth with several Inclosures relating to the dispute concerning the Boundary Line between that part of this Province called the Province of Maine and the Province of New Hampshire. I must desire that you will give these due Consideration as soon as you well can; as the business is of long standing."

Fra Bernard

Council Chamber Decem^r 30th 1767

Province of the Massachusetts Bay

To his Excellency Francis Bernard Esqr Captain General & Commander in chief In & over his Majesties Province of the Massachusetts-Bay   To the Honble his Majesties Council & To the Honble House of Representatives in general Court Assembled January 1768

The Petition of Josiah Richardson Esqr Agent to a Number of Petitioners (whose Names are herewith exhibitted whose ancestors were on the Expedition against Canada in the year 1690— Humbly shews That your Petitioner as agent as beforementioned preferred a Petition to this Court at their Sessions in June last which Petition was read & committed to a Com^{tee} of this Honble House which Com^{ttee} (as your Pet^r has been informed) thought The Prayer thereof reasonable but as it was so near the Close of that Session the s^d Com^{ttee} only reported that the Consideration of s^d Petition should be referred to the then next Session of this Honble Court at which Session your Pet^r Attended when to his Great Surprize your Pet^r finds by a Vote of this House of the 7th of January Instant that your Petitioner might have Liberty to withdraw his s^d Petition or Memorial Your Petitioner therefore most humbly prays That this hon^ble Court would reassume the Consideration of s^d Petition or Memorial & if this Honble Court shall think proper make a Grant of some of the unappropriated Lands of this Province to your Petitioner & his Associates or let your Pet^r be heard by a Com^ttee as The Rest of the Sufferers in the aforesd Expedition in the Year 1690 have Rec^d Grants from the general Court Your Petitioner Conceives that your Pet^r & his Associates are equally entitle to the same Grace & Favour we having proved our Heirship more than twenty years Ago & were prevented having our Grants compleated by the burning of the Court House —

all which is more fully expressed in the Pet^n above referred to and herewith exhibited or that your Pet^r & his associates may be otherways relieved as this hon^ble Court shall think proper & your Pet^r as in Duty bound shall ever pray

Josiah Richardson agent for the Petitioners

Deposition. 1768.

The Deposition of Simon Ayer of Haverhill of Laful Age who testifys and Says that he was at Newbury at the hous of Mr Whitman inholder in July the Twenty ninth 1765 At a Meeting of the Proprietors of Bakers Town so called when theer was aBought fifteen or sixteen of the Proprietors Meet together and that Maj^er Saml Gerish and Capt Moses Little Agent to said proprietors then Requested Security for the pay to them for thier Application for a New Township or that said proprietors would then Vote that their Agents should have the over Plush of Six Mile Squar or of a Certain measure then propos^d in Case they Shold Obtain a Grant — And that it was then Voted that the agents Shuld have the over Plush on Certain Conditions and further Testifys that he is Fuly Perswaded and of oppinion that their was abowet five or six Proprietors that then Voted away the over Plush Land and that it was then agreed and Voted that the agents shuld Lay out the township and Lotts for the proprietors on thier own Cost and Charge and Repay the Proprietors the money they had then Advansed.

Simon Ayer

Haverhill Jany 4th 1768 —

N B I Never knew of the meting at m^r Whitmors inholder in Newbury may ^th 27^d 1765 Nor the word Prinsible Proprietor till after it was all over —

Essex ss January 21st 1768 Then the within Name^d Simon Ayer apeared and made oath to the truth of the within declarences —

before   Nathaniel Peaslee Justice Peace

The above named Simon Ayer being asked whether he was a proprietor of backers town and he declared he was

Nathaniel Peaslee Justice Peace

Message   *Jany 19, 1768.*

Gentlemen of the House of Representatives

I hereby send you Copies of Advices I received from Fort Pownall some time ago with the proceedings of the Council thereupon and my Orders in pursuance thereof. From all these you will perceive that the Indians have been encouraged by the late reduction of the Garrison to an insolence, which had very near broke up all the Settlements in that part of the Country; and you must be convinced that if you would maintain your claim to the Lands on the East side of Penobscot, which is still disputed, and would encourage the improvement of the Country by population, you must provide for the security of the Settlers by making the Fort more respectable than it was when those disorders were committed.

It will be also necessary for the Security of the Fort to remove the Truck house out of it. At present when the Indians who come in to Trade must be allowed to enter the Fort. It is impossible with the present small Garrison to keep a Guard sufficient to prevent its being surprised. Whereas if the Truck house was removed to a small distance from the Fort, but under its cannon, It would be safe itself, and not endanger the Fort. A small expence will, serve to erect a building for that purpose.

I also lay before you a Petition of the Inhabitants about Fort Pownall. It is not pretended that a Chaplain is necessary to the Garrison of the Fort reduced as it has been. But the Chaplain which you established there was the only Minister of the Gospel within a circle of One hundred Miles diameter now generally peopled tho' but thinly. And as the Settlers are not able to maintain a Minister of themselves, It is a Charity of the highest kind to assist them in providing for their spiritual Wants, by keeping up Religion among them; of which they must otherwise be destitute.

I have not as yet received any advice from Fort Pownall that the Indians have made any satisfaction for the Mischiefs they have done, or given any assurance that they will not repeat the same.

Fra Bernard

Council Chamber January 19th 1768 —

Petition of Henry Y. Brown 1768.

Province of the Mass^a Bay

To His Excell: Francis Bernard Esq Capt Genl Govr &

Commander in chief   The Hon¹ his Majestys Council & House of Rep^ves for said Province in General Court Assembled   February 1768

Humbly Shews   Henry Young Brown

That on the 23ᵈ of January A: D: 1764 The General Court made him a Grant of a Township to be laid out on Saco River above Col° Joseph Frye's Township,   The Conditions thereof will appear by said Grant, he laid it out according to said Court's directions & returned them a Plan of the same:

On the 7ᵗʰ June following the Plan was accepted & the Lands thus laid out were confirmed to your Petit^r & his heirs & assigns forever.

In order to perform the Conditions of the Obligations he was under to settle said Lands he has been at the expence to move his Family & introduce a number of others into said Township where they have been at great expence in bringing forward said Settlement.

In Novr 1765 He informed the Gen¹ Court that the greatest part of said Township was claimed by the Province of New Hampshire, who then took the affair under consideration & directed him to proceed in the settlement thereof.

In June 1766. He was directed to Prosecute any persons who should enter on said Township under the New Hampshire Title & defend all actions brought against him or his Setlers at the expence & under the directions of this Government.—

Oct° 7ᵗʰ 1767. He was advised by His Excell^y & the Hon° Council not to proceed in Law against those claiming under New Hampshire until the General Court could have an opportunity to consider the papers received from his Excell & Governor Wentworth.—

After the great expences he has been at, and fatigue & trouble he has endured in the affair he is so situated that he is unable to reap any advantages by disposing of any part of said Lands but on the contrary is at continual expence in pursuing the directions of this Hon^l Court

Not only your Petit^r & his Setlers ; but this Province too he humbly apprehends will suffer by any longer delay in setling the Line

Wherefore he humbly prays this Hon^d Court will take some speedy & effectual measures to settle the Line aforesaid, that he may reap some advantage from his great labors, and otherwise releived as your wisdom shall dictate

And as in duty bound shall ever pray,

Henry Young Brown

Petition of John Cox

Province of the Massachusetts Bay To his Excellency Francis Bernard Esqr Capt General & Governour of said Province, the Honble his Majestys Council & House of Representatives in General Court assembled January 1768 —

Humbly shews John Cox of Falmouth in the County of Cumberland, That Samuel Waldo Esqr Coll^l of the Regiment in said County, in the Month of August 1758 impressed his Sloop called the Ranger, himself Master to carry about One Hundred & Forty Men belonging to said Regiment for Relief of St Georges when attack'd by the Indians, that your Petitioner with five of his People together with his said Sloop were imployed Six Days in s^d Service for which he has never yet received one Farthing, altho he humbly conceives he is intitled to Forty eight Dollars vizt Eight Dollars p Day for his, his Peoples & Sloops Service. He has repeatedly apply'd to Coll^l Waldo for Payment, and has been as often refused, & told by the Coll^o to apply to the Province for Pay who had paid the Men that were sent. Wherefore he now resorts to your Excellency & Honours for Redress, humbly requesting that Such Recompence may be made him for said Service as to you shall seem meet, and as in Duty bound will ever pray —

$\qquad\qquad\qquad\qquad\qquad\qquad\qquad$ John Cox —

The petitioner rec^d Pay for the same Sloop in the Kings Service in the Year 1760   129 Tuns and an half

In the House of Representatives Feby 9 1768

Resolvd that the Sum of Twelve Pounds be allowd & paid out of the publick Treasury to the Petitioner in full of the Services within mentiond

$\qquad\qquad$ Sent up for Concurrence

$\qquad\qquad\qquad\qquad\qquad\qquad$ T Cushing Spk^r

In Council Feby 1õ. 1768.   Read & Concurred

$\qquad\qquad\qquad\qquad\qquad\qquad$ A Oliver Sec^y

Consented to   Fra. Bernard

$\qquad\qquad\qquad\qquad$ *Resolve.*

In the House of Representa^{ts} Feby 15, 1768

The House taking under consideration his Excel^y Message of the 19th Jany with respect to Fort Pownall

Resolved that there be a farther Establishment of Eight privates for the defence of said Fort at the rate of one pound four shill^g p^r month, and also for One Chaplain at the rate of four pounds p^r Month, ending the 20th of June next

$\qquad$ Sent up for Concurrence   T Cushing Speaker

In Council 15 Feby 1765   Read & Concurred

$\qquad\qquad\qquad\qquad\qquad\qquad$ A Oliver Sec^y

$\qquad$ Consented to $\qquad$ Fra Bernard

Message. Feb. 16, 1768.

Gentlemen of the House of Representatives

In answer to your Message of the 13th inst. I find it necessary to inform you that soon after the Letter of the Earl of Shelburne was read in your House I ordered a Copy of it to be given to the Speaker to be used as He should think fit, upon condition that no other Copy should be taken thereof: I am very willing that the Copy in the Speakers hands should be communicated to you in Any Manner which is consistent with that restriction.

I know of no letters of my own which I think can be of any use to you upon this occasion.

I quite agree with you in Opinion that all effectual Methods should be taken to cultivate an Harmony between the several branches of the Legislature of this Government, as being necessary to promote the prosperity of the province: and I shall chearfully join with you in all proper Measures for so Salutary a purpose.

Fra Bernard

Council Chamber Feb. 16, 1768

Extract from Message to the Governor.

In the House of Representatives Febry 18th 1768

Ordered, That Mr Hancock, Major Fry Collº Richmond Coll Noyes & Collº Stoddard be a Committee to wait upon his Excellency the Governor, and present to him the following Answer to his Message of the 16th Instant.

T Cushing Speaker

" May it please your Excellency,

your Message of the 16th Instant has been read and duly considered in the House of Representatives, The manner in

which your Excellency was pleased to introduce into this
House the Letter from the Right Honorable the Earl of Shelburne, by giving Orders to the Secretary to read it without
leaving a Copy, appeared to be unprecedented and unparliamentary, but this made but a light Impression on the House,
when the Members recollected as far as they could the unfavorable Sentiments his Lordship thought himself necessitated
to entertain of the two Houses of this Assembly, and of some
particular Members in this House, whose Characters in the
Opinion of the House stand unimpeachable — Under this
Apprehension they thought it necessary for their own Vindication humbly to request your Excellency to favor them with
a Copy of his Lordship's Letter; and as it appeared to them
that his Lordship had formed his Sentiments of the two
Houses and their Members from your own Letters to which
he referred, the House thought they could not do themselves
and their Members Justice unless they could be favored with
a Sight of them also, and accordingly requested it of your
Excellency."

Bill for incorporating Phillipstown. 1768.

Anno Regni Regis Georgii tertii octavo.

An Act for erecting a Tract of Land of eight Miles Square
call^d Phillips town Joyning upon the North West end of the
Town of Wells in the County of York; into a Town by the
Name of

Whereas the erecting of that Tract of Land call^d Phillips
Town into a Town will greatly Contribute to the Growth
Thereof, and Remedy many Inconveniences to which the
Inhabitants and Proprietors may be Otherwise Subject —

Be it ennacted by the Governor Council and House of Representatives that the Tract aforesaid Bounded as followeth — viz Lying on the North West end of the Town of Wells West of Kennebunk River East of the Town of Berwick and North by Province Grants in part & in part by unappropriated Lands be and hereby is erected into a Town by the Name of   and that the Inhabitants Thereof be and hereby are invested with all Powers Privilledges and Immunities which the Inhabitants of the Towns within this Province do enjoye

And be it further ennacted that Benj^a Chadburne Esqr be and he hereby is Impowered to Issue his Warrant Directed to some Principal Inhabitant of said Town Requireing him to Warn the Inhabitants of said Town who have an Estate of Freehold According to Charter to meet at such Time and place as shall be therein set fourth to Chuse all such Officers as are or Shall be Required by Law to mannage the Affairs of said Town.

In the House of Representatives Feb. 19 1768

Read a first time — P.M. Read a second & third time & passed to be engrossed

    Sent up for Concurrence   T Cushing Speaker

In Council Feby 20. 1768 —   Read a first Time —

Read a second time and passed a concurrence to be engrossed.

                                    A Oliver Sec^y

Petition of Selectmen of Sanford. 1768.

To his Excellency Francis Bernard Esqr Governor & Commander in Cheif in and over the Province of the Massachusetts Bay &c: To the Honourable his Majestys Council and the Honourable House of Representatives in General Court assembled may 1768

The Petition of Benjamin Harmon Naptali Harmon and John Stanyan Selectmen of the Town of Sanford in the County of York in behalf of said Town Humbly Shews

That said Town was Incorporated into a Town the present year, and that the assessors have Taken the valuation as by Law Directed according to the best of there Understanding,

That there is a Considerable number of Polls Contained in the list of Valuation of People latly come in said Town from the Province of N. Hampshire in Very Poor Carcomstances and as your Petitioners apprehends there stay will be very Short as they have no Lands of there own, And that most of the Inhabitants of said Town are very Poor and unable to Support them Selves, That they are Destitute of a minister and School Master which by Law they are now obliged to be Provided with nor have they any Meeting House in said Town, That the Town is now obliged to Clear & Make new Roads through the Town Leading to other new Towns beyond them, the Lands in General but very Ordinary they Never had any help from the Proprietors to Enable them to support the Gospel or Making Roads in said Town and the setlers but Smal Tracts of Lands for Settlements, Tho: the Township is Eight Miles Square Your Petitioners apprehends that a Province Tax Even a Poll Tax would Greatly Distress the Inhabitants of s^d Town

Wherefore your Petetioners Humbly prays your Excellency and Honours that you will not Lay any Province Tax on said Town the present year on the Polls and Estates — That they may be Enabled to Settle the Gospel which they are now Engageing and in And Your Petitioners as in Duty Bound shall Ever pray

Benj^a Harmon
Naptali Harmon
John Stanyan

Deposition.

I Josiah Richardson of Lawfull age testifye and say that Ever since the year A D 1737 I have acted as an Agent for a numb^r of Petitioners whose anchestors ware in the Expedition to Canada in the year 1690 and in the year 1737 I in behalfe of my selfe and my assoctits prefered a petition to the Honarable Grate and Genarail Court praying for a Grant of Land to be Mad to us on account of our s^d anchester being in the s^d Expedition (as many oathers had) had before for their Grat Suffering and Services in the s^d Expedition and that by a Grat Number of memorials I have Revived the s^d petition from time to time and now I Do Testeyfye and Declare that to my Sertain Knoledge theire never as yet has ben aney Grant of Land made to them on account of their Anchesters being in the said Expedition witteness my hand this 23^d Day of may: 1768

Josiah Richardson

Middlesex ss may ye 23rd 1768

the above said Josiah Richardson Parsonaley appeared befor me the Subcriber one of his majests Justices of the Peace for the Countey of middle and after being Carfulley Examined and Duley Cautioned to Testeyfye to the truth mad oath to the truth of the above Declaration aboves^d by him Subscribed

before me   Jos: Buckminster

Prov^e of the Mass^{tts} Bay

To his Excellency Francis Bernard Esq Governor in chief in and over his Majestys Province of the Massachusetts Bay in New England; The hon^{ble} his Majesty's Council and House of Representatives in Genl Court assembled the 25th of May A D 1768 — Humbly shews

The Freeholders & other Inhabitants of the Town of Windham in the County of Cumberland legally assembled for this purpose at said Windham on the twenty eighth day of March A D 1768

That Your petitioners presented their petition to the Gen[l] assembly of this province in May 1767 —

Wherein they set forth that the Inhabitants of said Town were at " a great charge and expence in settleing and sup-
" porting public Worship amongst them and also that large
" sums were still wanting for clearing Roads and making
" them passable &c And that the proprietors of said Town
" had laid out and appropriated most of their Lands into
" hundred acre Lots which /except the very small part that
" was under actual improvement/ could not be charged with
" any Sort of taxes by the Town or proprietors tho' the clear-
" ing and preparing Roads is principally for the proprietors
" advantage Wherefore your petitioners prayed that the
" Assessors or Selectmen of y[e] s[d] Town for the Time being
" might be authorized and impower'd to assess on every Acre
" of the several 100 acre Lots in said Town not otherways taxed
" one penny yearly to be paid into the Town Treasury there
" to be applied to the uses aforementioned and that such
" payment might be inforced by such ways and means as to
" your Excellency and the Hon[ble] Court should seem meet "-
In answer to which petition a Memorial was presented to the General Court then sitting by Nathan Bowen Jeremiah Lee and Isaac Mansfield Esq[rs] a Committee of the proprietors of the Town of Windham in which they set forth that they did not oppose the Tax prayed for, but prayed that by a public Act of the Government The Assessors of the said Town of Windham for three Years then next ensuing might be authorized and impower'd to assess yearly one penny on every acre of every 100 Acre Lott in the said Town not otherways taxed, except ministerial & school Lands and that

the Assessors of s^d Town by such Act be impower'd to enforce the payment of such Tax by legal sale of so much of the delinquent Lands as shall be necessary to pay the said Tax and charges &c as by the petition and Memorial aforementioned Copies whereof herewith exhibited will more fully appear —

Upon which petition the third of March last the whole Court resolved, "That the assessors of the said Town of
" Windham for three years next ensuing be authorized and
" impower'd to assess one penny p acre on every 100 Acre
" Lot in said Town not otherways taxed, except ministerial
" and school Lands, & that ye s^d assessors be impower'd to
" enforce the payment of such Tax by Legal Sales of so much
" of the delinquent Lands as shall be necessary to pay the
" said Tax and charges thereupon arising; & that ye s^d Town
" be impower'd in their March meeting for the said three
" Years next coming to chuse two Collectors, one of them to
" be an inhabitant of Marblehead and that one half of the
" money raised by s^d Tax be paid into the hands of the Treas-
" urer of said Town of Windham to be by them applied to
" the paying the ministerial & other Town charges, the other
" half to be paid to the proprietors Treasurer to be by them
" applied to the opening and making passable such ways as
" still remain in a Wilderness state as by said Order on file
" will fully appear "

Now your petitioners humbly shew that many of the Inhabitants and proprietors of ye s^d Town of Windham are apprehensive that the authority given by the afores^d recited Resolve or Order of Court is insufficient for the purposes therein mentioned and that in Case Sale should be made agreeable to said Resolve of the delinquent Lands the payment of s^d Tax /especially as the Method or Manner of Sale is not therein particularly pointed out or described and they are at a loss to know what was intended by a legal Sale/

Differences and Disputes may hereafter arise & that Harmony, peace and Concord which has hitherto subsisted between the proprietors and Inhabitants of ye s^d Town of Windham /& which they wish still to preserve/ may be disturbed and broken Wherefore your pet^{rs} humbly pray your Excellency & Honors that the payment of the Taxes afores^d may be enforced by an Act or Law of the province explicitly determining the Method and Manner of such Sale of the delinquent Lands as may be necessary for raising the Taxes afores^d and also that your petitioners may be specially impower'd to chuse at a future Town meet^g two Collectors for the gathering the Tax afores^d for the ensuing year which was neglected at their Town meeting in March last by reason of the difficulties afores^d or otherwise relieve your pet^{rs} as in your Wisdom shall seem meet & as in duty bound shall ever pray & —

   Signed by Order of   Abraham Anderson
       the Town

Resolve

The following Order passed on the Petition of Abraham Anderson in behalf of the Town of Windham vizt

In the House of Represent^s March 3^d 1768

Resolved That the assessors of the said Town of Windham for three years next ensuing be authorized and impowered to assess yearly one penny p acre on every hundred acre Lot in said Town of Windham not otherwise taxed, except Ministerial and School Lands That the said assessors be impowered to enforce the payment of such Tax by legal Sale of so much of the delinquent Lands as shall be necessary to pay said Tax and Charges thereupon arising ; and that the said

Town be impowered in their March Meeting for the said three years next coming to chuse two Collectors, one of whom to be an Inhabitant of Marblehead and That one half of the Money raised by said Tax be paid into the hands of the Treasurer of the said Town of Windham to be by them applied to the paying the Minister and other Town Charges; the other half to be paid into the Proprietors Treasury to be by them applied to the opening & making passable such ways as still remain in a Wilderness State

   Sent up for Concurrence   T Cushing Spk^r
In Council March 4th 1768   Read & Concurred
            Jn° Cotton D Sec̃ry
   Consented to   Fra Bernard
   A true Copy   Exam^d p Jn° Cotton D Sec̃ry

Petition of Inhab^{ts} of Sebascodegin Island. 1768.

Province of the Mass^{tts} Bay

 To His Excellency Francis Bernard Esqr Governour and Commander in Cheif of said Province The Honble His Majestys Councill and the Honourable House of Representatives of said Province in General Court Assembled on May 25, 1768.—

The Petition of the Inhabitants of Sebascodegin Island in the District of Harpswell in the County of Cumberland.
   Most humbly Sheweth

That in the Act of Incorporation of said District about 11 Years past, said Island by the Name of Great Sebascodegin Island alias Shapleigh's Island, was included in said Act, & annexed to said District of Harpswell, that when this was done we were but few in Number, not of our Motion, or Choice, nor were we so much as advised with, yet we Submitted to this Act of Government from a Principle of Duty, and from the Encouragement then given us, that whenever we were able to support the Gospell among our Selves, that the Other Inhabitants Setled on Merryconeag Neck would readily consent to our being sett off as a distinct Parish: And in particular when the Revd Mr Samuel Eaton was setled this was publickly mentioned & conceded to, at a meeting of said Inhabitants, altho' no formal vote was passed, or any Record made thereof, yet this appeared to be the Sence of many then present. Your Petitioners beg leave to represent to your Excellency, & Honours, that there are now setled on said Island about fifty Families, and at their own Cost & Charge they have erected, & built a Meeting house on said Island to the Expence of Three hundred pounds, lawfull Money, and have now a Gentleman preaching to us in whom we are all well united and he would be encouraged to stay among us; altho' our Abilities are comparatively small, yet if we could obtain the Favour of this Court so as to be sett off a distinct Parish, it would greatly contribute to our Increase, and under the Divine Blessing & Protection to our future Prosperity, & Welfare by which our Ability to support the Gospell among us would be enlarged. For which purpose we have first applyed to our Christian Brethren for their Consent, who have (notwithstanding their former Encouragement given us, & not regarding the great Difficulties we are exposed to in Travell by Land as well as water, which in a tempestuous Season, which often happens, is impracticable for our Wives & Children) unkindly denyed their Consent to our being Sett off a distinct Parish, when by estimation many of the Inhabitants on said Island live at the Distance of 12, 13 & 14 Miles from the stated place of Worship on said Neck, which in the Winter Season is attended with great Hazard & Danger to our Lives to gett there, in crossing the River on many Accounts which might be mentioned.—

We acknowledge that by Agreement it is provided, that the Minister shall preach to the Inhabitants living on said Island One third part of the Year, but by reason of the above mentioned Difficulties in travelling, and the Infirmity of Body under which the Revd Mr Eaton Labours, this is not, nor cannot be fully performed, & we are thereby deprived of this Advantage for our Selves & Children.—

We are free to declare to this Honoured Court, that it is not from any disaffection to our present Pastor, whom we highly esteem & honour, nor from any want of Affection to our Christian Brethren that we are seeking this, but we trust from a Sincere Regard to the Divine Institutions, & that we may have the enjoyment of those Christian Priviledges, to which we think our Selves Justly entitled.

In a humble dependance on the Favour of this Honoured Court we hope that the Reasons and Motives offered on our part, will have that Influence with your Excellency, & Honours as to take the Prayer of this Petition into your wise consideration, and direct that the Inhabitants on said Island may be erected into a Separate Precinct, that so we may enjoy the Priviledges of the Gospell in common with other Christians, in a more decent & convenient Manner, or otherwise grant that Releif to your Petitioners as your Excellency & Honours shall in your Wisdom Judge meet: And your Petitioners as in Duty bound shall ever pray, &c

Abiezer Holbrook	Joseph Combs	Anthony Combs juner
Jonathan Holbrook	T Small jun	John Ross
Isaac Snow	Joseph Lincoln	Joseph Ross
John Snow	Josiah Wells	John Matthews
Elisha Snow	Simon Page	Paule Ray mon
Samuel Williams	John Rankins	Stephen De
William Thompson	Isaac Hall	Phillip Aubens
Joseph Thompson	Isaac Hall jun^r	James Stacpole
James Ridley	John Hall	Willam Stacpole

James Ridley juner Thomas Ross   Small
Simeon Hopkins   Joseph Hall   Samuel Mores
James Rankins   Nath¹ Hall   Ezeikel Clemons
Constant Rankins   David Welch   Wiliem Hasey
Nathanael Purenton Anthony Combs

Resolve, In the House of Representitives June yᵉ 2ᵈ 1768

Resolved that yᵉ Petitioners Notify the District of Harpswell by Leaveing An attested Coppy of this Petition with the Clerk of said District to shew cause if any they have on the second Wednesday of the next Seting of this Court why the Prayer there of should not be granted.

Sent up for Concurrence

In Council 2ᵈ June 1768   Read and Nonconcurred
                                        A Oliver Secʳ

Petition of the Selectmen of Gorham "*June 1, 1768.*"

To his Excellency Francis Bernard Esqʳ Captain General and Governour in Chief in and over his Majesties Province of the Massachusets Bay in New England The Honourable his Majesties Council and House of Representatives in General Court Assembled

The Petition of the selectmen of the Town of Gorham in the name of said Town Humbly sheweth That by reason of the Many Misfortunes that has happened in said Town within these few years and the settlement of a minister of the Gospel among us, brings on us a burthen which we find exceeding hard to bare and the exceeding scarcity of mony adds weight to that burthen, and inasmuch as two thirds of the lands in Gorham is owned by non resident Proprietors who are Equally benefitted in the raising Price of their Lands with those that are Resident proprietors, and that by the settlers improvements and their multiplication in said Town as to Numbers, and the Settlement of the Gospel here, We are humbly of the opinion that the non Resident proprietors are held in Justice to Contribute something towards the defraying the Charges of the Gospel Ministry among us for That who feels the benefit ought to feel the burden was never a bad maxim, we therefore Humbly pray that your Excellency and Honours would take the affair under your wise Consideration and Order so much upon the Acre on all unimproved Lands already Divided into Lots in said Town not otherwise paying taxes as Your Excellency and Honours shall in your Great Wisdom order and for such Time as may be Convenient which sum so ordered, be for the support of the Gospel in said Place and your Petitioners as in Duty bound shall ever pray

     Joseph Cates) Selectmen
     Edmund Phinney } of
     Hugh M^{c}lalen) Gorham

Memorial of James Small and others to be set from the First Parish in Falmouth to the District of Cape Elizabeth.

Province of the Massachusetts Bay in New England 1768
 To his Excellency Francis Barnard, Esqr Captain General and Governor in Chief in and over his Majestyes Province of the Massachusetts Bay in New England, and Vice Admiral of the Same —

To the Honourable his Majesty's Council. And the Honourable House of Representatives, in the Greate and General Court assembled

 This memorial Humbley Sheweth, that we your Memorialists and our Estates ware Some Years ago Set of from the (then) Second Parish in Falmouth to the first Parish in said Town by an Act of the Honourable Court. But finding it burdensom to cross the Water to attend Publick Worship, with the other Disadvantages attending the same,

Influenced your Memorialists some time ago to Petition to the Honourable Court Praying to be Set back again, the Prayer whereof has not as yet bin Granted. But when Said Second Parish was Incorporated into a District, we apprehended that we no more belonged to the First Parish in Falmouth, but to the District of Cape Elizabeth, and accordingly we have been Raited in said District to the Minister and Sundrey of us have Paid Said Raits and have got Receits, Yet Not With Standing they Continnue to Rait us to the first Parish in Said Falmouth.

Therefore as we your Memorialests do Receive Gosple Priviledges in Said District, we are desirous of Paying our Raits there. And whereas some of us the Subscribers under Stand that names have been lately returnd into the Secretaryes Office by a Committee of the First Parish in Falmouth Seting forth our Desires to be continnued to said first Parish, which Signing was Obtained in an unfair way.

Therefore we your Memorialests humbley Pray that we whoes Names are hereunto Subscribed May, with our Estates be Set from the first Parish in said Falmouth to the District of Cape Elizabeth, as your Memorialests in duty bound shall Ever Pray.

Saml Skillin	James Small	Loring Cushing
Anthony Strout	Jonathan Loveitt	humphry Richards
Eben^r Thorndike	Daniel Strout	George Roberds
John Robinson	Joseph Sawyer	Vallentin Wieman
Nathanell Jordan jun^r	Jonathan Mitchell	Robert Thorndike
Robert Thorndick Jn^r	Robert Stanford	Joshua Strout
Joseph Stanford	Samuel dyer	Thomas Cushing
Thomas Fickett	Isaac Loveitt	Josiah Stanford Ju^r
Samuel Dunn	Samuel Skillin Junr	

"Pet^n of James Small & others —
May 30, 1769 Read ord^d to ly June 6 1768.
Cap. Fuller, Dr Calef, Mr Nye. June 16, rep^t accepted."

Report. 1768.

The Committee appointed to take into consideration the petition of Ichabod Jones and others, have attended that Service, heard the petitioners and fully considered the same beg leave to report it as our opinion, that the Tract of land described in their said petition be granted to the petitioners their heirs and assigns forever Agreeable to the form of a Vote herewith Exhibited —

All which is humbly submitted

Vote. 1768.

In the House of Representatives June 7 1768

Voted That the Petition of Ichabod Jones and Seventy nine others his Associates, be so far granted, as that there be and hereby is granted unto him the said Ichabod Jones, and his Associates named in the Annexed petition, their heirs and assigns forever as Tenants in Common, One Township of Land situate lying and being to the Westward of St Croix about Eight or ten leagues, which Tract of land is now known by the Name of Machias, and is bounded as follows vizt beginning at a dry Rock at a place called the Eastern Bay near the House of Mr Samuel Holmes and extending North ten degrees West, ten Miles then West ten degrees South eight Miles, then South ten degrees East ten Miles, then East ten degrees North eight miles to the first mentioned bounds;

That they return a Plan of the same (taken by a Surveyor and Chain Men on Oath) to this Court for further Confirmation, on or before the first day of June next;

That they within Six years after they shall obtain his majesty's approbation of this Grant (unless prevented by War)

Settle the said Township with Eighty good Protestant Families, and build Eighty Houses, none to be less than eighteen feet Square, and seven feet Stud, and clear and cultivate five Acres of Land on each Share fit for Tillage or Mowing, and that they build in said Township a suitable Meeting House for the Publick Worship of God, and settle a learned Protestant Minister, and make Provision for his Comfortable and honourable Support: and that in said Township there be reserved and appropriated, four whole Rights or Shares in the Division of the same (accounting to one Eighty fourth part a Share) for the following purposes vizt One for the first Settled or Ordained Minister his heirs and assigns forever; one for the use of the Ministry, one to and for the use of Harvard College; and one for the use of a School forever: And if any of the Grantees or Proprietors of said Township shall neglect within the Term of Six Years as before mentioned, to do and perform according to the Several Articles respecting the Settlement of his Right or Share as hereby enjoined, his whole Right or Share shall be entirely forfeited and enure to the use of the Province, Provided nevertheless the Grant of the above Lands is to be void and of none Effect, unless the Grantees do obtain his Majesty's Confirmation of the same in Eighteen Months from this time —

And be it further Ordered as a Condition of the Grant aforesaid, that each Grantee give Bond to the Treasurer of this Province for the time being, and to his Successors in said office, for the sum of Fifty pounds for the use of this Province for the faithfull performance of the duties required, according to the Tenour of the Grant aforesaid: and that a Committee or Committees be appointed by this Court to take Bonds accordingly.—

And further Ordered That the said Committee be impowered to admit others as Grantees in the room of such persons contained in the list aforesaid, who shall neglect to appear by themselves or others in their behalf to give Bonds at such time as the Committee shall appoint —

And its further orderd that as this township is remote from the Centre of the Province and at a great Distance from his majesties Surveyor of his woods and timber, that the s^d Petitioner take Especial Care not to Cutt or Destroy any of his majesties timber on or about s^d Township.

  Sent up for Concurrence   T Cushing Spk^r
 In Council June 9th 1768 Read & Concurred
              Jno Cotton D: Secry
  Consented to —

Report.

The Committee appointed to consider the Petition of Henry Young Brown having attended that Service beg Leave to report, That they have received from him the following Proposals which they humbly submit to the Consideration of this hon^{ble} House vizt That if the Province will discharge him of & from one half the Debt due from him to the Province on Account of his Bond & pay half the Expences incurred by him and sundry other Inhabitants of the Tract of Land he purchased of this Province, in setling & improving the same & also the cost & Charges incurred by him in Pursuance of the Orders of this Court then he will release this Province from all Claims which he has or may or ought to have upon them in Justice Equity or Favor on Account of their Grant to him of the Tract aforesaid and any Votes Orders and Resolves passed by this Court relative to his Conduct in Defence of the same —

            Wm Browne p^r order —
 June 15th 1768 —

Petition of David Bean & others. 1768.

Province of the Massachusetts Bay

To His Excellency Fra: Bernard Esqr Captain General and Comander in Cheife in and over said Province the Honble his Majestys Council & House of Representatives in General Court assembled at Boston May — 1768

The memorial of David Bean Nathaniel Harmon and Josiah Simpson in behalf of themselves and others Grantees of a certain Township lying in the Territory of Sagadahock granted by the Genl Court in the year 1762   humbly Shew

That in the Grant of said Township a Proviso was therein contained that unless the said Grantees should obtain his majestys approbation of said Grant in Eighteen Months after that Time; that the said Grant should be void. That since the expiration of said Eighteen months the General Court by a Resolve lengthed out the Time for obtaining the approbation of his majesty which last Time is also expired —

That altho: the said Grantees have been at great Expence in bringing Forward said Settlement, there being now already thirty Families Settled in said Town, have not yet obtained his majestys Approbation and are in Danger of having said Grant become Void unless a further Term be allowed to them —

They therefore pray your Excellency & Honors will take the matter under Consideration, and grant unto said Grantees such further Time for obtaining s^d approbation as in your wisdom shall be tho^t best. & as in Duty bound Shall ever pray.

       David Bean
       Nath^{ll} Harmon
       Josiah Simpson

In the House of Representatives The 28th June 1768

Resolved, That the Prayer of this Petition be granted and that the Grantees of the Township lying in the Territory of

Sagadahock granted by the general Court in March 1762 to David Bean & others be allowed the further Time of Eighteen Months from this Day to obtain his Majesties Approbation
   Sent up for Concurrence   T. Cushing Spk^r
 In Council June 28th 1768 — Read and Concurred
          Jno Cotton D. Secŕy
 Consented to   Fra Bernard

Letter, Wm Tyng, " Sheriff of Cumberland " to Gov. Bernard

        Falmouth July 12th 1768
Sir

 I think it my duty to acquaint your Excellency, that last Evening a Number of Men (thirty or more) armed with Axes Clubs & other weapons, surrounded the Goal in this Town, broke it open, resqued from thence two men named John Huston and John Sanborn, who were convicted of a Riot at the last Assizes, held in Falmouth; - I have offered a Reward of four pounds for any of the resequers, and forty shillings for each, or either of the two Criminals, which I hope will meet your Excellencys approbation.—
   I am with great respect
     your Excellencys humble servant
          Willm Tyng

Letter, Dudley Carlton to Col. Goldthwait

 These are humbly to request the Favor of Coln^l Goldthrite to represent to his Excellency ye Governor, the true State and Circumstances of that Part of ye Province, to ye East and Northward of Penobscut River; relating to the Timber fit for his Majestys Use for the Navy, with ⏤ it is said to abound. And as it is a very wrong & Misrepresentation, as to those six Townships granted by the General Court to David Marsh & others, would humbly pray his Excellency to write home in Favor of the Proprietors, as there is a Number of them setled in Consequence of said Grant, in order to bring forward the Settlement, without suspecting but that his Majesty's Approbation might be obtained, as it would be the Enlargement of his Majesty's Dominions with Respect to his Subjects; & a Means of rooting out the Savages, where it has always been a Nursery for them. And if those Families that are Setled, must be removed, it of Consequence = be the Ruin of a great Number of Families, and break up some Societies, where they have, for several Seasons had the Gospel preached to them.

And if his Excellency would use his Influence in Favor of the Case, by setting it in a true & just Light, would greatly oblige his humble Petitioner, as in Duty bound shall ever pray

Dudley Carlton

Earl of Stirling's Advertisement.

To Be Sold.

A Tract of Land of one Hundred Thousand Acres, situate on the East Side of Penobscot River, in the Eastern Part of New England, on the following Conditions, vis.

The Tract is to be divided and laid out in One Hundred Lots, of 1000 Acres each, bounding Westerly on the said River.

The Purchaser of each Lot, is to pay One Hundred Pounds Sterling down, or secure the Payment thereof by Mortgage of the Land, or otherwise, and shall be entitled also to a Town Lot of Half an Acre, in a Town called, Alexandria, laid out at the Mouth of the River, and fronting on Penobscot Bay; the whole to be held free of Quit Rent for ever.

The Purchaser is, on each 1000 Acre Lot, within three Years after the first Day of July, 1769, to settle at least one Family, or shall then forfeit his Grant; in which Case the Consideration Money shall be returned, with Interest, at Five per Cent.

A Map of the whole, with a State of the Title, is to be seen at the Earl of Stirling's Office at Baskinridge in Somerset County; at John Smith's Esq; at Perth-Amboy; At Cornelius Low's, Junior, Esq; at New Brunswick; and at Isaac Ogden's, Esq; at Newark, allo in New Jersey; at Philip J. Livingston's Esq; in Bayard-Street, and at Mr Gerard Buncker's, near the Exchange, in New-York; at Jared Ingorsel's, Esq; at New-Haven, in Connecticut; and Messrs. Hazen and Jarvis's, at Newberry, in Massachusetts Bay.

All Persons inclining to be concerned in this Purchase, are desired to enter their Names at either of the above Places, on or before the first Day of November next, in Order that the respective Deeds may be prepared.

Penobscot Bay is one of the finest on the Coast of New England; it abounds with Sea-Fish; its Navigation is safe and easy to Ships of any Burden. That Part of the River, on which this Tract is laid out, begins within two Leagues of the Bay; the Lands are as good as any in America, taking so large a Tract together: The Town Spot and the Islands in its Neighbourhood, are admirably well situated for the carrying on the Cod-Fishery; the Rivers have great Plenty of Salmon. Those who have their Names first entered, will have the Advantage of taking the first Choice of their Lots as to Situation.

If this Offer to the Public be duly considered, it will be found the most advantageous one that has appeared, especially to Farmers who have large Families of Children, and who have no great Stocks to provide them with; the Terms are intended lower than any other that has been offered for Lands so commodiously situated, purposely to encourage the Settlement of this Country, the Proprietor having other Lands in the Neighbourhood.

July 22, 1768.

Earl of Stirling to Govr Bernard

Baskenbridge August 10th 1768

Sir

I have the honour to transmit to your Excellency some Proposals I have lately published for settling and planting a Tract of Land belonging to me, situate in the Eastern part of your Government; and which I have good reason to expect, I shall be able to effect, so far as to the amount of Two hundred families next Spring, I also send your Excellency a printed State of my Title to that Tract of Country by which your Excellency will find, that it is founded on the same original Patent, under which all the other Lands within your Jurisdiction are held.

His Majesty in Council has long since been informed of my Right and Intention herein; and I cannot but hope that the Settlers, on their Arrival within your Province will meet with every Encouragement from your Excellency that so laudable a Design merits. I have the honor to be Your Excellency's most humble Servant

Stirling

Reply of Council to Stirling

At a Council held at the Council Chamber in Boston Tuesday August 30th 1768.
Present in Council.
His Excellency Francis Bernard Esqr Governor.

Willm Brattle	Harrison Gray	Royall Tyler
James Bowdoin	James Russell	James Pitts
Thos Hubbard	Thos Flucker	Samuel Dexter

His Excellency laid before the Board, a Letter from the Earl of Stirling of the 10th August, signifying his Intention to settle a Tract of land, in the Eastern parts of this Province which he pretends a Claim to.

Advised that William Brattle and James Bowdoin Esqrs take the said Letter into Consideration and report the next Council day.

At a Council held at the Council Chamber in Boston Wednesday Sept 7th 1768.
Present in Council
His Excellency Francis Bernard Esqr Governor.

Samuel Danforth	Harrison Gray	Samuel White
Willm Brattle	James Russell	Jeremy Powell
James Bowdoin	Thos Flucker	James Pitts Esqrs
Thomas Hubbard	Royall Tyler	Saml Dexter

The Committee appointed to take into Consideration the Earl of Stirling's Letter, made a report, and also reported a Draft of a Proclamation, relative to the Business therein mentioned, the said report was accepted, and his Excellency issued a Proclamation accordingly.

The Report is as follows —

The Committee of Council to whom was refered the Earl of Stirling's Letter to his Excellency Governor Bernard, dated August 10th 1768, with the printed State of his title, to the Lands between St Croix and Pemaquid, in the Eastern parts of this Province, and his printed Advertizement for the sale of said Lands, having duly considered the same, are humbly of Opinion —

That in the Answer to said Letter, his Excellency be desired to inform the Earl of Stirling, that some Time after receiving from Mr Bollan the Province Agent, a Copy of a Petition, signed by said Earl and others to his late Majesty relative to the said lands, a Committee of the General Court prepared a State of the title of this Province to the Country between Kennebec & St Croix: that by said State it appears that the Persons claiming under Sir William Alexander, first Earl of Stirling, have no right, or title whatsoever to the said Country, or any part thereof, and that the Province of Massachusetts Bay, hath a clear and undoubted right, and equitable Title to the Soil & Jurisdiction of the said Country, and every part thereof, under such restrictions and limitations, as are expressed in the Province Charter.

That the General Court relying on the goodness of the Province Title, have granted twelve Townships on Penobscot River, and to the Eastward, on Condition that Sixty families at least should be settled in each, within a limited time: That a great part of the Families are already settled, and in some of the Townships the whole number: that it is inconsistent with his Majesty's Interest that the said Grantees should be disvested, that it would be manifest Injustice in the Government to suffer it, and that this Government cannot suffer it, unless it be done by his Majesty's Orders

The Committee think it would be proper that a Copy of the said State, should accompany his Excellency's Letter which they cannot but apprehend will induce the Earl of Stirling to desist from his Pretensions.

The Committee are further of Opinion that in order to

prevent any uneasiness in the Grantees aforesaid and their associates, arising from the Claim aforesaid, and to prevent any Persons purchasing or taking Leases of the lands advertized aforesaid, his Excellency issue a Proclamation assuring such Grantees & Associates of the Protection of this Government, and cautioning all Persons against purchasing or taking Leases of any of the said Lands under the said Earl of Stirling.

The Committee herewith present the Draft of the Proclamation, which with the foregoing Report, is humbly submitted to your Excellency and Honours.

William Brattle
James Bowdoin

The foregoing are true Copies.

Attest Jno: Cotton   D: Secry

Proclamation. Sept. 7, 1768.

By his Excellency Francis Bernard Esqr Captain General and Governor in Chief in and over his Majestys Province of the Massachusetts Bay in New England and Vice Admiral of the same.

A Proclamation

Whereas the Earl of Stirling hath published advertisements for the Sale of a large Tract of Land situated on the East side of Penobscot River and for Leasing another large Tract on Castine River; said Tracts being part of a Tract in the Eastern parts of this Province extending from St Croix to Pemaquid to which he has laid Claim by virtue of a Grant made in the year 1635 to William Alexander first Earl of Stirling by the Council established at Plymouth. And whereas by a State of the title of this Province to the Country between the Rivers Kennebec and St Croix prepared by a Committee of the General Court and Printed in 1763 by order of the said Court it is alleged that the persons claiming under the said first Earl of Stirling have no right or title whatsoever to the said Country or any part thereof and it is asserted on the behalf of the Province that the Province of the Massachusetts Bay hath a clear and undoubted right & equitable title to the Soil and Jurisdiction of the said Country & every part thereof under such restrictions and limitations as are expressed in the Province Charter.

And whereas the General Court have granted twelve Townships within the Tract claimed as aforesaid which Grants now lie before his Majesty for his royal approbation in consequence of which Grants a great number of Families have actually settled in the said Townships, in order to fulfill the Conditions of the said Grants if the same shall be approved, I have thought fit to issue, and do by and with the Advice and Consent of his Majesty's Council issue this Proclamation, hereby declaring the Intention of this Government to protect & defend the said Lands & the inhabitants thereof against the said Earl of Sterling & all persons claiming under him untill his Majesty's pleasure shall be known therein and cautioning all his Majestys Subjects against purchasing or taking Leases of any of the said Lands under any person or persons claiming under the first Earl of Stirling aforesaid.

Given at the Council Chamber in Boston the 7th day of Septemr 1768 In the Eighth year of the Reign of our Sovereign Lord George the third by the Grace of God of Great Britain France and Ireland King defender of the Faith &c—
By his Excellency's Command
God Save the King

Town of York. Petition. 1770.

Provce of the Masstts Bay
To His Honr Thomas Hutchinson Esqr Lt Governr The Honble His Majestys Council and House of Representatives in General Court Assembled Jana 10, 1770

The Select Men and Overseers of the Poor of the Town of York in said Province Humbly Shew

That Josiah Bridges of the said Town by the Providence of God some Years since fell into Distraction and became non compos Mentis whereby great Trouble and Expence for some Years last past and untill about a Month ago when he Died arose for his Support and Safety. That his Estate consist only of about Ten acres of Land lying somewhat remote uncultivated and of no Income.

That His Relations are not of Ability to pay & discharge the said Expence.

Wherefore Your Petitioners Pray this Court to License and Authorize them, or such others as the said Court in their Wisdom shall think fit to make Sale of the said Josiah's Estate aforesaid the produce whereof to be applied for and towards satisfying the Charges afores^d

And they as in duty bound shall pray &e

Danl Moulton	Sel^t Men
Saml Sewall	& Overseers
Jos Simpson Jr	of the Poor
Joseph Weare Jr	of York

Petition to Govr Hutchinson by Inhabitants of the Fifth Township.

To his Excellency Thomas Hutchinson Esqr Captain General and Governor of the Province of the Massachusetts Bay in New England.

The Petition of the Inhabitants of the fifth Township granted by this Province to Eastward of Mount Desart & commonly called Pleasant River humbly sheweth to your Excellency

That whereas there is now residing in this Township upwards of Sixty Families and neither Law nor Gospel embraced among us every one doing what's right in his own eyes and a great spirit of mobbing and Rioting prevails, Cursing, Swearing, fighting, threatning, Stealing, pulling down Houses and the like as we cant sleep a nights without fear and living to such a distance from any authority that we labour under a great disadvantage of obtaining relief in such matters, being twenty miles to the Eastward of Goldsboro' and upwards of twenty miles Westward of Machias and very difficult passing any way makes us apply to your Excellency to interpose in this affair to redress our Grievances, and We whose names are hereunto subscribed humbly implore your Excellency that you would appoint a Justice of the Peace at Pleasant River as it is our sincere and hearty desire to live under a proper regulation of the Common Laws of the Land, and there is one Capt Wilmot Woss a man of a good reputation who removed from Martha's Vineyard about three years ago and has a good Interest in this Township whom we recommend to your Excellency to be appointed if you in your goodness shall think proper with the advice of Council, & we pray your Excellency to lay this our Petition before our said Council as we flatter ourselves of your Excellency's protection of our Civil Rights as far as the due Execution of the Law will give us, which causes us to apply to your Excellency to cause them to be put in force as we profess ourselves to be Loyal Subjects and are ready to spend our lives and fortunes for his Majesty's Crown and dignity and the Laws and good government as your Petitioners are in duty bound to pray for.

N. B. If your Excellency shall think proper to appoint any other suitable person we have no objection.

Moses Plumer	Joseph Drisko Junr	Noah Michell
Samuel Disko	Nathl Buck	Samuel Nash
William Michell	John Drisk his **O** mark	Joseph Michell
Benjamin Look	Daniel Look	Ebenezer Coal

Chare Stevens	Robin Groas	James Bryent
Edward Cate	Owen Macdonald	William Hix
Seth Norton	Edmund Stevens	Thomas
Samuel Knowls	George Tinney	Joseph Tebbut
John Hall	James Nash	Samuel
Isaiah Nash	Joseph **X** his mark	Joseph Nash jun[r]
Samull Coffin	Isaac Smith	
Copy		T Hutchinson

Petition of B. Mulliken & M. Bridges, Agents.

To the Honourable Thomas Hutchinson Esq[r] Lieu[t] Governour & Commander in Chief of the Province of the Massach[ts] Bay in New England

To the Hon[ble] the Council & House of Representatives in General Court Assembled March 15th 1770

The Petition of Benjamin Mullikin and Moody Bridges Agents for the Prop[rs] of a Township Granted to the. said Benj[a] Mulliken & others June 25th 1765 Humbly Sheweth

That the Great & General Court of s[d] Province in Answer to a Memorial of your Petitioners (on the twelfth Day of June 1767 —

Resolved that Eight thousand Six hundred & forty five Acres of Land lying on the Easterly Side & Northerly end of a pond Called long pond Bounded as Stipulated in s[d] Resolve be Exchanged for an Equivalent of Land on the Westerly Side of s[d] Township &c —

That Pursuant to s[d] Resolve the said Proprietors appointed a Committee to take a plan of the said land lying between Saco River & s[d] Township in order to Exhibit a plan thereof to s[d] Court for Confirmation — Who Reported as followeth (viz)

That Saco River which the Proprietors Apprehended to be within One Mile of said Township they found to be Near five Miles from the Westerly line thereof —

That the land is Mountainous & Broken & that a pond Judg'd to be Six or Seven Miles in Length Intervening between said Township & said River prevents the Communication intended By Said Proprietors with s^d River —

That the whole of the said Tract of Land in the Opinion of the Com^{ttee} falls Short of an Equivalent for the Said Land on the Easterly Side & Northerly end of s^d pond —

That should the Proprietors Make up an Equivalent at the Southerly end of said Township it would take off so much of that Tract of Land between s^d Township & Pearson Town which land is Capacious enough for a Township as would leave it Insufficient for that Purpose —

Wherefore Your Petitioners Humbly Entreat your Honours to Quiet the said Proprietors in the Peaceable possession & Enjoyment of the said 8645 Acres of Land on the Easterly side & Northerly end of Long pond & Your Petitioners as in Duty Bound Shall ever Pray —

Moody Bridges
Benjamin Mulliken

Vote on petition of Ichabod Jones & others. 1770.

In the House of Representatives April 4, 1770

Voted, That the Petition of Ichabod Jones and Seventy nine others his Associates, be so far granted, as that there be, and hereby is granted unto him the said Ichabod Jones, and his Associates named in the annexed Petition, their Heirs and Assigns forever, as Tenants in Common, One Township of Land, Scituate, lying and being to the Westward of St Croix about eight or ten Leagues, which Tract of Land is now known by the Name of Machias, and is bounded as follows, vizt beginning at a dry Rock at a Place called the Eastern Bay, near the House of Mr Samuel Holmes, and extending

North ten Degrees West, ten Miles, then West, ten Degrees South eight Miles, then South ten Degrees East ten Miles, then East ten Degrees north eight Miles to the first mentioned Bounds.

That they return a Plan of the same (taken by a Surveyor and Chainmen on Oath) to this Court for further Confirmation, on or before the First Day of Janu^y 1771. That they within six Years after they shall obtain his Majesty's Approbation of this Grant (unless prevented by War) settle the said Township with eighty Good protestant Families, and build eighty Houses, none to be less than eighteen Feet Square, and seven Feet Stud, and clear and cultivate five Acres of Land on each Share fit for Tillage or Mowing; and that they build in said Township a suitable Meeting house for the publick Worship of God, and settle a learned Protestant Minister, and make Provision for his comfortable and honorable Support: And that in said Township there be reserved and appropriated four whole Rights or Shares in the Division of the same (accounting to one eighty fourth Part a Share, for the following Purposes Viz^t One for the first settled or ordained Minister his Heirs and Assigns for ever; one for the Use of the Ministry, one to and for the Use of Harvard College; and one for the Use of a School for ever: And if any of the Grantees or Proprietors of said Township shall neglect within the Term of six Years as before mentioned, to do and perform according to the several Articles respecting the Settlement of his Right or Share as hereby enjoined, his whole Right or share shall be entirely forfeited, and enure to the use of this Province.

Provided nevertheless, the Grant of the above Lands is to be void and of none Effect unless the Grantees do obtain his Majesty's Confirmation of the same in Eighteen Months from this Time.

And be it further Ordered, as a Condition of the Grant

aforesaid, that each Grantee give Bond to the Treasurer of this Province for the Time being and to his Successors in said office for the Sum of Fifty Pounds for the Use of this Province, for the faithful Performance of the Duties required, according to the Tenor of the Grant aforesaid: And that a Committee or Committees be appointed by this Court to take Bonds accordingly.

And further Ordered, That the said Committee be empowered to admit others as Grantees in the Room of such Persons contained in the List aforesaid, who shall neglect to appear by themselves or others in their behalf to give Bonds at such Time as the Committee shall appoint.

And it is further Ordered, That as this Township is remote from the Centre of the Province, and at a great Distance from his Majestys Surveyor of his Woods and Timber, that the said Petitioner take especial Care not to cut or destroy any of his Majesty's Timber on or about said Township.

  Sent up for Concurrence   T Cushing Spk^r

 In Council April 4th 1770   Read & Concurred

            Jno Cotton D. Sec̃ry

 Consented to 26 Ap 1770   T Hutchinson

Resolve.

In the House of Representatives April 7th 1770

Resolved that the Prayer of this Petition be Granted and that the Petitioners be and they are hereby Impowered to make Sale of the Real Estate within mentioned for the most the same will fetch and to make & Execute a Good Deed or Deeds of Conveyance thereof they observing the Directions of the Law for the Sale of Real Estates by Execo^s & Admin^{rs} & giveing Caution to the Judge of Probate for the County of York that the Proceeds of said Sale be applied to the purposes mentioned.

 Sent up for Concurrence   T Cushing Spk^r
In Council Ap^l 11th 1770 — Read & Concurred
           Jn° Cotton D. Secry
 Consented to —

Resolve.

In the House of Representatives April 9th 1770

 On the Petition of Benjamin Mulliken and Moody Bridges Agents for the Proprietors of a Township Granted to Benjamin Muliken & others June 25th 1765, Whereas the Petitioners made Application to the Great and General Court Dated the twenty seventh Day of May Anno Domini 1767 praying that the Court would receive back a Part of said Township and grant them an Equivalent in other Lands adjoining, but now finding said Exchange inconvenient, pray that they may hold the said Township according to original Grant.

 Resolved that the prayer of the said Petition be granted and that the said Proprietors, have and hold said Township according to the Extent described in the original Grant any Petition of said Proprietors or Resolve of this Court thereon notwithstanding, and according to said Proprietors Petition and the Intent thereof: the said Lands resolved on their said Application to be given them for an Equivalent is hereby received back as Lands belonging to the Province — the said proprietors fulfilling the Condition of the Original Grant

 Sent up for Concurrence   T Cushing Spk^r
In Council April 10th 1770   Read and Concurred
           Jn° Cotton D. Secry
 Consented to Ap 26 1770   T Hutchinson

Resolve. 1770.

In the House of Representatives Aprill y[e] 14 1770

Whereas the Gen[ral] Court in their present Session on the Petition of Capt. Sam[ll] Skillan and others Inhabitants of Cape Elizabeth Resolved on said Petion that from the time the Act of Incorporation of Cape Elizabeth into a District took place all the Inhabitants of said District included within y[e] Lines of said District ware & still are held to Pay Parish Taxes there & to no other Place — Since which the first parish have by Thomas Smith on their behalf Represented some Inconveincy that may attend the Carrying s[d] Resolve into Execution before the s[d] first Parish has an oppertunity to be heard upon the Subject matter of the s[d] Petition —

Therefore Resolved that all Proceedings in Consequence of said Resolve be stayd as fully as if it had not been, till the Second Wednesday of the next Sitting of the Gen[l] Court at which Time the first Parish may be heard upon s[d] Petition of Cape Elizabeth if they see fit to Shew Cause if any they have why the s[d] Resolve should not be Reversed

  Sent up for Concurrence   Thomas Cushing Spk[r]

In Council 16 Apr[l] 1770   Read and Concurred
             A Oliver Sec[y]

Consented to Ap. 25 1770   T Hutchinson

Report on Petition of D. Phips & others

The Committee on the Petition of David Phips Esq[r] & others praying for a Township in Consideration of their ancestors being in the Expedition against Canada in the Year 1690 Have attended that service and find that the Petitioners are the Descendents and Legal representatives of sundry persons in the Expedition aforesaid and that they nor their ancestors have not as yet received any Grant for the Hardships & Burdens Sustained By their ancestors aforesaid in said Expedition as all others has Done who have regulerly applied to the Gen¹ Court for the same Therefore are of opinion that the following Resolve pass —

In the House of Representatives April 24, 1770

Resolved That there be Granted to David Phips Esqr and Others mentioned in the Petition a Township of the Contents of Six miles and three Quarters Square to be Laid out adjoining to some former Grant in the unappropriated Lands in this Province to the Eastward of Saco River Proveded the Grantees within seven years Settle Eighty families in said Township Build a House for the public Worship of God and settle a Learned Protestant Minister and Lay out one 84th part for the first settled Minister one 84th part for the Ministry one 84th part for the use of a School in said Township and one 84th part for the use of Harvard College forever Provided also that they return a plan thereof Taken by a Surveyor and Chainmen under Oath into the Secretarys Office within Twelve Months

  Sent up for Concurrence   T Cushing Spk^r

Report on Petition of J. Fuller & others.

The Committee to whome was Refferred the Petition of Capt Joshua Fuller and others praying for a Township of Land in Leiu of a Township Granted to them & their ancestors in the year 1736 which Township was Cut off by the Running of the Line between this province and New Hampshire have attended that Service and find the Facts set forth in said Petition are True and y^t they had entered upon the settlement of s^d Township and expended therein six pounds ten shillings old Ten^r for Each Right amounting to £390 one hundred and Eighty pounds of which was paid to the Government, Therefore are of opinion that the following Resolve pass

In the House of Representatives april 24 1770

Resolved That there be Granted to Capt Joshua Fuller and others mentioned in the Petition, a Township of the Contents of Six miles and one Quarter Square to be Laid out adjoining to some former Grant & in the unappropriated Land in the province to the Eastward of Saco River Provided the Grantees within seven Years settle Sixty Families in said Township Build a House for the public Worship of God and settle a Learned Protestant Minister and Lay out one 64th part for the first settled Minister one 64th part for the ministry one 64th part for the use of a school in said Township and one 64th part for the use of Harvard College forever Provided also that they Return a Plan thereof Taken by a Surveyor and Chain men under Oath into the Secretarys office within Twelve month for Confirmation —

Sent up for Concurrence T Cushing Spk^r

Resolve. 1770.

In the House of Representatives April 26th 1770

Resolved that there be Granted to Capt. Henry Young Brown eleven Thousand Acres of Land to be Laid out in the Unappropriated Land within this Province to the Eastward of Sauco River, and Adjoining to a Grant of eight thousand five hundred and forty four Acres Granted to the said Capt Brown in the Year 1766, to extend on said Sauco River including the Grant aforesaid Not exceeding seven Miles and so to extend back from said River and on the back of the Grant aforesaid so farr as to compleat the eleven thousand acres aforesaid and That the aforesaid Capt Brown Return a plann of this Last Grant Taken by a Surveyor & Chainmen under Oath in Twelve Months to this Court for Confirmation And that the said Henry Young Brown Give security for the settleing the said Lands Now Granted and for the performing the Same Conditions required in the first Grant or sale of a Township to him the said Brown in the year 1764 — Which Grant of eleven thousand Acres aforesaid is Considered by this Court in full Consideration of All the demands that the said Henry Young Brown has against this province for the Lose of Lands, occationed by the Disputed lines between this Province and the province of New Hampshire and that the said Brown give the Govern^t a Quit Claim for all the Lands Included in the Township sold him by this Government in the Year 1764, that are between, Warren, and Bryants Lines exceepting Twenty Two hundred Acres Already Sold to sundry persons, and also One hundred Acres Taken out of his Own Farme and this Last Grant be also Considered in full consideration of all costs & charges the said Brown has already been at or may be put too by Reason of the disputed Lines aforesaid and that the said Brown give this Government a Discharge in full for the same

Also Resolved that the Treasurer of the Province be directed to give up to Capt Henry Young Brown his Bond for Two hundred pounds dated in 1764 being the purchas— Consideration of the Township aforesaid, and in Lieu thereof The said Brown do give a New bond to the Treasurer aforesaid for the use of the Province for Two hundred pounds with sufficient sureties to bare date the fifth day of May Next payable In One Year with Lawful Inter^t which Bond when paid shall be in full Consideration for all the Grants aforesaid

  Sent up for Concurrence   T Cushing Spk^r
 In Council Ap^l 26th 1770 Read & Concurred
            Jno Cotton D. Sec̃ry
 Consented to 26 Ap 1770   T Hutchinson

Report.

The Committe appointed to Consider and report upon the Petition of Capt Henry Young Brown have attended that service and beg Leave to Report that in april 1770 the Court had a State of Facts Laid Before them and upon Mature Deliberation had thereon they Granted to the Petitioner 11000 acres of Land which Grant was at that time Considered by the Court to be in full satisfaction for all the Demands the Petitioner had against the province for loss of Lands in his Petition mentioned That the Court at that time apprehended that the 11000 acres of Land Granted as afores^d was as good as the same Quantity lost by the Disputed lines mentioned in his Petition But your Committee are fully Convinced by the Testimony of a Number of Credable Witnesses who are well Knowing to both Tracts of Land that it falls Considerably Short in value — Your Committee are Therefore of Opinion that the Petitioner be allowed the sum of Fifty pounds more with the Interest thereof from the 5th day of May 1770 the same to be entered upon his Bond of two hundred pounds given the province Treas^r as the purchase Consideration of his Township in said Petition mentioned

All which is Humbly Submitted

Jonas Dix p^r Order

Lt Gov$^{r's}$ Speech. Sept. 1770.

Gentlemen of the Council, and Gentlemen of the House of Representatives —

It is now become in several respects more necessary for the General Court to proceed upon the Business of the Province than it was when I met you in your two last Sessions. Many of our Laws, which have been of great utility, are expired, some for the punishment of criminal offences, others which affect the course of our Judicial proceedings and the People call for the revival of them.— There are other affairs depending of a very interesting nature which had not then come to our knowledge and which may be determined before we can have another opportunity of acting upon them. The Council thought it not advisable for me to Prorogue the Court to a further time: Their opinion and advice, which always have weight with me, induced me to call you together rather sooner than I had before intended.

Pursuant to my Instructions and the established practice I caused the Acts and Doings of the General Court at the Session in March last to be transmitted to England by the first opportunity. Particular notice has been taken of a Grant made in that Session to a number of Persons who had settled upon Lands in the Eastern part of the Province and, it appearing that other Persons had also begun Settlements Eastward of Sagadehock, some under colour of Grants from the General Court notwithstanding that by the express terms of the Charter, such Grants <u>are of no force validity or effect until approved by the Crown</u>, others without any colour of Grant or Title whatsoever, these Settlements are deemed of great Importance in various lights, but in none more so than in that of the incouragement they have given to the waste and destruction of the Kings Timber which is a matter of the most serious consideration in respect to the Naval Strength of the Kingdom. It is made my Duty to inform you that, as the remedy for this great mischief ought properly and can only effectually come from the Province within whose Jurisdiction the Lands lye, it is expedient all Trespassers should be prosecuted, and, I am further to inform you, that the neglecting to exert every legal means to remove and prevent all unwarrantable intrusions will be imputed as a default for which the Province will stand responsible. From a sense of my Duty to the King and from regard to the Interest of the Province I must desire you to take this affair into your consideration and do what is necessary on your part. I will assist and concur with you to the utmost of my power.

Gentlemen of the House of Representatives —

In order to conform to the Laws of the Province and to maintain the Public Faith, it was necessary the Treasurer should issue his Warrants for the assessment of the whole Province Debt in the current year. If these Warrants have not been so far executed as to render an alteration impracticable and you should be of opinion that the burden will be too great for the People to bear, I am willing to consent to an act for affording the necessary relief by easing the present year of part of this Tax and charging the same Sum upon a future year.

A State of the Treasury will be laid before you by which it will appear that a Supply will be necessary Some Appropriations are quite exhausted.

His Majesty having thought fit to Order that the Garrison of Castle William, in the pay of the Province, should be withdrawn and that this Fortress should be Garrisoned by his Majesty's Regular forces, I am prevented from desiring you to make the usual Establishment. The last Establishment expired the 20 day of June last. I know you did not expect I should then dismiss the Officers and Men. I must now desire you to continue their Pay & subsistance from the expiration of the Establishment and, as they are discharged at a Season of the year when it will be difficult for them to find Employ I could wish that the continuance might extend, at least, to the 20th of November the usual time of making up the Roll. It is no more than justice to the Garrison to say they have behaved well and have some Claim to favour.

The Establishment of Fort Pownall being also recommended to you to provide for the revival and continuance of it.

Gentlemen of the Council and House of Representatives —

As the affairs which lye before you are of great moment and deserve your serious and mature deliberation, so they must take up much time. It is therefore more necessary that you should begin without delay and should proceed with all diligence.

I wish there may be a good harmony in the Legislature, and that we may unite in such measures as our common Interest, the Interest of the Province, requires of us.—

T. Hutchinson

Council Chamber September 1770

Petition of Joseph Frye. 1770.

Province of the Massachusetts Bay

 To the Honourable Thomas Hutchinson Esqr Lieu^t G & Commander in Chieff, To the Honourable his Majestys Council & House of Representatives in General Court Assembled

 The Petition of Joseph Frye humbly Sheweth

 That under the Patronage of this Government your Petit^r has Settled upwards of Fifty Families in a new Township (at present called Fryeburg) in the County of York, which is at such a distance from any Sea-Port-Town, the Inhabitants thereof have it not in their power to procure Sundry of the absolute Necessaries of Life, at those Short periods, which Nature often calles urgently for, and they being unable to purchase so many of them at a Time, as to answer Nature's Just Demand thro' the Year. They often Suffer for want —

 That as your said Petitioner is Determined with all possible Speed to move Himself and Family into s^d Township, and for remedy of that inconvenience, open a Store there, He presumes he may Say, It's Necessary he should be Legally

Authorized to Sell Spirituous Licquors, as Such Licquors are what Labouring Men stand in Need of. That as said Township is not Incorporated; there are no Selectmen to recommend any Person in it, to the Court of general Sessions of the Peace for the County wherein it lays, (which is what the Law requires) He cannot Obtain Licence from thence —

Wherefore Your Petitioner Prays your Hon^r & Hon^rs would please to impower Him to Sell Spirituous Licquors by Retail at his Dwelling House in s^d Township, by such a Meathod as you shall Judge Proper. And as in Duty bound Prays

Joseph Frye

Petition of H. Eggleston "Oct. 1770."

To his Honor the Leiu^t Governor, the Hono^ble his Majesty's Council and the Hono^ble House of Representatives.—

The Petition of Hezekiah Egglestone of Bristol in the County of Lincoln — Humbly sheweth,

That your Petitioner's Great Grandfather Richard Fullford formerly of a Place called Round Pond in said Bristol, about the Year of our Lord 1660 purchased a Tract of Land there whereon he lived, adjoining to a Plantation commonly called Muscongus, and belonging to the Family of the Peirces; that your Petitioner's said Great Grandfather lived on and quietly enjoyed the Premises 'till the Beginning of the present Century except the Interruptions given him by the Indians (in which Time the Deed of his s^d Land was lost) leaving Issue only one Son who was a Minor, and a Daughter who was your Petitioner's Grandmother and who married Samuel Martin, who as soon as the Troubles with the Indians were over again in 1715 settled said Lands, till he was beat off by the Indians in the War commonly called the three Year War between 1722 & 1725; that your Petitioner's said Grandfather Martin after he had thus resettled said Lands, took the Testimonies of sundry ancient Persons in 1717, who formerly lived adjoining, to fix the Boundaries and supply the Loss of his Father in Law's Deed of said Land; that afterwards Viz^t in 1739 your Petitioner's Great Uncle Viz^t Francis Fullford the only Son of said Richard again settled said Lands, whose Tenants have been in constant Possession 'till the late War; and lastly that your Petitioner is now in Possession of Part of said Tract — But so it happens that your Petitioner's said Grandfather thro' Ignorance of the Law, had the said Testimonies taken before one Justice of the Peace only and put on Record ad perpetuam Rei Memoriam. And whereas sundry Persons without any Pretence of Title have trespassed and settled themselves on said Land cleared and brought too by your Petitioner's Ancestors at great Peril of their Lives and Expence of Labour, your Petitioner is unable to recover the Possession of said Land unless relieved by your Honors; Wherefore your Petitioner humbly prays that your Honors would confirm or make valid in Law said Testimonies or otherwise grant him that Relief which to your Honors shall seem meet — And your Petitioner as in Duty bound shall ever pray —

Hezekiah Eggleston

Petition & Remonstrance of S. Livermore & others. 1770.

Province of the Massachusetts Bay

 To the Honour^{able} Thomas Hutchinson Esqr Lieu^t Governor and Commander in Cheif in and over said Province; To the Honourable his Majestys Council; and House of Representatives in General Court assembled the 29th Day of Octr 1770

The Petition and Remonstrance of Samuel Livermore, Leonard Williams, and George Badcock a Committee appointed by a Society who were Proprietors of a Township of Land granted to Nath^{ll} Harris Esqr and others by s^d General Court in the Year 1736, (as a Gratuity for their Service in the Reduction of Port Royal) humbly sheweth That the said Proprietors in Observance of the Condition of their Grant proceeded to lay out said Township and returned a Plan of the same to the same Court for their Approbation, which was approved of by them accordingly. That then the Grantees proceeded to perform the Conditions of their Grant by allotting out the House Lotts, and some began to build thereon and repaired to said Town with Design to dwell there, cleared Roads, and built a Saw Mill at the charge of the Proprietors, with many other charges, in the whole amounting to more than £1000 of the then Currency (as by the Book of Records of s^d Proprietors clearly appears) besides their Expence of Time & Labour.

But yet it happened that a War broke out, and many of the Inhabitants were killd, others taken Captive, others surprised, and discouraged : and immediately by the Settlement of the Bounds between this Province, and the Province of New: Hampshire to our great Loss & Disappointment the Town fell within the Bounds of New Hampshire Province, whereby the Proprietors were wholly deprived of all the Profit and Advantage, they expected to reap and enjoy for their Services aforesaid, and suffered great Loss not only in Time, but in Mony in laying out their Lotts, clearing Roads, &c. and have no way to obtain Relief but by the Interposition of your Honors —

Your Petitioners therefore pray your Honors would take the same into your wise Consideration, and appoint a Committee to enquire into the Equity of our Claims, and also the Claims of several others who were in the same Expedition, but have received no Favour therefor, & who desire to be admitted with us and grant Leave to remove our Pitch to some other Place, in some of the unappropriated Lands in s^d Province And your Petitioners as in Duty bound shall ever pray

     Samuel Livermore ⎫
     Leonard Williams ⎬ Com^{tee}
     George Badcock ⎭

Resolve in favor of Joseph Frye.

In the House of Representatives Octo^r 30th 1770

Resolved that the prayer of the foregoing petition be So far Granted as that the Court of Genl Sessions for the peace for the County of York are hereby Impowered to Grant the petitioner License to Retail Spirituous Liquours In said Township of Fryeburge at their next Term & until the time for Granting Licenses in said County by Law shall commence

  Sent up for Concurrence   T Cushing Spk^r

 In Council Oct^o 30th 1770   Read and Concurred

           Jno Cotton D. Sec̃ry

  Consented to   T Hutchinson

Resolve.

On the Petition of Hezekiah Egglestone in the House of Representatives Nov. 2, 1770 Read and Resolved that the Prayer be so far Granted that the Justices of the Inferior Court of Common Pleas or the Justices of the Superior Court of Judicature before whom any action is or may be depending Relating to the Lands mentioned in said Petition be

Impowered to admit the Testimonies **A** Refered to in said Petition to be plead as Evidence in the Case as valid in the Law the failure of Taking the Testimonies before Two Justices Quorum unus Notwithstanding.

 Sent up for Concurrence   T. Cushing Spk^r

In Council Novr 7th 1770 Read & Concurred as taken into a new draft

 Sent down for Concurrence   Jn° Cotton D. Secry

In the House of Representatives Novr 8 1770 Read & Nonconcurred & the House adhere to their own Vote with Amendment at **A** viz insert of Morrice Champney Richard Pearce Senr & John Pearce

 Sent up for Concurrence   T. Cushing Spk^r

In Council Novr 8 1770 Read and Concurred

          Jn° Cotton D. Secry

 Consented to

Resolve.

In the House of Representatives Nov. 6 1770 —

Resolved that the prayer of this Petition Granted and that their be Granted to the Petitioners and their associates a Township of the Contents of Six miles and three Quarters Square in Some of the unappropriated Lands in the Province of Maine to the Eastward of Saco River to Satisfie the Grant of the Township therein mentioned which they Lost by the Running of the line between this province and the province of New Hampshire and that the Petitioners at the Cost of themselves and their associates Cause the same to be Laid out by a Skillful Surveyor and Chain men under Oath and Return a Plan of the Same to this Court for their acceptance within twelve months and that Cap Heath & Coll Buckminster with Such as the Honourable Board Shall Join be a Committee to Examine the Claims which may be made to any of the former Propriators rights which are either Deceasᵈ or have Conveyed their rights to Others. And admitt such as shall make out the most Equitable Claims, and return a list of their names to this Court at their next Sessions to be admitted Grantees to sᵈ Grant. And that the said Grantees shall Hold the same to themselves their heirs and assigns forever upon the following Conditions viz. that the Grantees shall within seven Years settle Sixty families in sᵈ Township Build a House for the publick Worship of God and settle a Learned protestant minister and Lay out One Sixty fourth part for the first Settled Minister One Sixty fourth part for the Ministry and one sixty fourth part for the use of a School forever.

 Sent up for Concurrence   T Cushing Spkʳ

 In Council Novʳ 6ᵗʰ 1770 — Read, & ordered that this Petⁿ be referred to the second Tuesday of the next Session of the Genˡ Court,—

 Sent down for Concurrence   Jnº Cotton D. Secry

 In the House of Representatives Nov. 6, 1770   Read & Concurred

           T Cushing Speaker

Jonathan Longfellow's Memorial to Govʳ Hutchinson.

Provence of the Masachusets Bay   To the Honourable
 Thomas Hutchinson Esqʳᵉ Lieuᵗ Governor and Commander in Chief in and over his Majestys Said provence

 Jonathan Longfellow of Machias in the County of Lincoln, humbly Represents to your honor, that since your Memorialist was appointed by your honor, as one of his Majestys justices of the peace for said County, a number of the inhabitants of

Machias who are enemies to all law and government, have Combined together against your Memorialist, for no other Reason: but, for that of his being a Civil magistrate: they have at divers times put your memorialist in great Bodily fear, by menaces and threatning speaches; and on Saturday the third day of November, as your memorialst was in the publick highway, in the peace of God and the King, four of the said disaffected persons; vis Samuel Kenney, Jeremiah Obrion, James Southerland, and Joshua Webster, did attack the person of your memorialist, and in a violent manner threw him down uppon the ground; and then Beat, and mawled your memorialist with their fists, in a most Barbarous manner, so that your memorialist is wholly disenabled from going about his common buisness, and what makes his Situation still more unhappy is, that there is no Magistrate nigher than Gold⁸boro', which is about twenty leagues from this place; and those that where there, are now gone to Boston, and the Season of the year approaching, that makes it dificult passeing either by land or water; So that it is impossible for your memorialist to Receive any present Relief, in the disabled circumstances that he is now in.

Your memorialist would allso Represent to your honor, that, except he can have some other person⁸ appointed as Justices⁸ of the peace in this place, he must Resign his Commision; it being impossible for him to do his duty without being in continual danger of his life from the lawless party, who are daly giveing out threatning speaches against any Civil officer, that shall presume to take any one of their party; and that they are determined to Support themselves by Clubb law. Conscious of the deep wisdom of your honor, he most humbly Submits his hard case, and the agravated treatment he has Recieved, in consequence of his being appointed one of his majestys Justiceses: most humbly imploreing your honor to take the premises into Consideration, and grant such Releif, as your honor, in your known great wisdom and impartiality, shall deem most for the advancement of Justice, and the preservation of peace, order, and good government

 and as in duty bound Shall ever pray

         Jonathan Longfellow

Machias Nov^{mber} 8th 1770

Memorial of Inhabitants of Mass: Bay to Govr Hutchinson

Provence of the Masachusets Bay To the Honorable Thomas Hutchinson Esqre Lieu^t Governor and Commander in Chief, in and over his majestys Said provence.

 The Subscribers, inhabitants of machias in the County of Lincoln, humbly Represent to your honor; that they bare true and faithfull Allegiance to his majesty King George, and are willing and desireous of supporting Civil Government as far as lies in their power, and very much lament that they are obliged to Represent to your honor, that a number of their Neighbours, and fellow inhabitants, seem to be otherwise inclined, which by their Conduct is but too evident: they haveing by many Repeated and open acts of violence, Shewn their disaffection to all order and good Government. They have divers times put his Majesty's quiet and peaceable Subjects, in this place, in great Bodily fear; not only by threatning speaches; but likewise by heavy Blows. They have at divers times assembled together in a Riotious manner; pulled down their neighbours buildings; and have beat or abused all those, who offered to oppose them and on the third day of Nov^{mber} four of them, vis Samuel Kenney, Jerimiah Obrion, James Southerland, and Joshua Webster, did attack, in the publick highway, when in the peace of God and the King, the person whom youre honour was pleased to appoint, as a Civil magistrate in this place; and in a violent manner threw him down upon the ground then beat and brused him to such a degree, that he is now incapable of going about his common buisness. And what makes his Situation still more deplorable, is, that there is no magistrate within twenty leagues of this place, that he can apply to for Relief, and assistance.

Your memorialist^s would likewise Represent to your honor, the absolute necessity of having another Justice appointed in this place, and that it will be impossible to suppress the present disorders; excepting there is one or more persons appointed to that office.

Conscious of the deep wisdom of your honor, we most humbly Submit our Case. Most humbly imploreing your honor to take the premises into consideration, and grant such Relief, as your honor, in your Known great wisdom, and impartiality, Shall deem most for the advancement of Justice, and the preservation of peace, order and good Government

And as in duty bound Shall Ever pray

Abier Spague	William Corliss	Ephraim Andrews
Joseph Libbee	Daniel Hill	Stephen Jones
Isaac Larrabee	Stephen Young	Stephen Parker
Ezekiel Libbee	Samuel Rich	John Scott
Joseph Sevey	John Sinkler	Benj^a Foster
James Dilbeney	Jacob Foster	Reuben Libby
Wooden Foster	John Warren	J^{hn} Wooden Foster
Nathl Tinkler	Will How	John Bevveys
Samuel Scott	Benj^a Getechel	Isaiah foster
Thomas Knight	Japeth Shithen	Joseph Getechel
Amos Boynton	David Longfellow	William Albee
James Shaw	Nathan Longfellow	

Machias Nov^{mber} 9th 1770

Petition of Henry Young Brown 1770

To His Honour Thomas Hutchinson Esqr Lieu^t Governour Commander in chief in and over his Majestys Province of the Massachusetts bay the Honourable his Majestys Council & house of representatives Novr 13th 1770

Humbly Sheweth Henry Young Brown

That your memorialist preferred a Petition to the General Court which was considered last April praying for an allowence for that part of his Township which he purchased of this province that lies between Warrens & Bryants Lines and claim^d by New hampshire also for his Expencnces in laying out his first Grant and other necessary Expences he has been at in Consequence of orders from the General Court in October 1765 For which he hath not had an allowance

When the affair was under consideration it was thought that he could avail himself of one hundred and Fifty pounds out of what he had Rec^d of the Settlers he Sold to. and they be Quieted in their Lands under New hampshire. Since that, five of them have Recovered against him Two hundred and Seventy Eight pounds Exclusive of his own Expences which is above one hundred Dollars. all which he hath been oblig^d to pay. So that instead of having 150£ he has paid Considerable more than he Rec^d of his Settlers.

What he Rec^d out of the Treasury hath been Expended and accounted for to the acceptance of the Court and hath no reference to what he asks allowence for, that Expence being founded on an order of June 1766 which directed him to prosecute and defend actions with those claiming under New hampshire —

The land he was ordered to lay out in Lieu of his former Grant is not half so Good as his first Grant — Which first Grant the General Court ordered him to keep possession of and to Go on in his Improvements and Settlements and if he should meet with any difficualty he Should be Reliev^d this order pased after the matter had been Enquired into by a Committee Sent to View and Examine the foundation of the dispute which order prevented him from Secureing his Settlers under New hampshire which he could have done to great advantage;

Your memorialist humbly Conceives this court will not suffer him to be so Great a Looser by the dispute as is now Evident he must be if he Dont have further Relief

therefore he humbly prays your honour and honours would Reassume the Consideration of his former petition and grant him Such further Relief as you in Your Great wisdom Shall think proper as in duty Bound Shall Ever pray

Henry Young Brown

Trade with Indians. 1770.

In the House of Representatives Nov. 16, 1770.

Resolved that the Commissary General be & hereby is directed to hire a suitable house at Passamiquaddy for the purpose of Carrying on A Trade with the Indians there.

Sent up for Concurrence   T Cushing Speaker

In Council Novr 17th 1770 — Read & Nonconcurd

Jn° Cotton D. Secŕy

Petition of Pondstown. 1770.

Province of the Massachusetts Bay

    To his Excellency Thomas Hutchinson Esqr Governor and Commander in Chief the Honble his Majestys Council and Honorable House of Representatives of the province aforesaid in General Court Assembled at —

The petition of the Inhabitants of a plantation called Pondstown, Humbly Sheweth, That we the Subscribers inhabitants of s^d pondstown on the west side of Kennebeck River within the plymouth purchase might enjoy the Blessings of the Gospel and good Government amongst our selves, and be inabled to settle a Minister & School. We therefore most Humbly pray your Excel^y and Honors to incorporate us into a Town with all the priviledges, & Immunitys, with other towns within this province have, by the Name of   as your Exc^y & Hon^{rs} shall think proper by the following butts and bounds Viz^t begining on the west side of Cobbiseconte great pond at the Easterly end of Lott N° One, from thence to run a West North West course five miles from thence to run a North North East course about seven Miles from thence to run an East South East — seven miles or untill it Meets the Westerly line of the township N° One,— being five Miles from Kennebeck river & from thence to run Southerly untill it meet with the North Easterly end of Cobbiseconte Great pond, from thence to run Westerly on the northly end of s^d pond to the West side thereof — then to run Southerly on the Westerly side of s^d pond to the first mentioned bounds, as appears by plan annexd — As this Country is at present but little cultivated it will oblige us to be at a great Expence in clearing roads & to build a House for the publick Worship of God, a Ministerial house as well as a School & settling & supporting the Gospel, and many other charges will Naturly arise in a new Country and being poor in general, therefore we most Humbly Pray your Exc^y and Honours to Exempt us from paying province taxes for ten years to come and otherwise relive your petitioners as in Duty Bound shall ever pray

Kennebeck December 1770

John Chandler	James Bishup	Jonathan Emery
James Pullen	Ichabod How	John Blunt

Amos Stevens	Seth Delano	Samuel frost
Benjamin Fairbanks	Joseph Stevens	John Chandler Juner
Stephen Pullen	Joseph Brown	Samuel Stevens
James Craigg	Robert Waugh	Richard Humphrey
Moses Ayer	Joseph Chandler	Gideon Lambert
Elihu Smith	Moses Grele	Joseph Davenport
Joseph Grele	Wright Brown	Arther Dun
Nathan[el] Emry		

Act relative to York Bridge. 1771.

Anno Regni Regis Georgii Tertii undecimo

An Act to Enable the Proprietors of the great Bridge over York River in the first Parish in said Town to take Toll for the repair & amendment thereof.

Preamble.

Whereas the great Bridge over York River in the first Parish in said Town built in the year one thousand seven hundred Sixty one, appears to be of general use and public utility, and whereas the proprietors of the said Bridge have represented that the same is now in great want of repair and Amendment, and will very soon without it become useless, and have petitioned this Court for liberty to take a reasonable Toll of such persons as may have Occasion to pass and repass the said Bridge for the repair and Amendment thereof.

Be it therefore Enacted by the Governour, Councill and House of Representatives, That the said Proprietors shall, & hereby are Authorized and impowered to demand and receive the several Rates & fees hereafter expressed, which every passenger is required to pay before they have liberty to pass viz. For every footman who shall pass the said Bridge two thirds of a penny for every Man and Horse two pence, for every two Wheel chaize, chair or Sleigh & Horse with the Travellers therewith the sum of Four pence for every four Wheel carriage including the Passengers six pence for every Man with Team Cart or Sled the Sum of four Pence, for all horse kine or neat cattle two Thirds of a Penny, for Sheep or Swine four Pence a Dozen and so in proportion for a greater or lesser Number.

And Be it further enacted that the said Proprietors be and hereby are impowered to appoint some suitable Person to receive said Toll from Time to Time as there shall be Occasion, who shall be approved of by the Court of General Sessions of the Peace for the County of York, & who shall give such Security as the said Court shall from Time to Time order and direct: and the Person so appointed and approved, as aforesaid, shall faithfully & diligently attend upon his duty, and at all Times between the Hours of five in the morning & Nine in the evening be ready to admit any Person to pass the said Bridge upon the penalty of Twenty Shillings for any neglect and in case he shall not be present to admit passengers to pass the Bridge between the Hours of Nine in the evening & five in the morning he shall leave the passage free and open. And the person so appointed and Approved as aforesaid, shall from Time to Time as often as the said Proprietors shall Order & direct exhibet an Account of the moneys he shall recieve as aforesaid, on Oath if required, to the said Proprietors or their Treasurer, duly by them appointed, and shall pay the said Sum to him or them Accordingly, to be Applyed by the said Proprietors for the repair & amendment of said Bridge, as they or the major part of them shall Order and direct.

And be it further enacted that the passage of said Bridge shall be kept open and free for all Persons travelling to or from public worship on Lords Days — for the Inhabitants of the Town of York going to or from Public meetings of the

Town or Parish Post riders ministers of the Gospell on all Occasions, Constables and collectors of Taxes & all other officers of the said Town and Parish, while doing the Town or Parish business & members of the general Court going to or returning from the same.

And be it further enacted that no fee or reward shall be demanded or taken for drawing up and Opening the Bridge for the passing and repassing of Vessells, and the same shall be made and kept as convenient as may be for that purpose, as hath always been heretofore Accustomed.

And be it further Enacted that if the keeper of said Bridge shall at any Time demand or receive a greater Toll that what is allowed by this Act, he shall for every such offence be subject to the penalty of Twenty Shillings. And the said Proprietors shall keep, and exhibit to this Court under Oath when required an account of the Sums taken & Receiv'd for Toll as well as an Account of the Sums Advanced for the repair and Amendment of the said Bridge.

And all fines and forfeitures arising by this Act shall be one moiety to him or them that shall sue for the same, and the other moiety to his Majesty to and for the use of the Province

This Act to be in force for the space of Seven years from the Publication thereof and no longer.

In the House of Representatives
   April 10 1771   Read the first time
   April 12 1771   Read a Second time
   Apr 13 1771   Read the third time & passd to be engross[d]
      Sent up for Concurrence   T Cushing Spk[r]

In Council Ap[l] 15th 1771 Read a first time   16th Read a second time & passed a Concurrence to be Engrossed
                        Tho[s] Flucker Sec[ry]

Act of Incorporation 1771

Anno Regni Regis Georgii Tertii Undecimo —

An Act for incorporating a Certain Tract of land in the County of Lincoln into a Township by the Name of

Whereas the Inhabitants of a certain Tract of Land lying on the East and West sides of Kennebeck River in the County of Lincoln are desirous of enjoying the Priviledges that will arise to them by being incorporated into a Township

Be it enacted by the Governor, Council and House of Representatives, That the Tract of Land aforesaid butted and bounded as follows vizt beginning on the East side of Kennebeck River on the North line of lott Number Fifty and running from Kennebeck River on said line an East South East course five miles (being bounded thus far by the Town of   from thence to run Northerly about Eight miles more or less, on such a course as to meet the East end of a line running five Miles East South East from Kennebeck River along the Southerly side of lott Number One hundred and two, fronting on said Kennebeck River, from thence to run West North West on the last mentioned line to Kennebeck River, and to run on the same course across the said river to the end of five Miles on the West side thereof, from thence to run Southerly to the North Westerly corner of the Town of   aforesaid, from thence to run East South East five Miles on the Northerly side of said Town to Kennebeck River, and over said River to the first mentioned bounds; be and hereby is erected into a Town by the Name of   And that the Inhabitants thereof be and hereby are invested with all the Powers, Privileges and Immunities which the Inhabitants of any of the Towns within this Province respectively do, or by Law ought to Enjoy.

And be it further enacted that James Howard Esqr be, and he hereby is impowered to issue his Warrant directed to some principal Inhabitant of said Town requiring him to notify and warn the Inhabitants in said Town qualified by Law to vote in Town affairs, to meet at such Time and place as shall be therein set forth, to choose all such Officers as shall be necessary to manage the Affairs of said Town.

And be it further enacted, That the Freeholders of the said Town shall be, And hereby are empowered at their first Meeting to proceed to bring in their Votes for a Register of Deeds and also for a Treasurer for the s^d County of Lincoln qualified according to Law. And the Votes for such Register and Treasurer shall be at the same time Sealed up by a Constable of said Town who may then be chosen and sworn, and by him returned unto the Court of General Sessions of the Peace to be holden in June next at Pownalborough for said County, in the same manner as by law in like cases is provided for other Towns within this Province: which Court is hereby Authorized and required to receive the said Votes: which Votes with the Votes of the other Towns of said County shall be opened, Sorted and Counted as the Law directs, for the determining the choice of such Register and Treasurer, And such Choice shall be to all intents and purposes Valid and effectual in Law —

And be it further enacted That if by reason of Sickness or any other means the said James Howard Esqr shall be prevented from performing the Business (or any part thereof) to which he is appointed by this Act, then in that case William Cushing Esqr shall be and hereby is impowered to transact the whole or any part of said Business as fully and effectually as the said Ja^s Howard Esqr is by the several clauses of this Act empowered to Transact the same.

In Council April 23, 1771 Read a first Time 24 Read a second Time & passed to be Engrossed
    Sent down for Concurrence   Thos Flucker Sec^y

In the House of Representatives Ap. 24, 1771

Read a first Second & third time & passed a Concurrence to be Engrossed

T Cushing Spk^r

Act of Incorporation 1771.

Anno, Regni, Regis, Georgii, Tertii, Undecimo

An Act for Incorporating a certain Tract of Land in the County of Lincoln into a Town by the Name of

Whereas the Inhabitants of a certain Tract of Land lying on the East and West side of Kennebec River in the County of Lincoln are desirous of enjoying the privileges that will arise to them by being Incorporated into a Town.

Be it therefore Enacted by the Governor, Council and House of Representatives That the Tract of Land aforesaid butted & bounded as follows vizt begining on the East side of Kennebec River at the South line of a hundred Acre lot number one hundred & two, and on the north line of the Town of   and running an East South East course five Miles bounded thus far on said Town, from thence to run north-easterly about six miles on such a course as to meet the East end of the North line of a Tract of Land granted to John Winslow Esqr and others (which end is five miles distant from Kennebec River on an E S E Course) from thence to run West northwest on the last mentioned line five miles to Kennebec River, and to run the same course across the said River to the end of five miles on the West side of the said River; from thence to run Southwesterly about six miles to the Northwesterly corner of the Town of   aforesaid, from thence to run an East Southeast course on said Town to Kennebec River and over the said River to the first mentioned bounds; be and hereby is erected into a

Town by the Name of   ; and that the Inhabitants thereof be and hereby are invested with all the powers, privileges and immunities which the Inhabitants of the Towns within this Province respectively do or by Law ought to enjoy.

And be it further Enacted That James Howard Esqr be and he hereby is impowered to issue his Warrant directed to some principal Inhabitant in said Town requiring him to notify and warn the Inhabitants thereof, qualified by Law to vote in Town affairs, to meet at such time and place as shall be therein set forth, to choose all such Officers as shall be necessary to manage the affairs of said Town —

And be it further Enacted That the Freeholders of the said Town shall be & hereby are impowered at their s^d first Meeting to bring in their Votes for the choice of a Register of Deeds for the County of Lincoln, also for a Treasurer for said County qualified according to Law; and the Votes for such Register & Treasurer shall at the same time by a Constable who may be then Chosen & sworn be Sealed up and by him returned unto the Court of General Sessions of the peace to be holden in June next at Pownalborough for the said County in like manner as is provided by law in like cases for other Towns within this Province which Court is hereby authorized & required to receive the said Votes, which with the Votes of the other Towns of said County shall be opened, sorted & counted as the Law directs, for the determining the choice of such Register & Treasurer, such choice shall be to all intents and purposes valid & effectual in Law.

And be it further Enacted That if by reason of Sickness or any other means the said James Howard Esqr shall be prevented from performing the business, or any part thereof, to which he is appointed by this Act, then and in that case William Cushing Esqr shall be & hereby is impowered to transact the whole or any part of such business as fully and effectually as the said James Howard Esqr is by the several clauses of this Act impowered to transact the same

In the House of Representatives
 April 13 1771 read a first time
   23 1771 read a second time
   24 1771 read a third time & passed to be Engrossed
 Sent up for Concurrence   T Cushing Spk^r

In Council April 24. 1771 Read a first Time & a second Time & passed a Concurrence To be Engrossed
           Thos Flucker Sec^{ry}

 Begining on the East side of Kennebeck River at an Hemlock Tree standing on the Bank of s^d River, & one rod West North west of a large Rock & two miles & half a mile on a north North East Course from Fort Hallifax, & from said Fort to run East south East five miles to a Beach Tree mark'd thence to run South south west five miles & one hundred & seventy eight Poles, thence West North West to the North East Corner of the Town of   thence on the Northerly Line of said Town West North West five miles to Kennebeck river, thence to run across s^d River the same Course to the end of five miles on the West side of said River, butting thus far on the same Northerly Line of the s^d Town of   thence Northerly on such a Course so far as to meet the west end of a Line running from the Hemlock Tree abovementioned West North West five miles from Kennebeck River, thence to run East south East on the last mentioned Line five miles to s^d Kennebeck River thence across s^d River to the Hemlock Tree afores^d the first mentioned Bound.

Act of Incorporation. 1771

Anno Regni Regis Georgii Tertii Undecimo
 An Act for Incorporating a Certain Tract of Land called

Pond Town in the County of Lincoln into a Town by the Name of

Whereas the Inhabitants of a certain Tract of Land called Pond Town lying on the West side of Kennebeck river in ye County of Lincoln are desirous of enjoying ye Privileges that will arise to them by being incorporated into a Town

Be it enacted by ye Govr Council & House of Representatives, that ye Tract of land aforesaid, butted & bounded as follows viz: Beginning on ye West side of Cobbeseconte great Pond at the easterly End of the Southerly Line of a two hundred Acre Lot Number One, from thence to run a West North West Course five Miles; from thence to run a North North East Course about nine miles, till it meets a Line runing West North West from the North West Corner of the Town of   , from thence to run East South East on the last mentioned Line Seven miles more or less, to the Northwest Corner of the said Town; and from thence to run Southerly on the Westerly Line of the said Town; as far as the Northerly End of Cobbiseconte great Pond; from thence to run Westerly on the northerly End of said Pond to the West Side thereof, then to run Southerly on the Westerly Side of said Pond to the first mentioned Boundary, including also the said Pond as far South as the said Boundary; be and hereby is erected into a Township by the Name of and that the Inhabitants thereof be and hereby are invested with all the Powers Privileges and Immunities which the Inhabitants of any of the Towns within this Province do or by Law ought to enjoy.

And be it further enacted, That Ja^s Howard Esqr be, and hereby is empowered to issue his Warrant directed to some principal Inhabitant in said Township requiring him to notify and warn the Inhabitants in said Township, qualified by Law to vote in Town Affairs, to meet at such Time and Place, as shall be therein set forth, to chuse all such Officers as shall be necessary to manage the Affairs of the said Township.

And be it further enacted, That the Freeholders of the said Town shall be, and are hereby empowered, at their first Meeting to proceed to bring in their Votes for a Register of Deeds, and also for a Treasurer, for the said County of Lincoln qualified according to Law; and the Votes for such Register and Treasurer shall be at the same Time sealed up by a Constable of said Town who may then be chosen and sworn, and by him returned unto the Court of General Sessions of the Peace holden in June next at Pownallborough for the said County in the same Manner as is provided by Law in like Cases for other Towns within this Province; which Court is hereby authorized and required to receive the said Votes; which Votes with the Votes of the other Towns of said County shall be opened, sorted and counted, as the Law directs, for the determining the Choice of such Register and Treasurer And such Choice shall be to all Intents and Purposes valid and effectual in Law.

And be it further enacted, That if by Reason of Sickness, or any other Means the said Ja[s] Howard Esq[r] shall be prevented from performing the Business (or any Part thereof) to which he is appointed by this Act, then in that case William Cushing Esq[r] shall be and hereby is empowered to transact the whole or any Part of said Business as fully and effectually as the said Ja[s] Howard Esq[r] is by the several Clauses of this Act empowered to transact the same.

[The wild lands along the Kennebec began about this time to attract attention. There was a rapidly growing interest at this time in the incorporation of towns along the Kennebec river, and several were incorporated as here shown, four at this session of the General Court, namely, Winthrop, named for Governor Winthrop; Vassalboro, for William Vassal, one of the Assistants of Massachusetts; Winslow, for General John Winslow; and Hallowell, for the well known Hallowell family. The names were left by the General Court to be supplied by the inhabitants.]

In Council April 23, 1771. Read a first Time ye 24. Read a second Time & Passed to be Engrossed
 Sent down for Concurrence Thos Flucker Sec^ry

In the House of Representatives Ap. 24. 1771
 Read a first a second and a third time & passed a Concurrence to be Engrossed
         T Cushing Spk^r

Petition in behalf of George Town. 1771.

To His Excellency Thomas Hutchinson Esqr Captain General & Comander in Chief in & over his Majesties province of Massachusetts Bay — The Honorable the Council & House of Representatives in General Court assembled May 29 1771

 The Petition of James McCobb in Behalf of the Town of George Town humbly shews

 That said Town was fined in the Sum of Ten pounds for not returning a representative to the General Assembly the last year

 Your Petitioner prays this Hon^le Court that said fine may be remitted, & begs leave to offer the following Reasons

 The said Town being at the distance of one hundred & Eighty miles from Boston, it has been seldom that the Selectmen could have a Precept in Season: and particularly the last year the precept came so late that a Meeting of the Town could not be had, till the very day before the Election of Councellors, whereby it became impossible for the Town to return a Member timely enough for them to enjoy their full Share of the Right & Privilege of Representation

 But further your Petitioner would humbly represent, that the Inhabitants of said Town were in very distressing Circumstances occasioned by the Destruction of their Grass & Corn by Worms, many Persons having thereby lost four fifths of their Crops, & in Consequence a great part of their stock of Cattle in the Spring by which means they were greatly impoverish^d

Wherefore your Petitioner prays your Excellency & Honors to take the Case of said Town into your compassionate Consideration and afford them Releif And as in duty bound shall ever pray

James McCobb

In the House of Representatives June 11 1771

Resolved that the prayer of this pet^n be granted & that there be allow^d & paid out of the publick Treasury the sum of Ten pounds into the Hands of James McCobb Esqr for the Use of the said Town of George Town accordingly

    Sent up for Concurrence   Tho Cushing Spk^r

    In Council June 18th 1771   Read & Concurred

Thos Flucker Sec^y

    Consented to   T Hutchinson

Extract from Speech. May 30, 1771.

Gentlemen of the Council and Gentlemen of the House of Representatives

"It is with pleasure that I now inform you that the account which I thought my self warranted to transmit to England, the last Fall of the general disposition in the people of the Province to promote Order and a due submission to Government gave the greatest satisfaction to His Majesty, who has nothing more at heart than to see his Subjects in a State of happiness Peace and Prosperity. By making these the great Objects of my Administration I shall advance the real Interest of the Province and at the same time do that duty to the King which he requires of me.

The common inferior business of the Province necessary to be acted upon at this Session I need not particularly point out to you. The state and circumstances of that part of the Province which lies to the East and North of Penobscot River, where settlements are every day making by persons who have no colour of Title, I am required by the King to recommend to your serious consideration. I think the people deceive themselves with a groundless expectation of acquiring a Title by force of possession. I know that His Majesty is displeased with such proceedings and I have reason to apprehend that a longer neglect of effectual measures, on our part, to prevent any further Intrusions and to remove those already made will occasion the interposition of Parliament to maintain and preserve the possession of this Country or District for the sake of His Majesty's Timber with which it is said to abound. I recomended this important business to the Assembly of the last year at their Session in September. The Council thought it necessary then to be acted upon, but the House referred it to the next Session and then let it drop without further notice."

T Hutchinson

Council Chamber Cambridge 30 May 1771.

Report on Petition of S. Livermore & others 1771

The Committee to whom was referd the Petition of Samuel Livermore Esq[r] and others have enquired into the Facts therein set Forth and Judge them to be True and therefore of Opinion that the following Resolve pass

In the House of Representatives June : 11 : 1771

Resolved, that the prayer of this Petition be granted and that there be Granted to the Petitioners and to the Assigns or Legal Representatives of the Original Grantees in the said

Petition mentioned their Heirs and Assigns a Territory of the Contents of Six Miles and three Quarters Square in some of the unappropriated Lands in the Province of Main to the Eastward of Saco-River adjoining to some former Grant to satisfie the Grant of a Township therein Mentioned which they Lost by the running of the Line Between this Province and the Province of New Hampshire and that the Petitioners at the Cost of themselves and their Associates Cause the same to be Laid out by a Skilful Surveyor and Chainmen under Oath and return a Plan of the same to this Court for their Acceptance within Twelve Months and the said Grantees shall hold the same to themselves their Heirs and Assigns forever upon the following Conditions, vizt that the Grantees within Seven Years Settle Sixty Families in said Township, Build a House for the Public Worship of God and Settle a Learned Protestant Minister and lay out one 64th part for the first Settled Minister, one 64th part for the Ministry One 64th part for the use of a School and one 64th part for the use of Harvard College forever —

  Sent up for Concurrence T Cushing Spk^r
 In Council June 11th 1771 Read & Concurred
           Thos Flucker Sec^y
  Consented to T Hutchinson

Message. June 19, 1771.

Gentlemen of the House of Representatives

 There is only one part of your Message presented to me yesterday which I think it necessary, at present, to make any Observations upon.

 In my Speech to the two Houses at opening the Session I expressed my Opinion of the necessity of effectual measures to prevent any farther Intrusions upon the Eastern parts of the Province and to remove such as have been already made.

The Council in a very obliging Address or Answer declare their willingness to do every thing they can in conjunction with the other Branches of the Legislature to convince the Intruders that they are under a mistake if they expect to acquire Title by force of their Possession.

You tell me that I am sensible some of these Settlements are in consequence of Grants made by the General Assembly of this Province agreeable to the Royal Charter and if any settlements are made there without any colour of Title you apprehend that the penalty provided by Charter and the appointment of Surveyors is sufficient to prevent Trespasses on the King's Woods and that there is no necessity, at present of the Interposition of this or any other Legislature for that purpose.

The words in the Charter are "that no Grant of any Lands lying &c^a shall be of any force validity or effect until We our Heirs and Successors shall have signified our or their Approbation of the same." Now a Grant cannot give a colour of Title without having some force validity or effect. It is immaterial whether the Settlements are with or without Grants from the Court. In either case the Settlers are alike Intruders for none have the Royal approbation. I know what the Penalties are in the Charter and in divers Acts of Parliament for Trespasses made upon the King's Woods. I have not asked you to join with me in more effectual measures for punishing such Trespasses. I desired your assistance in removing such persons as have already intruded and in preventing all others from intruding upon the Lands, for by means of such Intrusions Trespasses are easily committed without any great danger of discovery let the Surveyors be ever so vigilant & attentive to their duty.

You have avoided a direct Answer and I have no encouragement that you will join in removing the Intruders with or without what you call Grants or in discouraging others from making further Intrusions. I am bound to explain to you my Intention in my Speech to repeat my recommendation and my apprehensions of the consequences of your neglect, that I may never be charged with having failed giving you that warning which I ought to have done

T Hutchinson

Boston 19 June 1771

Committee appointed. 1771

In Council June 21ᵗ 1771

Ordered that Wᵐ Brattle James Bowdoin & James Otis Esqʳˢ with such as the honˡᵉ house shall Join be a Committee to Consider the Circumstanes of those people who are Settled on Lands In the County of Lincoln to the Eastward of Penobscot River under Grants from this Court, and Report what they shall Judge propper to be done Respecting them

Sent down for Concurrence Thoˢ Flucker Secʸ

In the House of Representatives June 21 1771   Read & Nonconcurred

T Cushing Spkʳ

In the House of Representatives June 22 1771

Reconsidered & Concurred & Mʳ Speaker Mʳ Fisk Mʳ Otis & Coll Worthinton are joynd

T Cushing Spkʳ

The Comᵗᵉᵉ of both Houses appointed by the Order annexed having Considered the Affair in the said Order mentioned beg leave to report yᵉ following draft of a Letter of Instructions to their respective Agents in London, to be sent to them in yᵉ name and behalf of the Two Houses respectively: which is humbly submitted

Wᵐ Brattle by order

In Council July 1ˢᵗ 1771:
 Read & accepted as taken into a new Draft
  Sent up for Concurrence   Jn° Cotton D. Secry
In the House of Representatives July 1. 1771
 Read & Concurred   T Cushing Spk*

Act of Incorporation 1771.

Anno Regni Regis Georgii Tertii Undecimo.

An Act for Erecting the New Plantation called Narraganset N° One in the County of York into a Town by the Name of

Whereas the Plantition called Narraganset N° One in the County of York into a Town will greatly Contribute to the Growth thereof and remedy many inconveniences to which the Inhabitants & proprietors thereof may be otherwise Subjected

Be it enacted by the Goverᵣ Council and House of Representatives that the Plantition Called Narraganset N° One in the County of York — Bounded as followeth (to wit) Southwesterly on Saco River Southeasterly on Pepperellborough and Scarborough Northeasterly on Gorham Northwesterly on Peircentown So Called, be and hereby is Erected into a Town by the Name of [Buxton *] and that the Inhabitants thereof be and hereby are invested with all the Powers, priviledges & immunities which the Towns within this province do injoy.

And be it further Enacted that Rushworth Jordan Esqʳ Be and hereby is impowered & Directed to Issue his warrant directed to some principal Inhabitant in sᵈ Town, requiring him to warn the Inhabitants of the sᵈ Town who are Freeholders to meet at such time & place as shall be therein set

---
* So named for **Buxton on River Wye, England.**

forth who at said first meeting shall be empowered to Chuse all such officers as are or shall be required by Law to manage the affairs of s^d Town and they are further impowered when so assembled to chuse a moderator to regulate s^d Meeting.

In the House of Representatives June 24, 1771
  Read a first time
  June 27 Read a second time
  June 27 177_ Read a Third time & passed to be Engrossed
    Sent up for Concurrence   T Cushing Spk^r

Resolve.

In the House of Representatives June 27th 1771

One plan of the Township of Land Taken by Nath^ll Dwight Sarveyer in the favour of William Bullock Esqr & others Containing within s^d Plan Twenty three thousand & forty acers of Land which is agreable to the order of the Gene^l Court: Resolved that the Tract of Land afores^d be & Remain to said proprietors & there Heires & assigns uppon there fulfiling the Condit^s hereafter mentioned viz Said Proprietors to Settle the Tract of Land afores^d, with fifty families & Errect & build fifty Dwelling houses thereon none Less than Eighteen feet Squair & Seven feet Stud & Clear & Cultivate Seven acres of Land on Eaich Right or Share fit for Tillage & Mowing within Seven yeares from the Date hereof & within s^d Time builde a Sutable Meeting House for the publick worship of God: & Settle a Lerned protestant Minister & make Suteable provision for his Comfortable Support: & allso within s^d Township there be reserved & appropriated one Sixty third part thereof to the first Settled or ordained minister his heires & assigns for Ever & one Sixty third part thereof for the use of the ministry & one Sixty third part for the use & Benefit of a School for Ever & furthermore Said proprietors are to agree with Such person or persons Now in the possession of aney of the Lands within the bounds of the Township aforesaid as shall be Estemated Just & Eaqutable: not Less than one hundred acres to Each person thereon so as to Quiet them in there possession thay allowing s^d Proprietors the Value of the same as tho no Improvement had ben made thereon; & in Case the Grantees and Settlers shall not agree upon the Value of s^d Lands it shall be Determined by a Committee of this Court & if the Grantees or proprietors of s^d Tract of Land should faile or neglect within s^d Seven yeares of Complying with the Conditions afores^d thay shall forfeit there Right to said Tract of Land, which in that Case shall revert to the province

  Sent up for Concurrence   T Cushing Spk^r
 In Council June 28th 1771 Read and Concurred
           Jno Cotton D. Secry
  Consented to   T Hutchinson

Report of Commissioners on Machias Septr 12th 1771.

Pursuant to your Excellency's Instructions, you will permit us to make the following Remarks —

1st The quality of the Land at Machias is very good, capable of making extraordinary Farms, from the produce whereof the Grantees may live very comfortably and have a surplusage for market, and considering the great improvements in so short a time which they have made We believe that will soon be the case, provided they meet with no obstructions.

2^{ndly} We cannot by our view which was very considerable or by the best information we could get, find that the Pine Trees growing there are capable of making masts for his Majesty's Royal Navy, they being what is called Saplings. There is an extraordinary Harbour with several ways of entrance into it and a number of Navigable Rivers within the bounds of Machias. About four miles up the River called Eastern River on one branch of it there is a very large Pond which they call a Lake, about twelve miles in length and three or four miles in wedth with a variety of Fish in it as well as in the River aforesaid: the Rivers abounding with Salmon and Salmon Trouts &c. of large dimensions. The Rivers there all communicate with the main River which empties itself into the Ocean. There are a considerable number of Mills in said place, the people very notable, sober, peaceable, and industrious, a few excepted, who tho' not so peaceable are very industrious.

3^{rdly} That there might be as much peace and good order at Machias as in the other twelve granted Towns, we would humbly offer it as our opinion that the authority which is now there should be strengthned. This we believe would be greatly for his Majesty's service and the honor of Government. It was with great pleasure that we had an opportunity of Swearing Mr Sinkler an Inhabitant there into the office of a Deputy Sheriff. That there should be such an Officer there was absolutely necessary, especially as there neither was nor could be a Constable in that place, it not being Incorporated: but there being but one Goal in the County wherein it lies & that Goal near 70 leagues distant by water and for several months in the year inaccessible, involves in it a thousand legal difficulties which might be removed if there was a Goal at and in Fort Pownall, where there is a convenient Room which would extremely well answer that purpose and in no wise hurt the Garrison. But this cannot be done with your Excellency's permission which we doubt not will be granted, as it will be so much for his Majesty's real service. And if we should be so happy as to have your Excell^y view it in the same point of light We persuade ourselves for the reason aforesaid that you will be pleased to express your sentiments,— with your permission to the Court of General Sessions of the peace at Pownalborough that the same by them may be made a Goal during the Governor's pleasure.— Machias is about 36 leagues from Fort Pownall and about 90 from Boston.

4^thly It was with pleasure and at the same time with grief, we heard the good people at Machias express their ardent desires that they might be in a legal capacity to maintain the preaching of the Gospel among them and that they and their Children might be taught to fear God and honor the King. That they are sincere in it we have abundant reason to believe when we consider that whilst we were there the Reverend Gentleman that went down with us preached twice a day the two Sabbaths we were at Machias and one Lecture to an audience consisting of about 150 or rather two hundred persons and Baptized 13 Children. We are sure your Excell^y feels for these people and for those in the Towns abovementioned and will do every thing for them touching the premises that possibly can be done, consistent with your duty to his Majesty.

5^thly The number of Males at Machias from sixteen & upwards are about 150 and of Families upwards of Sixty.

6^thly As to the quality of the Land at Gouldsboro' what bounds upon the Harbour we thought not very extraordinary, but we were informed that that was the worst of the Land; at Frenchmans Bay, part of Gouldsboro' where Mr Justice Nathan Jones lives, the Land is very good, but no Pines fit for Masts grow there, being chiefly Saplings. Whilst we were at Gouldsboro' Capt Smith in a Ship from and belonging to Bristol in England and bound there, was in the Harbour which is a mighty good one (tho' dangerous to enter without a good pilot, having some ledges of Rocks near the

entrance) informed us that he had either lost a mast or
wanted a spare one, and that he could not get one in the
whole Township. The people in general we are informed
are honest, sober and peaceable. The Lands in the other
granted Townships by what we saw of them and by what we
heard are good, very much improved for the time and very
much in the same situation with respect to Pine Trees fit for
his Majesty's Royal Navy as at Machias and Gouldsboro'.
The people in general are sober industrious, peaceable and
well affected to Government and make great Improvements
of the Lands granted them. This we had ocular demonstra-
tion of, when we came between the Islands and the main
from Mount Desart to Fort Pownall, which is about 20.
leagues. We anchored on a Saturday (24 August) near
Naskeeg point within the Reach called Egamogging Reach
18 miles in length very strait and about a mile wide
extremely pleasant; good improvements in many places on
each side thereof; an Inhabitant having about 100 Cocks of
fine English Hay upon about five acres of Land as we
judged. This is in the Township N° four: We were
detained here by reason of a calm and the Tide against us
till Lords day noon; the people ashore upon their knowing
there was an Ordained Minister on board, entreated that we
would go ashore and that the minister would perform Divine
Service amongst them and Baptise their Children, there not
having been a Sermon ever preached there. It gave us
great satisfaction to see such a disposition in them and that
providence had given us such an opportunity to oblige them.
We went ashore, divine Service was carried on and nine
Children baptised and one adult, tho' these people had only
one hours notice. We apprehend there are 500 Families at
least in the thirteen granted Townships. Notwithstanding
the Pine Trees afores^d are generally of the Sapling kind, yet
as we are informed in the rear of said Townships there are

some very fine **Trees** fit to Mast the Royal Navy, the Land there being stronger and better, but without the clearing of the Land in said granted Townships they cannot be transported to the Water side without very great expence. We were at Mount Desart, the Land there is extremely good, saving the mountains which are a Desart and from whence Monsieur Champlain gave it that name— We suppose there was or might have been mowed there a thousand Tuns of fine Salt hay this year, and a vast quantity of fresh and English Grass. There are on it many stately Trees fit for Royal Masts.

7^{thly} It is most certain that the people who have settled and are settling in the 13 Townships have this intention to make further Improvements and to spend their days there: But that they went there only for the sake of the Timber and when they have cut that off intend to quit the Lands is without the least color of truth: for can it be conceived that persons who have laid out their Money and strength upon these Lands by clearing and making such profitable Improvements thereon, so that in fact they now support themselves and Families, should ever voluntarily quit the same, especially when a great number, perhaps far the greatest never was concerned in logging, Masting, or a Saw Mill. This your Excellency may depend upon as a fact; and it is the opinion of the most thinking amongst them and their practice is accordingly that upon the whole and in the conclusion those who are least concerned in logging will be the Richest. They gave us numbers of instances to support their sentiments by way of comparison and we must confess that we were intirely of their mind.

8^{thly} We do not find that there hath been much if any spoil or waste made on the Lands aforesaid by cutting Trees fit for Masts for the Royal Navy and we are so far from apprehending that the settling these Townships with Inhabitants can, supposing there was a number of Trees fit for the Royal Navy therein, have any tendency to destroy said Trees, that we believe quite the contrary and for this plain reason, that there is less hazard of detection in committing Trespasses where there are no settled fixed Inhabitants than in a place where there are numbers of such Inhabitants, many of whom from a sense of duty or for a Reward would turn Informers and we are from our own observations certain that there is no Trading Maritime Town destitute of Informers, and the reason of the thing holds equally good with respect to Informers in the above case.

Lastly When we consider the description given by Monsieur Champlain who we apprehend was the first European that reconnoitred the Eastern shore and gave the River St Croix its name, we are convinced that the River St Croix mentioned in the Royal Charter can by no means be the River Passamaquoda, but that the River Passamaquoda being an Indian name was known thereby: When we consider also that there is a living Witness (whose Deposition we wish might be taken in perpetuam rei memoriam) who will Swear that about Sixty years ago he used to trade at St Croix, that by the Indians he Traded with (who were born there & always lived there and by the oldest of them who had it from their Fathers) the River St Croix aforesaid was known by that name, and that St Croix River was East of Passamaquoda. When we consider these things and many more we could mention it is plain to us that the River St Croix which we call by that name and which is East of Passamaquoda is the true River St Croix and the Eastern boundary of this Province as mentioned in the Charter. Notwithstanding which we are well informed that there are Grants made by the Governor or Government of Nova Scotia of Grand Manan, some of the Islands of Passamaquoda Bay and of Land upon the main and settlements thereon, all

West of St. Croix. And we are also informed that the same Lands are very good.

The above Remarks are humbly submitted to your Excellency by

William Brattle
James Bowdoin
Thos Hubbard

Boston Septem^r 12th 1771
    A true Copy
        att^d Tho. Flucker Sec^y

Memorial of Arthur Savage 1771.

To His Excellency Thomas Hutchinson Esqr Governor of The Province of The Massachusetts Bay. &c &c

Arthur Savage Comptroller of His Majestys Customs for the Port of Falmouth, begs leave Humbly to represent to Your Excellency

That on the Evening of the 12th Currant setting in my House at Falmouth in company with my Nephew Mr William Savage just before nine of the Clock, some person gave a violent stroke at the door of the House of your Memorialist, upon which my Nephew abovemention^d took a Candle, and went to the door, and unbolted the same, Immediately on which I heard a rushing in the Entry, and turning me head towards the door of the Room, I see a number of disguised persons entring the same, Upon which your Memorialist rose and Spoke to them, and asked them their Business with Him, and was answered by the persons in disguise, that they had come to know who was the Informer, and immediately seazed me, I answered the persons in disguise That I could not lett them know who the person was, They replyed with an Oath That I should tell, and forceably hauled me out of my

House, Upon which I told them they need not treat me Ill, as if I must go with them I would walk without hauling me — being forced immediately into the Street, I desired my Nephew beforementioned to call Mr Benjamin Titcomb (who lives opposite to me) Said Titcomb came into the Street, and I lett him know " That I was forced out of my House " by a number of persons armed with Clubs, and in disguise, " and what they Intended against me I did not know, and " desired the assistance of the said Titcomb"; Upon which one of the disguised persons replyed, " We come to know " who was the Informer and by God you must and shall tell, upon which said Benj^a Titcomb said, applying himself to your Memorialist.— We want to know who the Informer is, which we shall be glad to know — and left me, Immediately on which I asked Mr William Savage beforement^d to keep by me, The disguised Persons then violently pushing me, and hauling me by my Arms down a lane leading towards the River, Mr Wm Savage soon disapeared, and I was left in their custody, without any person to assist me, Said disguised persons hurreing me along the side of the River where no House is, but at a considerable distance, and frequently stopt and surrounded me, and with horrid Oaths and threatnings demanded whether I would let them know the name of the Informer. I still refused to satisfy them, and continued in telling them it was contrary to my duty so to do, and demanded of them wether I had in any way or manner Injured any of them they the disguised persons replyed I had not, but by the Almighty God I should tell them who the Informer was, I repeatedly answered them to these demands, that I would not lett them know who he was, lett the Consequences be what they would, Upon which they continued forcing me along to the extream parts of this Town, and soon after a loud Yell was given and they surrounded me, (being upwards of twenty five persons) and with verry threatning expressions told me they where armed, I answered I could not help it, upon which the person who appeared their leader presented a Pistle towards me, and told me "That by the living God I now must lett them know, or take the consequence, and at the same Time three or four others by me shew their Pistles — upon which I lett them know what I was acquainted with respecting the matter, which they obliged me twice at the place to Swear to, and immediately turned, and brought me up the lane w^r they had carried me down, and stopped at the door of the House of Benj^a Titcomb beforemention^d, where they the disguised persons asked for Liquor, and obliged me there to swear to what I had before done — Upon which upon mentioning my Swearing That if I knew any of them I would not make a discovery — They the disguised persons in the most Solemn manner, called God to wittness "That if I knew "any of them and should discover them, they would destroy "me, or words conveying that meaning — they then fired two or three Pistles in the Air, and left me in the Street opposite to my House, after being in their custody near One Hour.

Your memorialist would further Acquaint Your Excellency that the next day being the 13th in Company with the Collector, and deputy collector he waited on the Justices of the Inferior Court, then sitting at Falmouth, and made known to them perticularly the circumstances before related, Who remarked that it was a high handed Riott — bore Testimony against it, and told me all they could do was to Issue Warrants in case any of the persons where known, Your memorialist answered that he could not say who the persons where.

On Thursday 14th Mr William Savage beforement^d having committed to writing what he knew respecting the Riott Aforement^d, was desirous (at the request of your memorialist) to make Oath to the same — I attended him to the House where the Justices of the Inferior Court where Setting, and taking Enock Freeman Esq one of said Justices into another Room the said writing was offered to said Freeman with the desire of the said W^m that he might be admitted to make Oath to the same which the said Enock refused to administer — I then called out another of the said Justices, and after sending for the beforement^d Benjamin Titcomb, and reading the said writing to him (the words aledged to be spoken by him he having admitted to be True) the said Justice declined administering an Oath, and was of Opinion It was proper to lay it before the Court — Soon after which on the same day Your Memorialist with Francis Waldo Esqr Collector of said Port, William Tyng Esqr Sherrif of the County of Cumberland, and Mr Wm Savage beforement^d, applied to The Justices of the Inferior Court then setting, and presented the said writing, and prayed that the said William might be admitted to make Oath to the Same, which said Justices after a debate on the matter for an Hour or more Voted that he should not be admitted to make Oath to the same three of which Justices voting directly against an Admission, and two of them where of Opinion that if it could be admitted it must be with Mr Benjamin Titcomb beforement^d Oath to his deposition on the Same paper, and to be used together. And as Your memorialist had the greatest Reason to think his life in danger, and as he could not receive the desired support from the Justices of the County, he tho^t it his duty (after deputiseing a Sutable person to act for him in the Custom House) to repair to Boston and pray the protection of Your Excellency.

He therefore Humbly prays That Your Excellency would be pleased to consider the distressed situation of Your Memorialist, his Wife, and family, who he has been obliged to leave at Falmouth, and that your Excellency will be pleased to grant him such Relief as in your Wisdom you may judge the nature of his case calls for, And as in duty bound shall ever pray &c.

A Savage

Boston November 27th: 1771.

Mr Savage attending the Governor & Council further saith that he Certainly knew Jonathan Armstrong & Stone Masters of Vessels Living in Falmouth to be of the Company Mentioned In this Memorial, and that he verily Believes Thomas Sanford a Master of a Vessell was the person who presented the Pistol to his Breast — and that the reason Assigned by One of the Justices of the Sessions for not Admitting his Nephew William Savage to his Oath was, because the deposition Might possably be sent To the Commissioners at Boston and by them be sent to England the Consequence whereof Might be fatal to the Town — he further said that Collonel Powell & Mr Bradbury two of the Justices said that If Mr Wm Savage was Admitted to his Oath, that Mr Benj^a Titcomb should Likewise that they might appear Together

A Savage

November 27th 1771. Sworn to before the Governor & Council

Attest Thos Flucker Sec^y

Proceedings of the Council Regarding the Riot at Falmouth.

At a Council held at the Council Chamber, in Boston, Wednesday November 27th 1771. Present His Excellency Governor Hutchinson John Erving Willm Brattle James Bowdoin Esq^{rs} Thos Hubbard Harrison Gray James Otis James Pitts Esq^{rs} Stephen Hall

His Excellency communicated to the Board, a Letter from William Tyng Esq[r] Sheriff of the County of Cumberland, to him, dated the 4th Instant, together with a Copy of a Letter from Arthur Savage Esq[r] Comptroller of his Majesty's Customs, at the Port of Falmouth, to the Commissioners at Boston with their Letter to his Excellency the Governor thereupon, and said Savages Memorial to him; all relating to a violent Assault upon the Person of the said Savage, by sundry of the Inhabitants of the Town of Falmouth, on the Evening of the 12th Current, as particularly set forth in the several Papers aforementioned; when a Motion was made for M[r] Savage's Attendance who was accordingly sent for, and being asked whether he knew any of the Persons, concerned in the Riot? answered that he certainly knew Jonathan Armstrong and   Stone, both Masters of Vessells, living in Falmouth, to be very active therein, and that he believed Thomas Sanford of Falmouth aforesaid Mariner, was the Person who presented the Pistol to his Breast, as mentioned in his Memorial. He was further asked whether he knew the Reason why the Justices of the Sessions then sitting refused to admit his Nephew William Savage to his Oath; to which he answered that one of them said, the Deposition might possibly be sent to the Commissioners at Boston, and by them to England, the Consequence whereof, might be fatal to the Town, he added that Col[o] Powell and M[r] Bradbury, two of said Justices, said, that if M[r] Savage was admitted to his Oath, M[r] Benjamin Titcomb, ought likewise to be admitted that they might appear together.

Whereupon it was advised that his Majesty's Justices of the Superior Court, now sitting in Boston, be desired to attend the Governor and Council, of which they were made acquainted by the Secretary; they attended accordingly when his Excellency informed them of the whole of this matter; They expressed their to do all that was incumbent on them to bring the Rioters to Punishment, & desired the Complaint might be laid before them, which was advised to, and laid before them accordingly.

Ordered that the further Consideration of this affair, be referred to the next sitting of the Council.

A true Copy from the Council Minutes

Att^t Jno Cotton D. Seõry

To the Right Honourable the Lords Commissioners of His Majesty's Treasury

The petition of the Proprietors of the Kennebeck Purchase lying in the County of Lincoln in the Province of Massachusets Bay. Humbly Sheweth,

That your Petitioners are Proprietors of a large Tract of Land lying on each side of the Kennebeck River: their Title to which appears by the paper annexed N° 1, which they humbly submit to Your Lordships Consideration, together with a State of Facts relative to the said Tract, N° 2.

That in the Patent & Deeds from which your petitioner's Title is derived, there is no Reserve of White pines suitable for Masts for the Royal Navy, nor any other Reservation whatever, except a certain part of the Ore of the Mines of Gold & silver which shall be had & obtained within the Premises, & which shall be for, or in lieu of all services & Demands whatsoever.

That as they have the Property of the White pine Trees growing on the said Tract, so they are not disturbed in that property by any of the Acts of Parliament made for the preservation of white pines in America suitable for Masts for the Royal Navy. And this it is humbly apprehended will appear by the Extracts from the said Acts hereunto annexed, N° 3.

That knowing of what Importance it is, that there should be a supply of Masts for the Royal Navy, they have to the utmost of their power endeavoured to preserve the White pines growing on the said Tract and they have been influenced thereto by their own Interest also: it being much more beneficial to reserve such Trees for the use of the Navy, than for any other use whatever.

That the Means necessary for procuring such Masts there, could not be had before the said Tract was in a considerable degree settled.

That the settling it, besides the granting away many thousands of Acres of Land on no other Condition than of Settlement, has already occasioned to the said proprietors an Expence of above Eight Thousand pounds Sterling since 1749 besides a large sum that has been expended by Individuals of them.

That from this Expence & their great Exertions they have hitherto reaped no Benefit: and it will be many Years before they can expect any, unless the Mast Trees can be made to procure it for them.

That the Benefit of those Trees they are deprived of by the Agents of the Mast Contractors, who under the pretence that they grow in the King's Woods take them away at pleasure.

That the said Agents could not have procured those Trees without the means furnished them by the Petitioners by the Exertion & Expence abovementioned: And now it has become practicable by those means to procure Masts on the said Tract they are unjustly endeavouring to engross the Advantage of it to themselves. One of the said Agents, Mr Perry, lately had an Interview with one of your petitioners and was informed that your petitioners would allow his getting Masts provided a reasonable Compensation was made for them: and it was proposed to him that the Masts should be procured for him at the same rate the late Contractor Mr Henaker allowed for them, but he said they would turn out too dear to the present Contractor: whereupon he was told it was unreasonable to make an extra profit for the Contractor at the Expence & to the great Damage of Your Petitioners.

That the persons employed by the said Agents having no Interest in the Soil & its Growth, are wholly regardless of the Damage they do to either: and through ignorance or to make Advantage by it cut down many Trees unfit for Masts for the Navy which they afterward convert into Lumber thereby making great Destruction of the Timber to the great Detriment of your Petitioners.

That for the redress of these Grievances they have applied to Governor Wentworth Surveyor General of the Woods, but His Excellency has informed them his Office being only executive he could grant no redress; & proposed (in a manner that does Honor to his politeness) that the Matter should be settled by a Judgement of Court in a Suit to be brought for that purpose.

That the entering into a Law Suit having the appearance of refusing the Masts for His Majesty's Services (I would probably be so represented by the said Agents) & being ready to accept a reasonable Compensation for them, Your Petitioners choose rather to lay their Case before your Lordships, humbly praying your Lordships to take the same into Consideration, & grant or procure them such relief as in your great Wisdom you should think fit.

    James Bowdoin James Pitts ⎫ Committee
    Silv. Gardiner Benjn Hallovell ⎬ of the said
    William Bowdoin   ⎭ Proprietors.

Boston New England 18th December 1771

Thomas Scammell to Govr Hutchinson

Portsmouth January 2nd 1772—

Sir

I take the liberty to inform your Excellency that I had the honour of receiving yours of the 21 instant, and that I am extremely sorry (as you expected it) that I did not wait on you; I will therefore, as near as I can, give you an account of my proceedings since I had the pleasure of seeing you.

Immediately after, I set out for Portsmouth and at my arrival waited on his Excellency Governor Wentworth in consequence of my 6th and last Instruction, which enjoins me to obey such other Instructions as I shall from time to time receive from the Surveyor General. I soon found after I left Boston that the Summer was the most improper time for inspecting the Woods. The Surveyor General pointed out to me the impropriety of such an attempt; that the Flies &c would be very troublesome, and that the Country people born on the skirts of the Woods durst scarce ever make such attempts. However that no reflexion might be cast on my Conduct, I took the liberty to inform him, if he thought proper, I would try whether they would have the same effect on me — this his Excellency willingly assented to, and prevailed on Colonel Bagley (who is personally known to you Sir) to accompany me. We accordingly set out for Kennebec and soon arrived at Doctor Gardiners at Cobbiseconta (from a Report I received that the Banks of that Stream abounded with good Oak Timber) The Doctors Son made one of the party, we landed and found some Oak Timber — had not long been on shore before I was too sensible of the Surveyor General's kind caution; the flies had such an effect on me, that after my arrival at the Doctors, I found myself somewhat indisposed, and therefore was obliged to return. That no time might be lost, and from experience finding that tis much easier to prevent than remedy, I determined to send the Colonel to the Eastward to remove any prejudices that the people might entertain from my appointment. He set out accordingly and I have the pleasure to inform your Excellency that it fully answered our expectation. The people in general were prepossessed with very strange notions one of which was that I was coming down with an arm'd force to dispossess them, and burn their Mills. As soon as the nature of my Commission was explaind to them their prejudices vanished and they wished to see me. Immediately after the Colonel's return I hired a Vessel and engaged him to go with me; Before we sailed I received from the Surveyor General Instructions to confine myself, in this Expedition, to the Sea Coast and Rivers; This appeared to me to be a well concerted scheme tending much to prove his great knowledge in whatever is necessary for the preservation of his Majesty's Woods. We sailed for Gouldsborough, arrived and went on shore but could not make any important discovery. We sailed from thence for Eastern River, Blue hill Bay and Penobscot; At the latter place, the commanding officer (Col^o Goldthwait being at Boston) afforded us every assistance in his power. We sailed up the River and anchor'd off the mouth of Condeskeeg Stream. Captain Fletcher accompanied us and informed me that the Indians was very desirous of seeing me — we saw one and had a conference. I desired the Captain to acquaint him that I should have occasion frequently to employ them as guides in exploring the Country. That his Majesty required all the large Trees for Masts &c for the Royal Navy and nothing would recommend them more to his Majesty's notice and protection than their affording me every assistance & information in their power; went on shore and walked some miles about the Woods. The best Pines, tho' not extraordinary, we found near this stream. I fully intended paying the Indians a visit and prepared accordingly, but was prevented by the heavy rains which fell the day before. We sailed and Anchor'd in Kennebec River and observed with the greatest circumspection the appearance of the Woods, and are of opinion that very few pines near the Sea shore, are fit for Masts &c &c for the Royal Navy. I cannot pretend to assert at what distance from the Sea they are good, this must be left to a future inspection. I shall consult the Surveyor General respecting my report, and your Excellency may depend on having an exact Copy. In my report I shall be careful not to mention anything but what myself or Deputy have seen, little dependance is to be placed on the peoples account of the state of the Country. The internal part now claims my attention; I have therefore ordered a party for that purpose, from whose diligence and activity I form the greatest expectations. As my District has an extensive Sea Coast, and a very great part not inhabited, I therefore wrote to their Lordships for a Vessel of thirty Tons and a flat bottom Boat, and am in daily expectation of their Lordships Order: In which I took the liberty to inform them of your Excellency to the following effect, "As "part of my District is the Eastern part of Mass[a] Bay I "therefore conceived it consistent with my duty to wait on "his Excellency Governor Hutchinson to apprize him of my "arrival and to procure the best information of the state "and limits of the unclaimed Lands; His Excell[y] received "me with the greatest civility, enjoyed the Civil and Mili- "tary power to be aiding and assisting — that I might "depend on his protection and consult him in all matters "relating to my office within his Government."

I entreat your Excellency's pardon for the liberty I have taken and assure you that I shall on every occasion be happy in convincing you how much I am with the greatest respect Your Excellency's much obliged and obedient humble Servant —

Copy   Tho[s] Scammell

Govr Hutchinson to the Earl of Hillsborough

Boston 3 January 1772

My Lord

The Proprietors of what is called the Plimouth Patent, being a Tract on each side the River Kennebec, have applied to me to transmit to the Lords of the Treasury a Petition and Proposal relative to the Masts within the Patent. I acquainted them that it was most regular for me to transmit it to your Lordship and to submit to you the presenting it, that I should say nothing concerning their Title — which is a Subject of Controversy in the Courts of Law here and which was revived about the year 1750. I am bound to observe to your Lordship that the whole of the Western side of Kennebec River is included in the Patent to Sir Ferdinando Gorges and although this Patent was dated after that under which the Kennebec Proprietors claim from the Council of Plimouth yet it is founded upon a patent or patents from the same Council of a prior date to that of the Kennebeck Proprietors.

The history of the Country East of Kennebec your Lordship is well acquainted with. This Tract as well as the Country East of it, settles with great rapidity and one of the Proprietors acquaints me that 150 new families are going out upon it the next Spring.

Mr Scammell is returned from his survey of the Eastern Country and had what assistance he desired from Fort Pownall. He is now at Portsmouth in New Hampshire. I have wrote to him to remind him of making some return to your Lordship but have received no Answer.

In consequence of a Warrant from the Chief Justice two of the persons concerned in the Assault upon the Comptroller at Falmouth have been apprehended & by a Justice of Peace there recognized in a sufficient Sum with Sureties for their appearance to answer at the next Assizes and upon information brought to me of the names of five or six others concerned I have directed the same Justice to proceed with them in like manner and I hope they will all be brought to exemplary punishment.

Being still without Letters from your Lordship I have thought it for his Majesty's Service further to prorogue the General Court to the 19th of February

I am with very great respect My Lord Your Lordship's most humble & most obed^t Servant

Tho' Hutchinson

Letter, Dr. Franklin to Hon. Thos Cushing & Committee

London Jany 13, 1772

Gentlemen,

On my Return from a late Tour thrô Ireland and Scotland for the Establishment of my Health, I found your respected Letter of June 25, with the Papers therein referred to relating to the Townships settled eastward of Penobscot River.

I immediately waited on Mr Agent Bollan, to consult with him Agreable to your Instructions; who inform'd me, that in my Absence he had by himself thoroughly considered the same, having formerly had Occasion to be well-acquainted with the whole Affair; and had suggested to his Constituents the Council a Plan of Accommodation, to be propos'd to Government here if they should approve of it, and that he hoped by the Meeting of Parliament (before which little Publick Business is done here, so many of the Lords of the Council being out of Town) he might have their Answer; and it would otherwise be to little Purpose to attempt any thing sooner. I make no doubt but the Proposal has been communicated to the House of Representatives if they have since had a Meeting, and that we may soon receive their farther Instructions thereupon.

The Town now begins to fill, the Members of Parliament & great Officers of State coming in daily to celebrate the Queen's Birthday, & be present at the Opening of the Session, which is fixed for next Tuesday. It is given out that nothing relating to America is likely to be agitated this Session; i. e. there is no Purpose either to abrogate the old Duties or lay new ones. For the first I am sorry, believing as I do that no Harmony can be restored between the two Countries while those Duties are continu'd.

This with the other Aggrievances mentioned in your Letters of June 29 & July 13, your Agents will constantly attend to, and take every Step possible in their present Situation (unacknowledg'd as they are here) to obtain the Redress that is so justly your Due, and which it would be so prudent in Government here to grant.

In yours of July 9, it is mentioned that the House desire I would annually send an Account of the Expence I am at in carrying on the Affairs of the Province.— Having Business to do for several Colonies almost every time I go to the Publick Offices and to the Ministers, I have found it troublesome to keep an Account of small Expenses, such as Coach & Chair Hire, Stationary, &c. and difficult to divide them justly. Therefore I have some time since omitted keeping any Account or making any Charge of them, but content myself with such Salaries, Grants or Allowances as have been made me. Where considerable Sums have been disburs'd, as in Fees to Council, Payment of Sollicitors Bills, & the like, those I charge: But as yet I have made no such Disbursements on the Account of your Province.

Please to present my Duty to the House of Representatives, and believe me to be with great Esteem & Respect Gentlemen, Your most obedient hum^l Servt

B Franklin

Govr Hutchinson to the Earl of Hillsborough

N° 21   Boston 31st Jany 1772
  My Lord
    It is my duty to acquaint your Lordship with every material occurrence relative to the Country East of Kenebeck.
    I have been informed, within a few days past, that a person has taken possession of a small Island a few leagues from Fort Pownall and not claimed by private persons where he found great quantities of Limestone and soon after sold one half of the Island, the whole not exceeding 17 acres, for One hundred and fifty pounds sterling and the partners have burnt the last year four or five hundred hogsheads of Lime for a Market. The people have at all times been capricious in the choice of new settlements; the present caprice is to this part of the Country, and I expect a very great increase of Inhabitants there in the course of the next summer unless I am enabled to check it by some other aid than that of the General Court.
    Except in this town, there is now a general appearance of contentment throughout the Province and, even here, the persons who have made the most disturbance are become of less importance. A Gentleman who has assisted them much by his money and by the reputation which his fortune gives him among the people seems weary of them and I have reason to think is determined to leave them. The plain dispassionate pieces in favour of Government which are now published with freedom in our News papers and dispersed through the Province have done great Service
    I have the honour to be most respectfully
           My Lord Your Lordship's most humble
                    & most obedient Servant
                           Tho' Hutchinson

Petition of James Chase & others 1772.

Province of the Massachusett Bay   To his Excellency Thomas Hutchinson Esqr Captain General and Commander in Chief in and over his Majesties Province of the Massachusetts Bay   To the Honorable his Majesties Council And House of Representatives in General Court convened in May 1771 —

The Memorial of the Subscribers hereto, Inhabitants of or Proprietors of Lands in a Plantation in the County of York on the East side of Saco River called Narraganset N° One — Humbly Sheweth —

That the Bounds of said Plantation are as follows. viz. South Easterly at the Heads of Biddeford & Scarborough, South Westerly by Saco River, North Westerly by Pearson Town (so called) and North Easterly by Gorham.

That there is settled within the bounds of said Plantation upwards of Sixty Familys that a Meeting House is there built, and that for a Number of years past they have had a Minister of the Gospel regularly settled there — That the said Plantation was never Incorporated and that the Inhabitants by Reason thereof lay under Great Difficulties and Discouragements which would be removed if the said Plantation was Erected into a Township — and the Inhabitants had the Benefit & Priviledges of Town order —

Wherefore The Memorialists pray your Excellency and Honours by an Act of the Great & General Assembly to Erect the said Plantation into a Town according to the bounds & limits afores^d And to Grant to the Inhabitants thereof all the Powers, Priviledges, and Immunities that the respective Towns in this Province Do by Law Exercise & Enjoy — or otherwise Releive Your Memorialists as in your Great Wisdom your Excellency & Honours shall think fit — And your Memorialists as in Duty bound shall ever pray —

James Pike   Amos Chase   Joseph Adams

Joshua Wyman   Richd Greenleaf   Tristram Gordon
Joseph Woodbrige   John Lane   James Jewett
Robert McDonald   Sam^ll Greenleaf   Josiah Groffaim
Ambrose Berey   Simeon Fitts   Cutting Bartlet
Martha Milliken wid Abraham Somerby   Richard Elvins
Cutting Moodey   Snell Wingate   Samuel Noyes
Philip Fowler   John Thurston   Henry Adams
Benjamin Thurston Tomas Berry   Benjamin Elwell
Ebenezer Greenleaf Cornelius Fellows   Nathaniel Low
Gustavus fellows   Nathanel fellows   William Cuningham
Samuel Fellows

       In the House of Representatives
        April 11th 1772 —

Ordered that the within named Petitioners notifie the Inhabitants & Proprietors of the Plantation mentioned in said Petition by Posting up On the meeting House in said Plantation a Copy of this Petition with this Order thereon twenty days before the third Wednesday of the General Court that they shew cause if any they have why the prayer thereof should not be granted, and that the proprietors make no further Grants or Assessments

    Sent up for Concurrence
      John Hancock Spk^r pro Temp^e

In Council.   April 13. 1772   Read & Concurr'd
        Jno Cotton   D. Secry

In Council June 6th 1772 — Read again, & revived & ordered that the within named Petitioners, notifie the Inhabitants, or Proprietors, of the Plantation ment^d in said Petition, by posting up on the Meeting House in said Plantation, a Copy of this Petition, with this Order thereon, twenty days before the second Wednesday of the next sitting of the General Court, that they may shew cause if any they have, on the said second Wednesday, why the Prayer thereof

should not be granted, & that the proprietors in the mean time, make no further Grants, or Assessments
    Sent down for Concurrence
                Jn° Cotton   D. Secry

Confirmation to Capt. Joshua Fuller 1772

In the House of Representatives April 22 1772

Resolved that the Plan of the Township hereunto Annexed, Containing the Contents of Six Miles and One Quarter Square (Exclusive of the Allowance of One thousand nine hundred Acres for the River & Ponds in said Township, and Eight hundred & forty Acres for Swag of Chain, being one thirtieth part thereof) bounded as followeth, beginning at a heap of Stones at the South west Corner, running North 73 Deg^s East fifty one Chains and thirty to little Amarascoggin River, thence by said, One hundred and fourteen Chains to a White Pine Tree on the Easterly Side of said River, thence North 43 Deg^s East, three hundred and forty Chains to a Spruce Tree on Sylvester Canada line, thence North 4 Deg^s West five hundred & forty two Chains to Stake and Stones, thence South 68 Deg 30 minutes West five hundred twenty seven Chains thence South 14 Deg^s East Six hundred Eighty Eight Chains to the heap of Stones first mentioned Granted in June A.D. 1771 to Capt Joshua Fuller and others mentioned in their petition be Accepted and hereby is Confirmed to the said petitioners their heirs and Assigns forever they Complying with the following Conditions, Viz^t the Grantees within Seven years Settle Sixty families in said Township, build a house for the Public Worship of God and Settle a learned Protestant Minister, and lay out one Sixty fourth part for the first Settled Minister, one Sixty forth part for the use of the Ministry, one Sixty fourth part for the use of a School, and one Sixty fourth part for the use of Harvard College forever, Provided it doth not exceed the Quantity aforementioned nor interfere with any former grant —

Sent up for Concurrence

T Cushing Spk^r

In Council April 22. 1772   Read & Concurred

Thos Flucker Sec^y

Consented to   T Hutchinson

Confirmation to David Phips and others, 1772.

In the House of Representatives April 22^d 1772

Resolved that the Plan of the Township hereunto Annexed, containing the Contents of Six Miles and Three Quarters Square (Exclusive of the Allowance of One Thousand Acres for Swag of Chain and Two Thousand Acres for Ponds & Rivers) Bounded as Followeth Beginning at a Pine Tree on the Westerly side of Amarascoggin River, Thence across said River on The Head Line of a Township Granted to Samuel Livermore and others Due East Two Hundred and Thirty Two Chains Twenty Five Links to a Stake and Stones, thence North on Province Land Five Hundred and Twelve Chains to a a heap of Stones, thence West on Province Land Three Hundred and Eighty Eight Chains to a heap of Stones, thence South Forty Three Deg^s West Five Hundred and Thirty two Chains on Province Land to a Pine Tree, thence south Nineteen Deg^s East on Province Land Two Hundred and Sixty Chains to a stake and stones, thence on Province Land in part, and in part on the Township aforementioned to the Pine Tree first mentioned Granted in June A. D. 1771 to David Phips Esqr and others mentioned in their Petition, be Accepted and hereby is confirmed to the said Petitioners their Heirs and Assigns forever, they Complying with the Following Conditions, Viz^t The Grantees within seven years Settle Eighty Families in said Township, build a house for the Publick Worship of God, and Settle a Learned Protestant Minister, and Lay out one Eighty Fourth Part for the First settled Minister, one Eighty Fourth Part for the use of the Ministry, one Eighty Fourth Part for the use of a School, and one Eighty Fourth Part for the use of Harvard College forever. Provided it doth not exceed the Quantity aforementioned nor Interfere with any Former Grant.

   Sent up for Concurrence
          T Cushing Spk^r
In Council April 22^d 1772 Read & Concurred
         Thos Flucker Sec^y
 Consented to
         T Hutchinson

Resolve, confirming Plan of Township to S. Livermore & others. 1772.

In the House of Representatives April 22^d 1772

Resolved that the Plan of the Township hereunto Annexed containing The Contents of Six Miles and Three Quarters Square (Exclusive of the Allowance of one Thousand Acres for swag of Chain being one 30th part Three Thousands and Forty Two Acres for Ponds and Rivers) Bounded as Followeth Viz^t Beginning at a heap of Stones on the Westerly Side Amarascoggin River at the North Easterly Corner of a Township called Sylvester Canada, Thence North Sixty Four Deg^s West one Thousand and Forty One Poles to the Corner, thence North Two Thousand one Hundred Ninety and Four Poles to the Corner, Thence

North Sixty Five Deg^r East One Thousand One Hundred and Four Poles to Amarascoggin River, Thence East Seven Hundreds and Seventy Nine Poles, across the aforesaid River to the Corner Thence south Three Thousands one Hundred and sixty Eight Poles to a Pile of Stones to the Corner, thence Eight Hundreds and Eighty Two Poles to the Corner First Mentioned. Granted in June A D 1771 to Samuel Livermore Esqr and his Associates, mentioned in their Petition be Accepted and hereby is confirmed to the said Petitioners Their Heirs and Assigns Forever, They Complying with the Following Conditions Viz^t The Grantees within seven Years settle Sixty Families, in said Township, Build a House for the Publick Worship of God, and settle a Learned Protestant Minister, and Lay out one Sixty Fourth Part for the First settled Minister, one Sixty Fourth Part for the Use of the Ministry, one Sixty Fourth Part for the Use of a School, one Sixty Fourth Part for the Use of Harvard College Forever Provided it doth not exceed the Quantity aforementioned nor Interfere with any former Grant —

   Sent up for Concurrence

           T Cushing Spk^r

In Council April 22^d 1772. Read and Concurred

           Thos Flucker Sec^y

   Consented To

           T Hutchinson

Resolve Confirming Grant to Hon. James Otis & others. 1772.

In the House of Representatives April 23 1772.

Resolved that the Plan of the Township hereunto Annexed Containing the Contents of Seven miles Square, (Exclusive of the Allowance of One thousand & Eighty

Acres for Swag of Chain being one thirtieth part, also an Allowance of three thousand & Sixty Acres, for Ponds in said Township) bounded as followeth beginning at the Northwest Corner of Raymond's Town, and the line running Northeast partly on Raymond's Town & partly on Province land, two thousand nine hundred & thirteen rods to a Corner, thence running North 25 Deg^s West, two thousand five hundred & twenty rods to a Corner, thence South 65 Deg^s West One hundred & Ninety five rods, thence North 25 Deg. west five hundred & forty rods thence South 65 Deg^s West One thousand two hundred & Ninty Six rods to Bridge's Town line, thence South 25 Degrees East, three thousand One hundred & Sixty nine rods, thence South 65 Deg. West One thousand four hundred & Eighty rods, thence South 40 Deg^s East nine hundred & thirty rods to the bound mark first mentioned, Granted in June A. D. 1771 to the Hon^r James Otis Esqr and Mr Nathaniel Gorham in behalf of themselves & others mentioned in their Petition, be Accepted and hereby is Confirmed to them their heirs and assigns for ever, in lieu of and in full Satisfaction for the loss of lands mentioned in their petition, by running the line between this Province & the Province of New Hampshire; they Complying with the following Conditions Viz the Grantees within Six years Settle thirty Families in the said Town, build a meeting house and Settle a learned Protestant Minister and lay out one Sixty fourth part of said Township for the first Settled Minister, one Sixty fourth part for the use of the Ministry, and one Sixty fourth part for a Grammar School, and one other Sixty fourth part for the use of Harvard College forever provided it doth not exceed the Quantity aforementioned nor interfere with any former Grant.

   Sent up for Concurrence

          T Cushing Spk^r

In Council Ap¹ 23ᵈ 1772 —   Read & Concurrᵈ
                                Jnº Cotton D. Secry
        Consented to
                                        T Hutchinson

Petition of the Inhabitants of Boothbay.

To His Most Excellent Majesty, George the third, by the Grace of God, of Great Britain, France and Ireland King, Defender of the Faith &c. &c.

The Petition of the Subscribers, inhabitants of Boothbay in the County of Lincoln and Province of the Massachusetts Bay, Most Humbly sheweth,

That many of us the Subscribers and the Ancestors of others of us, in the Year of our Lord one thousand seven hundred and thirty one, were settled on the lands in said Boothbay (then called Townsend) by Colonel Dunbar, who acted by Commission from the King, whose encouraging proposals, published in his Majesty's name, induced us to leave our habitations in the Western parts, and venture into this then howling wilderness, on what we thought the Royal word.

That, the said Dunbar settled us as tenants holding said lands immediately under the Crown, promising in his Majesty's name, upon demand, to give us deeds, under the King's Seal, of any quantity of Land, less than a thousand acres each, as might be desired by each settler, (next adjoining to the two acres he then laid out for each, in fee simple for ever.

That, having thus, as we thought, the promise of our King, we proceeded to build us little hutts and to clear and cultivate, as we were able, an inhospitable desert, in the midst of Savage beasts, and yet more savage men: and altho' the said

Dunbar's power, was, some years thereafter, superceded, yet judging that all his publick Acts of office must necessarily have had the Sanction of the Crown as long as his said Commission was not revoked; and nothing doubting but his Majesty's Royal justice would ever defend, to his dutiful Subjects, the rights and possessions which his Royal Authority had conferred, we still continued in possession of said lands; tho always oppressed with every kind of hardship horrible to humanity on earth; at the distance of near two hundred miles from any market; without any of the conveniences of trade or navigation; often without any other sustenanc than a little Shell-fish called <u>Clams</u>, which, dug out of the mud at low water, was our only food, and water from the brooks our only drink for many weeks together; without any convenient houses, and often without any convenient clothing to defend ourselves and families from the inclemency of our severe winters; kept in continual alarms by the savage enemy, who ranged the wilderness all around, and who, in the year 1745, broke forth in such numbers, and carried on their murders, burnings, and depredations with such violence, as totally routed our whole settlement, and forced us to seek shelter for ourselves and families at near two hundred miles distance; where all our little substance was soon spent in the maintenance of our families so far from home.

That, four years after, when the rigor of the war was abated, we again ventured back and resumed our old possessions, tho' in circumstances rendered still more distressing by the losses and damages sustained by our so long banishment; whist the murders frequently committed on our neighbours kept us in continual terrors; ever under arms; and, on every new alarm, obliged to pen up our families in a little Garrison of <u>our own building and our own defending</u>, no assistance having ever been given us by the Government, either for sustenance or protection; tho' numbers of our men were called into the Provincial Army, and sent to the defence of other places; whist scalping or captivity was frequently the fate of some, and ever the expectation of us all.

That, matters continuing thus with us 'till the late peace with France, our settlement was then in most forlorn circumstances; but that happy event encouraged us to resume the cultivation of our lands, and soon changed the face of our affairs; for, tho' utterly neglected and disowned till then, no sooner was the peace of these parts secured by the cession of Canada, than we began to be harrassed with enemies of a new sort, swarms of persons pretending themselves proprietors of our lands, infested us from divers parts of the Country, demanding the possession of said lands and threatning us with prosecutions and utter ruin if we refused.

That, said Proprietors (so called) were opposite to one another as well as adverse to us, claiming by pretended Indian deeds, ancient occupations, and other pretences never before heard of, none of which deeds have ever been approved by the General Court, nor any of the said claims justified by a course of law:

That, tho' our lands are naturally poor, much broken with rocks, and fitted chiefly for grass, and hence, to this day, scarce any of us can raise the necessary provisions for more than a few months in the year, yet as we know not where to seek a place of residence for ourselves or families, on this side the grave, if we should be driven from these our Ancient possessions, therefore the said Proprietors, by threats prevailed on some, and by promises cajoled others of us so far that several have bought their lands three times over, from three opposite setts of competing claimers; none of whom have ever done anything to defend us from the others, and all of them still leave us open to the challenges of we know not how many more; by one or other of whom we are daily threatned and disturbed.

That, your Petitioners have applied to the General Court to be quieted in our possessions, but hitherto without effect; and it being now publickly rumored that various persons, around your Majesty's throne, are applying for grants of the Eastern lands in this Province, with design of reducing the Settlers to rack rents on leases of years, or turning them off entirely, we are thereby put into great fears lest, our true case being unknown to your Majesty, the said lands should be granted to some others, and so your Petitioners be reduced to utter ruin.

That, notwithstanding all our distresses, by the blessing of God, we are still preserved, and our numbers encreased; in the year 1764 we were incorporated into a Town, by the name of Boothbay; in the year 1766 at our own sole charge, we erected and finished a convenient Church, settled a Gospel Minister, and still endeavour to support the cause of Christianity amongst us; and to contribute, from time to time, as required, our full proportion towards defraying the Expences of Government, tho' we still live very poor, many of us, some part of every year, being almost quite destitute of the necessarys of life, and few, if any, having any other subsistance for ourselves or families than by cutting down fire-wood and carrying it to Boston.

That, your Petitioners beg leave to assure your Majesty, that the above is a relation of facts strictly agreeable to truth, and that, without any exaggeration, much more might be added, as by the depositions accompanying this Petition may more fully appear; and we hope it may not be deemed unseemly arrogance to add, that we are as truly loyal, dutiful, and affectionate Subjects, as any others in your Majesty's Dominions, that we have never taken part in any of the seditious proceedings, for which many in the Provinces have rendered themselves justly obnoxious to your Royal displeasure, having never had a representative in the General

Court, and having positively refused to send one to the convention of deputy's that met in Boston whilst the Court was under sentence of disolution; and having ever signified, in our little sphere, our abhorrence of all steps, by whomsoever taken, in opposition to lawful Authority.

Therefore, as loyal and affectionate Subjects to the best of Kings, who have (many of us) for more than forty years, without aid from any but Almighty God, possessed and defended a remote part of your Majesty's Dominions, which we first entered and have ever since held in dependence on what we thought the promise of your Majesty's Royal Grandfather by his representative, and which promise we still esteem equal to any Sealed Charter; as Protestants, decended from Ancestors many of whose lives and fortunes have been sacrificed in the cause of religion and the Royal House of Hanover, and who are still prompt to prove themselves not unworthy to be called their Sons, by standing ever ready to devote our lives to the defence of your Majesty's Royal person, family, and Government; Permit us Great Sire, to cast ourselves, our Wives and helpless little ones, at your Majesty's royal feet, humbly to implore a share in that Princely tenderness, that so strongly bespeaks a father's heart to all that have the honour to meet the notice of your Royal mind; and earnestly to beseech your Majesty to take our case into your most gracious Consideration, and to grant to us, our heirs and Assigns a Quietus in our several possessions, in said Boothbay, in such way and manner as, to your Majesty, in your royal wisdom and goodness, may seem meet; And your Petitioners, and their Posterity, to the latest generation, in gratitude for a favour, to which We and they must be indebted for their very beings in the world,

As in duty bound, shall ever pray

Robert Murray	Sam[1] Adams	Daniel Knights
Soloman Burnum	Samuel Brier	Joseph Perkins

Thomas Kennay	Saml Ketley	Thomas Kenney
Giles Tebbets	Samuel Kenney	Eleaz^r Sheerman
abigh Kenney	Ebenez^r Hanasdon	John Kenney
Joseph Hervendon	Henry Kenney	James Tebbets
James Dey	John Leishman	Moses Dey
Saml Barter Tert^s	Israel Davis	Nich^s Barter
John Dawse	Saml Alley	Joseph Cunhill
Joshua Alley	And^w McFarland	Joseph Floyd
And^w McFarland Junr	John Lerote Junr	Ephraim M^{tt}farland
John fullerton	John Murray ^{mc}farland	Joseph Craven
David Reed	Ebenezer Fulerton	Joseph Reed
James Fullerton	John Holton	Neil Wylie
Samuel McCobb	James McCobb	George Lewis
Andrew Reed Junr	John Barter	Benj. Kelley
John Tebbets	Thos Kelley	Samuel Wylie
Andrew Reed 3^d	Aaron Kelley	Samuel Montgomery
Samuel M. Cobb Junr	John Reed	Ichabod Tebbets
William Wiley	William Kennedy	Alex Wiley
William McCobb	John Wiley	John Call
Robert Wiley	Saml Barter	Robert Wiley Junr
Benj^a Barter	Thomas Kennedy	Jno Alley Junr
James Kennedy	Nathl Tebbets J^r	John Booker Jun
James Auld	Jacob Booker	John Ingraham
Paul Wombly	Samwill Harris	Jno Dresser Davis
John Murray	J^{no} Murray	David Decker
John Alley	John M^{tt}Cobb	John Beath
William Fullerton	Edwd Emerson	John Lerote
William Reed	Jonathan Daws	John Matthews
Samuel Cortew Junr	Joseph Barter	Patrick Kincaid
Patrick McKown	William Lewis	Jeremiah Beath
William Moon	Nathl Lampson	Israel Davis
Nathanael Tebbets	Charls Davis	Joseph Giles
Bicomian Rent	Joseph Farnam	Nehemiah Hervenden
Solomon pinkham	Daniel Heriss	

Letter, Benjⁿ Foster & others to Rev. James Lyon

Mechias June 6th 1772

Reverend Sir

It having pleased God in his Holy Providence to bring you to this place, and by you to afford us an opportunity of hearing his Word preached in a manner we apprehend agreeable to the Purity Simplicity and Evangelical Nature of the Gospel of our Lord and Savior, wherefore, imploring the most humbling sense of our unworthiness and the Divine Goodness in thus regarding our destitute condition by directing you to this Place, and beseeching his continual Blessing, we a Committee Chosen and appointed by the Proprietors and Inhabitants of Mechias in legal Meeting assembled, do in their behalf and Stead tender you our grateful acknowledgements for your faithful Labors hitherto among us, and intreat you to accept of this our invitation and Call to Settle with and become our Pastor and Teacher, and knowing it to be our duty as far as God shall be pleased to enable us to provide for the decent and honorable support of the Gospel, That we may make your Ministerial Labors among us as easy, and your Life as agreeable as our poor Circumstances will allow, we do on your acceptance to Settle with, and become our Pastor & Teacher, during your Natural Life, or your abilities to perform the duties of a Minister of the Gospel, as the will of the Lord and the Necessities of this People may require, agree to give or grant you Eighty Six pounds Lawful Money of the Massachusetts Yearly for your Support, which sum we hereby agree to pay you in the Common pay of this place, now Merchantable Pine Lumber at the annual market price among us, and we engage you shall or may recieve the same between the first day of May and the first day of October yearly, & we do further vote and agree to give you Eighty pounds Lawful Money, one half to be paid you this year in the Specie & time above mentioned

the other half the year ensueing in like manner to enable you to Build or provide yourself a dwelling House or Settlement; earnestly commending ourselves & ours to your Pastoral Care we are — Reverend Sir,
Your faithful friends & Servants,
Benj^a Foster
Samuel Scott
Stephen Parker

Petition of Benjamin Foster and others.

To his Excellency the Governor, the Honorable his Majestys Council and the Honorable the Representatives of the Massachusets Province

May it please your Excellency & Honors

Emboldned by a Sense of our Duty, the Indispensible obligations we are under to Settle a Minister of the Gospel among us and provide for his Comfortable Support, that temporal Cares may not perplex and divide his Time; and encouraged by the Merciful dispensation of Divine Providence in bringing a Gentleman of a truely Christian Character to this place, in a manner to us altogether unexpected; we your Excellency's & Honors humble Petitioners being a Committee chosen by the Proprietors & Inhabitants of Mechias, to agree with and devise means for the support of said Gentleman vizt the Reverend Mr James Lyon — Assess the Inhabitants for said purpose and make provission for his regular Settlement as our Pastor, and knowing the deficiency from authority to Assess or lay any Tax for the support of the Gospel and oblige the Assessed, however reasonable & Just, to pay the same, Pray that your Excellency & Honors in great goodness from your distinguishing regard to our Holy Religion, agreeable to the Vote of this place, passed for said purpose, and the Call to said Reverend Gentleman founded on that Vote, Copy's of which we beg leave to lay before your Excellency & Honors, would be pleased to enable or authorize us Your humble Petitioners and future Committee's to Assess, Levy & Collect such Rates or Taxes from the Inhabitants for the above Purpose as shall be necessary proportionate & Just, and as in duty bound shall ever pray.

Benj^a Foster
Samuel Scott
Stephen Jones
Stephen Parker

Mechias June 8th 1772

In the House of Representatives June 26, 1772.

Read & Ordered that Cap. Herrick Mr Chadwick & Cap. Searl with such as the Hon^l Board shall joyn be a Committee to take this Petition into consideration & report.

Sent up for Concurrence.

T. Cushing Spk^r

In Council June 26th 1772 Read & Concurred and Wm Brattle & Thomas Hubbard Esq^{rs} are joined——

Jn° Cotton D. Secry

The Committee have attended the within service assigned beg leave to report the Bill accompanyin the same

W Brattle by order

Answer of Rev. James Lyon

To the Committee of the Church & Congregation of Mechias
   Gentlemen

Having duely I trust considered your destitute circumstances in this Place and your kind and unanimous invitation to me to settle with you in the important work of the Ministry, it appears to be my duty as far as I can judge to comply with your request. And I do hereby declare my acceptance of your Call in the fullest manner I am capable & do chearfully tho' with fear & trembling take upon me the pastoral charge and care of your Society during my natural life or while God, in his Holy Providence shall enable me to perform the duties incumbent on a Minister of the Gospel, Provided the General Court of this Province shall see fit to empower you and your Successors in Office to collect what you here voted for my Support, If otherways I shall think myself free from the above obligation.

Ja^s Lyon

Mechias June 8th 1772

Memorial of J. Wyman & others   1772

Province of the Massachusetts Bay   To his Excellency Thomas Hutchinson Esqr Governor The Honourable his Majesties Council and House of Representatives of said Province in Genl Court Assembled June 1772

The Memorial of Joshua Wyman and others Inhabitants or Proprietors of a Plantation in the County of York in said Province Called Narraganset N° One Bounded on Scarborough and Biddeford South Easterly on Saco River South Westerly on Pearson Town (So called) North Westerly And on Gorham North Easterly — Humbly Sheweth — That the said Joshua with Amos Chase and above thirty one other persons of s^d Inhabitants or proprietors in May 1771 Made their petition or Memorial to the Govr Council and Representatives of said Province — Praying that for the benefit of said Inhabitants And said Proprietors, his Excellency And their Honors would by An Act of the General Court Incorporate said Plantation According to the bounds and Limits thereof as a Town with all the powers And priviledges that other Towns in this Province enjoy by Law — That in consequence thereof it was Ordered in the House of Representatives on the 11th day of April last that the petitioners Should Notify the Inhabitants and Proprietors of the said Plantation Twenty days before the third Wednesday of the then next Session of the General Court to shew cause why the prayer of said Petition Should not be granted: That the same Order was read and Concurr'd in Council on the 13th of the Same Month — That it was Never Assented to by his Excellency the Governor and is of None Effect and That the Inhabitants and proprietors are under Many and great difficulties and discouragements by reason that said Plantation was never Incorporated — Wherefore we humbly pray that your Excellency and Honours will take the matter into Your wise consideration And by an Act of the Great and General Court incorporate said plantation According to the bounds and limits thereof into a Town (by some proper Name) with all Necessary powers and priviledges — And we shall as in duty bound ever Pray

Joshua Wyman
Enoch Bartlet
Jere^h Hill

In the House of Representatives June 10th 1772

Resolved that the petitioners give Notice to the Inhabitants and proprietors of s^d Plantation by Posting an attested Copy of this Memorial and Order at the Meeting House Door in said Plantation fourteen days before the first Wednesday in July Next to Shew cause (if the Genl Court is then Sitting) why the prayer of said petition shall not be Granted — And in case the General Court shall not then be Sitting then the said Inhabitants and proprietors are directed on said Notice

to Appear and make their Objections on the Second Wednesday of the Next Session of the General Court
  Sent up for Concurrence   T Cushing Spk^r
In Council June 10th 1772   Read & Concurred
           Jn° Cotton D. Secry
In Council July 1st 1772   Read again together with the Answer, & Ordered that this Petition be dismissed
  Sent down for Concurrence   Jn° Cotton D. Secry
In the House of Representatives July 1, 1772
Read & non concurred & ordered that the petitioners have leave to bring in a Bill for the purpose of their Petition
  Sent up for Concurrence   T Cushing Spk^r
In Council July 1st 1772   Read & Concurred —
           Jn° Cotton D Secry

Saml March's Petition. 1772.

 To His Exelency Thomas Hutchinson Esqr Capt General and Commander In Cheiff In and Over His Majestys Province of the Massachusetts Bay — To the Honble His Majestys Councill and House of Represtitives. In Generall Court assembled

Humbly Shews: Samuel March of Scarborough in the County of Cumberland in said province — That the said Town of Scarborough have Ever Shewn their willingness to Bear their full Share of the Expences of Government in all Respects according to their abilitys and have not failed to Send Some person to Represent them in the Greate & General Court more than one or two years in Twenty years Last past — Excepting the years 1770 and 1771 (which Defect if any) your petitioner is Verry Sure was not owing To any

Slight of privelidge or unwillingness in his Constitutents to pay their full Share toward the Support of Government — but So it was that as their was no one present that Could Represent the Distrest Circumstances of said Town to your Exelency & Honors in its True Light, when those matters were Considered by the General Court the Said Town was fined for their aforesaid neglect the Sum of ten pounds for the year 1770 — which hath been allready assessed on the Inhabitants of said Town and allso the further sum of fifteen pounds for such neglect in the year 1771 which has not yet been paid — and as said Town of Scarborough has of Late been not only at Greate Expence In Setling a minister and allso at the Expence of pay for two ministers for a Long time together the setled minister being unable to attend on the work of the ministry — but the said Town has been also and Stands Obliged to pay allmost five hundred pounds Lawfull money within a few years Last past a Second time by means of Defective Collectors near three hundred pounds thereoff being Not yet paid — Besides the said Town of Scarborough have Verry Lately Expended the Sum of One hundred pounds more for Repairing the meeting Houses in said Town: adding allso the Verry Greate Loss the Said Town has Sustained by the Late terrible fire which Raged in Said Town To Such a Degree that many of the Inhabitants thereof Suffered Greate Loss thereby which they have not yet nor is it Likely they will for a Long time Recover altho the General Court in their Greate Goodness and Compassion was pleased to make them a Verry Considerable Grant for the then present Releif of Some of the unhappy Sufferers thereby

Wherefore your petitioner Most Humbly prays your Exelency and Honors To take the Several matters in the above representation of facts Into your wise Consideration and Remitt to the Said Town the Several fines above mentioned

or other ways Releive them In Such way and manner as to your Exelency and Honors May Seem meet —
and as in Duty Bound shall Ever pray

Sam[ll] March

In the House of Representatives June 11 1772

Resolved that the Prayer of this Petition be granted: that there be allowed & paid out of the publick Treasury into the Hands of Samuel March for the Use of the Town of Scarborough the Sum of ten pounds, being the sum assessed on said Town for neglecting to return a Representative to the General Assembly in the year 1770 — and also that the fine laid on said Town for omitting to return a representative in the year 1771 be remitted.

Sent up for Concurrence   T Cushing Spk[r]

In Council June 17th 1772
     Read & Concurred   Tho[s] Flucker Sec[y]
     Consented To   T Hutchinson

Objection against the Petition.

To his Exellency the Governor, The honorable Council And Representatives of the Province of the Massachsetts Bay in New England in general Court assembled

The Petition of the Inhabitants of Narragansett No 1 in the County of York is most humbly presented

In Objection against the Petition of a Number of the Proprietors of this Place for the Incorporation of it into a Town, we beg leave to offer to your Wisdom & Lenity the following Considerations

We perceive ourselves unable to bear any further Taxes (except a far Minor Part of Us) by Means of our Debts,

And the unavoidable Difficulties of feeding & Clothing our Families in this infant-Settlement: Furthermore,

We pray your Excellency & Honors to Consider the Township Consists of 120 Rights & That the Petitioners for an Incorporation are only three or four, & they not Owners of more than six or seven Rights.

The Bounds between this Place & Gorham & Scarboro are not Settled. These Towns regard not the Line run by a Committee of a former general Court 8 or ten years past. We Sued them at law for Trespass within said Line, & also for the Title to the Land & lost about 5 or £600 old Tenor, & recovered Nothing. Should We be incorporated in this unsettled & quarrelling Condition, We know not what Loss & Sufferings we may meet with. Some of the largest Proprietors of the Township are by no means desirous of an Incorporation in this state, & one of them was a Signer to the Petition for the Corporation before He had weighed this matter, & therefore repents what he then so immaturely acted. Some Families from Scarborough are now on the Gore, so called, a Strip of valuable Land Containing twelve Lots which are within the Line aforesaid run by the general Court. these Lots, if lost, must be a great Loss to the Proprietors, as well as to Us the Inhabitants of the Place. And Gorham Claims 40 Rods within said Line upon the Seven miles long. And besides this, that is, granting the said Line to stand good, Gorham will have about 70 Acres more to a Right than we have, whereas they ought by the Grant of these Townships to have been No longer than We. Considering these great Disadvantages, & that there are not as we know of four Men In the Place who desire an Incorporation, We humbly hope It will not take Place. We therefore most earnestly beseech your Excellency & Honors that we may not be incorporated till our Limits are finally adjusted, & we more able To bear the Expences & Charges of a Town by granting This Petition, you will lay Us under new & great Obligations, as now in Duty bound, ever to pray &c

Narragansett June 17. 1772

Saml Sands	Daniel Leavit	Jacob Bradbury
John Owen	Isaiah Brooks	John X Garland (his mark)
Thomas Bradbury	Matthias R	John Nason
Benj^a Donnel	John Boynton Ju^r	Eben^r Wentworth
John Hopkinson Jun	Richard Clay	Jabez Lane
humphry adkinson	Sam^{ll} Hovey	Job Roberts
Benj^a Bradbury	Joseph Bradbury	Joseph Laint
Samuel Merrill	Jaob Bradbury	William Bradbury
John Kimball	Nathan Elden	Joseph Woodman
Abel herdy	John Hopkin	Joseph Woodman Junr
Timothy Hasaltine	Daniel X Clay (his mark)	Joseph Donnell
Samuel heseltine	Asa Stevens	Caleb Hopkinson
Ephraim Sands	John Eaton	Joshuay Kimball
Abel Merrill	Samuel Leavit	Joshua
Matthias R	Jr.	

Act of Incorporation. 1772.

Anno, Regni, Regis, Georgii, Tertii, Duodecimo

An Act for Incorporating the Plantation called Narraganset Number one in the County of York into a Town by the name of

Whereas it has been represented to this Court that the plantation called Narraganset number one lying on the East side of Saco River in the County of York is competently filled with Inhabitants who labour under great difficulties and discouragements by means of their not being Incorporated into a Town.

Be it therefore enacted by the Governor, Council and House of Representatives That the said Narraganset N° one bounded Southeasterly at the heads of Bideford and Scar-

borough Southwesterly by Saco River, Northwesterly by
Pearson Town so called and Northeasterly by Gorham, be
and hereby is Incorporated into a Town by the Name of
and that the Inhabitants thereof be and hereby are invested
with all the powers, privileges & immunities which the
Inhabitants of other Towns in this Province by Law enjoy.

And Be it further Enacted That Jeremiah Hill Esqr be
and hereby is directed to issue his Warrant to some principal
Inhabitant of said Town, requiring him to warn the Inhabitants thereof to meet at such time and place as shall be
therein set forth, to chuse all such officers as Towns are by
Law impowered to chuse in the month of March annually:
at which said Meeting all the then present Inhabitants shall
be admitted to vote

In the House of Representatives

July 7 1772 Read the first time

     8 1772 Read the second & third time & passd to be engrossd

    Sent up for Concurrence   T Cushing Spk^r

In Council July 8th 1772 Read a first Time

        8th Read a second time, & Passed a Concurrence to be Engrossed

                     Jno Cotton D. Sec̃ry

Consented to

Memorial of the Associated Ministers of York.

To his Excellency Thomas Hutchinson Esqr Governor The honourable his Majesties Council; and The honourable House of Representatives of The Province of the Massachusetts Bay.

The Memorial of the associated Ministers of the County of York humbly sheweth:

That many of the new Settlements in the Eastern Parts of this Province are without the Preaching of the Gospel; and by Reason of their Poverty, and other Difficulties they labour under, are unable at present to settle and maintain a learned and Orthodox Ministry, as by the Law of this Province is required,

That unless some Provision be made for their Instruction, they must remain for a considerable Time in a great Measure destitute of the Means of Religion; and in danger of loosing the Knowledge and Sense of their Duty to God, and their King, and one another; and sinking into Ignorance, Irreligion, and all Manner of Disorder.

That it appears to your Memorialists that it must be in many Respects for the public Emolument, as well as the temporal and religious Interest of these new Settlements, that some speedy and effectual Measures be taken for the Preservation of Christian Knowledge and Virtue, among those scattered Inhabitants of the Wilderness.

Your Memorialists therefore beg Leave, to lay the Premises before Your Excellency and Honours, in Confidence of your paternal Care for the Advancement of Religion, and the Welfare of this Province; and humbly to propose to the Consideration of your Excellency and Honours, whether the providing of one or more Missionaries for the Instruction of those destitute People, be not a Matter of public Concernment, that the Knowledge and Sense of our holy Religion may not be lost among them

And your Memorialists shall ever pray &^{c}

Benjn Stevens ⎫ In the Name of the
Isaac Lyman ⎬ associated Ministers

Answer

In the House of Representatives July 9, 1772.

Whereas application has been made to this Court by the

Associated Ministers in the County of York, by their Memorial setting forth that many of the New Settlements in the Eastern Parts of this Province are without the Preaching of the Gospel; and that they are unable to support the same; and praying that one or more Missionaries may be provided, at the expence of the Province, for the Instruction of those Destitute People And it appearing that good & valuable Purposes may be answered by making Provision for the same. Therefore Resolved that there be allowed and paid out of the Publick Treasury in the month of October Annually for three years next ensuing the first Day of September next a sum not exceeding the sum of Eighty pounds to the Trustees hereinafter named, to be by them applied for supporting One Missionary of sober life & conversation for promoting Christian Knowledge in the Eastern Parts of this Province in such Places as are destitute of the Preaching of the Gospel, and are unable to support the same among themselves, such missionary to officiate at such Places as he shall from time to time be directed by said Trustees. Provided said Trustees shall annually at the end of each year account to this Court for the Sum or Sums by them expended in support of said Mission.

Resolved also that the Rev[d] Benjamin Stevens of Kittery & the Rev[d] Isaac Lyman and the rev[d] Samuel Lancton of York be the Trustees for the purposes abovementioned and that they or either Two of them be empowered to receive the above Grants & to appoint the missionary as above & him dismiss and another appoint in his Room as to them shall seem fit

   Sent up for Concurrence T. Cushing Spk[r]
 In Council July 10[h] 1772
   Read & Concurred   Tho[s] Flucker Sec[y]
   Consented to   T. Hutchinson

An Act to encourage the Preaching of the Gospel.

Anno Regni Regis Georgii Tertii Duodecimo.

An Act to encourage the Preaching of the Gospel to the Inhabitants of a certain place known by the name of Machias in the County of Lincoln.

Whereas there are a great number of Persons residing at a place known by the name of Machias in the County of Lincoln within this Province who profess to be of the principles or Persuasion of the Churches of this Province known by the name of Congregational Churches and to be desirous for their spiritual benefit that the Gospel should be Preached among them, which may likewise tend to the maintenance or support of Civil order; And whereas the persons residing as aforesaid have not been incorporated into a Town, District, Precinct or Parish and cannot provide for the support of the Gospel in such way and manner as Towns, Districts, Precincts and Parishes by the Laws of this Province are enabled to provide.

Be it therefore Enacted by the Governor Council & House of Representatives That Jonathan Longfellow and Stephen Jones Esq^{rs} Messrs Ichabod Jones, Stephen Parker, Benjamin Foster and James Eliot or the major part of them be & hereby are authorized & impowered upon Oath to Tax all the Inhabitants of Machias annually, excepting those that are professed Churchmen, Baptists or Quakers, not exceeding the Sum of one hundred and twenty pounds annually for the support and maintenance of the Gospel amongst them as the major part of said Inhabitants shall at their meeting vote and determine ; upon notice being given to them eight days at least by notification in writing being posted up at the several places where said Inhabitants attend Divine Worship on the Lords day.

And be it further Enacted that the said Jonathan Longfellow, Stephen Jones, Ichabod Jones, Stephen Parker, Benjamin Foster and James Eliot or the major part of them shall have and hereby is given them the same power and authority to Tax said Inhabitants for the purpose aforesaid and the same power to appoint a Collector or Collectors for collecting the said Taxes as the Inhabitants would have had where they incorporated into a Town or District, and the Collector or Collectors thus appointed and sworn to the faithful discharge of their office, shall have the same power and authority to Collect the said Taxes committed to them as if they were legally chosen by said Inhabitants for that purpose.

And s^d Committee shall have & hereby is granted unto them or any three of them the Power of a Town District or Precinct Treasurer unto whom the money collected as afores^d shall by the Collectors be paid.

This Act to continue & be in force for the space of three years from the first day of April 1772.

In Council July 14th 1772 Read a first & a second Time & passed to be Engrossed

Thos Flucker Sec^y

In the House of Representatives July 14, 1772.

Read & ordered that the further Consideration of this Bill be referd to the next Session.

Sent up for Concurrence   T. Cushing Spk^r

In Council July 14th 1772

Read and Conc^d — Jno Cotton D. Secry

Govr Hutchinson to the Earl of Dartmouth

No. 6   Boston 13th November 1772.
My Lord

Having received a letter from Mr Goldthwait Commanding officer of Fort Pownall and of a Regiment of Militia in the Eastern part of the Province I take the liberty to cover a copy as an addition to the state of that Country which I have already sent. Upon a review of your Lordship's directions I find that I have not fully complied with them, having made no mention of my opinion upon the steps proper to remove the difficulties which have hitherto obstructed the regulation of the settlements there.

The inducement to people to flock from the settled parts of this Province and New Hampshire and to prefer the Sea coast and Islands and Rivers there to the inland parts of either Province is the profit which arises from the pine and Oak Timber which, being near the Sea, is purchased of the Settlers for transportation to Europe or for the supply of the Inhabitants of Boston Portsmouth &c. A very great quantity has been carried to England and the King has paid no inconsiderable sum as a bounty for bringing away his own Timber without his licence. As the settlers increase this mischief increases. A restraint therefore from further settling seems to be the first steps necessary, and this would effectually be made if all Timber cut there wheresoever carried, was made liable to a forfeiture; but this would take away the present means of support from a thousand or fifteen hundred families and make most of them, for some time, miserable, and would also be sensibly felt by the Seaport Towns of both Provinces which have their principal supply of fewal from this Country. The Assembly I think without any good reason have repeatedly refused their aid in order to restrain these unjustifiable settlements and there is no prospect of their agreeing to such measures as may answer His Majesty's purpose. It seems therefore necessary for the preservation of His Majesty's interest the Country should be subject to His sole direction. To effect this an offer may be made of the Lands West of Merrimack River which were taken from this Province by the new boundary with New Hampshire in 1737 as an equivalent for the Country East of Kennebeck. Or the absolute property of the Country West of Penobscot may be vested in the Province provided all claim be relinquished to the Country East of Penobscot and if the line of the Province of Main might be allowed to run from the head of Newichewanock River, North West instead of North two degrees West, as I conceived it ought to run until His late Majesty in Council otherwise determined, this would not, being added to the Lands, West of Penobscot, make more than an equivalent for the Lands East and would make the proposal more likely to be accepted. In the Grant to Sir Ferdinando Gorges the line upon the Sea Coast is said to be Northeastward when the course of the Seacoast, which was then well known, is Northeast, and the plain intent of the patent seems to be a Tract of 120 miles square & that being the length upon the Sea, upon this construction the other three sides would be equal.

I cannot answer for a compliance with any proposals whatsoever but one advantage will arise from them. A refusal will facilitate and render unexceptionable a Parliamentary consideration the only remaining step, which will be absolutely necessary and which the repeated refusal to take proper care of this Country may, alone, be sufficient to justify.

* * * * * * * * *

Tho Hutchinson

Province of the Massachusetts Bay   To his Excellency Thomas Hutchinson Esqr Captain General and Commander in Chief in and over said Province

To the Honorable his Majesties Council and House of Representatives in General Court assembled, January Anno Domini 1773 —

The Petition of the Proprietors of a certain Tract of Land situate in the County of Lincoln in said Province at or near a Place called Pemaquid in the Eastward Parts of said Province granted by the Council of Plymouth in great Britain in the Year One Thousand Six hundred and thirty one, To Robert Aldsword and Giles Elbridge, known by the Name of Pemaquid Lands humbly sheweth —

That your Petitioners and their Ancestors, and Others whose Estate in the Lands aforesaid they now hold have been at great Pains and Expences in making Surveys Plans and Divisions of the Tract of Land aforesaid, and in bringing forward Settlements and making improvements there, and in many other Ways, in managing, ordering, and disposing the Affairs of said Pemaquid Propriety or Company, for a Course of Thirty Years past —

That in the Course of these Transactions, they have frequently voted to raise Monies for necessary Purposes relating to said Propriety, and have ordered such sums to be laid and Apportioned on the several Proprietors, according to each Proprietors Interest in the Land and to strict Equity — And they have stated Accounts, paid and received Monies and done other Things as appears in the Companys Book of Records and in the Company's Book of Accounts —

But in some Instances, through Error and want of Information in the Law, in Voting sums of monies to be raised, and in forming Assessments of those sums upon the Proprietors they have not as they are now advised conformed in all things to the strict regulations of the Law, tho' they have in all Respects conformed to the Principles of Equity and good Conscience, as they shall be able fully to prove to the Satisfaction of this Honorable Court or any Committee thereof, upon Inspection of their said Books of Records, Proceedings and Accounts —

That some of said Proprietors have not paid their respective Quotes, and Proportions of the Expences and intended Assessments aforesaid but are considerably in Arrear — But on Account of the Irregularities aforesaid your Petitioners and the said Company are informed that they cannot proceed to collect and lay said Quotas or to make sale of the Lands of said delinquent Proprietors, for the Payment of their just Proportions aforesaid, which are still in Arrear, and unpaid, without great Hazzard of Lawsuits and Perplexities both to your Petitioners, and the delinquent Proprietors aforesaid.

Wherefore your Petitioners humbly pray the Interposition of this Honorable Court, for the Ratification of their past Proceedings, and that the said Company or Propriety may be impowered to proceed to collect and levy, the said Sums that are still in Arrear by sale of the delinquent Proprietors Lands, or otherwise According to Law; any want of Conformity to the strict Regulation of the Law, relating to the Votes, Assessments, Proceedings of Proprietors of common and undivided Lands, notwithstanding: and your Petitioners as in Duty bound shall Pray —

Seth Sweetser	John Savage	Habijah Savage
Bart^w Kneeland	Stephen Minot	Rachel Noble
Stephen Miller		

Petition of Selectmen of Winthrop, 1773

To His Excellency Thomas Hutchinson Esqr Governor in Chief of His Majestys Province of the Massachusetts Bay The Honorable His Majestys Council and the Honorable House of Representatives in General Court Assembled The Petition of the Selectmen of the Town of Winthrop in the County of Lincoln in said Province

Humbly Sheweth

That the Inhabitants of said Town are all New Settlers So new that Six years ago thair was but two familys in the

Compass of the said Town as it is Incorporated that the nearest place of the said Town to Kennebeck River is the distance of five miles and the Roads all New and all most impasable with Teams dureing the Sumer Season So the said Inhabitants cannot have the advantage of Lumbering as People that live on Kennebeck River thair whole dependance being upon what they Raise from the land the said Inhabitants are poor in General and of Consequence money very Scarce among them and hard to be procuered Your Petitioners Therefore Humbly Pray that Your Excellency and Honours would take our Case under your Wise Consideration and for the Reasons aforesaid and the Consideration of the Expence we must be at in Building a meeting House for the Publick Worship of God would Exempt the said Inhabitants from paying any Tax to the Province for the Tarm of five years next to Come or otherways Grant Relief as Your Exelency and Honours in your Wisdom Shall See meet and your Petitioners Shall ever pray &c

Dated March ye 8th A D. 1773 at Winthrop

Jonathan Whiting } Selectmen
Gideon Lambart } for
Ichabod How } Winthrop

Petition of Members of the Church of England.

To his Excellency the Governor the Honble his Majestys Council & the Honble House of Representatives in General Court Assembled

The Petition of a Number of Persons Members of the Church of England usually attending Public Worship at St Paul's Church in Falmouth — Humbly Sheweth —

That in the Year of our Lord 1765 your Petitioners at great Expence erected a Church & obtaind a Missionary from the Venerable Society for Propogating the Gospel in Foreign Parts which Missionary they laid themselves under an obligation to support & hitherto have supported the said Missionary by laying a Tax upon the Pews in the said Church together with a small Tax upon Persons who were not owners of Pews yet usually & frequently attending Public Worship in the said Church —

And whereas your Petitioners being assessed heretofore by the first Parish in said Town agreeable to the Law of this Province now in force has been found to be attended with many inconveniences they humbly pray your Excellency & Honors would be pleased to enable & permit the Assessors of said first Parish to omit rating the members of the s^d Church for the future the Minister & Wardens giving in a List of said Members to said Assessors on or before the first day of September next & on or before the first day of September annually afterwards & certifying thereon that the Persons therein named are members of the Church of England and usually & frequently attend the Public Worship of God with them on the Lords Days —

And your Petitioners further pray that said members of said Church of England may have the further priviledge granted them of raising assessing & levying all ministerial Charges independent of any other denomination of Christians in said Falmouth in such ways & means as they hitherto have done or otherwise as your Excellency & Honors shall judge most expedient.

And your Petitioners as in duty bound shall ever Pray.

Jon^a Webb	J Johnson	Edward Watts
Zebulun Noyes	Moses Shattuck	Jos: Domett
Abra^m Osgood	David Wyer	Samuel Mountfort
Jedidiah Preble	Fra^s Waldo	Edward Oxnard
Thos Oxnard	Tho: Child	David Wyer Ju^r
G. Lyde	W. Simmons	John Waite
Step^n Waite		

At a legal Meeting of the first Parish in Falmouth by Adjournment May 17th 1773. The said Petition was laid before the Parish, whereupon,

Voted that the parish join in the first prayer of said Petition that the Assessors may be permitted to omit rating said Members of the church of England for the future upon the Minister & Wardens giving in a List and certifying thereon as mentioned in said Petition;

The Second prayer of said Petition for the Grant of further priviledges they submit to the Wisdom of the Legislature.

Attest Theo Bradbury Clerk of said Parish.

In Council June 8th 1773 Read & Ordered That William Brattle & James Bowdoin Esqrs with such as the honbl house shall join be a Committee To Consider this petition & report

Sent down for Concurrence   Thos Flucker Secy

In the House of Representatives June 11, 1773.

Read & Concurrd and Mr Stickney Coll Warren and Coll Murray are joynd.

T. Cushing Spkr

The Committee above named have attended the service assigned them Report that the prayer of the Petitioners be granted, & that they have liberty to bring in a bill accordingly.

W. Brattle by order

In Council June 18th 1773. Read & accepted, & ordered that the Petitioners have Liberty to bring in a Bill for the purposes in their Petition mentioned —

Sent down for Concurrence

Jn° Cotton D. Secry

In the House of Representatives June 18, 1773.

Read & Concurrd

T. Cushing Spkr

Petition of Selectmen of North Yarmouth. 1773.

To his Excellency the Governor and the hon^ble the Council of his Majestys Province of the Massachusetts Bay in New England at their Session in May 1773

The Petition of the Selectmen of the Town of North Yarmouth, on behalf of said Town   Humbly Sheweth

That one Edward Doring, a transient Person, formerly a native of Ireland, Some time in July last came to said Town, and on or about the last of the same Month was taken sick at the House of Captn Solomon Loring, Inholder in said Town; whereupon said Loring finding him to be a person of no property, made application to the Selectmen of the Town, to provide for his Nursing and doctoring, and the Selectmen gave Orders to said Loring to provide accordingly —

That on the 20th of August the said Doring died there, and said Loring has debted the Town for Nursing doctoring and funeral Expence, as by the Attested Accounts accompanying this Petition may appear £4: 19: 4. Lawful money

That the Selectmen, on behalf of the Town, have taken pains to inform themselves of the circumstances of the said Doring, & can't find by all their enquiries that he had obtained a legal Settlement in any Town within this Government; nor can they find that he has left any Estate, real or personal towards defraying the Charges of his Sickness and burial —

Wherefore your Petitioners pray, that said Sum of £4: 19: 4. may be refunded to the Town of North Yarmouth out of the Province Treasury, and Orders given for that Purpose, agreeable to the Law of this Province in such Cases made and provided —

And your Petitioners, as in Duty bound shall ever pray —

North Yarmouth   Solomon Loring   ⎫   Selectmen
     May 31. 1773   Jonathan Mitchell ⎬   of
                       Silvanus Prince   ⎭   North Yarmouth

Deposition.

Stephen Holt of Lawful Age Testifieth & Saith That he was one of the first Settlers in a Township Granted to Captn John Lovewell & others known by the Name of Suncook.— That the Grantees with great Labour & Expence brought forward their Settlements Soon after the grant of s^d Township was made Notwithstanding the opposition made by the Proprietors of Bow who Claimed a Tract of Land by Virtue of a Grant made by the Goverment of New Hampshire of the Contents of Twelve miles Square which Included Suncook & was made near the Time of the Massachusetts grant — That they were Encouraged by the People of the Massachusetts Government to Perfect their Settlements Notwithstanding the opposition made by Bow & Accordingly Persevered in their undertaking & Endeavoured to Defend their Rights in the Common Law of New Hampshire when many of them were held to Answer there by Process or be Defaulted —

That many Actions were Continued from Term to Term till the Defendants were almost Ruin'd — That the Proprietors of Pennicook being under like Circumstances (saving only that Pennicook was purchased with money & Suncook was the Price of Blood) Apply'd to the great & General Court of the Massachusetts Province for Relief & obtained a grant of One hundred pounds Sterling to Defend their Cause in England and the Suncook Proprietors Embark'd in the Same Cause According to their Ability Contributed to the Pennicook Agent for his Aid to them in the Common Cause. But so it is though the Actions at home were Determined in some sort in favour of the Massachusetts Grantees yet the point of Property most Essential to be Determined was Carefully Avoided, and after this New Actions were Commenced So that the Proprietors of Suncook as well as those of Pennicook have been Continually Harrassed & Worried in the

Law from their Infant State 'till within these two or three years last past they have almost all of them, Purchased their Improvements & them only at an Extravagant Lay, and all the unimprov'd Lands Revert to the Proprietors of Bow.

The Deponant further Saith that he was an Inhabitant of Suncook for the Term of Ten Years & Since his Removal he has been Conversant with the Proprietors, been Concern'd in Defending Sundry Rights & that he has no Knowledge of any one of the Inhabitants having Received any Consideration from the Province of the Massachusetts Bay, nor from New Hampshire, on Account of their Loss in Suncook; but on the Contary is well assured that there is not one Individual of s^d Prop^{rs} of Suncook but what has Sustain'd more Loss than Double the Value of his Right when Granted, and that many Others have been Entirely Ruined And were Obliged to part with their Farms Valued at more than £100 Sterling to Defrey the Chargs of their Vexatious Law suits.
Andover May 31, 1773   Stephen Holt

Essex ss. Andover May 31, 1773

Then Mr Stephen Holt appear^d personally & made Oath to the forewritten Deposition, by him Subscrib^d
         Before me Samuel Phillips Just^s Pacis

Petition of James Miller and others   1773

To His Excellency Thomas Hutchinson Esqr Captain General Governor & Commander in Chief in & Over his majestys Province of the massachusetts Bay &c —

The Honourable His majestys Councele & House of Representatives in General Assembly Convened —

The subscribers humbly Shew —
that your Petitioners Purchased from the Heirs of Brigadeer Waldo a tract of Land Near Six miles Square Situate on the

Western Side of Penobscot Bay Bounded Begining at the Westerly Bounds of the township of Frankfort from thence Westerly Round the Harbour Called Passageesewokey to Little River from thence up Said River as far as Salt Water flows then Crossing Said River to a Black Burch tree Computed to be thirty Seven Chains from thence South Sixty Eight Degrees west two Hundred & seventy three Chains to A Burch tree from thence North twenty two Degrees West three Hundred & Twenty two Chains to a rock maple tree one rod Westerly from a quarry of stones from thence North Sixty Eight Degrees East six hundred & two Chains to the Westerly Line of said Frankfort from thence South thirty Seven Chains to the Largest of Halfway Creek Ponds from thence Down said Creek to the Bounds first mentioned and Whereas the Vendors Could not Convey jurisdicktion the Vendees have no Legal Power to Vote assess or Levy taxes for any Publick use & many of the Vendees being Now Settled on the Premises & Scarcely able in Point of Circumstances to Perform their own Settlements Suffer Greatly Being Destitute of the Gospell Schools mills Bridges &c and Whereas the Vendors Did not Oblige the Vendees to Settle the Premises Sundry of them are non Residents and Should the Premisses be Incorporated in Common form the Poor Residents must Suffer all the inconveniences of Being the first Settlers & pay all the taxes for the publick uses aforesaid: and the non Residents have the advantage of Lumber from their Lands increasing Everey Day at the Expence & By the Labour of the Residents —

Therefore your Petitioners Humbly Pray your Excellency & Honours to Incorporate the Premisses into a township by the Name of Belfast & Grant them all the Privileges & Invest them with all the Legal Authority Necessary to Enable the Said Purchassers to Hold Legal meetings & to Chuse all Necessary Officers the Vote to be Numbred

According to the Interest of Each Purchasser Present at Said meetings to Vote & Levey taxes from time to time to Expedite Said Settlement from all the Purchassers of said Premisses, Whether Resident or non Resident According to their Intrast in said Premisses Numbring as afores^d and in Case any Purchasser Neglects or Refuse- to Pay any tax Voted as afores^d for the Space of Sixty Days Next after the Day Said Vote was Recorded A Commttee Chosen as afores^d be Impowered to Sell at Publick Vendue giving thirty Days Notice Before Said Sale as much of Purchassers Land as will Pay Said tax or taxes & all Incidental Charges Returning the Overplush if any to the Purchasser Every meeting to be Notified by the Clark of said town in the most Publick Place in said Belfast fifteen Days before said meeting, giving an Explict account in writing under his hand of time & Place & of what to be acted at Said meeting & that what sover tax the Residents are obliged to Pay be assessed & Levied in manner as afores^d for teen years Next after the Date of Said Incorporation & after that Period to be assessed Levied and Paid as other towns assess & Pay their taxes —

and your Petitioners as in Duty Bound Will Ever Pray &c

James Miller	John Tuffts	Ephraim Stimson
William	John Durham	William Patterson ^{jun}
Nathaniel Patterson	John Davidson	William Glechlan
John Gilman	Richard Stimson	Robt Patterson
James Patterson	John Stel	John Mitchel
Samul Morrison	Mo^s Barnett	John Brown
John Moor	Sam^{ll} Houston	Sam^{ll} Houston Ju^r
James Macgregore Junr	David Hemphill	John Barnet
John Durham Juner	Joseph Morrison	Alex^r Wilson
Samuel Marsh	Joseph Gragg	John Tuffts
Alexander Little	John Cochran	James Gilmore
David Gilmore		

Act of Incorporation, 1773.

In the thirteenth Year of the Reign of King George the third

An Act for Incorporating a Certain Tract of Land on the Westerly side of Penobscot Bay into a Town by the name of

Whereas the Inhabitants of a Certain Tract of Land on the Westerly side of Penobscot Bay in the County of Lincoln are desirous of being incorporated into and invested with the Powers and Priviledges of a Town,— therefore,

Be it Enacted by the Governor Council and House of Representatives that the Tract of Land aforesaid Bounded as follows Viz^t Beginning at the Westerly Bounds of the township of Frankfort from thence Westerly Round the Harbour called Passagusnoskey to little River from thence up said River as far as Salt Water flows then Crossing said River to a Black Burch tree Computed to be thirty seven Chains from thence South Sixty eight Degrees West Two Hundred & twenty three Chains to a Burch tree from thence North twenty two Degrees West three hundred & seventy two Chains to a rock maple Tree one rod Westerly from a quarrey of Stones from thence North Sixty Eight Degrees East Six hundred & two Chains to the Westerly Line of said Frankfort from thence South thirty Seven Chains to the largest of halfway Creek Ponds from thence down said Creek to the Bounds first mentioned; be and hereby is erected into a Town by the Name of

And that the Inhabitants thereof be and hereby are invested with all the Powers, Priviledges and Immunities which the Inhabitants of the Towns within this Province respectively do, or by Law ought to enjoy.

And be it further enacted That Thomas Goldthwait Esqr be, and he hereby is impowered to issue his Warrant directed to some principal Inhabitant in said Town to notify and Warn the Inhabitants in said Town qualified by Law to vote in Town Affairs, to meet at such Time and Place as shall be therein set forth, to choose all officers as shall be necessary to manage the Affairs of said Town. At which said First meeting all the then Present Male Inhabitants that shall be arrived to ye age of Twenty one years Shall be admitted to vote

In the House of Representatives
Read the first time June 14 1773
June 15 Read a second time
June 21, Read a third time & passed to be Engrossed
   Sent up for Concurrence   T Cushing Spk^r

In Council June 21^t 1773 Read a first & a Second Time & passed a Concurrence to be Engrossed
               Thos Flucker Sec^y

Act of Incorporation. 1773.

Anno Regni Regis Geo. Tertii Decimo Tertio

An Act for Incorporating a Plantation called Broad Bay into a Town by the Name of

Whereas the Inhabitants of the Plantation called Broad Bay in the County of Lincoln have Represented to this Court that they labour under many great difficulties and Inconveniences by reason of their not being Incorporated into a Town ——— Therefore

Be it Enacted by the Governor Council and House of Representatives that the said Plantation commonly called and known by the name of Broad Bay Bounded as follows Viz^t To begin at the Northwest Corner Bound of the Town of Bristol in said County at a Stake standing on the Bank of the Duck-Puddle-Brook so called, thence running Northerly by said Brook and pond, to the Northerly end of said pond to a pine Tree marked on four sides, thence to run North five hundred and Sixty Rods to a pine Tree marked on four sides thence to run North twenty two Degrees & thirty Minutes East seventeen hundred Rods to a spruce Tree marked on four sides, thence to run East southeast eleven hundred and twenty Rods to a Birch Tree marked on four sides thence to run South seven Degrees East sixteen hundred Rods to a Maple Tree marked on four sides, thence to run south Nineteen Degrees West nine hundred and sixty Rods to a spruce Tree marked on four sides, thence to run Southeast one hundred & sixty Rods to a Firr Tree marked on four sides, thence to run South fifteen Degrees East three hnndred and twenty Rods to a stake standing on the Bank of little Pond so called thence Easterly by the Shore of said Pond to the Easterly part thereof, thence South fifteen Degrees East to a stake standing on the Bank of the Southerly Pond so called thence Easterly by the Shore of the said Pond to the easterly part thereof, thence South fifteen Degrees East one hundred Rods to a spruce Tree marked on four sides, thence running South twelve Degrees West three hundred and twenty Rods to a spruce Tree marked on four sides, thence running Northwest four hundred Rods to Goose River, so called, from thence southerly down said River in the middle thereof to its Entrance into the Bay, thence Northerly & westerly by the Shore of the Bay round the Back-Cove, so called, thence to continue by the Shore Southerly & westerly to the southerly Part of Passage Point otherwise called Jones's Neck, thence Westerly across the Narrow of Broad Bay River untill it strikes the southerly part of Havenars point, so called, thence Westerly round the Shore of said point and Northerly by the Shore of the eastern Branch Broad Cove, thence round the Head of said Cove Westerly & Southerly untill it comes to a red Oak Tree standing on the Land of Jacob Eaton being the Easterly

Corner Bound of the Town of Bristol aforesaid thence to run Northwesterly on said Line of Bristol to the first mentioned Bounds be and hereby is erected into a Township by the Name of

And that the Inhabitants thereof be and hereby are invested with all the Powers Privileges and Immunities which the Inhabitants of the Towns within this Province respectively do, or by Law ought to enjoy. And be it further enacted That Alexander Nichols Esq[r] be and hereby is impowered to issue his Warrant directed to some principal Inhabitant in said Township, to notify and warn the Inhabitants in said Township to meet at such Time and place as shall be therein set forth, to choose all such Officers as shall be necessary to manage the Affairs of said Town, at which said First meeting all the then Present male Inhabitants arrived to Twenty one years of age shall be admitted to vote

In the House of Representatives June 12, 1773.

Read a first time

June 15, 1773   Read a second time

June 26 1773   Read a third time & passed to be Engrossed

    Sent up for Concurrence

                            T Cushing Spk[r]

In Council June 26[t] 1773   Read a first time & 29 a Second time & passed a Concurrence to be Engrossed

                            Jn° Cotton D Sec[y]

Petition of Noah Johnson & others

Province of the Massachusetts Bay   To His Excellency the Governor, To the Honourable His Majesty's Council & House of Representatives in general Court Assembled The Petition of the Subscribers hereto Humbly Shews —

That in the Time of the War with the Indians called the three year War, Capt John Lovewell and a number of Men under his Command Voluntarily Engaged in the Service of Their King and Country, and bravely Exerted Themselves therein, by Pursuing the Indians in the Wilderness, where They repeatedly met with & Destroy'd some of Them. And finally, viz on the 8th Day of May A D 1725. He with thirty four Men, met with a Large Body of Them at Pigwacket, and had a Long & very warm Engagement with Them in which He, and a Considerable part of His Men Lost Their Lives. But the Indians were so severely handled in this Engagement, It Struck Them with so much Terror, That the Government looked upon Lovewell & His Men so Eminently Serviceable by This & Their former Bravery, as That They were Worthy of Some particular Regard from the Publick — In Consideration whereof, The Government granted a Township of Wilderness Land at Suncook, To the Heirs of the said Capt John Lovewell, To the Heirs of those of His Men that fell with Him in the Engagement, To those who Liv'd thro it, and to a Number of such Other Men as the Government then thought were the most Proper to be admitted with Those who had been in said Engagement, and to make a Suitable Society for the Settlement of a New Township —

That in Consequence of said Grant, and in Compliance with the Conditions thereof, The Grantees Settled said Township, Some by Their own Persons and Others by Their Assigns; And as no Body at that Time, had any Suspicion of Danger in the Title of the Land the People who Settled thereon, carried all the Interest They had in the World with Them, and Laid it out on Their Respective Rights, and therewith bestow'd a great deal of Labour with Their own hands to bring Their Lands to be Profitable to Them, Trusting that They and Their Posterity Should Enjoy the Fruit

of Their Labour without Interruption — But by the running
the Line for a Divisional Line between this Province and
the Province of New Hampshire, said Township was taken
into the Latter — Soon after This, there came a number of
Men and laid Claime to the same Land, Alledging it was a
Township granted by the Province of New Hampshire to
Them by the Name of Bow.— And from thence forward
Sues for the Land, and so worried the Massachusetts
Grantees and Their Assigns from Time to Time in Law,
That they found Themselves obliged, either to leave Their
Possessions or buy Them — And being in such an unhappy
Situation, They knew not well what to do. Some bought
the Lands They had Subdu'd & lived upon, but Others, who
would not buy, were Intirely ousted of Theirs. So that
upon the whole, the Massachusetts Grant has been Obliged
(by the Laws in Hampshire) to give way to the Hampshire
Grant, and the Township (by that means) wholly Lost to
Those of the original Grantees who never Sold Their Rights,
and in a great Measure to Those who Settled therein by Purchase. Some of the Latter having had some Considerations
from those of the Original Grantees of whom They Purchas'd
Their Lands, They did not wholly Loose Theirs, but as the
Considerations They Rec^d were much Short of the Damages
They Sustain'd, They were greater Loosers than Those were
that they Purchas'd of — But in Fact both are Loosers, so
there is become more than one Sufferer on one & the Same
of many of the Rights in said lost Township — wherefore
your Petitioners, who are some of the immediate Sufferers
by said Loss take Leave to Pray, That in Lieu of said Township, your Excellency & Honours would be Pleas'd to grant
a Tract of Wilderness Land belonging to the Province
Sufficient for a Township, to Such of the original Grantees
of said Township as are Living, To the Heirs of such of
Them as are Dead and to Those who Settled therein by Pur-

chase, So that the same may be Shar'd among all the Loosers, in Proportion to the Damages They have Respectively Sustain'd; with Liberty to lay it out to the Eastward of Saco River, adjoining to the Northwardly part of the Township, granted to Benjamin Mullikin Esqr and others.

And as in Duty bound Prays

Noah Johnson	Thomas Harwood	John Chamberlin
James Whitney	John Lovewell	Richard Eastman
Francies Doyne	John Knox	Joseph Brown
Joseph Baker	David Abbot	Samuel Abbot
John Whittemore	Andrew Bunten	Moses Tyler
Benjamin Hall	David Lovejoy	Robert White
Patrick Galt	James Cuningham	Caleb Lovejoy
Andrew Galt	Ephraim foster	Sam^{ll} McConnell
Ephriam Blunt	John Man	Robert Moore
Moses Foster	Nathanael Holt	David Chandler
Benjamin Holt	Benj^a Stevens Junr	William Ayer
Abiel Austin	Zebediah Austin	

Thomas Barnard } Heirs of Revd Mr Barnard late of
Edward Barnard }   Andover

Deposition of Benjn Holt 1773.

I the Deponant aged Sixty four Years Testify & Say That I was the Lawful owner of the Substance of three Rights in the Township at Suncook which was granted to Capt John Lovewell & others — That I Settled upon a Tract of my said Land, and have lived in said Township about thirty nine years, and have been knowing to and have been a large Sufferer in the Loss of said Township, which has been recovered & taken from the Inhabitants who Settled therein under the Government of the Massachusetts-Bay, by a number of Persons, who Claim'd the greatest Part of it by virtue of a grant (as They said) from the Government of New-Hampshire for a Township by the name of Bow — By the Proprietors of the Mason Patent and by the Proprietors of the Township of Chester. That I know of no Compensation being ever made to the Sufferers for that Loss, by the Government of Massachusetts-Bay or New-Hampshire, Except Ross Wyman, who (as I have heard) has had a Grant of some land from the Government of the Massachusetts-Bay in lieu of his Loss — Also That the Bow-Proprietors gave (as I have been told) the Late Revd Mr Whittemore fifty acres of the Land He was Settled upon, and to one Francis Doyne twenty acres He was Settled on in s^d lost Township — And as for my Self besides the loss of my Lands I have been put to greater Expence than I can readly tell having been Ejected out of two Tracts of Land by two Actions which were continued in the Law for about fifteen years.

Benjamin Holt

York ss.   Fryeburg Octo^r 23^d A D 1773 the above named Benj^a Holt Personally appear'd and made Solemn Oath to the Truth of the foregoing Deposition by Him Subscribed

  Before me   J Frye Jus^t Peace

Govr Hutchinson to Lord Dartmouth.

Boston 26th October 1773   My Lord,

I could not obtain the Report of the Attorney and Solicitor General in 1731 until I had finished my Letter of the 16th to your Lordship; I have since met with it & perceive that it makes a distinction between a Country possessed merely by Conquest and a Country yielded by Treaty, & Supposes the Country between Kennebeck & Nova Scotia to fall under the first part of the distinction. I observed to your Lordship that I had no right from my Knowledge of the Civil Law, which has never been my profession to be positive upon any point. I had always received it that whenever Lands which had been lost by Conquest though ceded upon a Treaty were recovered by the Crown or State which had lost them, the subject also recovered his private property. I have heard that the French many years after the Cession of St. Christopher's, & the Spaniards also after the Cession of Jamaica, made it their practice to devise the Estates they had formerly possessed in those Islands respectively. This must have been upon the principle of Jus Post liminii after the Country had been given up by Treaty. I recollect, on the other Hand, that the Duke of York had a Grant of what is now New York in 1664 & kept possession until 1673 when it was recovered by the Dutch. It was soon after restored or ceded to England by Treaty. The Duke thereupon took a new Grant which looks as if there was then some doubt of this doctrine of Postliminii in general, for in that Case there was no more than a Suspension of property only & not what the Report of the Attorney & Solicitor General calls an Extinguishment the Country never having been ceded to the Dutch by Treaty. I have supposed the Duke might take this new Grant Ex Abundanti & to remove all Exception or Cavil.

If I have been mistaken in my Notions of Postliminii & the yielding up a Country by Treaty extinguishes the Right which the Subject had in it, the Massachusets can have no just claim to the Country East of Penobscot, for though the Charter is of a later date than the Treaty of Breda yet it is of an earlier date than the Treaty of Ryswick when all that had been before ceded by the Treaty of Breda was again ceded or restored. This however will not effect the Country West of Penobscot because it was never ceded by Treaty, nor has ever been in possession of any Europeans except the English.

   I am &c.   Thos Hutchinson.

Deposition. 1774.

the Deposition of Cap[t] Joseph Baker and John Knox all of Lawful Age Testifyeth and Saith that they have Lived upwards of thirty years in a place formerly Called Suncook which was Granted to Cap[t] Lowells men by the Grate and Genereal Court of the Massetuchetts Bay — and further Saith that the township So Granted has fell into the Province of New Hampshire and is Intirely taken away from the Settlers and Grantees aforesaid, by the title of New Hampshire and that they have Been oblig'd to Purtches of them at their own Price in order to Secure their Emprovements, and further Saith that they have not Rec[d] any Satisfaction from the Court of Either of the Said Provinces for the Loss of said Township Exept the Court has made some Retaleyation to Ross Wyman one of the Grantees —

and further adds that they have Expended Severeal thousands of Pounds in the Law in order to Defend said township.

       Joseph Baker
       David Lovejoy
       John Knox

Province of Newhamp[r] Rockingham ss Penicooke January 8th 1774 the Subscribers Joseph Baker David Lovejoy & John Knox all appeared & Made a solemn oath to the truth of the above Deposition

     Coram Jn° Bryent Jus[t] Peace

Province of the Massachusetts Bay — Cumberland ss — Falmouth Jan. 18th 1774 —

To his Excellency Thomas Hutchinson Esq[r] Cap[t] General & Governor in Chief in and over his Majestys Province of the Massachusetts-Bay The Honourable his Majestys Council, and House of Representatives in General Court assembled

The Memorial of Samuel Freeman of Falmouth aforesaid Merchant, humbly sets forth That in the Year 1764 this Court granted a Township of Land near Mount Desert, to one Ebenezer Thorndike and others, That the Grantees of said Township have been impower'd to hold Meetings as Proprietors, and have employed Persons to run out the same &c — and thereby incurr'd some considerable Charge, to pay which they have assess'd the several Rights in said Township, chose proper Officers to collect the same, but the Proprietors not having obtained the Kings Approbation of said Grant, they have not been able to collect the Monies so assess'd and the Persons to whom the Proprietors are in debt want their Money and one of them lately brought an Action against, and recovered Judgment and Execution, which Execution was put into the hands of an Officer, who therewith arrested your Memorialist, and though your Memorialist has a considerable Sum himself due from the said Proprietors, he was obliged to settle the same or go to Goal, which your Memorialist looks upon to be extreme hard and unequal — and their can never be an End of Lawsuits in this Way, for your Memorialist may also sue the Proprietors and upon recovering Judgment, may levy Execution on the former Plaintiff, being a Proprietor or any other, and they again may do the same, and so continue to the End of Time —

Wherefore, your Memorialist, humbly prays, that this Honourable Court would take the Premises into their mature Consideration, and provide some remedy for your Memorialist, that he as well as the other Creditors of the said Propriety may recover of the several Grantees their proportion of the several demands due from the said Proprietors in such a manner as shall put an end to said Demands, either to distrain or sue the several Proprietors aforesaid for their proportion as aforesaid, or by any other way or means relieve your Memorialist as Your Excellency and Honours shall, in your great Wisdom think proper — And your Memorialist as in Duty bound shall ever pray

Saml Freeman

Indorsed

Saml Freemans petition
Jany 18th 1774
Feb. 14, 1774 read & com{d} Coll Leonard
Mr Freeman of Eastham
Cap. Herrick

May 2 1774
refer{d} till next Session

Petition of Wm Elder 1774

To his Excellency Thomas Hutchinson Esqr Capt General & Governour in Chief in and over his majesties Province of the Massachusetts Bay in New England the Honble his Majesties Council and House of Representatives in General Court Assembled

The Petition of William Elder of Windham in the County of Cumberland Humbly sheweth that he was in the year one thousand seven hundred and seventy one chosen Assessor, with William Cofferin and William Knights for said Windham, the Papers Relative to the taking a Valuation of the Estates in said Town, Came very late to hand and one of the Assessors viz: Wm Knights having contracted for procuring a Number of large mast for his Majesties Navy was detained in pursuit thereof for a long time in the Woods, in all which time he never knew of the said Papers being Come to hand both which Cases Occationed a delay of taking said Valuation, and when they the Assessors entred upon the affair of valuation, and the Town Clerk living Remote and no Justice in the Town and they strangers to the Duty of their Office (as might well be expected from a New Plantation but lately incorporated) and they observing that they were subject to a fine of fifty pounds if they did not return the Valuation att or before a Certain Day Rashly took the Valuation of said Windham before they the Assessors had taken the Oath prescribed by Law, which two of them soon after did viz Your Petitioner and Wm Cofferin.

That altho there never has been any objection or exception taken against the Valuation, as Partial, unjust or unequall either by any one individual, Town, or Province, since it was taken, notwithstanding one Caleb Grashom of said Windham either from malice, ill nature, or Averice, or some other motive brot his Action for the forty pounds Penaty and at the Superiour Court recovered Judgment, for said forty pounds Anno 1773 and your Petitioner Moved that the execution might not be issued for the whole, but for the Moiety, belonging to the Proprietor, that your Petitioner might lay his case before the General Court, as to the other Moiety for their Consideration, Your Petitioners Circumstances are but low, his interest in the world but small and has found that the paying the prosecutor his half of the Penalty has very much distressed him, and if he is finally oblidged to pay the other half to the Province, it will just Compleat his ruin and absorb all his interest. Your Petitioner therefore, Humbly prays that your Excellency and Hon^s would take your Petitioners Case (which — truly Pitiable) under your wise Consideration, and remit, release and discharge your Petitioner— the payment of the Moiety Due to the Province, and your Petitioner as in Duty bound shall ever pray

 Windham January 25, 1774   William Elder

 In the House of Representatives Feby 10th 1774 —
 On the Petition of William Elder Shewing that he was Chosen one of the Assessors for the year 1771 for the town

of Windham in the County of Cumberland, and that there was an act made & Passed the same year by the Grate & General Court of this Province Intitled an act for Inquiring Into the ratable Estate of this Province and among other things it was Enacted that the assessors of Each town should take a list of the poles & Estates & before they Entred upon said bisness they should be first sworn to the faithfull Discharge of their Trust under the penalty of forty Pounds fine one moiety for the Informer or he or them that should sue for the same & the other moiety for the use of the Province and it appearing to the Court that the Petitioner Did (Simplely & not with a wicked Intent & Desire to Cheat or Defraud) assist in taking the list of Valuation for said town before he was Sworn & thereby Incured the Penalty in said act, and that one Caleb Grasham of said Windham has since brought his action against the Petitioner for the fine afores^d & at the Superiour Court at Falmouth in the year 1773 recovered a Judgment against the Petitioner for the recovery of forty Pounds the Penalty afores^d. But the Petitioner has not yet paid the moiety or half part of said fine belonging to the province

Therefore Resolved That the moiety or half part of said fine or forfeiture accruing to the Province thereby, be & hereby is remitted to the said William Elder & that he be wholly Discharged therefrom.

  Sent up for Concurrence   T Cushing Spk^r
In Council Feby 10th 1774 — Read & Concurred
            Jn° Cotton D. Secry
  Consented to   T Hutchinson

Petition of Timothy Walker Jany 26 1774

To His Excellency Thomas Hutchinson Esqr Captain General & Governor of the Province of the Massachusetts Bay —
To the Honorable His Majesty's Council and House of

Representatives of said Province in General Court assembled Boston Jany 26, 1774

The Petition of Timothy Walker Junr on behalf of himself and Associates humbly sheweth

That They and their Ancestors in the Year 1725 for a valuable Consideration purchased a Township of a little more than Seven Miles Square of this Goverment at a Place then called Pennicook afterwards Rumford on Merrimack River. That not at all doubting the Authority of this Goverment to make the said Grant, the Grantees, notwithstanding the extream difficulty & Cost of effecting a settlement so far up in the Indian Country at that Time, yet so vigorously applied themselves thereto, that in the year 1733,— consequent upon ye Report of a Committee sent by them to view the same, the then General Court of this Province declared that the Grantees had to full satisfaction fulfilled the Terms of their Grant & incorporated them by the Name of Rumford, That by the determination of the Boundary Line between this Province and that of New Hampshire by his late Majesty in the Year 1740 the said Townships fell near Forty Miles to the Northward of the dividing Line, That about the _ 1749 a Society under a Grant from the Province of New Hampshire began to molest us in our Posssssions and sued us in several Actions of Ejectment and always recovered against us in the Courts of New Hampshire. In this distressed State of our Affairs we applied to this Goverment to enable us to lay our Case before his Majesty by Way of Appeal, That by virtue of several Grants from this Goverment amounting in the whole to about the original purchase Consideration together with simple Interest for the same and also by much larger Sums raised amongst Ourselves we have been enabled to prosecute two Appeals to his Majesty, and altho' in each we obtained a reversal of the Judgment that stood against us here, yet the Royal Order extending in express Terms no farther than the Land sued for, the advantage fell far short of the Expence, And our Adversaries went on troubling us with new suits. Thus exhausted and seeing no end of our Troubles, we have been reduced to the necessity of repurchasing our Township of our Adversaries at a Rate far exceeding its Value in its rude State, That we have been at considerable expence in taking a View of a Tract of Land on Ammoroscoggin River on the Easterly side of Fullers Town (so called) which we apprehend would answer for a Township. We therefore Humbly Pray That your Excellency & Honours would be pleased so far to pity our hard Case as to make us a Grant of a Township at the said Place to be on each side of Ammoroscoggin River of equal extent with that formerly granted us by this Province on such reasonable Terms as you shall think proper. And your Petitioners shall as in Duty bound ever pray

Timothy Walker Junr
in behalf of himself & Associates

In the House of Representatives Feby 3, 1774

Whereas it hath been represented to this Court by Timothy Walker Junr in behalf of himself and Associates that in the Year 1725 they purchased of this Province a Township of Land of Seven Miles square, which by the runing of the Line between this Goverment & New Hampshire in the Year 1740 was cut off to that Goverment, by which means the Original Purchasers have been vexed with many expensive Lawsuits, and at last were oblidged to purchase the same Lands of Claimers under New Hampshire, Having enquired into the Matter, this Court find that the Facts set forth in said Petition are true; and that the Cost of defending their Title at the Court of Great Brittain have exceeded the Grants made to them by this Government to enable them to carry on the prosecution there.

Therefore

Resolved that there be granted to the Original Proprietors of the Township granted by this Province by the Name of Pennicook their Heirs or Assigns, who were Sufferers by said Township falling into New Hampshire a Township of Seven Miles Square to be laid out in regular Form on both sides of Amoscoggin River and easterly of and Adjoining to Fullers Town (so called)
otherwise Sudbury Canada laid out to Josiah Richardson Esqr & others Provided the Grantees within Six Years Settle Thirty Families in said Township and lay out one full Share to the first settled Minister, one full Share for the Ministry and one full Share for the School and one full Share for Harvard Colledge and provided the Petitioner within one Year return a Plan thereof taken by a Surveyor & Chainmen under Oath unto the Secretary's Office to be accepted and confirmed by the General Court.

And in Order that Justice may be done to the Sufferers it is further resolved That Mr Webster and Col^o Gerrish with such as the Honourable Board shall join be a Committee to repair to the said Township of Pennicook, who shall there enquire into and make out a List of the Sufferers, and that they return a List for Confirmation to the General Assembly, and that said Committee give suitable notice of the Time of their Meeting by Publishing an advertisement in the Essex Gazette and in one of the Portsmouth News Papers three Weeks successively, Two Months before the Time of their Meeting, That any Person claiming Right to the Grant aforesaid may appear and lay in their Claim.

   Sent up for Concurrence   T Cushing Spk^r

In Council Feby 3^d, 1774. Read & Concurred & Samuel Phillips Esqr is joined in the Affair

             Jno Cotton D. Secry

    Consented to   T Hutchinson

Petition of Inhab^{ts} of Freetown, 1774.

To his Excelency Thomas Hutchinson Esqr Captain General and commander in Cheif in and over his Majestys Province of the Massachusetts Bay in New England To the Honourable his Majestys council and the Honourable House of Representatives of said Province in Generall Court Assembled January 26th A: D: 1774.

The Inhabitants of a New plantation in the County of Lincoln in said Province Called Freetown and Jeremi Squom Island Humbly Sheweth that your Petitioners consist of more Than one Hundred Familays have long Laboured under the Disadvantage of being unincorporated by which we are deprived of many Blessings of civil Society, being destitute of the Power of Settleing a Gospel Minister of Jesus Christ and Of chusing a school Master and of Raising Taxes for their Support and Likewise the Assesing the Province & County Rates And of Laying out Roads for the Benifit of said Plantation all which is to the great Disadvantage of the Inhabitants of said Plantation and Whereas your Humble Petitioners have Raizd a Frame for a Meeting house for the further Promoting of the Gospel and are very desirous to Settle a Minister of the Gospel among us Your Petitioners humbly Pray your Excellency and Honours to take this our Petition into your wise consideration and that The Said Distrest Plantation Bounding Northerly on new Castle Easterly on the Town of Boothbay Southerly on the Cross river So called and Westerly on Sheepscott River mount Sweeg bay So as to include Jeremi Squom Island the said New Plantation Being about Seven miles in Length and five in Breadth May be Incorporated into a Town, and be invested with all The rights and priviledges Belonging or appertaining to an Incorporated Town agreable to the Royall charter and the Severall Acts of the Province Relative to Towns Incorporated And your Humble Petitioners as in Duty Bound will ever Pray &c

Petitioners

Moses Davis	Willam Cliford	John Cuningham
Solomon Baker	Jonathan Allbee	David Trask
John Chase	Solomon Trask	Ebenezer Gove
Isac Clifford	Nathaniel Leeman	Henery Leeman
John Leeman	William Clifford	Solomon Gove
Nathan Gove	Nathnael Winslow	Joshua Cross
Joseph Richards	James Allen	Thomas Ringe
Zachariah Dodge	Jonathan Moore	Stephen Merrill
Willam Cuningham	Thomes Ross	James Moore
John Patrick	Noar Colby	James Chase
Simon Morrill	Sam^{ll} Hiron	Asa Gove
Jonathan Hutchings	George Canfield	Huff Samuel Wilber
Rogles Colby	John Johnson	Joseph Mery
Nathan Webster	Daniel Webster	Joseph Brown
Daniel Gardner	Simon Pearl	Daniel Glover
Hubbard Stevens	Bengimand Laythan	Caleb Cross
William Cross	Noah Cross	Samuel Trask Junr
Joseph Trask	Samuel Trask	Benjamin Allbee

Petition of Joseph Josselyn. 1774.

Province of the Massachusetts Bay To His Excellency Thos Hutchinson Esqr Capt General & Governor in Chiefe over said Province to the Honble his Majestys Council & House of Representatives in General Court Assembled January the 26th 1774 —

The Petition of Joseph Josselyn of Hanover in the County of Plymouth Esqr Humbly Sheweth that there was a Grant of a Township made by the Great & General Court in June A D. 1732 To Benjamin Smith and Others for Services Done in the Naraganset Indian War,— which Township was laid out on Merrimack River in the year 1733, and Commonly called N° 5. Your Petitioner having Purchased of the Heirs of Benjamin Bates one of the Soldiers in that War his Right which was afterwards laid out in said Township to your Petitioner who has been at Considerable trouble and Cost from Time to Time in Bringing on the Settlement agreable to the terms of said Grant—

But after Some Years, upon Runing the Line Between this Province and that of New Hampshire, the whole of said Township was taken into that Province, and Your Petitioner was thereby deprived & Excluded from all Property and Benefit of his said Lands.—

Wherefore He Prays your Excellency and Honours to take this his Case into your Wise and Compassionate Consideration and in your Wisdom and Goodness make him Such a Grant of Some unappropriated Lands of this Province as shall appear to you Just & Reasonable or Otherwise Relieve him in this Case as to you Seems meet.—

And as in Duty bound Shall Ever Pray

Joseph Josselyn

In the House of Representatives March 3, 1774

Resolved that there be granted to the Petitioner Joseph Josselyn his heirs & Assigns forever a Tract of Land of four hundred Acres to the Eastward of Saco River adjoining to some former Grant in lieu of and in full Satisfaction for the land taken from him as Mentioned in this Petition, Provided it does not Interfere with any former Grant & that the Petitioner return a Plan thereof to this Court taken by a Surveyor & chainmen under Oath within Twelve Months for their Confirmation

  Sent up for Concurrence   T Cushing Spk[r]

In Council Mar. 3[d] 1774   Read & Concurred

J[no] Cotton D. Seĉry

  Consented to   T Hutchinson

Resolve.

In the House of Representatives February 5th 1774

On the Petition of Noah Johnson & others Representing that the Government formerly Granted to the Heirs of Capt John Lovewell & to the Heirs of those men that fell with him in the Engagement at Pigwacket & to those that were with him in sd Engagement & others, a Tract of Land at Suncook, who held the Same & made Large Improvements thereon, But by the Running the Line between this Government & New Hapshire the sd Township fell within the Latter, and the Proprietors thereby have lost the Benefit of sd Grant, and praying that they may have a Grant of Land in Compensation for their Loss Therefore Resolved that in Lieu of sd Township there be Granted a Township of Land of the Contents of Seven Miles Square on the Easterly side of Saco River & Adjoyning to a Township Granted to Benjamin Mulliken Esqr & others To such of the Original Grantees of sd Township as are Living to the Heirs of them that are Dead & to such of the Settlers in sd Township as have been Sufferers by the sd Townships falling into New Hampshire who have not had their Loss made up to them.— Provided that the Grantees within Six years Settle thirty families thereon, Build a meeting House and Settle a Learned Protestant Minister, and lay out one Sixty fourth part thereof for the first Settled Minister, One Sixty fourth part for the Ministry, One Sixty fourth part for the School and one Sixty fourth part for Harvard Colledge & Return a Plan of sd Township into the Secretaries office within twelve months for Confirmation —

And that Justice may be Done among the Claimers for a Compensation for their Loss in sd Township Resolved That Coll Gerrish and Mr Webster with such as the Honble Board Shall Joyn be a Comttee at the Charge of the Grantees to Repair to the sd Suncook and hear the Claimers & Determine who shall be Admitted Grantees in s^d Township, make out a List of their Names and their respective Shares & Lodge the Same in the Secretaries office within Ten Months for Confirmation of the General Court, and the s^d Com^tee shall Give notice of the Time of their meeting by Advertiseing the same in the Boston Gazette, in the Essex Gazette & New Hampshire News paper three weeks Successively two months before the Time of their meeting that all Persons may have opportunity to bring in their Claims —

  Sent up for Concurrence   T. Cushing Spk^r

In Council Feby 5th 1774 — Read & Concurred, and Samuel Phillips Esqr is joined —

             Jn° Cotton D. Sec̃ry

Consented to   T Hutchinson

Petition of Saml Whittemore & Amos Lawrence. 1774.

To his Excelency Thomas Hutchinson Esqr Cap General and Commander in Cheif in & over his majesties province of the Massachusetts Bay and to the Hon^bl his majesties Councel & House of Representitives in Genl Court assembled at Boston Feby 1774 — The memorial of Sam^ll Whitemore and Amos Lawrence in behalf of themselves & others Hum^bly Sheweth That they Petitioned the Grate & General Court praying for a Grant of land in Lieu of a Township Granted to Cap John Flint & Company which Township fell into New Hamsheir by the late runing of the Province line which Petition was Committed to a Commetee who Duly Examined into the reason of the same and reported (on the last Day of the Courts Setting in June last) that in Lieu of said lost Township there be Granted to the Prop^rs the original Grantees of said lost Township their heirs and assigns a township of the Contents of Seven miles Square on the East

Side of the Soco river Provided they Settle thirty families in said Township within Six years & lay out one Sixty fourth part for the use of the first settled minister one sixty fourth part for the ministry one sixty fourth part for the Gramer School & one Sixty fourth part for the use of Harvard College & take a plan thereof by a Surveyor & Chainmen under oath & return the same into the Secreta^y office in one year — which report was Excepted by the House and sent up to the Hon^{bl} Board for their Concurance. But the Hon^{bl} Board Did not Cuncur— the Vote of the House — and your memoriale^t have Been Informed the reason Given was because the Court was Just ariseing & that there was not then time, and by Some means or other the Petition & report is lost — Wherefore your memori^{ts} in behalf of themselves & the other Prop^{rs} pray your Excelency & Hon^{rs} would be pleased to take their Case into your wise Consideration & make them a Grant Simeler to the above mentioned report and your memori^{ls} in Duty Bound shall Ever pray

       Saml Whittemore
       Amos Lawrence

In the House of Representitives Feby 8 : 1774

on the Petition of Sam^{ll} Whitemore & Amos Lawrence in behalf of themselves & others prop^{rs} of a Township Granted to Cap John Flint & Company of the Contents of Six miles Square, praying for a Grant of land in Lieu of said Township which fell within the Province of New Hamsheir upon the late runing of the Province line, and it appearing to this Court that the Petitioners have Expended much Labour & money in Clearing roads bringing forward the Settlement of said township & have been thereby Grate Sufferers for which the Grantees have had no Consideration from this Province or the Province of New Hamsheir —

Therefore resolved that in Lieu thereof there be Granted to the oridginal Prop^{rs} & Grantees their legal representitives heirs or assigns a township of the Contents of Seven miles Square Provided the Grantees Settle thirty families in said township within Six years & lay out one Sixty fourth part for the use of the ministry one Sixty fourth part for the first settled minister one sixty fourth part for the use of the Gramer School & one Sixty fourth part for the use of Harvard College Provided also that said Township be layd out in that part of the unappropriated lands belonging to this Province on the Eastward of Saco river adjoyning to some former Grant (Except the Tract of land Petition— for by Suncook prop^{rs} & return a plan taken by a Surveyor and Chainmen under oath into the Secretarys office within one year for Confermation —

  Sent up for Concurrence   T Cushing Spk^r
In Council Feby 8th 1774 Read & Concurred
             Jno Cotton D. Sec̃ry
  Consented to   T Hutchinson

Henry Young Brown 1774

To the Honble House of Representatives

A State of Facts respecting the Petition of Henry Young Brown February 8, 1774,— as follows Viz^t—

In January 1764 the General Court made him a Grant of a Township to be laid out on Saco River above Coll^o Fryes Township, to lay it out according to order.—

In June 1764 he returned a plan that was accepted and the land confirmed to him his heirs and Assigns forever he then Gave bond for Two Hundred pounds as a consideration for said Township, as also a Bond to perform the Settlement of the Town, he immediately proceeded to lott out the Town, made Roads & settled Twelve Families in one year.—

In October 1765 he informed the Court that New Hampshire Claimed the Greatest part of the Town, they then looked into a report of the Honble Benj^a Lincoln Esqr and others who were sent by the Court to view the foundation of the dispute between the two Governments, and on the first day of November they Ordered him to keep his possession and go on with his Improvements and Settlement and promised him relief if he met with any difficulty in consequence of this Order: He was prevented from making advantageous terms with the Grantees under New Hampshire, as also with his own Settlers

In June 1766, the Court further Ordered him to prosecute any that Entered under the Grant of New Hampshire, and defend himself and Settlers against New Hampshire Claim, at the Expence of the Government

He attended Strictly to their orders, lay his Accounts before the Court from time to time and received his pay.

On the Twelfth of June 1769 He received Ninety five pounds in full Satisfaction for the Ballance of his Account for the Expences of Law Suits agreeable to the order of June 1766, as will appear by said Resolve of Court of 12th of June 1769: There was then a Committee appointed to proceed to Pigwackett, and Take a View of what had been done by him and Settlers, the Committee Reported in April 1770; Their Report was rejected. Another Committee was appointed to take the matter into consideration, they reported for said Brown to have Eleven Thousand Acres of land which was the same Quantity he lost, and that to be considered in full Satisfaction for all Damages he had or might sustain, the Report was objected to by him as insufficient to make him whole for the following reasons. 1st For that he was prevented by the order of the General Court of November 1st 1765 from making advantageous Terms with the Grantees under New Hampshire, and thereby have saved his

Expences of laying out his Town and Lotting out the same, and for making Roads and geting his Settlers.

2dly by said order he was prevented from settling with his own Settlers, who offered him advantageous Terms, he being subject to Damages by the Deeds he had Given.

And 3dly That the Land proposed for him was not half so good as his first Grant. The Major part of the Committee supposed that he would not be subject to Damages by his Deeds to his Settlers, but rather make a great Saving, and that the Land proposed for him was as good as his first Grant, by that means he humbly conceives they were led to make such report as Induced the House to pass the Resolve of April 1770. Since that his Settlers have recovered sundry large sums against him which he has been obliged to pay.

He has now settled the whole dispute and is able to make it appear that the former order of Court was founded on some mistakes that he never received one penny out of the Treasury but what he accounted for to the Court, agreable to the Order of June 1766, and had no reference to what he now asks allowance for, which is founded on an order of Court of first of November 1765.

He has not only, in a great measure lost the laying out his first Town, loting the same, Clearing Roads, getting on his settlers which every Gentleman acquainted with New Towns must know is attended with great Expence, as also the Damages recovered against him by his Settlers. But he has also been prevented from making proper Advantages of his Land that did not fall within New Hampshire Claim, by a Claim under Major Phillips

All which he humbly submits to the consideration of your Honors.

Henry Young Brown

The evidence to support the Facts, that do not depend on the Records of the Court, and within the knowledge of some of the Members, are ready to be offer'd when called for.

I pray it may be kept in View that all the money I Rec^d out of the Treasury was for Service performed in consiquence of an order of the General Court June 1766 and has been accounted for.

Court of Appeals Octr Term 1770
Henry Young Brown Appellant
Saml Osgood & al.   Appellees

Judgment for the Appellees to recover dam^s	180 —
Costs	24.10 —

Att^r Geo: King D Sec^y

Entry of the Action	4.10 —
Copy of the Case	2. 9. 6

This may certify whom it may concern. That I the subscriber with others being in search of a Township of Land to the Eastward of Saco River—View^d a Tract of Land between Bridgeton & the River aforesaid, but found it to be Generally so Broken a Tract, as rendered it of but Little Value for a Township therefore rejected it; and made a Different Pitch—

Boston Feby 10th 1774 —   Alex^r Shepard Junr
Newton

Account Allowed.

In the House of Representatives Feby 16, 1774

The Account of Revd Benjamin Stevens, Isaac Lyman and Samuel Langdon a Committee appointed by the Genl Court to Employ Missionaries for the Eastern parts of the Province being presented for Allowance it Appearing that the said Account is Just and Reasonable and that they had expended the Sum of Seventy pounds four shillings and seven pence half penny part of the sum of Eighty pounds Granted for that purpose,

Resolved that the Same be allowed And that the said Committee be further accountable for the Sum of Nine pounds fifteen shillings and four pence half penny yet Remaining in their hands.

 Sent up for Concurrence   T. Cushing Spk^r
 In Council Feby 16th 1774.   Read & Concurred —
          Jno Cotton D. Secŕy
 Consented to   T. Hutchinson

Act of Incorporation 1774.

Anno Regni Regis Georgii Tertii Decimo Quarto

An Act for incorporating a Plantation called Freetown & Jeremy Squam Island, into a Town by the name of

Whereas the Inhabitants of a new Plantation commonly called Freetown and Jeremy Squam Island in the County of Lincoln, have represented to this Court the great difficulties they labour under in their present situation, and have earnestly requested that they may be incorporated into a Township;—

Be it enacted by the Governor, Council and House of Representatives, that the Tract of Land including Jeremy Squam Island, bounding Northerly on New Castle, Easterly on the Town of Boothbay, Southerly on the cross River, so called, And Westerly on Sheepscott River, and Mount Sweeg Bay, so as to include said Island, be and hereby is Erected into a Town by the name of   And that the Inhabitants thereof be, and hereby are invested with all the powers, priviledges and immunities, which the Inhabitants of the

Towns within this Province respectively do, or by Law ought to enjoy.

And be it further enacted, That Thomas Rice of Pownalborough in the said County of Lincoln Esquire, be and hereby is empowered to issue his Warrant directed to some principal Inhabitant in said Township, to warn the Inhabitants of said Township to meet at such time and place as he shall therein set forth, to choose all such Officers as shall be necessary to manage the affairs of said Town, at which said first meeting all the then present Male Inhabitants arrived to twenty one years of age shall be admitted to Vote —

In the House Representatives Feby 14, 1774
Read a first time
Feby 15 Read Second Time
Feby 16 Read a Third time & passed to be Engrossed
 Sent up for Concurrence   T Cushing Spk^r

In Council Feby 16^h 1774 Read a first Time
 17th Read a second time & passed to be Engrossed, with the Amendments at A. & B Viz^t dele Glynborough —
 Sent down for Concurrence
         Jno Cotton D. Secry

In the House of Representatives Feb. 26 1774
 Read & Concurred   T Cushing Spk^r

In the House of Representatives Feb^r 24, 1774

On the Petition of John Gardner & others in Behalf of themselves & others Proprietors of a Township of the Contents of six Miles square granted to John Whitman Esq And others called Number Six in the Line of Towns between Merrimack & Connecticutt Rivers Whereas it appears that the Proprietors of said Township Expended much Labour & Money in making Roads & otherways bringing forward the

Settlement of said Township and that the whole of the said Township fell within the Limits of New-Hampshire on the runing the Line between this Government & the said Government of New-Hampshire for which the Grantees have received no Consideration from this Province or the said Province of New-Hampshire

Therefore Resolved that in Lieu thereof there be granted to the Proprietors & legal Representatives or Assigns of the Original Grantees who were Sufferers by losing their Lands A Township of seven miles square in the unappropriated Lands belonging to this Province provided the Grantees Settle thirty Families on said Township within Six years And lay out one Sixty fourth Part for the Use of the Ministry one sixty fourth Part for the first Settled Minister & one sixty fourth Part for the grammar school And one Sixty fourth Part for the use of Harvard Colledge provided also that said Township be laid out adjoining to some former Grant in that Part of the unappropriated Lands belonging to this Province lying Eastward of Saco River and Coll Whitcomb & Capt Gardner of Cambridge with such as the Hon^{bl} Board may Join be A Comittee to determine who are to be admitted as Proprietors in said Township & if any of the Grantees of said Township Number Six shall appear to have been hertofore compensated that said Committee shall admit other sufferers in their stead the Expence of the said Committee to be paid by the Grantees provided also that the said Proprietors Return a Plan taken by a Surveyor and Chainmen under Oath into the Secretarys Office within one year for Confirmation

    Sent up for Concurrence   T Cushing Spk^r

In Council Feby 24th 1774 Read & Concurred & Artemas Ward Esqr is joined —

               Jno Cotton D Sec̃ry

    Consented to   T Hutchinson

Petition of John Gardner & others 1774

Province of the Massachusetts Bay To His Excellency Thomas Hutchinson Esqr Captain General & Commander in chief in & over s^d Province

To the Honourable His majesties Council & To the Honourable House of Representatives in general Court assembled February 26th 1774

The Petition of the Subscriber– in behalf of ourselves and others Grantees of the Township Number Six in the Line of Towns humbly Sheweth

That the Great & General Court of this Province at their Session A D 1735 Granted a Township of the Contents of Six Miles square being Number six In the Line of Towns between Connecticut & Merrimack Rivers that the Grantees were at very considerable Expence in clearing Roads Buildings Mills &c on said Township. that by the late runing of the Line Between this Government & the Government of New-Hampshire the said Township was taken into the said Government of New-Hampshire, & your Pet^{rs} and their Associates have lost their whole Interest therin together with the Money Expended in bringing forward the Settlement of said Township

Your Petitioners therfore most humbly request that your Excellency & Honours would in your known wisdom & Justis Grant to your Petitioner– & the other Grantees and Proprietors of s^d Township Number Six in Lieu thereof a Township in some of the unappropriated Land in the Eastward Part of this Province or otherwise Relive your Petitioners as your Excellency & Hon^s In your Wisdom shall think proper & your Petitioners as in Duty bound shall ever pray

       John Gardner
       Stephen Maynard
       Seth Rice

Report.

The Committee of both Houses on the Petition of Seth Sweetser & others, belonging to the Company or Propriety owning Lands known by the Name of Pemaquid Lands, And the Answer of Thomas Drowne, Agent for Several of the Proprietors, In Answer thereto, have attended the service; And the said Agent having been fully satisfied by the Petitioners, and having declared, that he has now no remaining Objections — the Committee report — That the Payer of said Petition be granted, and that the Proceedings of the said Company or Propriety relative to, and at their Several Meetings be ratified and Confirmed & declared to be valid, to all Intents & Purposes in the Law; any Informality in their Proceedings, relative to, Or at said Meetings Notwithstanding

   which is submitted

             James Pitts
 p order

In Council Mar. 1st 1774 — Read & accepted, & ordered that the Prayer of the Pet^n be granted, & that the Proceedings of the Pemaquid Company so called relative to & at their several Meetings, be & hereby are ratified & confirmed, to all Intents & purposes in the Law; any Informality in their Proceedings relative to, or at said Meetings notwithstanding —

  Sent down for Concurrence Jno Cotton D. Secry

 In the House of Representatives March 1, 1774
   Read & Concurred   T Cushing Spk^r
   Consented to   T Hutchinson

          Boston March 3^d 1774

 I the Subcriber Certify that upon condition I may have the advantage of the fifty pounds Propos'd in your report and a confirmation of the Eleven thousand acres of land therein mentioned I promis and Engage to Give the Goverment a full Discharge from any further demands respecting the land in dispute between Warrins & Bryents lines: Also from all demands Respecting all Law suits which has or may arise in Consequence of said disputed line.

Test   Henry Young Brown

Petition of John Brown & others 1774.

To his Excellency Thomas Gage Esqr Capt genneral Governor & Commander in chief in and over his Majesties Province of The Massachusetts Bay in New England and To the Honnourable ye Council and house of Representatives Conveen^d at Boston

Whereas a Certain Number of People Purchased a Certain Tract of Land of the Hiers of Brigadier Waldow Said Land Lying on the Westerly Side of Penobscut Bay and is Incorporated into a Town By the Name of Belfast and Whereas s^d Purchasers Entered into an Obligatory Bond To make an Immediate Settlement Upon the said Land and s^d Bond Not Being Authentick, the one half of said Purchasers Declines Settlement Which renders us the Inhabitants unable To Carry on In the Form of a Town Being Neither in a Capacity To maintain a gospel Minister To Build a Meeting house To have the Priveledge of Schools Neither to Repair roads and to Build Bridges &c — And Therefore we think Our Circumstances in a Worse Condition than they were Before our Incorporation — and Whereas a Party of The Nonresidenters Insisted Upon the Incorporation of said Town and wanted us the Inhabitants to Sign with Them which we Refused to Do untill they Came to an Aggreement to have the Land Taxed which they Assented too and then We the

Inhabitants Signed with Them — And Now we are Incorporated in the Common Form Which Renders it Disaggreeable to the Inhabitants and Contrary to the Prayer of our former petition Which gives us Reason to Think that Our Circumstances and Abbilities Relateing to the Settlement of the place Was Not Rightly Represented —

Therefore We your Humble Petitioners Begs that your Excellency & Honnours Would Be pleased to Considder the Difficulties of our Case at present — and Further Begs if it might please your Excellency & Honnours for to pass an Act For to Tax all the unsettled Lands in said Town and To Invest Us Who are the Inhabitants of said Town with Full Power and Authoritie To Sell as much of the Delinquents Land at Publick Vendue as shall Pay their Taxes In equal proportion to Defray all Necessary Charges from Time to time. And if your Excellency & Honnours Would Think it Proper to Lay a Tax upon the Land By the Acre we have thought that Two pence p^r Acre Lawfull is as Little as we Think will Do yearly For some Term of years Or as Long as your Honnours Think Proper —

And we Who are your Humble Petitioners who are in Duty Bound Will Ever Pray

Belfast May ye 16th 1774

		John Brown
James Gilmore	John Tuffts	David Hemphill
John Tufft	John Barnet	William Nickles
James Patterson	Benjn Nesmith	James Murray
James Miller	Tolford Durham	John Durham
Nathaniel Patterson	William Patterson	David Glimor
John Davidson	Sam^{ll} Houston	Alex^{dr} Clark
William Petterson		

Resolve.

In the House of Representatives June 11, 1774
Resolved that the Petitioners Notify the Propriators of

the Lands in the Town of Belfast with a Copy of this Petition By Inserting the Substance thereof in Two of the Boston News papers Three Weeks Successively and also by Serveing the Clerk of said Propriaty with a Copy of s^d Petition & this order forty Days before the Next Siting of the General Court, that they shew Cause (if any they have) on the Second Wednesday of the next Sitting thereof why the Prayer thereof should not be granted.

  Sent up for Concurrence   T Cushing Spk^r
 In Council June 14th 1774 —   Read and Concurred —
           Jn° Cotton D. Sec̃ry

Boothbay Petition. 1774

To His Excellency Thomas Gage Esquire Captain General and Governor in Chief in and over his Majesty's Province of Massachusetts Bay in New England

To the Honorable his Majestys Council, and To the Honorable the House of Representatives of said Province, in General Court assembled.

The Petition of the subscribers chosen selectmen of the town of Boothbay in the County of Lincoln in said Province for the year of our Lord one thousand seven hundred and seventy four,

Most humbly sheweth

That agreeable to the directions of the Royal Charter, the town of Boothbay held their anniversary meeting for the choice of town officers for the current year, at the Meeting house in said town, on the seventh day of March last, and then and there did publicly elect such officers as the law directs, and pass such other votes for the internal affairs of the town as were authorized by the Warrant by virtue of which said meeting had been called; and adjourned to the thirteth day of

But before the said appointed meeting by Adjournment, it was discovered that, by an inadvertency of the constable, the certificate required by law to be returned by him on the back of the March warrant was omitted; and this omission having, thro' hurry of business, escaped the notice of the Moderator & Clerk at said Meeting, the whole transactions of the town at said Meeting were finished under this circumstance of illegality; and so are apprehended to be null & void. and it being then impossible legally to call another Meeting in the Month of March for remedying that mistake, the town is thereby deprived of the powers & privileges of a corporation, and all the public business of the year remains at a stand, therefore

Your Petitioners, having been chosen Select-men of said town for the present year, judge it incumbent on them to take necessary steps to have this inconvenience removed as speedily as possible; and therefore pray your Excellency & Honors, that, as early in your present session as may be, An act of the Great & General Court may pass, restoring us to the forfeited privileges of a town, and empowering some such person as you shall think proper to issue a warrant for calling a town meeting for the choice of the necessary officers of the present year, and for transacting anew the whole business contained in the said March warrant: and your Petitioners as in duty bound shall ever pray.

Dated at Boothbay
June 3^d 1774

William McCobb
Patrick McKown
John Beath

Resolve.

In the House of Representatives June 15 1774

Resolved that the prayer of the Petition (of William McCobb and others in behalf of the Town of Boothbay in the

County of Lincon) be granted and that the Select Men for the year 1773 or the Major part of them, be and hereby are authorized and required to issue out their Warrant Directed to one of the Constables of said Town for the year 1773 Requiring him to warn the Freeholders and other Inhabitants Qualified according to law to vote in Town affairs to meet together at such time and place (in said Town) as shall be expressed in said warrant to chuse such officers as Towns by law are Authorised to Chuse in the Month of March Anually —

    Sent up for Concurrence   T Cushing Spk^r

In Council June 15th 1774   Read & Concurred

                         Jno Cotton D. Secry

    Consented to   Thos Gage

At a Meeting held in Buxton June 20, 1774.

The Inhabitants being duly assembled & Thos Bradbury J^r being Chosen Moderator to regulate said meeting, the Town chose Capt Jno Elder & Capt. Jno Lane & Messrs Samuel Hovey, Jno Nason & Saml Merrill to be a Committee to draw up some Resolves in Behalf of the Town, & in Concurrence with the Committees of Correspondence in Boston, & with all the Friends of american Liberty in the Several Enlish american Colonies . . . . In order to Shew that we heartily join with them in abiding by the Constitutional Rights of America. The Town passed the following Resolves

Resolved 1st That Self Preservation is the first Law of Nature And y^t Taxation whout Representation is subversful of our Liberties

2. Whereas An Act has been passed in the british Parliament for blocking up the Harbour of Boston till such Time as an unreasonable Demand is Complied with —

resolved y^t we Deem this as an Attack upon Us which tends utterly to destroy our civil Liberties — For the same Power may at Pleasure destroy the Trade And Shut up the Harbors of any other Colonies in Their Turne And thus bring on a total End to our Liberties & Privileges

3. resolved y^t this Town approoves of the Constitutional Exertions & Struggles made by the Several Colonies of Enlish America for the Prevention of so dread a Catastrophe as will follow Taxation whout Representation — And y^t we are, & always will be ready in every Constitutional way to give all Assistance in our Power to prevent So dire a Calamity.

4. resolved y^t a Dread of being enslaved ourselves, & tansmitting the Chains to our Posterity is the principal Inducement to these measures.

5. resolved y^t this Town return their Sincere Thanks to all The Friends of America, And to the Town of Boston in Particular who have always nobly exerted themselves in the Cause of Liberty.

Voted that the Town Clerk transmit a true Copy of these Resolves to the Committee of Correspondence in Boston

The above is a true Copy   attestatur

John Nason ⟩ Town Clerk

Bond.

Know all men by these presents that We Dummer Sewall of Georgetown in the County of Lincoln Gentleman and Jordan Parker of said Georgetown Yeoman are holden & stand firmly bound unto the Provincial Congress now setting for the Province of Massachusetts Bay or to their Successors or any person that shall be appointed by the People for the head of the Province aforesaid, in the sum of two thousand pounds to be paid to the said Congress or their successors as aforesaid to which payment well & truly to be made we bind our selves our heirs Executors & Administrators firmly by these presents Sealed with our seals Dated the fourth day of May Anno Domini seventeen hundred & seventy five.

The Condition of the above obligation is such that Whereas Edward Parry Esqr has been taken by, & now is in Custody of, Coll^{or} Samuel Thompson as a suspected Enemy to the rights of America Now if the above bounden Dummer & Jordan shall keep the said Edward in safe Custody till he shall be released by order of the Provincial Congress & that the said Edward shall not either by himself or any for or under him, remove the masts spars booms boards & now laying in the mast dock in said Georgetown & shall not write to any of the officers of the Army or Navy for protection or against the Country then the above obligation to be void otherwise to be in force —

Test   Dum^r Sewall   Seal.
  J^{no} Wood   Jordan Parker   Seal.
  J^{no} Hobby

Damariscotta Resolves, &c. March 6, 1775.

March the 6th in the year 1775
Then the Inhabitance of a place Cauled Damiscota being withoute the bounds of Eany Township in the County of Lincoln mett to Gather to Consider of the Distresed state and Condishon of North americk under the present Reign which are so notorous to ous that we should be glad never to hear of them again.

we have pased these Resouls

1   that wee will abide by the Douings of the grate and genereal Congres of North Americk from first to last

2   Resouled to obey all orders that shall be given oute from our provinchal Congres

3ˡʸ Resouled to Stand with our brearthen the Suns of Liberty in the Defence of Rights and Libertys against all tiranical doings let it Com from what quarter it will at the hazzard of our Estats and Lives.

4ˡʸ Chose a Committee to Inspect Import and Export according to the order of the Congres

5ˡʸ Chose three officers and Inlisted a Company the same Day

a trew Coppy attested by the Committee
this to be communicated to
the Provincial Congress

Anthony Chapman
Thomas Flint
Nathan Chapman

Letter from J. Brown   March 29, 1775.

Montreal March 29ᵗʰ 1775

Gentlemen

Immediately after the Reception of your Letters & Pamphlets, I went to Albany to find the State of the Lakes and established a Correspondence with Doctʳ Joseph Young. I found the lakes impassable at that time —

About a Fortnight after I set out for Canada and arived at Sᵗ Johns in 14 days having undergone most inconceivable hardships the Lake Champlain being very high, the small streems Rivers, and a great Part of the Country for Twenty Miles each Side the Lake especially toward Canada under Water; the Lake Champlain was partly open & partly covered with Dangerous Ice, which breaking loose for Miles in length eaugh [off] our Coast drove us agᵗ an Island and frose us in for 2 Days after which we were glad to foot it on Land —

I deliverd your Letters to Mess. Thos Walker & Blake and was very Kindly rece'd by the Committee of Correspondence at Montreal, from whom I received the following State of Affairs in the Province of Quebec. Govr Carleton is no g^t Pollition, a Man of a Souer morose Temper, a Strong Friend to Administration, and the late Acts of the British Parliament, which respect America, perticularly the Quebec Bill, has restrained the Liberty of the Press that nothing can be printed with^t examination & Licence Applycation has been made to him for printing the Address from the Continential Congress and a refusal obtain'd. All the Troops in this Province are ordered to hold themselves in readiness for Boston on the Shortest Notice, 4 or 5 hundred Snowshoes are prepared for what use they know not — Mr Walker has wrote you about three Weeks Since, and has been very explicit, he informs you that two Regular Officers Leiut^s have gone of in disguise, supposed to be gone to Boston, & to make what discovery they can through the Country — I have the pleasure and satisfaction to inform you that through the industory and exertions of our Friends in Canada our Enemies are not at present able to raise Ten Men for Administration. The Weapons that have been used by our Friends to thwart the constant endeavours of the Friends of Government (so called) have been chiefly in Terrorem. The French People are (as a Body extremely ignorant, and Bigotted The Curâ or Priests having almost the intire government of their Temporals as well as Spirituals — in Laperare a Small Village about 9 Miles from Montreal, I gave my Landlord (a Roman Padde) a Letter of address, and there being Four Curàs in the Village praying over the Dead Body of an old Frier, the Pamphlet was soon handed them, who sent a Messenger to purchase Several — I made them a Present of each of them one, and was desired to wait on them in the Nunnery with the holy Sisters, they appeared to have no Disposition unfriendly toward the Colinies but chose rather to stand nuter —

Two Men from the N. Hampshire Grants accompanied me over the Lakes the one was an old Indian hunter acquainted with the St Franceway Indians and their Language, the other was a captive many years among the Caughnawaga Indians which is the Principal of all the Canadian Six Nation and western Tribes of Indians, whom I sent to inquire and Search out any intreigues carrying on among them, these Men have this Minute returned and Report that they were very kindly received by the Caughnawaga Indians, with whom they tarried several Days: the Indians say they have been repeetedly applyed to and requested to Join with the Kings Troops to fight Boston, but have peremptorily refused, and still intend to refuse. they are a very Sinsible Polliticke People and say that if they are obliged for their own safety to take up arms on either side that they shall take part on the Side of their Brethern the English in N. England; all the Chiefs of the Caughnawaga Tribe being of English extraction Captivated in their infancy — They have wrote a Friendly Letter to Col° Israel Putnam of Pompfret in Connecticutt in Consequence of a Letter which Col° Putnam sent them, in which Letter they give their Brother Putnam assurance of their Peaceable Desposition — Several French Gentlemen from Montreal have paid the Governer a Visit and offered him their Service as officers to raise a Canadian Army and join the King's Troops, the Govr told them he could get Officers in plenty but the difficulty consisted in raising Soldiers.

There is no prospect of Canada sending Delegates to the Continental Congress; the Difficulty consists in this, Should the English Join in the non importation agreem^t the French would immediately monopolize the Indian Trade — the French in Canada are a set of People that know no other way of

Procuring Wealth and honor but by becoming Court Sycophants, and as the introduction of the French Laws will make room for the French Gentry, they are very thick about the Governer — You may depend that should any movement be made among the French to Join ag^t the Colonies your Friends here will give the Shortest Notice possible and the Indians on their part have ingaged to do the same, so that you have no reason to expect to be surprised with^t Notice, should the worst Event take place —

I have established a Channel of Corrispondence through the N. Hampshire Grants which may be depended on. Mr Walker's Letter comes by the hands of Mr Jeffries once of Boston, now on his Way thither which together with this is a full Account of Affairs here — I shall tarry here some time — but shall not go to Quebec as there are a Number of their Committee here —

One thing I must mention to be kept as a profound Secret, the Fort at Tyconderogo must be seised as soon as possible should hostilities be committed by the Kings Troops. The People on N. Hampshire Grants have ingaged to do this Business and in my opinion they are the most proper Persons for this Jobb. this will effectually curb this Province, and all the Troops that may be sent here —

As the Messenger to carry this Letter has been waiting some time with impatience must conclude by Subscribing myself Gentlemen your most Obed^t humble Servt

J Brown

To Mess
    Saml Adams } Comittee of Correspondence
    Doct^r Jo^s Warren &^{ce} } in Boston

I am this Minute informed that Mr Carleton has ordered that no wheat go out of the River untill further Order, the Design is Obvious —

Boston april the 6th 1775

Sr

I have let Fort Hallifax with all the land adjoining to it to mr Ephraim Ballard the Bearer of this   I ask your Countenance, favour and advice to him and that you will Introduce him into the premissis and give him all other assistance in your power which will oblige your very humble Servant

      Signed Silvester Gardiner

To Doctr John McLeeline
 at Fort Hallifax
  per Mr Ballard

Letter from the Selectmen of Falmouth.   April 26, 1775.

Falmouth April 26th 1775

Gentn

At this Alarming and Dangerous Time, we find our Stock of Powder, greatly deficient, therefore have sent some Money by the Bearers to purchase where they can find it, and if they cant find any this Side Cambridge, have desired them to wait upon You for Advice, presuming that you can direct them where it may be had.

We rely on Your Conduct, under God, in our Righteous Cause, for Deliverance from our present Calamities, and are, Gentlemen

Your Most Obedt huml Servts

Enoch Freeman	
Benja Mussey	Selectmen
John Brackett	of
William Owen	Falmouth

Postt the Bearers are Capta Joseph McLellan & Capt Joseph Noyes

Superscribed
To the Committee of Safety near Boston

Letter from H. Mowatt. 1775.
[To Edward Parry ?]

Canceaux Falmouth April 29 1775

Sir

I am just this moment informed that you are interrupted in your occupation by the misled people of the place where you are, I therefore think it incumbent on me as a Servant under the Crown, to warn those Infatuated people of the Consequences that will insue from the detaining or interfering with you, or any other of his Majesties Loyal subjects in their lawful avocations. & I do by the same Authority authorize you to make known to me without loss of time your present Situation, & the Names of those that have presumed to molest you. Should a reply to this Letter not appear by the time that I have a Right to expect it, I Shall Naturally Suppose that it has been interrupted, & you may depend, as soon as I know that to be the case, that assistance shall soon release you, or any other Subject whose treatment may furnish me with a just cause of Complaint. My best Compliments to Mr Barnard I hope he is not in the same predicament with yourself please to acquaint him that I Received his Letter, & that I have been in hourly expectations of seeing him for some days past I also hope to have the pleasure of Seeing you very soon. I am Sir
  Your most Obedient Humble Servant
          H: Mowat

Letter of Samuel Thompson.

I this minut have an opertunity to Informe you of the State of our affairs at the Eastward that we are all Stantch for Countys Except three men and one of them is Deserted the other two is in Ioins — as for the vessels which attemtd to Carrey Stuff to our enemies are Stopt and I am about to move about two hundred of white pine masts and other Stuff got for our Enemies use Si^r having heard of the Cruiel murders they have dun in our Province makes us more Reselute than ever and finding that the Sword is drawn first on their side that we shall be annimated with that noble Spirit that wise men ought to be untill our Just Rights and Libertys are Secured to us Si^r my heart is with everey tru Son of America thŏ my Person Can be in but one place at once. tho verey Soone I hope to be with you on the spot if aney of my Frinds enquier after me Informe them that I make it my whole business to persue those measurs Recomended by the Congresses. we being uppon the sea coast and in danger of Being invaded by Pirats as on the 27th of ins^t there was a boat or barge Came in to our harbour and Rver and sounding as they went up the River Si^r as powder and guns is much wanted in this Eastern Parts and allso Provisions Pray Sir have your thoughts Somthing on this matter against I arive which will be as Soone as busness will admit Si^r I am with the greatest Regard to the Countrey at heart your Ready frind and Hum^le Servt

           Samuel Thompson
Brunswick April ye 29th 1775

Letter from Brunswick. May 3^d 1775.

           Brunswick May 3^d 1775
Gentlemen

We, whose Names are hereunto Subscribed Beg Liberty to Inform You of our Situation, as we are Chosen by this Town to Examine into the Circumstance of it, which we have done, and find the Town very Deficient as to Arms & Amunition, and have Sent By Water to Salem, But have Just had Our Money Return'd Back Without Arms or Ammunition: at present we Have not More than one quarter of a pound of

powder to a man throughout the Town, nor more than one
firelock To two Men; and in this Defenceless State we are
Obliged to Apply to You to Assist Our Trusty friend whom
We have Sent Capt Nathaniel Larrybee: and as we think it
Would Be Unsafe to Transport Powder by Water we have
Ordered Him to Take Only one hundred weight and for him
to Consult With you how and in What way it Would be
Safest to Get Arms and more Powder Down To us. We
Should Esteem it as A favour, to be informed from You, by
way of Letter, Every Conveniant Oppertunity of Our Publick
Affairs. We are, Gentlemen, Yours, Ever to Be Commanded
        Aaron Hinkley
        Benj^a Stone
        Sam^{ll} Standwood
        James Curtis

Extracts from Letter of Hon. Enoch Freeman. May 5, 1775.

Extract of a Letter from The Hon^{bl} Enoch Freeman dated
   Falmouth May 5, 1775 —

"We have lately heard that the Penobscott Indians are
highly exasparated at Capt Goldthwaite for suffering the
Tender to dismantle the Fort there, and carrying off the
Powder; and Truck Trade stoped, as we are inform'd; and
that there was a Number of Men round about there, going to
take Goldthwaite for delivering up the Fort, into their Custody, but what they intend to do with him I don't hear.
Perhaps it would be prudent for the Congress to send down
there, and secure the Indians in our Interest, by keeping the
Truck Trade open, supplying them Powder, or any other
Method in their Wisdom, upon mature Consideration they
may think best — A hint on this Head is enough" ——

"The Selectmen of this Town have this moment agreed with one Mr Jabez Matthews and one David Dinsmore of New Glocester to go over to Quebec to make Discovery, whether any Canadians are in motion to come on our back Settlements, or to excite the Indians to do it; And I have wrote to Mr Remington Holby of Vassalborough, to procure one or two to go with them as Hunters; And they are charged to be cautious not to let the Canadians have Reason so much as to suspect their Business, and they will depend on your endeavouring to get the Congress to order them adequate Satisfaction out of the Public Fund. If they discover any evil Designs, we shall be glad to know it, that We may prepare accordingly for our Defence: If they find there is no Design upon us, it will be a great satisfaction to this Eastern Country —

"I could write a good deal in favour of sending such an Embassy, but as my Time is almost wholly taken up on Public Matters, I have little Time to spare."

Attest   Saml Freeman

In Provincial Congress — Watertown May 5th 1775

On a motion made by Capt McCobb, That some measures might be taken to preserve a Number of large Masts, Plank &c now lying in Kennebeck River, and to prevent their being carried to Hallifax where they must be appropriated to the Injury of this Country —

Order'd — That the Consideration thereof be refer'd to the Committee of Safety, and that Cap McCobb be desired to attend the said Committee, and give them all the information He can relative thereto —

A true extract from the minutes

Saml Freeman Secr^y P. T.

Letter from Dummer Sewall   1775.

Georgetown May 6th 1775

To the Honnorable Congress of the Province of the Macechusetts Bay, Gen^t — The Committees of Inspection of Georgetown Woolwich have Mett & Resolved that it was not Expediant to moove the Masts lying in the Dock in Georgetown that Edward Perry Esqr had Contracted for, inasmuch as he Declared he would not Ship said Masts nor hew them — The Committee of Safety from two Towns in the County of Lincoln Met & Resolved that it was not Expediant to Moove said Masts or Injury Edward Perry Esqr — Notwithstanding Col^o Thomson of Brunswick thought otherwise, and hath taken said Perry Prisoner, & Declar'd he would Moove the Masts or Destroy them, so that the said Perry was Obliged to get Bondsmen of two Thousand Pounds that he would not Depart Georgetown or Ship s^d Masts by himself or any other or write to any officer in the Navy or Army till the Will & Pleasure of the Congress should be made known to Messrs Dum^r Sewall & Jordan Parker who a_ Bound for s^d Perry; he the s^d Col^o Obliged the said Perry to pay 42/ Cost — I therefore Humbly Pray that your Will may be made known to the said Dummer & Jorden, as soon as may be that the said Perry may be releieded & the Bondsmen Liberated their large Bonds —

I am your Honnours Harty Freind & Humble Servent

Dum^r Sewall

Superscribed

To the Honnourable President of Provintial Congress.

Letter from Edwd Parry.   1775.

George Town May 10th 1775

Sir

I am very much obliged to you for your kind Letter of the

29th ult. p̱ Lambert, which was interupted and demanded with my other Letters &c at Brunswick by Samuel Thompson of that place and broke open, Copies of which have been industriously circulated thro' the Country by the different Committee men &c, several parts thereof being misconstrued or misunderstood by the illiterate — I should have answered your Letter sooner but did not know how to procure any safe conveyance — On the 4th inst Thompson attended by a number of Armed Men to the Amount of Forty or upwards insisted on my being his Prisoner, and to go with him; or give Bail Bond with two Securities in Penal Sum of £2000 payable to the Provincial Congress, the condition of the Bond compelled to be given, is that I should be kept in safe Custody by my Sureties, until released by the Congress — that I should not nor no one for or under me remove my Masts, Plank &c now here, nor write to any Officer of the Army or Navy for Protection, or against the Country — I prefer'd giving the Bond rather than to risk myself with them — A State of my Case has been sent to the Congress, who I hope will think it reasonable to release me; but such is the unfortunate Temper of the Times, that I am Apprehensive I shall be unable to proceed with my Business and fulfill my Engagements for Halifax Yard for the present and I think it will be extremely hazardous for some time to attempt it unless affairs take a Sudden Turn

 I am with great Respect Sir your oblig^d & most obed^t Hle
   Servant

        Edwd Parry

Mr Bernard is also under Bond, and in the same Situation.

There are some Reports spread here of an attempt to Surprize the Cançeaux

To Henry Mowatt Esqr Commander of His Majesty's Ship
 the Cançeaux

Letter from Edwd Parry. 1775

George Town Kennebec May 10th 1775

William Tyng Esqr Dear Sir

I reced your favor of the 29th April by Lambert which was intercepted by Thompson and broke open with my other Letters — I should have answered Capt Mowats kind Letter, but did not know how to convey it sooner, I beg you will deliver him the inclosed — I suppose you have heard of my being in Thompson's Clutches The Letter to Capt Mowat mentions the particulars — my best Complim^{ts} to Mrs Tyng & Mrs Ross &c— May God Send us peace and Good order again—

I am with great Respect Dear Sir your oblig^d & assured friend & humble serv^t

Edwd Parry

fav^d by Mr Ayers of Portsm^o

George Town Kennebec River May 10th 1775

Sir

I beg leave to lay before you that Mr Samuel Thompson of Brunswick one of the Delegates of your Congress has attended by about Forty or upwards of His Minute Men &c Armed, restrained me from following my lawful Occupation, and has detained me here, and compelled a Bond to be given the 4th instant with two securities for me in the penal Sum of £2,000 lawful money payable to you or the Heads of the Province for the time being that may be appointed by the People — The Condition of the Bond prevents me or any Person for or under me from removing certain Masts, Spars, Oak Plank &c that are now under my care in this River and procured for the Service of His Majesty's Navy — and that I should be kept in safe Custody here until I may be released by your Orders — he has also required that I shall not write to any Officer of the Army or Navy for Protection — He Grounds his pretences for these Violences to me by a Resolve of your Body (as he says) passed the beginning of April — The Subject matter of which as near as I can recollect is — " That Col° Samuel Thompson be appointed to notify certain " Towns in the Eastward, that one Perry was gone down " thither to Ship Masts, Plank &c for the Dock Yard at Nova " Scotia, and that he and they should use all possible and " effectual means to prevent the same being done."—

And likewise the People &c I employ'd have been intimidated and influenced from carrying on their work to my great detriment by Persons who appear by their Conduct to place Reliance on your Approbation — I imagine you will not justify but disavow these injurious proceedings — and I expect you will order without delay the Bond to be cancelled and myself released from my present confinement

I am Sir your very humble Servant

Edwd Parry

To The President of the Delegates of the Province of the Massachusets Bay assembled in Congress at Concord

Letter from Falmouth Comm^{ee} of Correspondence to The Provincial Congress   May 14, 1775.

Falm° 14th May 1775

Hon^d Sir

the Committee of Correspond^{ce} in this Town beg leave to inform you that Some Time past we received Advice from George Town, that Col: Thompson was fitting Vessels there, with Design to attempt the taking the Kings Ship Canceaux stationed in this Harbour commanded by Capt Mowatt, a Gentleman, whose Conduct since he has been here, has given no Grounds of Suspicion, he had any Design to distress or injure us; but on the other hand, he has afforded his Assistance to sundry Vessels in Distress. As we thought such an Attempt had the Appearance of laying a Foundation for the Destruction of this Town, the Comittee of Correspondence met & wrote to the Comittee of Correspondence of George Town desiring they would prevent their Coming; we also wrote to Col: Thompson, desiring him to desist from such an attempt, as it would through the Town into the greatest Confusion imaginable: we sent an Express, & received his Answer, that he had dropt the Design of Coming —

But, on Monday night [May 10] he landed upwards of Sixty Men, on the Back side of a Neck of Land joyning to the Town, who came there in a Number of Boats, & lay undiscovered till about the middle of the Next Day; at which Time, Capt Mowatt, the Doctor of the Ship, & Parson Wiswall, were taking a Walk on said Neck, when a Detachment from Col: Thompson's Party rushed from their Concealment, surrounded the Gentlemen, & made them Prisoners, & conducted them to the Colonel, who was with the main Body, on the back Side of the Neck. Capt. Hog, who now commanded the Ship, immediately clapped Springs on his Cables. She laying within Musket Shott of the Town, & swore if the Gentlemen were not Releas'd by Six o Clock, he would fire on the Town. He fired two Canon, & although there were no Shott in them, it frightened the Women & Children to such a Degree, that some crawled under wharfs; some ran down Cellar, & some out of Town, Such a Shocking Scene was never presented to View here — The Gentlemen who were in Custody, were conducted to a publick House Where Capt Mowatt declared, if he was not released it would be the Destruction of the Town. Every Gentleman present used their Utmost Endeavours to accomodate the Matter. Col: Thompson consented that a Comittee should be chose,

consisting of Officers from his Party and Gentlemen from the
Town, to consult in what manner the affair could be accom͞-
odated; but, as it was late, the Com͞ittee chose to defer the
Consideration of it till next Morning. Capt Mowatt then
requested, he might go on Board his Ship that night & he
would pawn his Word & Honour, he would return next
Morning, at what Time, and at what place should be
appointed. Coll. Thompson consented, provided Coll Freeman & Brigadier Preble, would pass their Words, that the
several Gentlemen should return according to their Promise,
& also pawn their Word & Honour, if the Gentlemen fail'd
coming, that they would deliver themselves up, & stand by
the Consequences, which was consented to. Capt Mowatt
not coming according to Promise, which was to have been at
Nine o Clock the next Morning, the Sponsors appeared
according to Promise, & were confined. Capt Mowatt wrote
to them, & let them know he had fully determined to have
comply'd with his promise, but he had sent his man on Shoar
to carry some dirty Linen to his washing Woman & to bring
of some clean: that said man made Oath, that two of the
Body under Arms, one of which, swore by all that was sacred,
the moment he came on Shore he should have what was in
his Piece, and the other, that he should never return on
Board again with his Life: that two more of his men made
Oath, they heard several of the Men under Arms say, the
moment he came on Shore they would have his Life; this
was what he wrote to plead an Excuse for not complying
with his promise. Coll. Thompson told the two Gentlemen
under Confinement, that he must have some Provision &
Refreshment for his Men, which they procured, to the
Amount of thirteen or fourteen Pounds L Money; on which
they were dismised.— about ten o Clock, he sent an Account
to them for Time & Expence, amounting to 158..18 L M.
and gave them till next morning, nine o Clock, to return an

Answer; which they did, in the Negative, he said he would have Satisfaction before he left Town. He then seized all the Goods he could find belonging to Capt Coulson & Wm Tyng Esq. They also carried off one Boat belonging to Coulson, & one other to Capt Mowatt; they also obliged Capt Pote to furnish them with some Provision & a small Matter of Cash: they also brought one Man on his Knees, for speaking disrespectfully of the Coll. & his Men. Coll. Thompson, we doubt not, is a true Friend to his Country, & a Man of Courage & Resolution, but, as our Town lays so much exposed to the Navy, that, had he succeeded in his Attempt, (which there was not the least Probability of) it must have proved the Destruction of this Town & the Country back, who are in the greatest Distress for want of Provisions. We have only related plain Facts, that the Honourable Members of the Provincial Congress may not be imposed on with false Accounts, to whom Please to coṁunicate this Letter

 We are with Great Esteem Gent^n Your Most Obed^t Humb^l
  Serv^{ts}
   Jedidiah Preble Chairman

Letter from Col. Jedidiah Preble to The Comm^{ee} of Safety at Cambridge. May 15, 1775.

          Falm^o ye 15th May 1775
Honourable gentlemen

 These wait on you by Colonel Phinney who brought all the Papers necessary for Inlisting a Regiment in the County of Cumberland, I advised with the Committee of Correspondence, who are of opinion it would be difficult for our County To spare a Regiment to be moved out of the Province, of Maine, as we Lay much Exposed to the Navy by sea & the

Indians and french on our Back Settlements if they should be Employed against us, but Should be glad to do Every thing in our Power for the defence of our Just Rights and Dearer liberties, our men are Zealous in the cause of their Country, and ready to venture Every thing for the defence of it, Colonel March informs me your Honours had appointed him a Colonel and gave him orders to Raise a Regiment in this County, and to Appoint all his officers, this he Acquainted me with after I had Delivered Colonel Phinney the papers back again, which he brought to me, it is impossible we can spare two Regiments out of this County, & they have both made Considerable Progress, am much afraid there will be some Difficulty in settling the affair, I am persuaded the men in general would prefer Col^n Phinney and so should I for that Reason, as I look on Colonel Phinney to be Equal To Colonel March in Every Respect —

Should have done my self the Honour to have waited on you in person, but am still in a poor state of health, and so Exercised with the gout, that I Cannot ware my Shoes I purpose to visit the Camp When Ever I am able to undergo the fatigue of so long a Journey, I wish Courage and Conduct in our officers, Resolution and a spirit of obedience in our soldiery, and a Speedy End of all our Troubles — I am your Honours most obedient Humble serv^t

Jedidiah Preble

Letter to the Eastern Indians. May 15, 1775.

In Provincial Congress Watertown May 15, 1775
Friends & good Brothers

We the Delegates of the Colony of the Massachusetts Bay, being come togeather in Congress to consider what may be best for you & ourselves, to get rid of the Slavery designed to be brought upon us have thought it our duty to write you the folowing Letter —

Brothers, the great wickedness of such as should be our friends but are our enemies, we mean the ministry of great Britain, have laid deep plots to take away our liberty & your liberty, they want to get all our money, make us pay it to them when they never earnt it, to make you & us their servants & let us have nothing to eat, drink or ware but what they say we shall, and prevent us from having guns & powder to use and kill our Dear and wolves & other game, or to send to you for you to kill your game with and to get skins & fur to trade with us for what you want But we hope soon to be able to supply you with both guns & Powder of our own making.

We have petitioned England for you & us and told them plainly, we want nothing but our own & dont want to hurt them, but they wont hear us and have sent over great Ships & their men with guns to make us give up and kill us, and have killed some of our men, but we have drove them back & beat them, & killed a great many of their men — The Englishmen of all the Colonies from Nova scotia to georgia have firmly resolved to stand togeather and oppose them: — our liberty & your liberty is the same, we are Brothers and what is for our good is for your good. And we by standing togeather shall make them wicked men afraid & overcome them and all be free men — Capt Golthwait has given up Fort Pownall into the hands of our enemies. We are angry at it & we hear you are angry with him & we dont wonder at it — we want to know what you our good Brothers want from us of Cloathing or warlike stores & we will Supply you as fast as we can. we will do all for you we can & fight to save you any time & hope none of your men or the Indians in Canada will join with our enemies. you may have a great deal of good influence on them.— our good brothers the

Indians at Stockbridge all join with us & some of their men have listed as Soldiers & we have given them that listed each one a Blankit & a Ribbond & they will be paid when they are from home in the Service and if any of you are willing to list we will do the same for you.—

We have Sent Captain John Lane to you for that purpose and he will show you his orders for raising one Company of your men to join with us in the war with your & our Enemies.

Brothers we humbly beseach that God who lives above, and that does what is right here below to be your friend & bless you to prevent the designs of those wicked men from hurting you or us.

Brothers If you will let Mr John Prebble know what Things you Want He will take Care to inform us and we will do the best for you that we can.

Passed

Ord. to be authenticated & sent forward.

Cambridge May 20th 1775

Honble Genl Prebble   Sir

This Committee received your favour of the 15th Instant, touching this Colony & note your Just Observations on the Subject —

The Committee, after the Resolutions of the Congress for Establishing an Army of 13600 Men, thought the exigencies of the Times & the exposed Situation of the several Towns near Boston, made it absolutely necessary that the Army should be immediately raised, & that for the facilitating of this important Business it was Expedient that orders should be issued to such Men as are Recommended as proper persons for such important trusts. Accordingly, orders were issued to as many Col^s as were sufficient to Complete said Army: but from the Delay which appeared in the Army's being formed, by the slow progress made in the inlisting Men, & the Exposed Situation of the Colony Camp by the going off of numbers from time to time, it was rendered necessary, that further orders should be issued for completing the Army with all possible speed, & in consequence of that determenation, among others, Col. March received orders for the inlisting of a Regiment for the Service of this Colony, &, we understand, has made some considerable Progress in enlisting Men for said Service: We are also informed by your Honour that Col. Phinney has received enlisting Orders from you, & has engaged in the Business of enlisting Men to complete a Regiment, and we are further Informed by your Honour that it is impracticable that two Regiments should be raised in the County of Cumberland, & being told by Col. Phinney, that many of the Men that would be raised in your County could not be supplied by the Town from which they are enlisted with fire Arms & Blankets, this Committee taking into Consideration the exposed Situation of your County & the probability of the Armys being Completed without drawing Men from those parts of the Colony which are more immediately exposed, would Recommend, Sir that you would use your influence that a stop be put to the raising any Men in your County until it may be known by the returns from the Several colonels authorized for the raising Regiments wether it may be necessary to take any Men from your County, and should this necessaty take place this Committee will endeavour to give your such early Intelligence as may be necessary. The Request of this Committee to your Honour, we flatter ourselves will not be conceived by you as carrying in it the least disrespect to Col: March or Col: Phinney, but solely from the probability of the Armys being Compleat without taking Men from those parts of the Colony which are more immediately exposed. We should be glad to see your Honour at Head Quarters, which we hope your health will soon admit, & with you we Join in the hope of soon seeing a speedy end to the great Difficulties this distressed Colony now Labours under — We are, Sir with the great_ Respect, your Honors Humble Servants

P. S. please to Inform the within mentioned Colonels of this determination y^{rs} &c

Letter from Abiel Wood to the Comm^{ee} for the County of Lincoln. May 22^d 1775.

Pownalboro. May 22^d 1775

Gentlemen

I am Informed you are to meet Tusday or wednsday and that there is Sum matters to be alledged against me I should - Don my Self the honour as to wated On you but am Obleaged to proceed to the Southward in my Sloop In order to Git In Sum Corn and Porke Before the first of July and One Days Delay may be attended with the Loss of my Vessell and Cargoe —

You may be asured that I Ever have ben Determin^d to Abide by the Result of the Continentall Congress and have Sufferd more then Three Hundred pounds Starling by Countermanding my order for Goods and Ships. it is true I Ever Disaproved of the Destruction of the Tea and maney Resolves of the provential Congress But I never had aney thing In harte but the Good of my Country and I am now Convinced that the Salvation of my Country Depends On Our Fermly Uniting and I am Determind to Stand by my Country so Long as I have Life and one Farthing of Interest In it. if it appears that I have Dun or Said aney thing unfrindly To the Country You Will I hope Impute it to Error In Judgment and not Designed and Over Look it and I shall make amends by my future Conduct —

I am Very Respectfully Your Humble Se^{rt}

Abiel Wood

Boothbay May 23ᵈ 1775

Sir

Pursuant to the order of Congress, & in compliance with the request of the Committee of the County of Lincoln, we have the honor to inform you that the town of Boothbay has not beheld with indifference the important contest between tyranny & patriotism at this Memorable Era: firmly attached to the cause of this injured country which they cannot but consider as the cause of virtue — of religion — & of God, their heart & hand has been ever ready — devoted to its defence:

Conscious of their obscurity & insignificance they have forborne taking any public part in the wise & laudable measures so generally adopted for redress of grievances, which the soul of slavery alone could endure: — they have not however been negligent of the means in their power, of co-operating with their brethren, in conducting their internal police at home: —

When the tea act took place they recorded some rational & spirited resolves, unanimously passed in town-meeting — suspended the use of that baneful herb — & all commerce with such as withdrew from the useful non-importation agreement.

In July 1774 they generally adopted a non-consumption covenant, but little different from the printed formula & chearf^{ly} bound themselves to abide the results of the Continental & provincial Congresses — in March 1775 they drew up a number of resolves, in which a steady & persevering exertion of all their powers, in support of the measures directed by both those august bodies, was unanimously engaged: Committees of Correspondence & Inspection were appointed, & the town stipulated to support them in the discharge of their trust at all hazards — & these Committees have sat on business once every week since their appointment; & no infringement of the orders of Congress is suffered within their bounds. — the officers of the Militia by request of the town, resigned their Commissions in March last — two Companies were erected, under officers then elected by the people : out of which, two Companies of minute-men have been since drawn : — our little force is under arms once a week — the Minute Companies often[r] — & have made no inconsiderable improvements in the military exercises : — a guard of ten men is established in the several parts of the town — besides four appointed for centries at a public store resolved on : a plan for provision & defence has been concluded on, & voted : a Committee of Safety appointed : — & the delegate newly chosen to attend Congress, directed immediately to pay into the hands of Henry Gardner Esq[r] receiver general 14£-6[s]-7[d] lawf : being the total of their Province-tax for the year 1774

They reflect with pain on their having paid the whole of the Province rates of the two foregoing years, to the public traitor formerly at the head of the treasury — but the recollection that it was done in April 1774 is some alleviation of this grief : —

They have Voted to indemnify their Constables for collecting & paying whatever — town — county — or Province rates it may be necessary to raise during the unsettled state of this Colony — they are cordially disposed to lend their best aid to their distressed Country in all respects — & firmly determined to part with their liberties only at the price of their possessions & lives.

We have the honor to be, with the greatest respect Sir, your most obedient & very humble Servants

the Committee of Correspond[ce]

Signed in behalf, & p[r] order : John Beath Secr[y]

To m[r] Dummer Sewal
in behalf of the County Com[ee]

Superscribed :
On public Service To M[r] Dummer Sewall In behalf of the County Committee at Georgetown

Letter from Partridgefield to the Provincial Congress.
May 27, 1775.

To the Honourable the Provincial Congress held at Watertown

Gentlemen: The Select Men of the Town of Partridgefield having Received a Message from the Provincial Congress Dated at Concord March ye 31st 1775 Requiring the Speedy Payment of Some Money to Henry Gardiner Esqr of Stow: They Immediately warned a Town Meeting: And the Inhabitants being Assembled and taking into Consideration the Present Circumstances of the Town: they Unanimously Voted: that Considering the Present Circumstances of the Town they were not Able to Pay the tax Required of them by the Provincial Congress: And Also Voted that the Town Clerk Should write to the Congress and give them Some Information Concerning the Present Circumstances of the Town. A Specimen of which is as follows Viz

This Town is but New and but few People in it And the Generality of them Are People of Low Fortunes And it is not Long since we were at Great Expense (for us) in Setling A Minister in the Town. And as our farms are mostly New And our Land not Quick to Produce A Crop; we are Obliged Every year to buy A Great Part of our Provision: And this Year Especially As the Blast and Vermin Destroyed A Great Part of our Grain the Last Year; We have no Town Stock of Ammunition Nor Do we know how to Procure it. As all the money we Can Get must Go to Purchase the Necessaries of Life. I Am Apt to think there is As many men Gone And going from this town in Defence of the Liberties And Previliges of America As from Any Town in this Province if not more; According to the Number of People in this and the other Towns. And we would be As free with our money as with our Men if we had it And Could Possibly Spare it.

The taxes which the Great And General Court of this Province Was Pleased to Lay Upon this Town We Petitioned to be Releived of And not Altogether without Success And we hope the Congress will be Graciously Pleased to Excuse Us for not Complying with their Requirments when it was not in our Power to do it

Signed in the Name And in Behalf of the Town Partridgefield May ye 27th 1775

                        Nathaniel Stowell Town Clerk

Letter from Wm Shirriff D. Q. M. G. 1775.

                        Boston 29th May 1775

Dear Sir

I have received your obliging favor, and return you many thankes for the trouble you have taken, and readiness you have shewn in giving your Assistance so Necessary at present for the good of the service. The Hay will be most Acceptable and I am in hopes Captain Princes Vessel has taken a part on Board As he promised me he should return immediately, and I will send you another one, as soon as possible I shall want three or four Thousand Tons of Hay and I wish with all my heart poor Annapolis could furnish it — but all it can furnish I will take, and if they are Industrious they may get a great deal of Money for their Vegetables Poultry Butter Eggs &c. — And may come directly into this Port, without any expence whatever and will be sure to find every encouragement and Assistance that can be given them. On the Other hand if they give themselves Airs, and follow the Cursed example of these Mad Men they will Consider how easily Governm{t} can Chastise them, and they may rely upon it they will, and that immediately too — but I hope They will Consider Their Interests better and make all the Money they can. They never will have a fairer opportunity.

I have wrote to Messrs Day & Scott at Halifax respecting Forage, and have desired them to Consult with you about the Quantity that may be procured at Annapolis, as they are to furnish the Remainder from Windsor, & that Neighbourhood.

Procure Hay screws at any rate, and the whole should be carried to a particular place most convenient for that purpose as Also for Shiping of it — You have not Advised me in what manner I am to make you remittances, for Expenses to be incurred in the above Service, therefore shall expect it pr Next. We are in the same Situation As when wrote you last — except the addition of twelve hundred Troops lately arrived from England, The Regiment of Horse and Eight Other Regts are hourly expected — when I hope you will hear better Accounts from us. I am hurried to Death therefore have only time to add my Compts to all friends & to wish you every happiness being truely Dear Sir Your faithfull and Obedient Servant

Willm Shirreff

P. S If you can possibly add to the Quantity of Old Hay pray do and don't mind the Expence — W. S

Boston May 30th 1775

This Charter Party or Agreement made this Day between Majr William Sherriff Dy Qr Mr General, on the one part & Ephraim Perkins of the County of York in Cape porpus, on the other part.

Witnesseth that the said Perkins being Owner of the Sloop Molly himself Master, burthen about Eighty Eight Tuns Doth hereby Covenant and Agree, that the said Sloop shall proceed from this Harbour to Nova Scotia, and there take on Board such Laden, as shall be directed by the said Majr Wm

Sherriff & proceed Imediately back to this Port. Said Perkins Maning Victualing & paying all Charges of the Voyage.

In Consideration of which the Above said Maj^r Wm Sherriff, Doth promise to pay to the said Perkins for the Run or Voyage of said Vessell, One Hundred and Eighty Dollars, and Six Dollars p Day Demurrage if Detained longer then Ten Working Days at the Port where she Loads, and Six Days where She Delivers her Cargo —

For the true and faithfull performance of the above Agreement we each of us Bind our selves in the penal sum of five hundred pounds Sterling money of Great Brittian

In Witness hereunto we have sett our hands and Seals this Thirtyeth day of May in the Year of our Lord. 1775 —

  Witness   Willm Shirreff
Jos. Goldthwait   D Q M G   (Seal)

Letter from Wm Shirreff

Mr Epharim Perkins   S^r

You will emediately proceed with the Sloop Molly under y^r Command to Windsor in the Bay of Funda & Receeve Such orders As Mr Jones will give You Respecting your Cargo. Making every dispatch that^s Possible. taking Care to touch at No Other Harbour unless it be absolutely Necessary —

       Jos: Goldthwait
        for William Sherriff
Boston May 30. 1775   D Q^r M G^1

Letter from Wm Shirreff. 1775.

         Boston 30th May 1775
Gentlemen/

The bearer Mr Josiah Jones with the Sloop Polly Ephraim Perkins Master is Charterd for Windsor in Nova Scotia in order to Receive from you Hay, and Oats — Am therefore to desire you will use every endeavor to Dispatch him as soon as possible agreeable to my Letter wrote you via Halifax the 29th Ins^t

Please to forward the Inclosed by Express to Annapolis.

I am Gentlemen Your most Obedient humble Servant

Willm Shirreff

To Messrs Day & Scott at Windsor Nova Scotia

Letter from Winslow to the Comm^{ee} for the County of Lincoln. June 3, 1775.

The Committee of Correspondence for the Town of Winslow hereby represent to the Committee for the County of Lincoln, the following State of said Town, vizt

There are Forty-four Families in the Town; One Half of whom have neither Bread nor Meat, but are entirely supported by Fish —

Twenty Guns are wanted; and there is no Ammunition in Town, except in the Hands of Ezekiel Pattee Esqr

On Thursday the twenty fifth Day of May last, at a full Meeting, the Town unanimously voted to adhere to all the Resolves of the Continental and Provincial Congresses the Preservation of their Lives, Liberties and Privileges.

Winslow June 3, 1775.

Ezekiel Pattee
Jonah Crosby
Joseph Carter
John Tozer
Zimri Heywood

Comittee of Correspondence for Winslow

Account of taking a sloop belonging to Arundel. 1775.

To the honourable Congress of the Province of the Massachusetts Bay in New-England now sitting,— the Committee of the Town of Arundel in said Province Sendeth Greeting

Whereas, a Sloop belonging to the Town of Arundel about three Weeks ago, saild out of this Harbour, and disposed of her Cargo at Plymouth, and having receiv^d her Effects, upon her Return, was seiz^d and carried into Boston, and there detained by general Gage for sometime, and her Effects taken into his Custody for which he pay^d near the prime Cost:— After which a Proposal was made to the Master of said Sloop, by the Officers of the Troops to inlist into the Governours Service with a Promise of a large Reward for his Service therein:

The Master being now under Confinement and knowing no Means of obtaining his Liberty now tho't this Proposal the only way to make his Escape, and obtain his Liberty, and therefore comply^d with the same, and accordingly receiv^d Orders to sail immediately for Anapolis, to bring a Quantity of Hay, and other Stores for the Use of the Troops in Boston. A Number of the kings Arms with Cartridges, were put on Board and two Young Men one named Josiah Jones, and the other Jon^a Hicks were put on board, one or both of which as SuperCargo in the Above Imployment, with a Packet of Letters, Orders & other Papers.

The Master then being prepard to go out sailed directly for this Port and arrived in this Harbour the second instant, with the Persons Letters &c. as above mentioned; who were immediately carried before the Committee of this Town and after Examination of both it was agreed by the Committee and they have accordingly sent the Persons and Papers under Guard to this hon^{le} Provincial Congress now sitting for Examination and to be dealt with as they in their United Wisdom shall think just, The Master and Mate of said Sloop we have hereby sent by whom an account of the whole Affair will be given.

Arundel 3ᵈ June 1775

    Benjᵃ Durrell   ⎫
    James Burnham ⎬ Commitᵉᵉ
    Thoˢ Wiswall   ⎬ of Town
    Jonaᵗ Stone   ⎬ of Arundl
    John Hovey   ⎭

Letter from the Committee for Waldoborough to the Committee at Pownalborough. June 5, 1775.

Waldoborough June the 5ᵗʰ 1775

To James Howard Esqʳ and to the Rest of the Honnorable Committe appointed by the Honnorable Congress

Gentlemen We Recᵛᵈ a Letter from you to Know how affairs Stand in our town upon the Recpt of your Leter we Called a town meating and we Chose a Commitie to Corrospond with you Gentlemen and we Voted unanymusly to abide by the Continentinel and Provencel Congress and you Desireed to Know how affairs Stand Relating ⁔ our Provence tax Gentlemen We Voted to Colect the mony as sone as Possable and Convey the same when Collected to Mʳ Henry Garner treasurer for the Congress —

Gentlemen We Shall Endeavour to Meat on the days appointed and We Shall Let you Know from time to time all that is Worthy of Notice — We with all Submission

  We Remain your servents &c

  P S We the Commite are Chose to Colect the above mony

        Jabesh Cole
        Andrew Schemle
        David Vinall
        Jacob Wenigeburla
        William farnsworth
            a Comittee for Walldoborough

Letter from Penobscot to the Provincial Congress.
June 7, 1775.

Penobscot June 7, 1775 —

Gent^n

We, the Subscribers, being appointed a Committee by the Inhabitants settled on Penobscot River; the Inhabitants of Belfast; Majabigwaduce, & Benjamins River, to make a Representation to you of the difficulties & distress the said Inhabitants are under, in respect to the scarcity of Corn & Ammunition occasioned by the interruption of vessels, which they depended upon for their supplies & also the impediments in exportation from the Seaport Towns by inefficient committees after the said Articles have been purchased We accordingly herewith send you the votes of said Inhabitants pass'd by them at a general meeting on Tuesday the 6th day of June instant which we are to pray your consideration of, being encourag'd thereto from the many instances of fav^r & assistance which the province have heretofore afforded to this infant settlem^t and without some, at this time we have real cause to apprehend that these promising settlements may be broke up. We are further to assure you that the said Inhabitants are ready with their lives & all y^t they have, to support the cause which this country is engaged in, in defence of their liberties & priviledges; and will hold themselves in readiness for that purpose. The said Committee are also to inform you that it was represented at the said Meeting that the establishment of Fort pownall is nearly expired: That the Commander of the s^d Fort in obedience to the commands of the Govr deliverd to his order the Artillery & some Arms belonging to the s^d Fort: That he also delivered to our own inhabitants in the different parts of this vicinity upon their application some Arms & Ammunition; reserving only a small quantity of each for the use of the soldiers belonging to said Garrison, which occasions the said

Fort at this time to be very bare in those respects. We are
also to represent to you that the Town of Belfast is in want
of about a dozen stand of Arms which is not practicable to
be got here. All which we are enjoined to lay before you,
Gentlemen, who represent the province in this unhappy time;
& to pray you to take the same into your consideration &
give them such relief as upon mature deliberation you judge
expedient. We are in behalf of the said Inhabitants Gent^n
Your most hum^{ble} Serv^{ts}

      Tho. Goldthwait
      John
      Jonathan Buck
      Edm^d Mooers
      Benj^a Shute
      Oliver Crary

Petition of Edwd Parry 1775.

To The Hon'ble Provincial Congress of the Massachusets
Bay convened and Assembled at Watertown

The Petition of Edward Parry Agent to the Contractor for
Masts, Humbly Sheweth

That your Petitioner has been detained in his Occupation
of shipping a small quantity of Masts and Lumber he was
providing for his Majesty's Dock yard in Nova Scotia on the
beginning of May last at George Town in Kennebeck River
by Lieu^t Col^o Samuel Thompson of Brunswick, and two
Bonded Securities required in the penal Sum of £2,000
Lawful money, payable to the Provincial Congress or the
Heads of the Province for the time being that may be
appointed by the People. The Condition of the Bond prevents me or any Person for or under me from removing certain Masts, Spars, Oak plank &c that are now under my

Care in said River, and procured for the Service of his Majesty's Navy, and that I should be kept here in safe Custody until I may be released by the Hon'ble the Provincial Congress's orders — the particulars of which are fully explain'd in the said Bond, which I suppose Col° Thompson has before this deliver^d unto your Honors.

Your Petitioner humbly begs leave to represent to your Honors that his being detain^d here so long, at such a great distance from New Hampshire, the Place he has used to reside at, is of great detriment and damage to him, and that he daily suffers considerable loss in his private Concerns — Wherefore he humbly prays your Honors would take his Case into your wise Consideration, and that your Honors would compassionately be pleased to order him to be released and the Bond cancelled, or order such relief as you in your great Wisdom may think proper, and your Petitioner will ever pray &c

Edwd Parry

George Town Kennebec River June 8th 1775 —

Letter from John Lane   June 9, 1775

Fort Pownall June 9, 1775

Sir

I have proceeded agreeable to my orders as you'l see by the inclosed journal, and have got one of the Chiefs to go as an Ambassador attended by three young men as far as Falmouth and I am in hopes to be able to get them as far as Watertown. I couldn't have tho't that, that they'd been so hearty in the Cause, and are very ready to assist us if occasion requires, the Cannada Indians are all of the same mind. The Indians are now here and we shall go to Casco Bay to morrow when I shall write more fully.

I am Sir with Respect Your much oblig'd Servt

Jn° Lane

The Honble Jos. Warren Esq

Letter from Elihu Hewes.   June 9, 1775.

Sir

as I have had the Pleasure of being well acquainted with your Wisdom and unalterable Principles from the first Instant of your Publickly Ingaging in the Glorious Cause which you now so nobly lead on in the Defence off — Should your High Appointment and the Complicated situation of affairs under your Inspection & Direction make my Scrawl too minute for your Notice I shall not wonder. — As I now live on Penobscott-River, about 23 Miles above Fort Pownall; the Settlem^t very New, the first Man that Pitch'd in my Neighbourhood has not been there more than 5 Years, Tis True Capt Jona^n Buck began near 10 years ago, but he Lives not more than 8 Miles above the Fort. The Inhabitants being Setled for above 20 Miles above Him. I find this a Country very good for both Tillage & Grass tho at present Cloath'd with a fine Growth of Pine, Spruce, Cedar, Hemlock &c Intersperc'd with large Spots of Rock & white Maple, Birch, Beach &c and some Oak; The River excells for Fish of various kinds, and easie Navigation for the Largest of Vessells. — The People firmly Attach'd to the Constitution you Precide in the Defence off. And I am confident will Support it to the Last Moment of their Lives, being willing in general to encounter any Difficulty rather than yeald to that Band of Tyranny, whose Plodding Pates have long been Projecting Methods to Enslave us: I am confirm'd in this Opinion by an Anecdote or Two that has come to my knowledge since my residence on this River: for I Live in the Neighbourhood of Col^l Thomas Goldthwait who was a Member of our Assembly (as you may Remember) for many Years and particularly in the Year 1762. From whom I had the following Story. Richard Jackson Esqr was then Agent for our Province; The Col^l says that then, in some of His Private Letters which he Wrote after his Appointment, He intimated his Fears, that it would not be in his Power to do the Province much Service as there was a Principle prevailing in England at that Time to render the Colony Assemblys useless. The Colo¹ also says Mr Bollin (who was Agent before Mr Jackson) was continually warning the Gen^ll Court of this Principle then prevailing in England, and yet no doubt you remember, both those Gentlemen were turn'd out of the Agency upon a Suspicion that they were not in the Interest of the Province. Certainly they were faithful as touching the most important Matter whatever part of their Conduct might give Umbrage to their Constituants. And there seems to be some Degree of Semelarety in the Case of the Above Gentlemen & Colo¹ Goldthwait. For one of your Members viz Capt John Lane who is now here says the Congress had rec'd very unfavourable Acco^ts of the Colo^ls Conduct: Whereas on a fair and impartial Examination it will appear that Colo¹ Goldthwait has been a Steady Uniform Friend to our Constitution. Should the Almighty Prosper us so as to bring on an Accommodation. Among other Grievances I look on the Greenwich Hospital-Money exacted from our American Seamen, to be a very Capital one. I hope the Congress will Compassionate the Case of this Infant Settlement as we are not got to the years of Tillage and raesing our own Bread and Cloathing, & like to be Shut from the Previledge of Importing.

We could now Manufactor our own Cloathing, but are destitute of Woll & Flax which is a very Material Grievance. Pray excuse the want of Order in these Hints

From Hon^bl Sir your Hum^l Ser^t in Haste

           Elihu Hewes

Penobscott River 9 June 1775

 P S I have wrote by this Oppertunity to Joseph Hewes Esqr on the Continental Congress we are Brothers Children and were bro't up together in the same Family your Favour in forwarding is Pray'd by Sir &c

Here is an Island in the Mouth of this River, Own'd by Isaac Winslow Esqr as he Saith, which contains 6 or 7000 Acres, I first setled on it, there is 10 or 12 Families of Good Connecticut Men who are Hearty in our Cause and Should Hold what they have Taken in their Own Right, The Reste Should be Deemd Forfit this my Privat Opinion made known to none but you.

Superscribed

To Joseph Warren Esqr Precident of the Provincial Congress for the Massachusetts-Bay

p̱ Fav^r Capt Buck
private Lett^r

Deposition of Samuel Smith. 1775.

I the Subscriber Being of Lawful age Do Testify That Being in a Coasting Sloop belonging to Arundel and on my Return from Plimouth was taken by a Cutter Belonging to Admiral Graves Squadron in Boston & carried in to that Port & their Detain^d Several Day^s & Being Solliscited By Admiral Graves^s Secretary to Enter into His majestys Service and knowing no other way wherein I Could Possibly make my Escape I Enter^d into s^d service to Go to Winsor in Nova Scotia for Hay & other things, and Haveing one Josiah Jones Put on Board as factor and Being Ready to Sail I Desir^d of ye Capt of our Convoy Leave to Sail But He told me I must not Sail til to morrow att ten o : Clock as their was a Number other vesels in ye same Employ & Should all Sail together I then Desir^d Leave _ Mr Jones to Hall off into the Road & obtain^d Leav it being Dark & I Got Consent of our factor m^r Jones to Sail I therefore Embrac^d the oppertunity & Emmediatly Sail^d for Arundel where I arriv^d in about twenty four Ours and Deliver^d up m^r Jones & one Jon^a Hicks who was Intraduc^d on Board my Sloop By m^r Jones But for what Purpos I cannot tell. and further Saith that Mr Jones Desird Me to oil and Clean the fire arms that was Put on Board to Defend our selves as He said the Rebels might attak us on our Passage

Watertown June 9th 1775   Samuel Smith

Provincial Congress. 1775.

A List of Persons met at Concord in Provincial Congress.
p. 85.

Kittery	Charles Chancy Esqr
	Edward Cutt
Wells	Mr Ebenezer Sayer
Barwick	Capt Wm Gerish

p. 86.

Falmouth & Cape Elizabeth	Enoch Freeman Esqr
Scarborough	Mr Sam^ll March
North Yarmouth	Mr John Lewis
Gorham	Solomon Lombard Esqr
Brunswick	Capt Sam^ll Thomson

Deposition of Eben^r Whittier. 1775.

Ebenezer Whittier of lawful age testifies and declares that some time in april Last Abiel Wood merchant Recommended the Coasters for Carrying up Boards and timber to the troops that the said Wood Being asked why he Didnt carry timber to the troops Hee the said Wood said Becaus He was affraid of the People and aded it was time Now to throw of fear He had Lost thousands by fearing to Supply the troops and on being informed by the Deponant the provential Congress had forbid the Supplying the Regular troops He the said Wood Said the most of the Congrees ware Damn'd Villains Saying their was Handcock adams & others acteid out of Selfish Views in destroying the tea and being told by the Deponant m^r Handcock did Not destroy the tea the said Wood offered to Give His oath before any Justice of Peace that Mr Handcock was the first Man that went on Board the Vessell to destroy the tea and that the Devil had made them Beleive that one of them Should be king another a Govenor and that they Should Be in Some Great Places of Honor & profit & their Veiws was to Stir up the People to Sedition in order to accomplis their designs this was Spoke Concerning mr Handcock & the Provential Congress April 1775 that the said Wood Spake Disrespectfully of the method Recommended by the Provential Congress for Chusing officers and that the s^d Wood Reported for truth that the Govinour of New york & twelve towns in this & Connecticut province Had Voted Not to abid by the Result of the Continental Congress and their By Eudevered to Discourage the People of this parish from approveing the Same.

Ebenezer Whittier

Lincoln ss June 9, 1775 Then the said Eben^r Whittier made Oath to the above Writing by him subscribed

Before me Thos Rice Just. Peace

Report on Jones & Hicks

The Committee appointed to examine the persons and papers sent this Congress by the Committe of the Town of Arundel have attended that service and after due perusal of said papers Josiah Jones & Jonathan Hicks therein refered to were brought before them and said Jones in his defence says he had no concern with the sloop Polly otherways than as a passenger in her to Nova Scotia. — notwithstanding which it appears clearly to this Committee, by s^d Papers as also by the evidence of Capt Smith Master herewith transmitted, that s^d Jones went on board s^d Sloop as supercargo in the service of Gen. Gage to bring hay & other articles to Boston to supply our enemies. — We find by s^d Jones's account of himself that he went to Boston soon after the memoriable Lexington Battle of the 19 of April last in company with John Ruggles of Hardwick who was ordred by a Committee to the said Town of Hardwick and that said Jones was knowing to the proceedings of s^d Committee against s^d Ruggles before they set out together from Weston to take refuge in Boston, that they left the comon road & went in the woods & dificult places to pass the Town of Roxbury.— This Committee upon the whole have not the least reason to doubt of s^d Jones's being a Notorious enemy to his Country & of his having been employed in the actual imployment of our enemies against the Just liberties of the people therefore beg leave to report the folowing Order. —

     In Provincial Congress 10 June 1775

Ordered that Josiah Jones, taken from the sloop Polly be sent with a sufficent guard to the Town of Concord in the County of Midsx and committed to the comon Goal there to remain untill the further Order of Congress or house of Representatives of this Colony. —

Said Jonathan Hicks in his defence says that since the public disputes respecting the liberties of the Country he has not liked the part that has been acted, in many respects, on either side therefore could not see his way clear to join with any —

Upon examination the Committe find by evidence that at Gardnerstown, while he lived there, he expressed himself highly against Committees of correspondence &c calling them rebels & useing other oprobrious language against the people who appeared for liberty and endeavoured to hinder their unity That also while he the said Hicks lived at Plymouth he was esteemed by the good people there inimical to the liberties of his Country by his general conduct and that at certain times he appeared very high and once drew his sword or spear upon certain persons.

Said Hicks upon the whole owns his general conduct has been such as the people for liberty call a Tory, but still he says he is against the oppressive Acts. s^d Hicks confesses that the evening after the Battle of Lexington aforesaid he left Plymouth & took shelter with the troops at Marshfield not thinking himself safe in the Country, that he went with them to Boston & there remained untill he went on board the Sloop Polly with Jones & says he designed for Hallifax there to tarry if he could find business in order to be out of the noise. —

Capt Smith Master, of s^d Sloop can give no Account of Hick's business on board, all he can say is, he in general appeared inimical calling the liberty People rebels &c — The Committee therefore beg leave to report the following order

In Provincial Congress Watertown June 10, 1775

Ordred that Jonathan Hicks taken from the sloop Polly be sent with a sufficient Guard to the Town of Concord in the County of Middlesex & committed to the comon Goal there to remain untill the further orders of Congress or house of Representatives of this Colony. —

Letter from Elihu Hewes.   June 10, 1775.

Honble Sir

I expect my Letters sent by Capt Buck will reach you before Capt Lane, who will be Impeded with his Charge. I hope none will Rob him of the Honour he alone deserves (under the Smiles of Heaven) for the Success he has met with in his Tour up the River — I hope we shall have more of his Company if our Trouble continue. you cannot Send a Man that can Act more for the Service and Interest of His Country.

I dare not Ask a written Answers to this or mine by Buck but a few words will be Highly Acceptable to

    Sir your very Hum¹ Ser^t

           Elihu Hewes

Extract of a Letter from Hon. Enoch Freeman.

Extract of a Letter from the Hon^{bl} Enoch Freeman Esq

"You informed me that the last Provincial Congress, did me the Honour to choose me one of the Committee of Safety for the Province. You may acquaint that Committee, that, was my Health and Capacity equal to my Inclination to serve the Public, I should cheerfully attend that Service without delay, but at present I cant possibly go up — Yet if I can be of any Service to the common cause, in the mean time, in these exposed parts of the Country, my utmost endeavours shall not be wanting, and as soon as I can find myself able, purpose to come up —

It wou'd perhaps be convenient for the Public that some Person or Persons here, shou'd be appointed, whose business shou'd be to execute the Orders of the Congress and Committee of Safety, and to communicate back to them from Time to Time, Intelligences and Occurrences that may affect the Public, without the trouble of getting a Quorum of Committee, and Selectmen together, who live at a Distance, which often causes great delay, and my Time is so often taken up, on one public Affair and another, that I am obliged to neglect my own business to my great Damage —

If the Congress shou'd allow the Regiment raised here in this County to be stationed among us for our Defence, it will be necessary that some body shou'd have the Care of them, besides their own Officers, to employ them in such a manner as shall be most for the Safety of the whole —

In this Service, I think I might be of as much or more Service to the Public, than if I was to go up to the Committee, as the Gentlemen there, are more acquainted with the Circumstances of that part of the Province than I am, I shou'd be of the less advantage to them. and I presume I am more acquainted with this part of the Province, and with their concurrence, may be of more service to the Public here than there; for here, new Emergencies may and do often arise, which require immediate attention —

I heard to Day, that lately there were a number of Indians of Androscoggin River consulting what Side to take, but could not agree among themselves. 'Tis Pity but some body here shou'd be employed to negotiate with them or any other Indians as opportunity shou'd offer —

A Man from Deer Island, near Penobscott, was here this afternoon, and gives a melancholy Account of the Distress the People are in that way for want of Bread owing to the stoppage of Trade — He heard that several Children had died of Hunger — What will become of them God only knows, we are not able to help them or our selves — I Dont know what can be done for them or us without some Vessel of Superior Force to the Tenders shou'd be provided to bring Bread kind among us — I just now heard that Cap John Cox was taken on his Passage to New York, with Spars, and carried into Boston —

Account of the Capture of the King's Cutter at Machias.
June 14, 1775.

"To the Honorable Congress of the Massachusetts' Bay."—

"Gentlemen We, the faithful & distressed inhabitants of Machias, beg leave, once more, in the most respectful manner, to approach your presence, & spread before you a just and full representation of our very critical situation.

On the 2^d instant Capt Ichabod Jones arrived in this River with two sloops, accompanied with one of the Kings Tenders: On the 3^d instant a paper was handed about for the people to sign, as a prerequisite to their obtaining any provision, of which we were in great want. The contents of this paper, required the signers to indulge Capt Jones in carrying Lumber to Boston, & to protect him and his property, at all events: But, unhappily, for him, if not for us, it soon expired after producing effects directly contrary in their nature to those intended. The next effort, in order to carry those favourite points, was to call a meeting, which was accordingly done. On the 6th the people generally assembled at the place appointed, and seemed so averse to the measures proposed, that Capt. Jones privately went to the Tender, & caused her to move up so near the Town that her Guns would reach the Houses, & put springs upon her Cables,— The people, however, not knowing what was done, and considering themselves nearly as prisoners of war, in the hands of the common enemy, (which is our only plea for suffering Capt Jones to carry any Lumber to Boston, since your Honors conceived it improper) passed a Vote, that Capt Jones might proceed in his Business as usual without molestation, that they would purchase the provision he brought into the place, and pay him according to Contract.—

After obtaining this Vote, Capt Jones immediately ordered his Vessels to the Wharf & distributed his provisions among those only, who voted in favour of his carrying Lumber to

Boston. This gave such offence to the aggrieved party, that they determined to take Capt Jones, if possible, & put a final stop to his supplying the Kings troops with any thing: Accordingly, they secretly invited the people of Mispecka & Pleasant River to join them; accordingly a number of them came & having joined our people, in the woods near the settlement; on the 11th They all agreed to take Capt Jones & Stephen Jones Esqr in the place of Worship, which they attempted, but Capt Jones made his escape into the woods, and does not yet appear, Stephen Jones Esqr only, was taken, & remains, as yet, under guard. The Capt & Lieutenant of the Tender, were also in the Meeting House, & fled to their Vessell, hoisted their flag, & sent a Message on shore to this effect: "That he had express orders to protect Capt Jones; that he was determined to do his duty whilst he had life; & that, if the people presumed to stop Capt Jones's vessells, he would burn the Town." Upon this, a party of our men went directly to stripping the sloop that lay at the wharf, and another party went off to take possession of the other sloop which lay below & brought her up nigh a Wharf, and anchored her in the stream. The tender did not fire, but weighed her anchors as privately as possible, and in the dusk of the evening fell down & came to, within Musket shott of the sloop, which obliged our people to slip their Cable & run the sloop aground. In the mean time, a considerable number of our people went down in boats and canoes, lined the shore directly opposite to the Tender, and having demanded her to surrender to America, received for answer, "fire and be damn'd:" they immediately fired in upon her, which she returned, and a smart engagement ensued. The Tender, at last, sliped her Cable and fell down to a small sloop, commanded by Cap.: —— Toby, and lashed herself to her for the remainder of the night. In the morning of the 12th They took Capt Toby out of his vessell, for a pilot, & made all the sail they could to get off, as the wind & tide favoured; but having carried away her main boom, and meeting with a sloop from the Bay of Fundy, they came to, robbed the sloop of her boom & gaff, took almost all her provision, together with Mr Robert Avery of Norwich in Connecticut, and proceeded on her voyage. Our people, seeing her go off in the morning determined to follow her. About forty men, armed with guns, swords, axes, & pitch forks, went in Capt Jones's sloop, under the command of Capt Jeremiah OBrian: about Twenty, armed in the same manner, & under the command of Capt Benjamin Foster, went in a small Schooner. During the Chase, our people built them breast works of pine boards, and any thing they could find in the Vessells, that would screen them from the enemy's fire. The Tender, upon the first appearance of our people, cut her boats from the stern, & made all the sail she could — but being a very dull sailor, they soon came up with her, and a most obstinate engagement ensued, both sides being determined to conquer or die: but the Tender was obliged to yield, her Captain was wounded in the breast with two balls, of which wounds he died next morning: poor Mr Avery was killed, and one of the marines, and five wounded. Only one of our men was killed and six wounded, one of which is since dead of his wounds.

The Battle was fought at the entrance of our harbour, & lasted for over the space of one hour. We have in our possession, four double fortifyed three pounders, & fourteen swivels, and a number of small arms, which we took with the Tender, besides a very small quantity of ammunition &c. Thus we have given your honors, as particular an account of this affair as possible. We now apply to you for advice, and for a supply of Ammunition & provisions (the latter of which we have petitioned your honors for already) which if we could be fully supply'd with we doubt not but with the blessing of Heaven we should be prepared to defend our selves. — We propose to convey the prisoners to Pownalborough Goal, as soon as possible, there to await your orders. We are, with deference, your Honors most Obedient Humble Servants —

By order of the Committee   Ja^s Lyon Chairman
Machias June 14th 1775   George Stillman Cler

Letter from Jedidiah Preble & Enoch Freeman.
June 14, 1775.

Falmouth June 14, 1775

Hon^d Sir

These wait on you by Collonel Phiney, who informs Us, he has order'd the Men lately inlisted in this County, to Guard the Sea Coasts, and Islands within said County, to secure the Cattle and Sheep from the Ravages of Cruisers from the Navy; But, as no provision is made for their subsistance, it cant be expected, they can continue to do duty without. We refer you to Collonel Phiney for particulars

Four Indian Chiefs ariv'd here this day, with Captain Lane, from the Penobscut Tribe. We hope their expectations will be answer'd, which will lay a foundation for the securing to Our interest the whole Tribe.—

We are, Honour'd Sir, Your most obedient humble Servants

Jedidiah Preble
Enoch Freeman

Hon^{bl} Joseph Warren, Esqr to be communicated

"*Letter from the Com^{tee} of Machias relative to fitting out an Arm'd Vessel — & Report thereon accepted.*"
June 17, 1775.

To the Honorable Congress of the Massachusetts Bay

Gentlemen, Since the express left this, by whom we transmitted an account of the taking of the Margeritta, one of the Kings Tenders, we have discovered, upon examining the Papers, that both Capt. Jones^s Sloops, of about 70 Tuns each, were, in the Kings service. And as the People are now obliged to provide for their own safety, in the best manner possible, the Committee of Safety have resolved, with the utmost expedition, to arm one of s^d Sloops, & to act only on the defensive.

We are deeply sensible of our own weakness & danger; & with becoming deference, we once more apply to your Honors for advice & support, if we are judged worthy of your Notice.

We are Gentlemen very respectfully &c

Machias June 17, 1775   Ja^s Lyon Ch. M.
    Mr Fox   Mr Lothrop
    Mr Woodbridge   Mr Johnson of Lynn

   In Provincial Congress Watertown July 7, 1775.

The Committee appointed to take into consideration a Letter from the Committee of Safety for the Town of Machias Relative to fitting an armed Sloop to act on the Defensive and to Report thereon Do Report in manner following (viz)

Resolved, that when and so soon as the Committee of Safety for said Town of Machias Shall have fitted and armed a Sloop for their Defence and Security and have procured a proper Person to Command Said Sloop and a Sufficient Number of hands to Man her and Shall Send the Name of such person to this Congress; then this Congress will Commission such a person to Take the Command of Said Sloop and to act on the Defensive for the Security and Defence of said Town of Machias.

Answer to Petition from Belfast, &c. 1775.

In Provincial Congress Watertown June 23 1775

On the Petition of a number of the Inhabitants settled on Penobscot River; the Inhabitants of Belfast, Majabigwaduce,

& Benjamin's River representing the difficulties & Distress said Inhabitants are under in respect of the scarcity of Corn & Ammunition, and praying for some Relief —

Resolved, That it be recommended by this Congress, to the Committees of safety, of the Towns of Glocester or Newbury-Port or to the like Committees of Safety or Correspondence of any other Towns within this Colony, to supply Capt Jonathan Buck one of the Petitioners, for the Use of s^d Inhabitants for their present Relief, with two Hundred Bushels of Indian Corn, or to that amount in Corn & Rye, and take in Return for the same Cordwood or such other payment as the said Buck may be able to make or His Security thear for and in Case the said Buck shall not make satisfaction for the same in a reasonable Time, it shall be allowed & paid out of the publick Treasury of this Colony and the said Buck shall refund the same as soon as may be and that Coll Goldthwait deliver up all the publick Arms & Ammunition in his possession to the petitioners or a Committee Appointed by them for that purpose —

And as to Powder they shall be Reasonably Supplyed therewith as Soon as the State of our magesen will admitt thereof

Receipt. 1775.

Dear Island June 23 1775

Received of Nathaniel Low Fourteen pounds Eleven Shillings and Two pence Lawful Money in Pertatas Solt Lead and hooks and Lines. Which We the Subscribers promise to pay the Above to the Provenchel Congress in Lumber As Soon as the Ports are Opned And We Can Sell Our Lumber

      Francis Haskell Samell Ruynels
      Josiah Crockett Nathan Dow
      Robert Nason   Courtney Babbidg
      Thomas Thompson

Report on John Lane's Account. 1775.

In provincial Congress June 23 1775

The Committee for examining the Account of Mr John Lane having attended that service found the said Lane's account well supported excepting a few inaccuracies in casting They therefore beg leave to report by way of Resolve viz.

Resolved that there be paid out of the publick Treasury of this Colony to Mr John Lane, the sum of forty four pounds eighteen shillings & eleven pence ½ for his expences in bringing to the Congress four of the Chiefs of the penobscott tribe of Indians, with an Interpreter & the Receiver General of this Colony is hereby directed to pay the said John Lane or order the afores^d sum of Forty seven pounds Eighteen shillings & 11^d ½

Accepted June 23

Resolve. 1775.

In provincial Congress June 23^d 1775

Resolved that there be paid out of the publick Treasury of this Colony to Mr John Lane or order the sum of nineteen pounds ten shillings & eight pence to pay the expenses of himself four Indian Chiefs & an interpreter from Watertown to Penobscott. And the Receiver General is hereby directed to pay the same sum accordingly.

Accepted

Resolve. 1775.

The Committee appointed to take into Consideration the petition from Mechias beg leave to report by way of resolve as follows

In provincial Congress Watertown June 26th 1775

Resolved, that the thanks of this Congress be and it is

hereby given to Capt Jeremiah Obrian and Capt Benjamin Foster and the other brave men under their command for their Courage & good conduct in taking one of the tenders belonging to our enemies, and two sloops belonging to Ichabod Jones; and for preventing the minesterial troops being supplied with lumber — And that the said tender, Sloops, their appurtenances & Cargoes remain in the hands of the said Captains Obrian & Foster & the men under their Command for them to use & improve as they shall think most for their & the publicks advantage untill the further order of this or some future Congress or house of Representatives — And that the Committee of Safety for the Western parish in Pownalboro' be ordered to convey the prisoners taken by the said Obrian & Foster from Pownalboro Goal to the Committee of Safety or Corospondance for the town of Brunswick, & the Committee for Brunswick to convey them to some Committee in the County of York and so to be conveyed from County to County till they arrive at this Congress —

    pass^d

The Com^{tee} appointed to Consider the petition of Edward Parry (Agent to the Contractor for Masts &c) taking said petition with several other papers accompaning the same into Consideration Beg leave to report by way of resolve (viz)

    In Provincial Congress Watertown June 26, 1775 —

Resolved That Coll Thomson be directed to repair to George Town and get assistance and remove said Masts and other Timber to a place of Safty The Costs not Exceeding forty pounds and as it appears Said Edward Parry is not Friendly to this Country that Coll Tomson send him as soon as may be to this Congress and that the Bond Given by Dummer Sewal and Jordan Parker be void when s^d masts are secured

    June 26. 1775   pass^d

Letter from Committee of Biddeford. June 28, 1775.

To the Honorable, the Provincial Congress

May it please your Honors As we have tho't proper to forward to your Honors, under Convoy of the Bearers, Messrs Noah Hooper and Edgecomb Nason; a Person who Calls Himself Thos Neat, we apprehend it to be our Duty as a Committee of Inspection, to transmit you an exact detail of our proceedings relative to him, that he may be dispos'd of as your Honors may judge expedient — therefore beg leave to represent, that on Saturday last, the Person in question arriv'd in this Town and being a Stranger — some of the Inhabitants were prepossess'd with a Suspicion of his being a Spy — The Committee in Consequence were immediately applied to — We attended — when he submitted to an Examination, and gave the following Account of himself — to wit, that he was a native of Britain — had liv'd several Years in America — had frequently travelled, and was well acquainted in most of the Southern Colonies, and had, previous to the present unhappy Crisis of the unnatural Contest between Great Britain and her Colonies, acquired the Birth of a Steward on Board his Majesty's Ship Senegal Capt Doddingston, Commander — that he left England in said Ship about 10 Weeks since — fully persuaded from the representations he had there receiv'd that the Disturbance in America was kindled by the Breath of a faction — by no means formidable that it might be easily quelled, and was universally disapproved by the Cool and dispassionate of all Denominations in the Colonies — that the first american Port they touch'd at was Boston — where they soon had Orders to repair to Falmouth, in Casco Bay, at which place he had been two Weeks — that on his arrival in America, he found, not a faction, but the whole Continent joined in Opposition to parliamentary Measures — that therefore he Could not in Conscience continue in a Service in which he must be Obliged to draw the Sword against America — for that Reason he had left the Ship and propos'd going to Philadelphia — where he had several friends and Acquaintance — and that he should have applied for a Pass prior to his leaving Falmouth, but that he imagined such application would be attended with Danger, as the Ship lay in the Harbor —

In Order if possible to be more fully ascertained of the truth of the above Declaration — we next day dispatch'd a Person to Falmouth to wait on the Committee there — who informed him that the Steward had departed the Ship — and that the Capt supposing he had been detained by the People, sent a Message to Col^o Preble to demand a Restoration of him — The Col^o return'd for Answer that he knew nothing of him, but that he was seen a little before going out of Town, Col^o Preble likewise inform'd the Messenger sent by us that he had had some Conversation with this person, and heared him say he intended to leave the Ship for the reason abovemention'd — He hired a Horse a little without the Town of Falm^o and came publicly to this place —

The above may it please your Honours is a true Account of what we have been able to Collect relative to the person in Custody — And as the People here are uneasy, and still apprehensive that he may be inimical to the Interests of America — we have judged it most elligible that he should be sent to the Congress that your Honors may give further Orders concerning him, as your Wisdom may direct

      Rishwth Jordan   ⎫ Committee of Inspec-
      Benj^a Hooper   ⎬ tion for the Town of
      Thos GillPatrick ⎭ Biddeford
Biddeford 28th, June 1775

    Coll Richmond
    Cap Stone
    Mr Langdon

In Provincial Congress July ye 1st 1775

 The Com^{ttee} appointed to Examine the within mentioned

Thoˢ Neat have attended that servics & are humbly of Oppinion that he Ought to be discharged & Set at liberty. & Do recomend him for a pass to be signed by the Sec^{ry} to go to New York there to Apply for a further pass as he proposes to go to Virginia.

Submitted —   p Ezra Richmond
                                           p^r order

Accepted

Report on petition of Thoˢ Donnell & others. 1775.

The committee appointed to Consider to petition of Thomas Donell and others of Frenchmans bay have attended that Service & beg leave to report by way of Resolve

           In provintial Congress Watertown July 8th 1775

Whereas Mr Philip Hodgkins has applied to this Congress for a Supply of Provision for Inhabitants of Frenchmen Bay & being at a good Distance from the Committees of Correspondence of that Place Therefore

Resolved That it be recommended & it is by this Congress accordingly recommended to the Governor & Company of the Colony of Conaticut that they suffer the Inhabitants of Frenchmen bay to purchess such Provisions in the said Colony as they stand in need of.

Accepted.

Letter from Bowdoinham. July 8, 1775.

                     Bowdoinham July ye 8 : 1775

Gentlemen   We have Lately Receiv^d from you Yo^r Resolvs or Rather a precept desireing us to Send a man to Represent us in a General Assembly at Watertown the Nineteenth Instant in Order to Chuse a Counsel & Assembly Which

Counsel you mention are to govern ye Colony till Some Other Alteration. — In which projection we Heartily Join: But in publick townmeeting: After Debating ye Matter It was Resolv^d that it would Not be prudence for us in our Present Circumstances to Send a man As we are at Great Distance It would be Attended with a Considerable Cost, But further Resolv^d that ye Select Men be a Committee To Write to Yo^r Hon^{rs} to let you know our present Situation & minds of ye Inhabitants in General —

It is Not Because of any dislike to Yo^r preposals that we do not Send a man, for we heartily Concur with ye Measures you have propos^d And heartily Beg the Almighty Will not only Bless them but Direct you further; — As to our Circumstaces our town is but A new Settlement & but a few Inhabitants; and we have Lately Suffered Very much by fire; Our Meeting-house Being Burnt & Several Dwelling houses Barns & other Buildings — With A Vast deal of fence & sevral feilds & Mowing land Burnt over; —

This Gentlemen with our former poverty is ye true Cause of our Not Acting more Generous than we do; But we are heartily Willing to Exert our Selves with Both life and fortune as far As is Needful & Joine With You in defence of ye priveledgs Which we are Contending for; — Gentlemen we desire Liberty Not only to Metion to You that we are Very Destitute Of Aminition But that You would Acquaint us Where we may purchase Some; As we have made Some Attempts to git But have fail^d hether-to   This from Yo^r Humble Ser^{nts}

Abr^m Preble \
Robert Fulton } A Comm^{tee} \
Abr^m Whittemore

Superscribed \
To y^e Provincel Congress of The Massachusetts Bay \
Now Setting At Wattertown

Stephen Jones' conduct justified. 1775

We the Subscribers Inhabitants of Machias, do testify and declare, that we have been frequently in Company with Stephen Jones Esqr since the Unhappy Contest arose between Great Britain and the Colonies: and he allways justified the measures taken by the Colonies: highly approved of the Resolutions of the Provincial & Continental Congress^s & condemn'd in the severest terms those Measures pursued by Administration, and the British Parliament against America. And we do realy believe, that he is, as sincere a Friend to the American Cause, as any man Whatever

Machias July 19th 1775

Japeth Hill	Daniel Stone	Morres OBrian
Benj^a Gooch	Ladwick Holway	James Elliot
Jabez West	Jona^t Pineo	Obediah Hill
Theodore Hill	John Chaloner	William Obrian
Joseph Gilichet	John Gooch	Gideon Obrian
Henry Griffiths	Joseph Getchell Jur	Samuel Reed
Stephen Smith	Wm Tupper	Daniel Meserve
Henry Watts	James Wheeler	James Gooch
Dennis Obrian	Jabez Huntley	Job Burnum
Samuel Shaw	Samuel Milbery	Willm
Benj^a gooch Ju	Jonathan Knight	Solomon
Stephen Young	John Morrson	Joseph Hill
Daniel B	Joseph Munson	Abraham Clark
William Albee	William Chaloner	Isaac Taft
James Dillany	James Cole	Ebn^r Beal

We are Gentlemen Your mo. obed^t Serv^{ts}

Thos Brackett Thomas Thompson
Sam^{ll} Oates Cornelius Turner
Briggs Turner

Dated at Bristol ye 16th of July 1775

Thos Boyd Cler of ye Committee

Letter from Stephen Jones. July 22ᵈ 1775.

Machias July 22ᵈ 1775

Honoᵇˡᵉ Sir

As I have been represented as a person Counter Acting the Resolutions of the Honoᵇˡᵉ Congress. Justice to my Character requires me to Send you the inclosed, which, with what the Committee of Safety have done in my favour, hope will be sufficient evidence of my Attachment to my Native Country.

As I have heretofore Served my Country both in Millatary, and Civil Capacity. Shall most Gratefully acknowledge Any favours of that kind. And endeavour faithfully to discharge any trust reposed in me.

Sincerely wishing Success to the American Arms I am Honoᵇˡ Sir most Respectfully, your obedient Humble Servant

Stephen Jones

The Honoᵇˡᵉ President of the Provincial
Congress, or Honoᵇˡᵉ Speaker of the
Massachusetts House of Commons

—— *to James Warren Esqʳ*

Philadelphia July 24, 1775

Sir

In Confidence, I am determined to write freely to you this Time — A Certain great Fortune and Riddling Genius whose Fame has been Trumpeted so loudly, has given a silly cast to our whole doings — We are between Hawk and Buzzard — We ought to have had in our hands a Month ago, the whole Legislative, Executive and Judicial of the whole Continent, and have compleatly Modelled a Constitution, to have raised a Naval Power and opened all our Ports wide, to have arrested every Friend to Government on the Continent, and held them as Hostages for the Poor victims in Boston — And then opened the Door as wide as possible for Peace and

Reconciliation, after this they might have Petitioned and Negotiated and Addressed &ca if the would — Is all this Extravagant? — Is it wild? — Is it not the soundest Policy?

One Piece of News — seven Thousand Weight of Powder Arrived here last night — We shall send along some as soon as we can — But you must be patient and Frugal.

We are lost in the extensiveness of our Field of Business — We have a Continental Treasury to Establish, a Paymaster to choose, and a Committee of Correspondence, or safety, or accounts or something I know not what that has confounded us all Day.

Shall I hail you Speaker of the House or Counsellor or what? What kind of an election had you? what sort of Magistrates do you intend to make?

Will your new Legislative and Executive feel bold or irresolute? Will your Judicial Hang and Whip, and Fine and Imprison without Scruples? I want to see our distressful Country once more — yet I dread the sight of Devastation.

You observe in your Letter the Oddity of a great Man, He is a queer Creature — But you must Love his Dogs if you Love him, and forgive a Thousand whims for the sake of the Soldier and the Scholar.

Yours

N. B.

This Letter was Anonymous, but wrote in the same hand with that Addressed to Abigail Adams.—

J. A. to Mrs Abigail Adams.

Philadelphia July 24th 1775

My Dear

It is now almost Three Months since I left you, in every part of which my Anxiety about you and the Children as well as our Country has been Extreme.

The Business, I have had upon my Mind has been as great and important as can be intrusted to One Man, and the difficulty and intricacy of it Prodigious, when 50 or 60 Men have a Constitution to form for a great Empire, at the same Time that they have a Country of Fifteen hundred Miles extent to Fortify, Millions to Arm and Train, a Naval Power to begin, an extensive Commerce to regulate, Numerous Tribes of Indians to Negotiate with, a standing Army of Twenty Seven Thousand Men to raise, Pay, Victual and officer, I really shall pity those 50 or 60 Men.

I must see you er'e Long — Rice has wrote me a very good Letter and so has Thaiter, for which I thank them both. Love to the Children

J: A.

I wish I had given you a Compleat History from the Beginning to the end of the Journey of the behaviour of my Compatriots — No Mortal Tale could equal it — I will tell you in future, but you shall keep it secret — The Fidgetts, the Whims, the Caprice, the vanity, the Superstition, the Irritability of some of us is enought to —

Report.

In the House of Representatives, Watertown July 25, 1775

Motion of Major Dumer Sewall: for being Discharged from the Bond he is under on account of Edward Parry Esq[r] Relative to his Conduct Respecting a quantity of Masts &c

Beg Leave to Report that Said Sewall is Willing to Remain Still Bound so far as Respects the safe keeping of said Masts &c: but Desires to be Discharged from the Residue of said Bond which your Committe are of opinion may be granted —

and your Committe are further of opinion that it will be

Unnecessary for Col⁰ Thompson to Remove said Masts to any other Place: all which is humbly submitted

      Abraᵐ Watson Jun Pʳ order

Address to the Continental Congress. 1775.

  House of Representatives Watertown July 28 1775

To the Honorable the Continental Congress now Seting at Philadelphia Whereas it hath been Made Appear to this Court by a Representation from yᵉ Committee of Correspondence of the Town of Bristol, in the County of Lincoln, in the Colony of the Massachusetts Bay, that the sᵈ Town of Bristol, and most of the Towns & Plantations in sᵈ County, Are in the utmost distress for want of provisions, and that it is extreame difficult to convay them any releaf by land. in there distressed Circumstances they most Earnestly beg of this Court to use our Influence with your Honors, that you would be pleased to permitt Mʳ William Savage to purchaise & Ship to them one or more Cargoes of provision. Therefore this Court Refer the matter to your Honors. Requesting that you would take it into your consideration and do thereon, as your Honors in your Great Wisdom Shall think Meete.

 passᵈ

In the House of Representatives July 28ᵗʰ 1775

 Read & accepted & orderd to be sent to the Honᵇˡ Continental Congress

  Sent up for Concurrence   Jaˢ Warren Speakʳ

July 28 1775

 In Council read & concurred as taken into a new Draught
      Attʳ P Morton Secʸ pro tem.

Address to the Continental Congress. 1775.

Colony of the Massachusetts Bay

To the Honorable American Congress at Philadelphia.

May it Please your Honors The distress'd Situation of the Eastern Parts of this Colony exhibited in the Petition (accompanying this Address) from the Committee of the Town of Bristol, and the impracticability of conveying provisions to them by Land will excuse this Court for troubling the Congress with an Address in their behalf — The two Houses of Assembly humbly request your Honors to take their Prayer under your wise consideration, and act thereon as in your Wisdom you shall think proper —

In the House of Representatives July 28th 1775. Read and ordered that the foregoing Address be sent to the American Congress

Ja^s Warren Speaker

Representation of Bristol. 1775.

The Committee of the Township of Bristol in the County of Lincoln in the Province of the Massachusets beg leave to represent to the Honourable the Provincial Assembly now Assembled at Watertown the very Distress^d Situation that all degrees of the People are in for want of Provisions of every kind and in short of every necessary in Life, their Situation is still made more bitter & alarming from the reflection that the same want is General from the River of Kennebeck to the most Easternmost part of this Province And We are made Acquainted that there is a Standing Resolve of the Honourable Contenental Congress that No Provisions Shoud be Sent from the Southern Colonies to this Province for fear of such Supplies falling into the hands of the King's Troops or Men of Warr —

It is our Study and desire that every Resolve of the Continental Congress shou'd be held sacred by us; We are Sensible that it may happen somtimes that Individuals or particular places may be Injured by Resolves which may notwithstanding be of great Utility to the Whole Continent in producing a repeal of the Many Obnoxious Acts & forwarding a reconciliation between the Colonies & Mother Country — Yet We must Petition & Beg that you will take our Peculiarly distressd Situation under Your Wise Considerations and Grant Yourselves and also procure a Liberty from the Honourable the Contenental Congress to permit the Bearer of this Mr Wm Savage to Ship Us one or More Loads of Provisions from such places to the Southward and West^d as May best Suit him; And as the above named Mr William Savage has been amongst Us And Made himself fully Acquainted with our distressd Situations We beg leave to refer You to him for such further Information as You may require from him; Having no doubt that you will Complye with this our most Earnest desire —

July 29th 1775

In Council read & ordered that the foregoing address be signed by the Secretary & forwarded to the Honble American Congress

P Morton Sec^{ry} pro tem.

Report, on petition of D. Scott & others   1775

Watertown July 29th 1775

The Committee appointed to consider the Petition of Daniel Scott and others from Pownalborough praying that Thomas Rice Esqr of that place may be discharged from a Seat in this Honourable House and that a precept may be issued for a new choice &c, having attended that Service beg leave to report the true state of facts that appeared upon examining the evidences & hearing both parties, so far as seems to concern his election or right to a Seat in this House, which are as follows viz : —

One Savage who voted at the meeting, was objected to as not being qualified according to Law, & was called upon to make oath — this was after y^e vote was declar'd & entered—

$Doct^r$ Rice Objected that it was too late to dispute the vote after it was entered and desired the meeting should be dissolved — the vote was calld and it pass for dissolving by a majority of two and s^d Savage did not make oath That 12 men appeared at the meeting and declared y^t Mr Rice was not Legally Chose as many were not voters & desir'd to have it reconsidered but the meeting was immediatly dissolved without scrutinizing y^e vote — all which facts are Humbly submitted

$Nath^{el}$ Freeman Chairman
pr Order

Order.

In the House of Representatives August 3^d 1775

Ordered That Mr Bryant, Capt Goodman and $Coll^l$ Cutt with such as the Honble Board shall join be a Committee to examine Mr Edward Parry who has been brought from Georgetown to this Court in consequence of a Resolve of the late Provincial Congress of the 26 June last — & report what is best to be done with him

Sent up for Concurrence Ja^s Warren $Speak^r$

Augt 3^d 1775

In Council read & concurred, & Mr Lincoln and Mr Chauncey are joined

Attest   P Morton $Secr^y$ pro tem.

Bond. 1775.

Know all men by these presents that We John Hobby and Obe Hubbs of George Town in the County of Lincoln, Merchants, are holden and stand firmly bound unto the Provincial Congress now setting for the Province of Massachusets Bay, or to their Successors, or any person that shall be appointed by the People for the Head of the Province afores[d] in the Sum of Two thousand pounds to be paid to the said Congress or their Successors as afores[d] to which payment well and truly to be made, we bind ourselves, our heirs, Executors and Administrators firmly by these presents, sealed with our Seals, dated the fourth day of May, Anno Domini, seventeen hundred and seventy five.

The Condition of the above Obligation is such that Whereas John Bernard Esq[r] has been taken by, and now is in Custody of Coll[ln] Samuel Thompson as a suspected Enemy to the rights of America, Now if the above bounden John Hobby & Obe Hubbs shall keep the said John in safe Custody till he shall be released by order of the Provincial Congress, and that the said John shall not either by himself or any for or under him, remove his Vessel from Long reach in Kennebec River & shall not write to any of the Officers of the Army or Navy for Protection or against the Country, then the above obligation to be void, otherwise to be in force.

Signed sealed & delivered   Jn° Hobby   Seal
   in presence of   Obe Hubbs   Seal
Tim° Langdon
Henry Sewall

Report on Examination of Edward Parry, Mast Agent. 1775.

The Committee appointed to examine M[r] Edward Parry have attended that service and considering his close connec-

tion and dependance on persons employed by the Crown — his disposition to supply our enemies with Masts, Plank &c contrary to the known suntiments of this people, and that his being restrained from doing it he considers as Acts of violence
appear under his own hand beg leave to report as their opinion that the said Edward Parry be immediately sent to **A** <u>some inland Town which shall be more than seventy miles distant from all the seaports</u> in this Colony, there to be detained & provided for by the select men of such Town untill the farther Order of this Court — And if on any pretence whatever he shall presume to leave the **B** <u>Town</u> to which he shall be sent unless by order as aforesaid, he shall be taken & put under close confinement untill ye farther order of this Court

                     p order   Benj Lincoln

August 9th 1775
     In Council read & accepted   Sent down for Concurrence
                     Perez Morton Secr^y pro temp.

In the House of Representatives August 12, 1775
     Read & concurr'd with the following amendments   dele the Words "some inland Town which shall be more than seventy miles distant from all the Sea Ports" and insert the Town of H
       Sent up for Concurrence
                 Saml Freeman Speaker Pr Temp

August 12, 1775
     In Council read & concurred
                Perez Morton Secr^y pro temp
   Consented to

James Otis	Jabez Fisher	B Greenleaf
Moses Gill	Caleb Cushing	John Taylor
Benj^a Chadbourn	Benja^n White	Enoch Freeman
James Prescott	Eldad Taylor	S. Holten
Chas Chauncy	J Palmer	M. Farley

Account. 1775.

Dr Colony Massachusetts Bay for Sundry Expences on Wounded Men & Prisoners taken in the Margueretta arm{d} Schooner (Viz)

	£	S	D
To Nathll Sinclair for 3½ m° Shop Rent & fuel for wounded Men	1	1	0
Ralph Hacock for a schooner & Self to go to Annapolis for Surgeon for D°	3	8	0
Bartholomew Bryant for washing for D°	2	3	4
Nathan Longfellow for taking Ichabod Jones		6	
Bradbury Merill Making Cabbins for wounded Men & his keeping		5	8
Job Burnham for Boarding 3 wounded Men from ye 19th of Augt 1775 to the 7th October 7 weeks @ 36/	12	12	0
D° Washing Milk & Rum for D°	2	2	0
Love Kenney 3 days guarding prisoners & keeping		17	
John Thomas for Making 2 pr breeches for wounded		5	8
Amos Boynton for house Rent Nursing Veal Salmon fowls Rice washing & firing for John Berry 8 week @ 16/4½	6	11	0
Jabez West 3 Days guarding Prisoners & expences		17	
Joseph averell 13 Days attending 3 wounded men Night & Day @ 4/8	2	18	8
John Obrien for 35 Days on Express to the Congress to git information what Should be Done with the Margueretta Tender & the Prisoners	7	0	0
Abial Sprague for D° D°	7	0	0
Wm Tupper for Trouble in taking Ichabod Jones		6	
James Dyer 3 days guarding prisoners & expenses		17	
Obadiah Hill 15 gallons Milk for Hospitall		15	
John Watt & Wm Brown for Making Cradles Cruches & Coffins for wounded & Killed	3	12	0
Samll Milberry for attending James Coolbroth 2 Days Capt for D° 1/6 Diging Grave for D° 6/		18	10
	£55	16	2

Brought over	£55	16	2
James Farnsworth 10 Days Time in going to Annapolis after a Surgeon @ 3/	1	10	
To Horse hire after D° to Cornwallis 72 Miles		18	
To Man & Expence Going after D°	1	7	
To my Board 10 Days in going		16	8
house Rent for wounded Prisoners		9	
Nathan Longfellow for attending wounded Men		4	8
To 2 Day Board & washing for Cole & Taft 2 wounded men		9	6
To Making Cabbins Boards & Joice & Nails for D°		15	10
To 8 Q^{ts} Milk & 25 times assisting the Doct^r Dress the wounded		15	
To Baking 13 Times for D°		13	
To Rye Meal & Bear		3	
John Chaloner 19 Days attendance on surgeon as p^r a/c		4	8	8
Mess Smith & Stillman sending Supplies for wounded Men as per accomp^t	9	9	6
George Walker 3 days guarding Prisoners to Pleasant River & Expences		17	
Timothy Young Diging		6	
James Dillaway for Attending wounded from 27th of June — 19th of Augt 53 Day @ 4/	10	12	0
Committee for Sundrys advanced as per acct Rendered	9	11	5
Committee for Sundrys supl'd the Widow McNeel	1	8	9
Committee for sundry supplies as p^r ac^t	13	15	6
	£124	6	8

Lord Dartmouth to Major Gen¹ Howe

Secret   Whitehall 5 Septr 1775.

Sir

After having in my Separate Letter of this day's date said so much upon the ideas which have been adopted of the great risque & little advantage that are to be expected from the Army's continuing at Boston during the Winter season, unless a more favourable Prospect opens, & having also repeatedly suggested the advantages of recovering possession of New York, I have nothing to add upon those material Objects of your consideration, but as it is of very great Importance that you should know upon what ground we entertain confident hope of having a large Army in North America in the Spring, I should be unpardonable if I did not acquaint you that His Majesty's Minister at Petersburgh having been well instructed to sound the Empress, how far she would be disposed, in case of necessity, to assist His Majesty with such Force as the state & security of the Empire would admit; Her Imperial Majesty has, in the fullness of her affection for the British Nation, & of gratitude for the benefits she received under her late difficulties, made the most explicit declaration, & given the most ample Assurances, of letting us have any number of Infantry that may be wanted.

In consequence of this generous and magnanimous Offer, a Requisition has been made for Twenty Thousand Men, & it is proposed to send the greatest part of these Auxiliaries, as early as possible in the Spring to Quebec; And I trust we shall have at least an equal number of British Troops in North America to act with them, if Occasion requires.

                                 I am &c.

                                       Dartmouth

OF THE STATE OF MAINE 305

Letter from Joseph Simpson. 1775.

Watertown Sep[r] 9th 1775

Gentlemen   The Town of York the Last Valuation put in a Considerable Trading Stock and Tons of Vessels, which are now Useless within a Year past One half of our Vessels which followed the Foreign Trade are Lost or Taken by our Unnatural Enemies Whereby the Usial means of Subsistance of a Number of families are lost to the greate Damage of the Town   I hope you will take this into your Consideration and abate the Town what you in you_ Wisdom think Reasonable and you[l] Oblige your Hum[le] Serv[t]

Joseph Simpson

To the Committe for taking into Consideration the State of the Towns &c —

Accounts of Losses sustained at Falmouth, in October 1775.

Mens Names	Loss in Buildings	Personal Estate	Cartage	Sum Total
Enoch Freeman Esq[r]	790 0 0	304 0 0	10 0 0	1104 0 0
Stephen Longfellow	1035	74	10	1119
Jeddediah Preble Esq[r]	1715	645	10	2370
John Cox	523	142	5	670
Simeon Mayo	1810	334	10	2154
Paul Little	510	167	6	683
Benjamin Titcomb		316 10 0		316 10
Benj[a] Titcomb for Phillip Kelley	120			120
Jonath[n] Morse Ju[r]	225	46 10 0	3	274
Josiah Tucker	200	10	3	213
James Purrinton	506	40	3	549
Jane Sweetsir	309	6 10 0		315
Joseph Bayley	300			300
Melatiah Young	76	6	2	84
Colman Watson	153			153
Stephen Morse	40	3		43
John Stevenson	50	165 10 0	10	225 10
Moses Haskel	413	80 0 0	8	501

20

Mens Names	Loss in Buildings			Personal Estate			Cartage			Sum Total		
Benj^a Pettingill	365			25	10	0	3			393	10	
Benj^a Jenks	80			129	0	0	4			213		
Esther Stickney				13	0	0				18		
Jabez Bradbury	80	0	0	6	0	0	2			88	0	0
Nathl Hale	8			20			2			30		
Peter Woodbury	70									70		
Thos Newman	220			33			2			225		
Simon Gookin	15						2			17		
Pearson Jones				110			3			113		
Paul Cammet	26			30			2			58		
Joseph Hatch				7						7		
Jemima Harrison				20			2			22		
Margret Due				8						8		
Tucker & Newman Administrators of Jonath^n Thrasher	230									230		
Robert Dryburg				14			4			18		
Josiah Bayley	20									20		
Abijah Parker				10						10		
John Thurlo	400			8	5	4	3			411	5	4
James Swain				20	0	0	2			22		
John Archer				48			2	4	0	50	4	0
John Hans				9			1	0	0	10		
Thos Cobb	100									100		
James Frost				11						11		
Josiah Shaw				8						8		
John Butler	1066			451			6	0	0	1523	0	0
Enoch Freeman Junr				11	12	0				11	12	0
Will: Brown				7						7		
Joshua Lawrence	340	0	0	26			3			369		
Daniel Riggs	120									120		
Wheeler Riggs	13			6			2			21		
Joseph Ingraham	200			100			1	0	0	301		
Caleb Carter	39			16			1			56		
Abigail Crosby	120			10			2			132		
Willm Hoole				15			1			16		
Paul Prince & Co				500						500		
Philip Fowler				2	8	0				2	8	0
Saml Bradbury	154			12			2			168		
Danl Pettingill	269			81			3			353		
Mary Kelley				102						102		
Joseph Blancher				460						460		
Willm Hustin	250			13			2			265		
Saml Freeman Esqr	540			330			3			873		
Saml Freeman for Willm Horton				300						300		

OF THE STATE OF MAINE 307

Mens Names	Loss in Buildings	Personal Estate	Cartage	Sum Total
Geo: Burns	7	63	2	102
Will: Harper	389	116	4	509
Ebenzr Snow	125	20 10	3	148 10 0
Thos Bradbury	294	12 0 0	3	309 0 0
John Baker	228 0 0	23 0 0	3	234 0 0
Mary Coverly	120	30	2	152
Jonathn Lambert	100	50	2	152
Walton Stover	400	22	2	424
Edmund Mountfort	320	29	3	352
Noah Noyes	370	30	2	402
Peter Merrell	10	5	1	16
Mary Corsair		5		5
Jonathn Bryant	5	47		52
Ezekiel Hatch		114	2	116
Joshua Brown	170			170
John Burnam	450	100	3	553
Ebenzr Mayo	538	94	8	630
Moses Lunt	66	9	3	78
Jereh Veazy	70	14	1	85
Jeremh Berry	173	36	3	212
John Bradbury	36	6	2	38
Josiah Baker	200	6	2	208
Chipman Cobb	60			60
Ebenzr Gustin	100	4	2	106
Lucy Condon		4 10 0		4 10 0
Nathl Deering	320 0 0	95 0 0	1	416 0 0
Christr Kelly	369	33	4	406
Joseph Riggs Junr	240	5	2	247
Summers Shattuck		8 10 0		8 10 0
Jonathn Morse	140	24	2	166
John Nichols	150		1	151
Saml Mountfort	400	36	2	438
John Greenwood	60	106	2	168
John Veazy	56	7	3	66
Abrahm Stevens		9	2	11
Margeret Mabery	500			500
Mary Cunningham		13	1	14
John Wood		6	1	7
Pelatiah Fernald		36	1	37
Abrahm Osgood	26	44	2	72
Joseph Emery	100	59 10 0		159 10 0
George Warren	230	48	2	280
Thos Wyer	222	101	2 0 0	325
David Wyer		67		67
Isaac Randell	18	6		24
John Dole	4	4		8

DOCUMENTARY HISTORY

Mens Names	Loss in Buildings	Personal Estate	Cartage	Sum Total
Peter Warren		4 8 0	1 4 0	5 12 0
Jacob Adams		39	2 0 0	41
Edward Watts	80 0 0	108	4 0 0	192
Else Greely		6		6
Cornelius Brimhall	402	5		407
Enoch Moody		4	4 0 0	8
Cornelius Briggs	4			4
Thomas Sanford	150	28	6 0 0	184
Mary Horn		75	2 0 0	77
John Johnston		45		45
Thomas Sanford Administrator to Estate of Authur Howell	34			34
Zebulon Noyes	281	40		323
Moses Bagley	80			80
John Martin	199		3 0 0	202
Joseph Thomes	40	6 12 0	2 0 0	48 12 0
James Gooding Junr	6	18	2 0 0	26
Nathl G. Moody	170	30	3 0 0	203
James Flood	36			36
Enoch Ilsley	1623 0	978 0 0	6	2607 0 0
Isaac Ilsley Junr	200 0 0	10	2 0 0	212
Estate of Sarah Mosely Dec^d	466	40		506
John Thrasher	75	44	2 0 0	121
Amy Hilton	253	11	3 0 0	267
Joseph Sylvester	203	5	2 0 0	210
Silvanus Brown		10 13 0		10 13 0
Joseph Quinby Ju^r	310			310
Benjamin Rand	462	94	3 0 0	559
Moses Shattuck	180	268	3 0 0	451
Isaiah & Jos. Noyes	346	107	1 0 0	454
Joseph Quinby	470	40	3	413
Abijah Pool	204	8		212
Joseph Harding		6		6
Thos Motley	70	8	2 0 0	90
Jesse Harding		11		11
Josiah Riggs	720	33	3	756
Timothy Pike	500	96	5	601
Benj^a Waite	730 0 0	29 0 0	3	762 0 0
Henry Y. Brown		15		15
Henry Wheeler	40	25	1	66
James Gooding	404	10	3 0 0	417
John Waite	540	59	26 0 0	625
Heirs of John Waite Deceas^d	505			505

OF THE STATE OF MAINE 309

Mens Names	Loss in Buildings	Personal Estate	Cartage	Sum Total
Ephr^m Broad		80	2 0 0	82
Stephen Woodman	320	11	3 0 0	334
Moses Noyes	100		2	102
Will: Pearson	70	12	2 0 0	84
Timothy Noyes		10	2 0 0	12
Mary Bradbury	200	33	3	236
Mary Stickney	270	19	1	290
James Cobb	60			60
John Tukey Junr	450	47	2	499
Dudley Cammet	133	8	2	143
Saml Lowell		18	1	19
John Minot		14 0 0	1 0 0	15 0 0
Jonath^n Elwell	94 0 0	12	2 0 0	108
Town of Falmouth	288			288
County of Cumberland	800			800
Propr^rs of St Pauls Church	1200			1200
Committee for Joshua Moody	200	30		230
John Tyng Esqr	120			120
Nathl Coffin	673 6 8	48 6 0		721 12 8
Mrs Lowther		150		150
Revd Thos Smith	400	20	4 0 0	424
Anne Oulton & Comp	437	191	2 0 0	630
Harrison Brazier	122	24	2 0 0	148
David Woodman	107	25	2	134
Thomas Child		29	2	31
Abigail Cobham		56	3	59
Kent & Oxnard		392	3	395
Eph^m Jones	370	22 0 0	2 0 0	394
Moses Pearson Esqr	592	96 0 0	3 0 0	691
Ebenz^r Owen	330 0 0	110 0 0	2 0 0	445 0 0
Roland Bradbury	70		2	72
John Ingersoll	120		2	122
Stephen Waite	935	216	8	1159
Lemuel Cox		20	1 10 0	21 10 0
Wm Waterhouse	406	73	1	480
Moses Plummer	544	2	5	551
Joseph McLallen	30	87	4	121
Eliz^th Freeman		5 13 0		5 13 0
Zach^r Nowell		336 13 8		336 13 8
David Noyes	419	48	4	471 0 0
Jerem^h Pote	656	198	4	858
Mary Shearman		4		4
Jacob Bradbury	185	11	2	198
Thomas Cumming		1106	0 16 4	1106 16 4

Mens Names	Loss in Buildings	Personal Estate	Cartage	Sum Total
John Bayley			1 0 0	12 6 0
David Stodart	133	64	3 0 0	200 0 0
James Johnson		6 0 0		6 0 0
Lucy Smith	60 0 0			60
John Fox		150 0 0		150 0 0
Brackett Marston		6 1 0	6 0 0	12 1 0
				54741 19 0

NOTE. To this list was later added several names and the amount slightly changed. It was at the session of Congress in 1776 submitted to Congress by a committee of citizens consisting of Peter Noyes, John Waite, Enoch Moody, Daniel Ilsley, Nathaniel Wilson, Richard Codman, John Johnson, Jr., and Joseph Noyes. As finally corrected see Willis' History of Portland, page 900.

Letter from Committee of Safety at Machias. 1775.

To the Honorable Council and House of Representatives of the Colony of the Massachusetts Bay now setting at Watertown.—

Gentlemen, During the absence of Capt[n] Obrien, the Committee of this place commissioned Capt[n] Stephen Smith to take Charge of the Private-teer, & bring in here the Brigg Loyal Briton owned by Mess[rs] Archibald Wilson, James Anderson, John Greenlaw, David Black and John Semple who had sent her to S[t] John's River in Nova Scotia to load with Cattle &c. for the Army at Boston; & upon Capt[n] Smiths Arrival there, he found the said Brigg loaded & weighing Anchor. He thereupon took Immediate possession of her, without opposition and after taking the provision found in the Fort, burning the Fort, and taking a Corporal & two Privates, with two women & five Children he proceeded with his Prize & Prisoners, (M[r] John Semple of Boston and David Ross the mate excepted, who found means to Escape), directly to this Place. An exact Inventory of the Goods taken in the Brigg and in the Fort we send enclosed.

The Cattle, sheep, Hogs, smoked Salmon & Butter, we have divided among the people, who took them, except one third part reserved in the Hands of the Committee for publick use: The other things are all Stored, & await the orders of the General Court. The two private Soldiers, with their wives & Children, at their earnest request, we have sent back to St Johns, taking it for granted that they would be not only useless, but expensive lumber in the western parts of this Colony. William Miller the Pilot of the Brigg and three seamen are permitted to ship on board the Private-teer, and Captn Frederick Sterling only, the Master of the Brigg, and the Corporàl above-mentioned are sent to Court. Captn Sterling has much to say for himself, but his conduct is not altogether unexceptionable: All we can say is, that he is a North Briton. We have given him part of his private venture, & reserve the rest till the pleasure of the General Court is known. John Anderson Esqr was also on board the Brigg, as a passenger who was dismissed & suffered to return to his own Home, not because he appeared to be a cordial friend to the Cause in which we have embarked, but because he belonged to another Province.

Nothing material has since happened, for we can do but little

We now beg leave to return your honors our Humble & hearty thanks for the many favors already confered upon us, of which we shall ever retain the most grateful remembrance. It would give us the highest satisfaction to find ourselves able, thro' the aid you have graciously given us, both in the Land & sea Service, to protect & support ourselves without giving your Honors any further trouble: But such are our Necessitous circumstances, thro' the almost total failure of our commerce, upon which we have hitherto subsisted & by which we have rose to such magnitude, as to be in some measure worthy of your Honors attention, the Admiration of this Vast Continent and the dread of Halifax, and the brittish Navy, that we have no other alternative, but Either to "sink" or to make a most humble and dutiful application to our avowed, beloved, & beneficent Guardians. We are therefore under the disagreeable necessity of adding, That we have drawn a bill upon your Honors in favor of Mr Wm Shey of Philadelphia for a Cargo of provisions, a Copy of which, together with the Letter of advice given with it; we send enclosed. We could not but View the arrival of this cargo of provision as a very remarkable interposition of Divine Providence, in our behalf, & thought ourselves indispensably bound to treat the benevolent Instrument by which it came, with honor. But purchase we could not; Lumber would not answer, and all the Cash we could collect in the whole place was but barely sufficient to pay the freight. To suffer this provision to depart from us, & go elsewhere, would have been the heighth of distraction, as we were then in want, and armed Plunderers infested all our coasts, and picked up all the provision they could find; and especially when we add, we had no prospect of either Quails or Manna. The sacred laws of self preservation, therefore, deserved respect to Mr Shey, the tender obligations, that subsist between the Guardian & his beneficiary, & the Mutual affection of Indulgent parents & dutiful Children, all conspired to Justify; & even recommend a draught upon the General Court of the Colony. The bill is drawn, & a copy of it now lies before you. If it is duly honored, our Mills, our boards, our shingles &c our houses and not to mention the sloop Mechias Liberty, sloop Unity, the Margeretta, Diligent, Tatamagouch, or the Infidel reclaimed (once Loyal Briton) our all is yours, till the whole is repaid. This may soon be done, for we are both able & willing to pay the whole amount of said Bill in lumber on Demand. If this bill is not Honored, we tremble at the consequence!

On this occasion we send Mr George Stillman as our Representative who was chosen by the Town for that purpose. And with him we send the Accounts of our expence in bringing the Dead, who fell in the day of battle, or died by the wounds they then received, in taking care of the wounded, & in supporting the prisoners & conveying them to Head Quarters, except the Doct^{rs} Bill, & the persons who attended him, which we choose they should present themselves. The charges of those persons who were lately at the General Court, & Mr Stephen Jones's we have sent as they brought them in to us. But all the rest we have examined, and Approved. We are heartily grieved to see our expences run so high, but we see no way to reduce them any lower without doing apparent injustice. We have other enormous expences among ourselves which we never mean to mention in the ears of Government, for the greatest part of us have spent almost our whole time in public service since the taking of the first Tender. We are but an handful & every publick exertion required the most of our strength. And were your Honors graciously to add, to your parental bounty in the land & Sea Service of this place, which we esteem a rich & signal favor, all the Prizes we have taken, we should still be sufferers. We ask not a farthing more than we have merited; we expect, we are willing to suffer with our brethren, for it is honorable & Glorious to suffer in this Cause. Your Honors are well Acquainted with our infant state, with our critical situation, & with all we have done in support of the invaluable priviledges of America, & Great Britain, and we rest assured that you will not permit us to suffer beyond measure. We must now acquaint your Honors, that the Company of Militia at our western Falls have chosen Mr Jonathan Knight their Captain Mr Daniel Miservey their first Lieutenant, & Mr David Longfellow their second Lieutenant. The Company at Eastern River have chosen Mr Joseph Sevey Captain M^r

John Scott first Lieu^t & Mr Ephraim Chase second Lieu^t we pray therefore with submission that their commissions may be made out & sent down — The Town approves of Mr Benjamin Foster as a Magistrate, but prefers Mr Joseph Libbee to Mr Nathaniel Sinkler & humbly request that both these Gentlemen may be made Justices of the peace.

We also beg leave to recommend to your Honors Notice the Widow McNiel & her orphan children who are left under very poor circumstances. Mr John Berry who has a family Ebenezer Beal of Old York, a very old Man & Isaac Taft & James Cole, Young men, may not be, perhaps, unworthy of Notice. These were all badly wounded, and it is doubtful whether they will ever be capable of business as they were before, or not. The last mentioned is still confined. Before we conclude, we must observe that on the 8th Instant Eleven Deserters from the Somerset at Halifax arrived here, who informed us that the Tartar & two ships of war are now up the Bay of Funday, & that a Schooner of 14 Carriage Guns & 50 men, was fitting out at Halifax in order to Join two other Tenders, and proceed directly against this place. Eight of the said deserters are inlested on board the Sloop Machias Liberty. Should Armed Vessels come against us we should be in danger of falling a sacrifice, for we are very Scant of Powder; as almost all that was taken in the Diligent was destroy'd, some body poured water into it privately. We earnestly beg therefore, that your Honors would please to send us More.

We are Gentlemen most respectfully your most Dutiful & Humble Servants.

By order of the Committee of Safety

Ja^s Lyon Ch. M.

Machias Octr 14th 1775

P. S. Mr Stillman is accompanied by Dr Willm Chaloner

In Council Novr 11th 1775

Read & sent down

Perez Morton D^y Secr^y

Orders. 1775

Captain Isaac Danks, you are to proceed Immediately with yᵉ Schooner Falmouth Packet now under your Command, to Boston, taking Care to keep Under the protection of the Man of War, who Convoys you; When at Boston you are to wait on William Sherriff Esqʳ the Deputy Quarter Master General, Whose Orders you are afterwards Implicitly to follow. Respecting the Cargo, on Board of you, plase to Observe the following Instructions —

1ˢᵗ Eight Bundles of Hay Stowed in the Hold and two Barrels of Potatoes, are to be Delivered to Daniel Chamier Esqʳ Commissary General.

2ᵈˡʸ the Fifteen Oxen together with the Remainder of the Hay are to be Delivered to the Order of Major Sherriff.

3ᵈˡʸ Two Barrels of Potatoes are to be Delivered to Major Martin of the Royal Artillery.

4ᵗʰˡʸ The Potatoes and Turnips which are lose In the Hold you are to Acquaint Major Sherreff thereof and Deliver them to his Order; provided he wants them, either for himself, Friends or Hospital; If he Does not want them you must dispose of them, and pay the proceeds Into the Hands of Mʳ Archibald Cunningham

I sincerely wish you _ prosperous Voyage and _ your Real friend_

Day & Scott

October 20ᵗʰ 1775 Cumberland

Account of Loss & Damage sustained by Elisha Snow. 1775.

An Account and Estimate of the Loss & Damage which Elisha Snow of a Place called St Georges in the County of Lincoln and Colony of Massachusetts Bay has sustained by means of the Hostilities committed by the Ministerial Forces in America, is as follows, viz. On the eighteenth Day of August 1775, David Silvester of Pownalborough in said County hired the Sloop Three Brothers from Robert Hodge & Co. of said Pownalborough, Same Day said Snow hired three Quarters of said Sloop from said Silvester; on the 6th of September she sailed for St. Christophers there discharged her Cargo, and took in 18 Hogsheads of Rum (some Sugar, & other articles, the particulars uncertain) three Quarters of which (Rum) i. e. 1485 Gallons at 4/ p Gallon comes to £297. On the 6th of December said Sloop with her Cargo on her Return, on this side the shoals of Georges was taken by a 50 Gun Ship; the Master Benjamin Friswell, said David Silvester Super Cargo, and one Hand were taken on Board the Ship; the Sloop with the other Hands has not since been heard of

Elisha Snow

To the Hon. Joseph Palmer Esq. Chairman of the Committee for collecting the Accounts of Hostilities committed by the Ministerial Troops and Navy &c.—

At Watertown

The above contains an Estimate of the Loss (by means of the Hostilities &c. aforesaid) sustained by the Inhabitants of the Plantation called the Eastern Township on St Georges River, so far as has come to our Knowledge

Patrick Porterfield
Chairman of the Committee per Order

Memorial of Com^ee of Safety of N. Yarmouth & New Glocester. 1775.

North Yarmouth October 24, 1775.

To the Honourable his Majesty's Council and the Honourable the House of Representatives of the Colony of the Massachusetts Bay.

May it please your Honours The Destruction of the Town of Falmouth on the 18th current by a Fleet under the command of Captn Mowit (the particulars of which your Honours have doubtless been informed of) has greatly alarmed this part of the Country, which we fear is destin'd to Devastation and Ruin, by our cruel & unnatural Enemies — but our greatest fears at present are, that our Enemies design to take possession of Falmouth Neck, & fortifie an Eminence that overlooks the Town & Harbour there, as it has been reported that Captain Mowit has hinted that he expected to winter at Falmouth with as many of the Kings Ships, as the Country round wou'd afford subsistance for — Those of your Honours who are best acquainted with this part of the Country must be sensible that Falmouth affords a Harbour the most commodious for the Kings Ships to winter in of any perhaps between Boston and Hallifax — that the Hill on the Neck may be easily so fortified, as with a small garrison of men, and a Fleet below to defend it, they may defie all the Force of this part of the Country, if not the united Forces of the whole Continent to rout them — And shou'd such an Event take place, not only this County, but all the Eastern Shore with the whole Province of Maine, may be lost to the Country for ever — The Consequences of which wou'd doubtless be most severely felt by the whole Continent, not only in the heavy loss, of so great a part of the Country, to the Community, but by the great Advantage such an Acquisition wou'd be to our Enemy in furnishing them with plenty of Lumber of all sorts Masts for their Navy, with Provision &c —

We therefore beg that your Honours wou'd take the distressed state of this part of the Country into your immediate Consideration, and afford us such assistance as in your great wisdom you shall judge best, either by seconding our Petition to his Excellency General Washington praying Him to take this part of the Country under his immediate Protection &

send forces to fortifie & garrison the said Eminence on Falmouth Neck, or shou'd he decline it, by affording us such Assistance yourselves, in men and Military Stores (in both which we are greatly deficient for such an undertaking) as may secure us from becoming the inevitable Prey of our merciless Enemies, for shou'd they once get footing in Falmouth, we shall to all human appearance, be soon reduced to the wretched alternative of yielding ourselves up into the hands of those whose Tender Mercies are cruelty, or of flying with our families naked & forlorn of all earthly subsistance to some other part of the Country, dependent upon Charity for our daily bread! We hope your Honors wont consider & treat our Fears as chimerical & groundless —

For further particulars we beg leave to refer you to D[r] Russel the Bearer, a Gentleman who will be capable to give any further light and Information respecting the dangerous state of this part of the Country that your Honours may think proper to require — We are with great Respect and Deference your Honours most obedient and very Humble Servants

Jer: Powell p Order of the Committee of Safety for North Yarmouth

Isaac Parsons p[r] order of the Committee of Safty for New Glocester

In Council Oct[r] 28th 1775   Read & sent down
                    Perez Morton Dp[y] Secr[y]

In the House of Representatives Oct[r] 30 1775 —

Read and Order'd that M[r] Story Col[o] Thompson M[r] Cross & M[r] Pitts with such as the Hon[ble] Board shall appoint, be a Committee to take into Consideration the within Memorial together with a Letter from Jeremiah Powell Esq[r] accompanying and report

Sent up for Concurrence
                    William Cooper Speak[r] Pro Tem.

In Council Octo^r 30th 1775

Read & concurred & Benj^a Chadbourn, Jno Whetcomb & Cha Chauncey Esq^{rs} are joined

Perez Morton Dp^y Ser^y

Letter from Jer^h Powell. 1775.

North Yarmouth Octo^r 24. 1775.

To the Honourable Coucil, and to the Honourable House of Representatives of the Colony of the Massachusetts Bay—

May it please your Honours—Last Evening came up to this Town from the Halifax armed Schooner, belonging to a Fleet, viz the Canceaux the Semitry & the Spitfire, lying in Hog Island Road under the Command of Capt Mowit Three men Deserters from said Schooner, who ran away with the Yawl belonging to said Schooner, from a watering Place on Hog Island where they with one man more under the Command of a Midshipman were sent on Shore to take in Water—They came & delivered themselves up to some of our Militia who were at work erecting a Battery on the Shore—And give us the following Inteligence That on Monday the 16th Current the s^d Fleet arrived in Casco Bay. That the same Day their Orders were read to them which were to burn, sink & Destroy every Thing to the Eastward of Boston that they cou'd not conveniently carry off with them.

That Tuesday the Fleet went up to Falmouth & came too in a Line before the Town—That Wednesday Morning about 9, o'Clock they began to fire upon the Town, and about 2 Hours after the Fire began Boats were sent on Shore to fire the Houses by hand—that the men went on Shore unarmed, and to their apprehension not more than 20 were on Shore at any one Time. Further they say, that the greater part of the Buildings that were burnt were fired by Hand — The mens names are Charles Stuart Quarter Master, John Elliot and Daniel Streetland Foremastmen, the two first taken out of Vessels which they took, & are now detained in Boston Harbour, & the last impressed out of a Schooner at Halifax —

The men give a fair and honest Acc^t of themselves and agree very well in their Relation of the fore mentioned Facts— We have sent them to the Committee of Scarborough to be forwarded to the General Court at Watertown, where when they arrive your Honors will have Opportunity for further Examination as may be tho't proper — The Yawl in which they made their Escape is now in our keeping, And should be glad to receive Orders what shall be done with her.

I am your Honours most obedient and most humble Servant

      Jer : Powell Chairman
        of the Committee of Safety

In Council Octo^r 28th 1775 Read & sent down
        Perez Morton Dp^y Secr^y

Report. 1775.

The Committee appointed to Consider of Vessels taken into Custody between Penobscut & Machias beg Leave to Report, that the Schooner Falmouth Packet bound from Nova Scotia to Boston Isaac Danks Master brought into Gouldsborough & deliverd up to the Committee of Safety of said Place having Receiv'd & Examined the papers belonging to said Vessel have Detain'd her & her Cargo by Virtue of the Trust Reposed in us. Copy of his orders from his owners you have herewith — in the Name & by order of the Committee

           Saml Jordan

Gouldsborough Novem^r 1775
   To Whole General Court

"*Letter to Genl Frye.*"   *Nov. 14, 1775.*

Watertown Novr 14th 1775 —

Sir   You are directed upon the receipt of the Commission inclosed, immediately to repair to Falmouth to take the Command of all the men in the County of Cumberland raised for the defence of the Sea Coasts and if you find it necessary for the Safety of said Town and County you are directed to call together their Militia or part thereof and take the Command of them also, and discharge them as soon as the service will admit, you are also directed to do all in your Power to prevent the Enemy from making any further depredations in that County, & to that end you are Ordered to fortify such Advantageous Parts as in your Opinion will most Conduce to so Salutary a Purpose

In the name & by Order of ye Council

James Otis Presd^t

Report.   1775.

The Committee appointed by both Houses to take under consideration the circumstances of the Seaports of this colony and where it will be Necessary to keep forces during the Winter season and to make Report —
beg leave to make the following Report that they have attended that Service and are of opinion that it is Necessary that there should be stationed at Glocester Two hundred and fifty men at Marblehead one hundred men at Tarpaulin Cove one hundred & fifty men and at Falmouth in the County of Cumberland Three hundred men which may serve under a proper officer as a guard for all the Sea Coast in the Counties of York & Cumberland Excepting Kittery where Your Committee are of opinion there ought to be stationed not less

than fifty men and at Hingham Braintree and Weymouth Two hundred men.

James Prescott p^r order

In Council Decr 21 1775   Read & sent down

Perez Morton Dp^y Secr^y

Letter from Haunce Robinson & Wm Walton. Jan. 6, 1776.

St Georges Janu^{ry} ye 6/ 1776

Honrd Sir.

Having Received the Money Sent for Billitting of Capt Samuel Gragg Company Two Months We do Not Find that the Said Company Contained More Then Fifty Eaight Men Including offesers That Past Musster and Upon Taking Corn^{ll} James Cargill Advise We Have Not Payd any More & There Remains two Pound Eight Shillings Laful Money in our Hands, and we Bedg the feavour of Your Hon^r Directions. as We Desire Nothing But What is Honerabel

From Your Friends and Most obedient Humbel Servents

Haunce Robinson
Willm Watson

Superscribed

To The Honrd John Tayler Esqr in Watertown

Letter from Stephen Parker to Gen. Washington. Jan. 15, 1776.

Yarmouth Nova Scotia 15th Jany 1776

May it please your Excellency

Impelled by the triple tyes of affection for my Country, Attachment to Liberty, and concern for my family Interest and place of residence, I am embolden'd to break thro' the rules of formality, and inform your Excellency, that at Annapolis in this Government, a schooner with hands impressed, which had two Cask of Powder, and an equivalent in ball, ship'd by some officers in the Governments service, was sent to St Johns river, with orders to put the Powder, Ball, &c into the hands of the savages there, and stir them up to cut off the inhabitants of Mechias, having an Officer on board to whose care the matter was committed. Thrice they put out of the harbour & by violent winds, were drove back, the last time the vessel narrowly escaped being lost, which adverse Providence has induced them to lay by their design at present. At the same place a Ship of Six hundred tons, collecting stores for Boston, was lately cast away with entire loss of Vessel & Cargo — This intelligence may be relyed on.

Altho I am from circumstances, disagreably here at Present, my most fervent wishes are, that the Noble struggles for American Liberty may be succeeded. That your Excellency may receive all Wisdom, Valour, and Protection, in your exalted station, from the Supreme Parent of those Blessings, and be the happy Instrument of bringing our distresses to an honorable, speedy, and effectual close, is the unfeigned prayer of Your Excellencys most obedient devoted humble servant

Stephen Parker

This letter was wrote with a view of embracing the first oportunity to send it the General. John Frevoy of Yarmouth in Mr Stanleys schooner promis'd to call at my lodgings before he sailed for Marblehead last winter, but failing of calling I had not oportunity to send it, fearing to give it him long before he saild, lest it might be known in Nova Scotia —

Copy of Letter from Stephen Parker to Christopher Prince " Enclosed to Genl Washington." Jan. 16, 1776.

Yarmouth N Scotia 16th Jany 1776

Dear Sir

Neither for toryism or any other offence against Church or State am I here, a place not long since to me the least expected & at present the least desired. My scituation is from a similar to the peasant who secure in his cottage observes the rising storm with tranquil mind but more truely comparable to the trembling merchant that from a barren Cliff beholds the rushing tempest lash the furious waves which threaten each moment to devour his expectations & wealth. Dont ask me why. I draw aside the curtain of reserve & answer thus, my lot is providentially cast & the small property I own fixd in a place whose inhabitants have not been the least active in annoying & destroying what they deem'd inimical to this Countrys welfare. Their vigorous exertions have made it absolutely necessary to keep a continual guard for the defence of their humble possessions the price of their past labour & presage of their future livelihood which being wholly incompatible with those vocations that a daily support calls for have by consequence not only stagnated but almost annihilated trade their whole dependance & introduced want, distress & every concometant evil.

You may remember I intimated to you a design of visiting the Southward in a letter —

The first of july last I took passage for Philadelphia in hopes of meeting with some open door to remove my family there, but finding Lumber the only article I could export in lieu of my property if I Disposed of it, would bear no price or scarcely more than pay freight I was obliged to abandon the thought & return where in my way back happening at Nantucket I met some business that with succeeding circumstances brought me to this place, at which I arrived the first of November —

The conceptions Mrs Parker my friend & the inhabitants have of my long absence I am a stranger to but tis not improbable they deem me a prisoner in Boston as I have reason to think they have had no oportunity of hearing where I am, should a conveyance from Anapolis offer of sending my family word a line from you to Mrs Parker informing my design is to see her soon as possible, and if not disagreable your enclosing her this letter would lay me under very great obligations.

My dear Sir, is not this a dismal day, when our late peaceable habitations are invaded by hostile arms, Our safety, our lives held by the most precarious tenure, Famine threatning our once flourishing quarters, plunderers prowling from port to port, preying on the property of the distressd honest & industrious, and every evil with accumulated force sweeping, till now this happy land — In what direction or to what place shall we flee for safety. To Nova Scotia say you, I answer not, discord & disorder prevail here jealousy & distrust have seized the humane breast & expected dangers appall every countenance. Tis true the Royal word is past & government encourages with promises fair & doubtless faithful the loyal sufferer that shall shelter himself under this wing, but ineffectual scheme — will fanning breezes quench a rapid flame or smooth expressions tame the fiery courser O my Country — my Country — believe me Sir there is an unalienable tye, & the tenderest sensations forbid a divorse. In whom, or where, in every feeling heart. Can a woman dash the fruit of her womb against the poignards point, or call forth the savage of the desart to destroy her smiling sons & daughters? can she turn her once fostering hand on which her tender offspring proud of their parentage so fondly lean'd, against their breasts her own & every vital pore, forbid it Heaven —

But while I thus rove o'er the landskip of disorder I forget I may obtrude on your serene mind gloomy ideas & dismal presages Let the Sons of ambition inebriate at the fountain of Honour till they quench their insatiable thirst, The votaries of mammon drive thro golden mines till they cry enough of shining dust Rapine & violence bleed upon its own point and the authors of publick calamitys gasp out their contagious breath in a halter return but peace with humble fare and the gay like Indians fond for me may share all featherd fopperies.

I have only to add, my fervent prayers to the Almighty, that he would be pleased to bestow on you & yours every blessing with the full enjoyment of internal & external peace and tranquility assuring you I am

Dear Sir most sincerely your obedient humble Servant
Stephen Parker

Copy of Receipt. Jan. 18, 1776.

Machias January 18, 1776 —

Then received of Mr James Lyon Chairman of the Committee of Safety three Rolls of paper, whereon are several plans, that were taken out from among Mr Thomas Sprys baggage, & two small paper books, containing directions for sailing into divers harbors. And a piece of parchment or paper in a frame, containing signals &c. all which I have received for the use of the United Colonies, as I am in their service —

Aaron Willard

A true Copy   Ja^s Lyon

Letter from James Lyon. Jan. 19, 1776.

Machias Jan. 19, 1776.

Sir   I think it my Duty to remind you, as you have doubtly been informed of what we have done that we generously too generously returned to the officers taken in the Schooner Diligent all their private property, & among their things all the plans of this Continent, in their possession, which oversight we greatly regret, & for which we can make no apology but our distress & confusion at that time, which would not admit of our attending to this matter as its vast importance required. Lieut. Knights goods are all sent away Lieut. Spry's only remain in our possession. These goods by Capt. Willards advice we have examined & have found the scetches now in our hands, together with a valuable compass some slop cloathing &c which is recorded. I now, in behalf of the Committee, humbly ask, if Lieut. Thomas Spry has not forfeited all his right to said goods? I therefore beg advice & direction of the Honorable General Court, which we should be glad to receive as soon as may be —

By order of the Committee of Safety

I am your Honors most humble & obedient servant

Ja^s Lyon Ch M

The Honorable Ja^s Otis Esquire

Sir Capt. Willard can give you farther information, to whom I refer you.—

In Council Feby 15th 1776

Read & committed to Benj^a Lincoln Esqr with such as the Hon^l House shall join

Sent down for Concurrence   Perez Morton D Secr^y

In the House of Representatives Feb. 15, 1776

Read and concurred and Coll^o Lovel & Coll Bliss are joined

William Cooper Speak^r Pro Tem.

Letter to the Committee of Safety at Machias.

Gentlemen.

Yours of the 29th of January last by Cap^{tn} Willard to the President of the Council is now before us. The subject matter thereof hath been duly consider'd. Altho' we could wish that the plans in possession of Lieutenant Knight had been detained, yet we are far from censuring the Inhabitants of Machias for not doing it. We are inform'd they are now in his hands. Some steps will be taken to secure them. We approve the measures you have taken with regard to Lieutenant Spry's goods. You will safely retain the whole.

Ld George Germain to Maj^r Genl Howe

Whitehall February 1st 1776

Sir,

Since my letter to you of the 5th of January every effort has been exerted in the different Departments, to bring forward the Preparations for the ensuing Campaign in North America, and though the Severity of the Weather, almost beyond what has ever been known in this Country, very much obstructs the Service in the Naval Department, yet I am encouraged to hope that the Reinforcement for the Army under your Command will be embarked before the end of March, and that the Armament intended for Quebec may be ready much sooner.

The unfortunate Events, which have happened in Canada, make it necessary that we should not only exert every Endeavour for the relief of Quebec as early as possible, but also for having a Force there, ready to commence its Operations, as soon as the Season will admit.

The great Attention, which the King shews upon all occasions to the rank & Merit of His Officers, would have led His Majesty to have appointed Major General Clinton to command upon this Service, under Major General Carleton, but as His Majesty's Pleasure has been already signified that he should command the Body of Forces to be employed upon an Expedition to the Southward, & he is, by this time probably sailed for Cape Fear, in order to wait their Arrival, His Majesty has thought fit that Major General Burgoyne should act as Second in Command to General Carleton in Canada, and that he should proceed thither with the Eight Regiments from Ireland, which I hope will be ready to sail by the 20th of next Month.

If Quebec should fall before any Relief can be got thither and Major General Carleton should unhappily not survive the Loss of it, the King's Intentions are that, in such an Event, the Command of the whole of His Majesty's Forces in North America should devolve upon you. It is also His Majesty's Intentions immediately to appoint Majors General Clinton, Burgoyne, Lord Percy & Lord Cornwallis, Lieutenant Generals in America; The old Colonels, who now act as Brigadiers, are to have Commissions as Majors General; and the other Colonels will be appointed Brigadiers.

In case of Major General Carleton's death it will remain with you to dispose of the different Commands, as you, in your discretion, shall think fit. It will consequently be in your power to leave the Command of the Troops on the Side of Canada to Major General Burgoyne, or, if you think it more advisable you may appoint General Clinton to that Service; And it being His Majesty's Pleasure that Major General Lord Cornwallis should be employed in Canada, he & his Regiment are to be sent thither as soon as he joins the Army under your Command.

In the present state of Affairs in North America the Security of Nova Scotia & Newfoundland are Objects of Attention; and I am commanded by the King to signify to you His Majesty's Pleasure that the two Battalions of Marines, now serving under your Command, or any part of them you shall judge necessary, should be posted at Halifax, and that a Detachment of Major Gorham's Corps be posted at St.

John's in Newfoundland, as a Garrison will be wanted there. It is also his Majesty's Pleasure that as many of the private Men of the 65th Regiment as are fit for Service should be turned over to the 27th Regiment, and if there are more than will complete it, you will incorporate them in any other Corps; That the 27th Regiment, when so completed, be joined to the Army under your Command, and that the Commissioned & Noncommissioned Officers & Invalids of the 65th be sent home to England.

I must not omit to acquaint you, before I leave the Subject of Military Arrangement, that the Officers of the Guards have expressed such Spirit & Zeal for His Majesty's Service, that His Majesty has ordered a Detachment of a Thousand Men rank & File, with Officers in proportion, to serve under you in America, and I have only further to add, that the King is so desirous of expressing upon every occasion His Royal approbation of the General Officers serving in the principal Ranks in America, that He has declared His Intentions that he will not employ any General Officer from hence who may be superior in rank to Majors General Clinton, Burgoyne, Lord Percy or Lord Cornwallis.

This letter will be entrusted to the Care of the Commander of His Matys Ship Greyhound, who will also deliver up to you the Officers of the Privateer fitted out by the Rebels under a Commission from the Congress, & taken by one of Admiral Graves's Squadron. The private Men have all voluntarily entered themselves on board His Majesty's Ships, but the Officers having refused so to do, it has been judged fit to send them back to America, for the same obvious reasons that induced the sending back the Rebel Prisoners taken in Arms upon the Attack of Montreal in September last.

It is hoped that the Possession of these Prisoners will enable you to procure the Release of such of His Majesty's

Officers and loyal Subjects as are in the disgraceful Situation of being Prisoners to the Rebels, for although it cannot be that you should enter into any Treaty or Agreement with Rebels for a regular Cartel for the Exchange of Prisoners, yet I doubt not but your own Discretion will suggest to you the means of effecting such Exchange without the King's Dignity & Honor being committed, or His Majesty's Name used in any Negociation for that purpose; And I am the more strongly urged to point out to you the Expediency of such a Measure, on account of the possible Difficulties which may otherwise occur in the case of foreign Troops serving in North America

I am &c

Geo: Germain.

Loss at Majorbagwaduce. 1776

We the Committee of Safty for Majorbigwaduce Being Supplicated by Mr Daniel Wordwell of this District for our assistance to inable him to Make Known unto Mr Deane Mr John Adames Mr Wythe Committee appointed By the Honorable Continental Congress to Receive accounts of Losses Sustained by the Ministerial troops this is therefore to Cartify their Honors the Committee and all others to whome it may Concerne that the above said Wordwel Did on the twelveth Day of September 1775 Saile from this place in a Sloop (being his own proppety laden with Cord wood) for piscattaqua with other articals as hides and Cash in order to procure provision for him selfe and Nighbours being on his Returne whome was taken by a man of war belonging to the King and finily Lost vessel and Effects. the Said Vessel was taken by our Enemy September the 30th 1775 and we the Said Committee having Maid Strict Inquire into the premeses find

Said Vessel to be Burden^d Sixty three tuns Saven years old two good Cabels and anchers Second Sute of Sals about halfe worne Verey good Standing Rigin Sixty Dollars in Stors being the property of Said Wordwel and the whole dependence the Said Wordwel had for the Suport of himselfe and family the whole of the above we Judge to be worth the Sum of two Hundred and fifty Eight pounds Lawfull money on board s^d Sloop (belonging to the Distrest Inhabetants) when taken Leather Cash & Nails to the Value of thirty Dollars.

> Joseph Young
> Mark Hatch   } Committee
> Joseph Perkins

Majerbigwaduce february the 1st 1776 then Jeremiah Wordwel and Peter Mugrige Came before us the Committee of Safty for s^d Majerbigwaduce they being the two hands belonging to daniel Wordwels Sloop when taken by a man of wor and after being Examaned and duly Coshoned to declare the whole truth Seresly and Solomly declard it was in Every Surcomstance as Related by us

> Joseph Young
> Mark Hatch   } Com
> Joseph Perkins

Petition of Nathan Jones   1776

To the Honble the Council and House of Representatives of the Colony of Massachusetts Bay —

The petition of Nathan Jones of Gouldsborough, Humbly Sheweth,

That whereas sundry people of a place called Dear-Island, did in the Month of August last forcibly take and carry away a Vessell, Gundalo and Bull belonging to your petitioner, much to the damage of the Inhabitants in general, and of your petitioner in particular. And whereas your honors did in the Month of December last, pass an order that said Vessell should be detained untill further orders, Wherefore your petitioner humbly prays your honors would grant him a hearing upon said matter, and your petitioner as in duty bound, will ever pray &c

Nathan Jones

Watertown Feby 3^d 1776

Letter from Wm Cutter. Feb. 16, 1776.

To the Whole Court —

I would inform Your Honr^s As Joshua Fabyan Esqr and My Self was Appointed to Raise two Companys in the County of Cumberland We have Attended that Service and by Agreement with Esqr Fabyan I Eng^{ed} to Raise a Company in the Easterly part of the County — I would Acquaint your Hon^{r}s that I have Enlisted a Company in North Yarth Brunswick Harpswell New Glocester New Boston and Windham Consisting of Ninety Men Encluding officers — the above S'^{d} Company Mete thiss day & Chose for their Capt Mr Winthrop Boston Mess^r Nathan Merril & Robert Duning Lef^{ts} Mr Thomas Addams Ensi^n — then immediately Marched for Cambridge — where I hope they will soon Arive — I am with Great Respect Your Hum^{le} Sr^t

William Cutter

Report. 1776.

In the House of Representatives Feby 16 1776

The Committe appointed to take into Consideration the Petition of Nathan Jones of Gouldsborough seting forth that he had a Vessel Gundelow & Bull taken forcably from him & praying that he may have a hearing thereon — Beg Leave to Report by way of Resolve — Viz^t Resolvd that the Person or persons who have in Custody the Vesel Gundelow & bull of the said Nathan Jones be & hereby _ Directed to apply to the Committe appointed by this Court to Examine into the Reason & Justness of the Capture of any Vessel or Vessels that have or may be taken in Custody by any Committe of Inspection Safety of Correspondence of any Town place or District or other person between penobscott & Mechias on or before the Twentieth Day of March next in Order to determin the Justness of taking said Vessel Gundelow &c, and in case they Neglect so to do the Captor or Captors are hereby Ordered and Directed to Deliver said Vessel with all they took with her to Nathan Jones or his Order imediately after the Expiration of said time.

N° 5

In the House of Representatives Feb^{ry} 16th, 1776.

Joseph Palmer Esqr brought down a Report of the Committee on the Letter of M. Lyon of Machias received yesterday.

Pass'd in Council vizt

In Council Feb^{ry} 16th 1776. Read and accepted and Order'd that the first Letter herein mention'd be sign'd by the Secretary by order of the General Court, and be sent to the Committee of Safety at Machias, and that the last recited Letter be sign'd by the Secry by order aforesaid, and be sent to the Committee of Correspondence of Northampton

Sent down for Concurrence

Read & Concurrd

Deposition.

The Deposition of Jeremiah Wardwel of majerbigwaduce being of Lawfull age testifies and Says that I the deponant did on or about the 12th day of September in the year 1775 Sale from Said majerbigwaduce in the Sloop Trythena Laden with Cordwood for piscataqua in order to procure Stoores and upon our Returne on the 30th day of the same month was taken by a man of war (viz) the Livele and finely Lost Vessel and Effects the Vessel was when taken about 7 years old had 2 Cable and anchers Secont Sute of Sales about halfe worne Verey good standing Rigin had on bord that belonged to my fathe_ daniel wordwel about Sixty Dollers worth of Stors there was Leather Cash and Nails on bord said vessel when taken about thirty three dollers worth that belonged to the Inhabetants of said majerbigwaduce Said Vessel is burdened 63 tuns

Jeremiah Wardwell

Colony Massachusetts Bay Feby 20th 1776

Jeremiah Wardwell made solemn Oath to the truth of the above

   Before John Taylor
     Justice Peace thrô ye Colony.

Letter from Edwd Parry. 1776.

Gentlemen I take the Liberty of addressing myself to you, and acquaint you, that having many unsettled and domestic Affairs in New Hampshire, where I used to reside, I petitioned the Honble the General Court of this Colony to release me, that I might return thither, previous to their ordering me into this Town, and putting me under your Care: my Affairs there still continue in the same unsettled precarious state, and am also in want of cloathing and other necessaries, I supposed their intention was to confine me here only for a short time, as I enjoyed no Office or commission under the Crown, nor (as I thought) had done any Injury to the Colonies, the duration of time they intended to confine me may possibly be elapsed; and if not, I apply to you Gentlemen to grant me liberty to return to my Home some time this Spring, and will return here whenever I am required; If you do not think that you can consistently grant me permission, be pleased to request your Representative to communicate my desire to the General Court, and you will greatly oblige

  Gentlemen your most obedient humble Servant

              Edwd Parry

Sturbridge Feb. 27th 1776

To the Selectmen of the Town of Sturbridge

In Council April 5th 1776

 Read & Ordered that the Petitioner have leave to proceed to Portsmouth on the Parole of his Honor to collect his Cloathing & settle his Business there so that he exceeds not the term of three months

 Sent down for Concurrence   Perez Morton D Sec^{ry}

In the House of Representatives April 8th 1776

 Read & nonconcurr'd   J Warren Spkr

           Sturbridge March ye 11th 1776

 Sir We have received the inclosed application from Mr Edward Parry for leave to return to his home in New Hampshire; We should imagine that his desire is reasonable and may be Complied with, and have no reason to think his requisition would be any detriment to the Public Affairs of the Colonies; but as we Cannot see that we can Consistently grant him permission of our selves — we request of you to

Communicate his application to the Honorable the General Court, and signify the result to

Sir your Humble Servants

Daniel Fisk
Daniel Plympton } Selectmen
Moses Weld   for
John Holbrook } Sturbridge

To Capt Timothy Parker

Letter from Timothy Pickering.   March 19, 1776.

Salem March 19, 1776

Sir   The Selectmen of Salem this day delivered to John Obrien two hundred pounds of powder for the use of the privateers Diligent & Machias Liberty in the service of this colony, as will appear by the inclosed receipt. The said Obrien shewed us a letter from Francis Abbot written for you as Commisary General, to Richd Derby j^r Esqr requesting him to furnish Obrien with that quantity of powder; but as the town had purchased the whole his vessel brought home, Obrien applied to us; and as the necessity appeared to be urgent we supplied him upon certain expectation of receiving the same quantity of you when requested, to be delivered at Salem without any expence to the town, or paid for at the price mentioned in the receipt, as the selectmen sh^d chuse. Of all which they give you this early notice, & pray that provision may be made for replacing the powder on the shortest notice, if they should judge it necessary for the town's safety.

I am, Sir, your most h'ble Servant

Tim. Pickering j^r

By order of the Select men

Superscribed
To Richard Devens Esqr At Watertown

Letter from Major Daniel Ilsley.   March 20, 1776.

Falmouth March 20th 1776

To the Honourable Counsel for the Provence of the Massachusetts Bay —

May^t Pleas Your Honours — the Commission I hold under Your Honours Gives me the Command of the Sea Cost men Stationed at Falmouth — at Present — which is my Apology for troubeling Your Honours at this time — I Expected when General Fry left falmouth there w^d be a Co^{ll} appointed and Sent to take the Command in a Short time — as I Cant hear of aney appointment Neither have I Rec^d aney Instructions how to fortify or where — General Fry has a New Plan which no Doup^t Your honours has Seen — this Plan will Command the Ground with Equil Strength on Every Side which is not Nesecary two Sides of this fort will have So grate advanteg of the ground that it may be Defended by Small Arms against a Verey Powerfull Enemy and Shuld the general Vew this ground when the weather was more moderate he might Change his mind — I think there is too much work Dun on the foorts at falmouth to be Laid aside — the Judgment of the County was taken Before the work was begun — and I Cant think that the first Plan will be mateerially objected to by any that will View the ground — we have Now 300 men in falmouth and Capt Morten at Cape Elizabeth with 80 men the guards on the Sea Cost are not yet Stationed — the Reports of the Enemy Leaving Boston and others ariveing at Hallifax is the Reason for Keeping the Sea Cost men Near togather we might have Dun Sumthing in Prepareing Pickets &c But General Fry advised me Not til I Received orders — the Cariges for Cannon wheel & handbarows are makeing the Soldiers Came without Powder the greater Part of them and Many of them without Ball I have Supplid without medling with the Provence Powder we Shall Indeavour to Collect what Shovels and Pick axes

we Can til we no how we are to be Provided the frost is
Near a foot thick in the ground at this time But the weather
is Now Very warm and Snow is Chefly gon — our men are
Sickly and they must Suffer if they Continu — we have Lost
But one — there is no Phisician Nearer then three miles — I
hope Your [honours] will Consider our Sick and make Such
Provision as your honours in your Wisdom shall think Proper
 From your Obedient Servant at Com^d
Daniel Ilsley

In Council March 30th 1776
 Read & Sent down   Perez Morton D Sec^y
 Committed to ye Committee on ye Cumberland Petition —

Letter from the Committee of Brunswick. March 28, 1776

 To the Honourable the Great and General Court Holden
at Watertown In and for the Province of the Massachusetts
Bay — the Committe of Brunswick in ye County of Cumberland Humbly beg Leave to Report That Last Summer there
was a Cargo of molases Landed here belonging to Isaac Smith
Esqr and Left in Care of Aaron Hinkly Esqr with orders to
Sell a Considerable part of said Cargo When it wast first
Landed it was Sold for 13/6 or 13/9 old tenor Soon after it
Riss to 14/ then to 15/ then towards the Spring to 20/
The people Here were Very much Dissatisfied at its being
Sold at Such an Exorbitant price and Look^d upon it, Considering the Distress of the present day to be Extortionous and
Grinding the face of the poor and Directly Repugnant to the
Salutary Resolves of the Worthy and Honourable Congress
of the United Colonies and Distructive to the Glorious Cause
of America.
 about ten or twelve Days ago there was a Vessell Come to
Carry away what was Left of s^d Cargo ye Inhabitants Desired

the Committee to stop so much molases as was absolutely Necessary for this place the Committe accordingly met and thought proper to Stop ten Hog^{ds} and Set it at 15/ which we though_ would be Sufficient to pay what it was first set at with Intrest of the money and cost of Storeing So that we apprehend the owner will be fully made whole

Brunswick March 28, 1776

      Nath^{ll} Larrabee ⎫
      James Curtis   ⎪ Committe
      Sam^{ll} Standwood ⎬ of
      Thos Thompson ⎪ Brunswick
      And^w Duning   ⎭

Report. 1776.

The Committee appointed to make inquiry with respect to the Powder & other war-like Stores latly arived at Kenebeck have attended that Service and beg leave to report by way of resolve (viz)

    In House of Representatives May 2^d 1776

Resolved That out of said Ammunition there be replaced in such Towns in this Colony the Powder flints and lead by them delivered for the use of this colony or the conteneental army (which have not received Compensation for the Same and chuse to have s^d Powder &c) as sone as may be and if any of s^d powder and other warlike Stores are <u>lost</u> to be disposed of as the General Court shall order.

      Mr Hobart
      Coll Woodbridge
      Coll Davis

to make inquiry with respect to the Powder & other Warlike Stores lately arriv'd at Kennebec & report how it shall be dispos'd of —

N⁰ 6

In the House of Representatives May 3ᵈ 1776.

Order'd that the following Letter be sign'd by the President of the Council and forwarded to the Indian Chiefs of the Penobscot Tribes

Sent up for Concurrence.

Friends & Good Brothers.

This Letter is to acquaint You that we receiv'd your favor by Lieutenant Gilman dated at Penobscot River the 22ᵈ November 1775, by which you have acquainted us, that you made choice of Mʳ Jonathan Lowder for your Truckmaster, and finding that Mʳ Preble was appointed you were not contented, and that You want to know how the alteration came to be made, you say you have heard that it was alterd by means of two young Indians that came here; in Answer to this We tell you that we are sorry that you are not contented with Mʳ Prebble, and have so many complaints against him.

this alterations in the Truckmasters happened by a very great mistake, as both these Men were to keep at Penobscot, but we trust you will excuse it, as we were then very much troubled with the white people of old England, which we have since drove out of our Colony, you tell us that when you agree to a thing you mean to stand to it, we mean to stand to all the promises we have made to You, You may depend on it, that all we have promis'd You will be done by us, Capᵗ Lane is oblig'd to go to New York, he can't come to You this Summer, but we have order'd Lieutenant Gilman to keep at Penobscot &c with You. You desire us to mind nobody but the Heads of your Tribe. We desire You for the time to come to sign all the Letters you send us with your marks, that we may not be deceived.

Dear Brothers, We have the pleasure to tell you, that by the help of God we have drove them wicked people of old England out of our Colony, and we trust and believe we shall be able to keep them out, we have built forts in almost all our Towns that are near the water, we are also a building a great many ships of war, with which we intend to drive away their Ships, we have heard that our enemies intend to go to Canada this Summer, if they do we trust you will help us drive them away, if we should want You. Your letter came so late that a great many of our Court were gone home before we received it, therefore we shall order the farther consideration of it to the next General Court which will be in June, they will send You a Truckmaster that You will be contented with, who will trade with You, and supply You with such things as You will want, if they can be bought. We wish You a blessing, health and prosperity and are

Your Friends & Brothers

Extract from Letter of General Howe to Lord George Germain.

Halifax May 7th 1776

In obedience to your Lordships Commands for a more explicit Account of the Expedition to Falmouth, which was entrusted to Lieut^t Mowat of the Navy, assisted by a Detachment of Marines & Artillery, I have reexamined the Officer who commanded this Detachment, & find that his Orders from General Gage were, to embark on board several armed Vessels the 6th October 1775, & to aid & assist Lieut^t Mowat in annoying and destroying all Ships & Vessels belonging to the Rebels on the Coast, & in the Harbours to the Eastward of Boston: That they first examined the Harbour of Cape Ann, & finding the Attack upon it inexpedient they proceeded to Falmouth, & laid the armed Vessels before the Town on the Evening of their Arrival, after which Lieut^t Mowat sent an officer on Shore with a Summons to the

Inhabitants to deliver up their Arms & Amunition, acquainting them at the same Time, that his Orders directed him to destroy the Town, if they did not comply with his Demand, of which they should be allowed two hours to consider & to remove their Women & Children; shortly after three Persons, deputed by the Inhabitants, came on board requesting a longer Time, & it was agreed to wait their Answer until eight Clock next Morning, about which Hour the same Persons returned, & reported that the Inhabitants were determined to wait their Fate: Within half an Hour a Signal was made by Lieut^t Mowat, the Vessels began a Cannonade, and several Carcasses were thrown into the Town, which set Fire to the Houses, & in a few Hours consumed the greatest part of them: a Detachment was then landed who compleated the Destruction, & embarked without Loss. The small Vessels in the Harbour were burnt, sunk, or brought away the 18th October, and the Armament returned to Boston the 5th Novr without attempting any further.

* * * * * * * *

Petition of Stephen Parker. May 11, 1776.

To the Honourable Council and the Honourable Representatives of the Colony of Massachusetts Bay.

May it please your Honours — With the profoundest respect and submission I beg leave to acquaint your Honors that the fifth of july last I took passage from this place for Philadelphia in hope of obtaining a supply of provision for the Inhabitants here, as I had not cash to purchase the Reverend Mr James Lyon furnished me with a letter of recommendation to his friend Jonathan Smith Esq of Philadelphia, but after the most earnest application to that gentleman & others during a months stay in the City with offers of mortgaging a considerable interest till Payment for one hundred barrels of flour, finding no probability of success & having nearly expended the trifle of money I carried with me I took passage with Captain Edward Bacon of Barnstable in a sloop loaded with flour, belonging to Colonel Doane of Welfleet bound for said place, arriving at Barnstable, I made pressing suit to Colonel Doane offering him the same but was here unsuccessful, I then try'd Captain Solomon Davis, Melatiah Bourn Esq, and Colonel Joseph Otis of Barnstable for assistance but these gentlemen not being disposed to risque or Credit their interest and my money being gone I was obliged to sell two of three barrels of flour which I brought from Philadelphia for my family. I then met Mr Shubael Lovel of Barnstable who gave me encouragement of sending a small schooner with some provisions to Mechias, but failing of obtaining the provisions, or fearing to risque his vessel this also fell thro', my solicitude was now turn'd to get home with all speed and going from Highannas to Nantucket with Mr Lovell he mentioned my case to Mr Timothy Fitch there, who told me if I could obtain permission for exporting Lumber to the West Indies he would supply me with provisions, in consequence of which I prosecuted a journey to Watertown, waiting on Colonel Joseph Otis and the Honourable James Bowdoin, who furnished me with recommendatory letters to the Honourable James Warren, but Collonel Warren presuming the matter would not be acceptable to the Honourable House, I returned full of anxiety & distress to Nantucket being reduced so low as to fear I should either suffer or be obliged to solicit the hand of Charity. On arrival at Nantucket I let Mr Fitch know my Circumstances with the scituation of Mechias and inform'd him that I thought I could serve that place effectually if I could go to Nova Scotia & send or carry hay from thence which we always supplyd ourselves with from said government for the support of our Cattle. Mr Fitch coincided in sentiment with me & we purchased of Captain Dunham of the Vineyard Three hundred thirteen bushels of Indian & fifteen bushels of rye Corn which was increased by a trifle of said articles & some rye flour & bread Mr Fitch had by him & we were preparing to sail when five or six people at Nantucket appeared dissatisfied on which I was advised by the Inhabitants to make application to the Committee at Falmouth, This I did & informing them what pains I had taken and at what expense I had been to serve Mechias with my earnest desire of getting home with what I could procure I obtained their consent to sail, on which we left Nantucket in a Brigantine commanded by Captain Thomas Fossey and meeting with one vessel only which appeard to chase us, arrived at East passage, from which Place we immediately proceeded to Cape Forschue in the bay of Fundy & directly oposite Mechias, here I disposed of what was on board save a small matter sold Mr William Pitts at East passage (exclusive of what I was intitled to from a Commission allowd me & which I strictly reserved in provision to Carry to Mechias) to New england people only, who appeard real friends to the welfare of America. On arrival I engaged a Schooner of one Mr Tinkham & seven Load of Salt hay (no english being to be had) intending immediately on the Brig's sailing to proceed therewith for Mechias but the Hay proving very bad & none else to be got, I faild in this but embrac'd the first oportunity I could meet of getting to Mechias with my Provisions, at the expense of ten dollars.

May it please your Honors — Ignorance, inadvertence & absolute necessity were the sole cause of my setting foot in the government of Nova Scotia & during my continuance there which was at Cape Forschue, I neither corresponded countenanced or associated with any of the enemies of America but most warmly espoused the cause of Liberty &

bore unfeigned testimony against the iniquitous tyranical ministerial measures & acts of Brittish parliament, nor was this confined to my tongue alone but my hand witnessed the same as leisure & oportunity gave me leave, Copies of which I humbly crave leave to lay at the feet of your Honours most solemnly declaring them to be authentic —

May it please Honours, from the first of my leaving Mechias last july to my arrival a few days since I have not ceased endeavours to serve the place to the utmost of my ability and I do most solemnly declare that nothing has, is, or can be remoter from my heart than an inclination to aid or abet the enemies of America, Liberty & Freedom, and in this necessary contest am willing to risque my interest in Life and for this purpose did strictly recommend to Captain Fossay to bring a quantity of powder for the use of the Colony Therefore throwing myself at the feet of your Honours I most humbly crave for myself and distressed family your Honours Pardon and protection, and as in duty bound shall ever pray for your Honours consummate Happiness & prosperity —

Stephen Parker

Mechias 11th May 1776 —

Letter from Stephen Parker. May 13th 1776.

May it please your Honour

You may remember I waited on you some time last September with a letter from Mr Timothy Fitch craving your interest for permission to send a vessel to the West Indies, in consequence of which you were pleased to write Colonel Warren on the subject and recommend the same, on my arrival at Watertown, presenting your letter and informing the Colonel of my business, he advised me not to mention the matter to General Court, as thinking it would not be granted, I submitted, and returned, and having expended what money I was possessed in seeking after relief for the inhabitants of Mechias, I mentioned to Mr Fitch my real opinion was, if I could proceed to the Bay in Nova Scotia & procure a quantity of hay it would be of eminent service to our people, as a large stock of cattle must die if no hay could be obtain'd but what was cut in the place, we being supplied with hundreds of Tons from Nova Scotia yearly. Mr Fitch joined in sentiment with me and accordingly agreed to allow me a commission for transacting some business, procured three or four hundred bushels of Corn & advised me as soon as the Brig he sent was dispatched, to get a Schooner & proceed to Mechias the command of the Brig was given Captain Thomas Fossey who arriving at East passage, we immediately proceeded to Cape Forschue (alias Yarmouth) here I agreed for a Schooner of one Mr Tinkham, & seven Tons of salt hay, no english being to be had, reserved what my commissions came to in provisions, & expected to proceed directly to Mechias on the Brig's sailing, but finding the hay so damaged, as to be unfit for any thing, and my being obliged to give fifty dollars for the run, freight, or no freight, it being now first of january, I concluded from the difficulties of weather & disappointment in hay to seek passage another and cheaper way, & the very first that presented I embraced at the expense of ten dollars tho' only twenty five leagues distant, bringing with me in provision which Mr Fitch ship'd, what my Commissions intitled me to.

May it please your Honour, my ignorance of the resolves of the Grand Congress, my necessitous circumstances & real concern for my family, with my ardent desire of serving the inhabitants of Mechias, and not lucrative motives or the remotest thought of joining myself with the enemies of America, were the cause of my putting foot in the Government of Nova Scotia, and I here solemnly declare to your Honour that I went to a place (vizt Yarmouth) which is inhabited almost entirely by New England people and who appear to be as true friends to the welfare of America & grand cause of Liberty as any persons whatever nor have I corresponded with, or sold any articles to any other, having strictly avoided furnishing any inhabitant of Halifax, officer, soldier, seaman belonging to the Crown, or any transport engaged in the service thereof with one article great or small. On my arrival here, as I had been to Nova Scotia the inhabitants seem dissatisfied and to what length it may grow I know not, I therefore presume most earnestly to crave your Honours candor and interest with the Honourable Court in my behalf, for if I have offended 'tis not with any design or the least alienation from the great and glorious cause in which America is engaged, but the effect of Ignorance & pure necessity for from the first of my leaving Mechias for Philadelphia, which was early last july, my principles & declarations, publick & private have been immoveably fixt in the most steadfast attachment to the Libertys & prosperity of this suffering Land America. I beseech for the sake of my poor distressed ailing wife, and helpless children that I may not be deem'd an enemy to the welfare of my native Country, the Cause of America or the least cool thereto or be made to suffer by censure or otherways, for as I ever have been, I now am, and trust ever shall be ready to give the most solemn assurances of my fervent regard to the Laws, Dignity and Interest of this virtuous, oppress'd & most justly strugling Land.

I beg leave to lay these my earnest requests at your Honours feet, and subscribe myself with profound respect Your Honours most obedient humble servant

Stephen Parker

I presume to enclose a copy of my petition to the Honourable Court

Superscribed:
To The Honorable James Bowdoin Esqr
at Middleborough or Boston.—

Copy of Record. Complaint against Rev. Jacob Bayley.
May 24, 1776.

At a Meeting of the Committee of Correspondence Inspection and Safety for the Town of Pownalborough May 24th 1776

Upon the Complaint against the Revd Jacob Bailey for being unfriendly to the Cause of Liberty, Resolv'd

1. That the said Jacob Bailey has in adverse Instances since the Year 1774; discover'd an undue Attachment to the Authority claimed by Great Britain over the united Colonies, and thereby has given great Reason to believe That he does not wish Success to our Struggles for Freedom.

2. That he has been Guilty of a criminal Neglect in not reading Proclamations issued by the Continental and Provincial Congresses, for days of public fasting & Prayer, and thereby throwing Contempt upon said Congresses and virtually denying their Authority.

3. Therefore Resolv'd That the said Jacob Bailey give Bond to the Treasurer of this Colony, in the penal Sum of Forty Pounds, with one or more Sureties, condition'd That the said Mr Bailey appear before the General Court of this Colony when called thereto by said Court to answer for said Conduct, and in the mean Time That he shall not aid the despotic Measures of our unnatural Enemies, or by any Ways or Means directly or indirectly assist them in their Designs of enslaving the said Colonies, or in any Measure what ever counteract the good Designs of the said Colonies in obtaining their Liberty & Freedom from the tyrannic Measures of Great Britain; and that the said Mr Bailey shall observe & obey all the Orders, Resolves & Laws of the said Court & of the Continental Congress and in all Things behave himself

peaceably towards the People and Government of this Colony.

A True Copy Att: Cha⁸ Cushing Chairman

Letter from the Committee at Machias. May 25, 1776.

To the Honorable Council & the Great and General Court of the Coloney of the Massachusetts Bay In New England —

These may inform your Honors: that whereas Stephen Parker went from Machias with Letters of Recommendation from the Chaireman of the Committee to procure if possible for Machias aforesaid being then in great want & he proseeded to Philadelphia as he informes and proves by Letters brought and with out any suckses and on his Return back being at Nantucket he met with one Mr Timothy Fitch with whoom he says he agreed to send provisions to Machias and take Lumber there for in Case that Liberty Culd be obtained for the said Fitch to send the Lumber from Machias to the West Indies —

On Account of Which he the said Parker Says that he went from Nantucket to Water Town in order to obtain Liberty of Your Hono^{rs} for to trade to the West Indies but was advised not to Mention it and then he the said Parker Returned back to Nantucket and Ingaged to take a Brig belonging to the said Fitch and proceed with her to Capepersue In the Province of Nova Scotia and there to sell of the Provisions and by a load of fish for the s^d Brig and procure a Nova Scotia Register Which he Says he Went to Halifax and obtained and then ordered the said Brig to proseed to Jamaca —

But as there was some Dispute about provisions being Carrayed out of Nantucket with out a permit from some of the Committee on the Continen Said Parker applyed as we have ben informed to the Committee of Falmouth for a permit which was Granted accordingly for the said Parker to bring Provisions to Machias aforesaid and then he proseeded to Capepersue as aforesaid and Delt as afore said with out as he sayeth any intent of Bring the said provisions to Machias Exsept his Commissions on the Cargoe which he has actualy Brought in the Whole or in part —

And for the afore said Reasons we have thought proper to take the said Parkers Notes of hand which he had by him in to our possession and them safe to keep for Securety that he shuld Not Depart this plase until your Honers pleasure is Known and there fore we take this oppertuneyty to In form your Honers of our proseedings and hoop your Honers will Give us further Directions as you in Your Wisdom shall think Best for the peace and Wellfare of the United Coloneys — The Securetys taken amounts to £187 : 5–9. we thought best to Inform Your Honors and Not to send the person without it is Required and we shall be always Readey & Will Cheerfuly Obey your Honers Commands and any advice your Honers may think fit to Give us will be greatfully Acknowledged by your Humbel Sarvents

By order of the Committee

Wm Tupper Clerk

May 25 1776

In Council June 10th 1776

    Read & sent down

John Lowell Dp^y Sec^y P T

In the House of Representatives June 21st 1776

Read & committed to the Committee on the Petition of Stephen Parker

    Sent up for Concurrence

Tim^o Danielson Sp^r p Tem:

In Council June 21st 1776

    Read & concurred

John Lowell Dp^y Sec^y P T

Letter from Hon. Charles Chauncey. May 27, 1776.

Sir/ Being conscious of acting with integrity, and of having done my duty (so far as the narrow limits of my capacity would allow), while a member of the Honble Board; and it being possible, that I may be chosen again this Year. I have to ask the favor of you, to inform, the Honble Assembly; That notwithstanding the great reluctance I have, in declining so Honorable an appointment, Yet, when I realize my inability, to perform the duty attending it; my want of health, and the unhappy situation of my Family together with my being so much affected with a sense of my own insufficiency; should such an appointment take place, for these reasons, I shall be obliged, to resign the important trust, and have come to a determination so to do. At the same time I must assure, that no other Motives induce me hereto, but those herein expressed.

As the unfeigned love I bear towards my Country, has not in the least abated, the same principles, ardor & Zeal, by which I was at first actuated, still remain fixed, & determinate, and I am ready whenever it appears necessary, to hazard every thing in the Publick service. —

Hoping that Heaven will smile on all your deliberations, I am with sincere respect, and the greatest regard, to the Honble Assembly, Sir, your most obedient & humble Servant

Cha. Chauncy

The Honble President of the
Council of the Colony of Massach^tts Bay

Bond of Rev. Jacob Bailey. May 28, 1776.

Know all Men by these presents That we Jacob Bailey of Pownalborough in the County of Lincoln Clerk and David Bailey of Pownalborough aforesaid yeoman are holden and stand firmly bound & obliged unto the Honorable Henry Garnder of Stow in the County of Middlesex Esqr Treasurer of the Colony of the Massachusetts Bay in the Sum of Forty Pounds to be paid unto the said Henry Treasurer as aforesaid or his Successors in said office To the true Payment whereof we bind our Selves our heirs Exec^{rs} & Adm^{rs} Jointly & Severally firmly by these presents. Sealed with our Seals. Dated the Twenty Eighth day of May A. D. 1776 —

The Condition of this present Obligation is such That whereas on the Twenty Fourth day of May A. D. 1776 the Committee of Correspondence, Safety and Inspection of the Town of Pownalborough aforesaid did pass three Resolves in the Words following viz.

"1 That the said Jacob Bailey has in diverse Instances since the Year 1774, discovered an undue attachment to the Authority Claimed by great Britain over the United Colonies and thereby has given great Reason to believe that he does not wish Success to our Struggles for Freedom.

2 That he has been Guilty of a Criminal Neglect in not reading Proclamations issued by the Continental and provincial Congresses for days of publick Fasting & Prayer, & thereby throwing Contempt upon said Congresses, & Virtually denying their Authority.

3. Therefore resolved that the said Mr Jacob Bailey give Bond to the Treasurer of this Colony in the penal Sum of forty pounds with one or more sureties Conditioned that the said Mr Bailey appear before the General Court of this Colony when called thereto by said Court to Answer for said Conduct, and in the Mean Time that he shall not Aid the despotick Measures of our Unnatural Enemies, or by any ways or means directly or indirectly Assist them in their designs of enslaving the said Colonies, or in any Measure whatever counteract the good designs of the said Colonies in Obtaining their Liberty & Freedom from the tirannic Measures of Great

Britain and that the said Mr Bailey shall observe & obey all the Orders Resolves & Laws of the said Court and of the Continental Congress, and in all things behave himself peaceably towards the People & Government of this Colony."

Now if the said Jacob Bailey shall appear before the said General Court of this Colony when called thereto by said Court to answer for said Conduct, and in the Mean Time shall not Aid the despotic Measures of our Unnatural Enemies, or by any ways or means directly or indirectly Assist them in their designs of enslaving the said Colonies, or in any Measure whatever Counteract the good designs of the said Colonies in obtaining their Liberty & Freedom from the tirannic Measures of Great Britain & further if he the said Jacob Bailey shall observe & obey all the orders Resolves & Laws of the said Court and of the Continental Congress and in all things behave himself peaceably towards the People & Government of this Colony then this Obligation to be Void, otherwise to remain in full force & Virtue

                                Jacob Bailey   Seal

Signed Sealed & Deliv^d   David Bailey   Seal
   in Presence of
    Obadiah Call Junr
    Caleb Barker

Representatives.

Representatives at Watertown, May 29, 1776
York County.

York,	Joseph Simpson Esq.
Kittery,	Edward Cutt Esq.
Wells,	Joseph Storer Esq.
Berwick,	Col. Ichabod Goodwin
Arundell,	Benjamin Durrill
Biddeford,	James Sullivan Esq.

	Cumberland
Falmouth	Hon. Jedidiah Preble Esq.
	Samuel Freeman Esq.
	John Wall Esq.
	Mr. Joseph Noyes
North Yarmouth,	John Lewis Esq.
Scarborough,	Joshua Fabyan Esq.
Cape Elizabeth,	Mr. James Leach
Gorham,	Mr. Caleb Chace
Harpswell,	Snow

Letter from James Sullivan.   June 4, 1776.

Biddeford 4th of June 1776

Sir   Since I left the court I have recollected that there is no Truckmaster at Penobscot to supply the Indians on the Bay of Funday and the Saint Johns Tribe — When their Chiefs were up in the last Summer, they informed the Court that they had Six hundred fighting men — Brigadier Preble was appointed truckmaster for them but believe that he never Accepted the office one Lowder was Nominated by the Indians but Nothing has been done — as the Country of these Indians are within Nova Scotia & Contiguous to Halifax there is great danger of their being inticed to take part with the more Savage British Troops in which Case our Settlements in Machias &c will be broken up & a very great Number of persons will become a public Charge — as the Indians are ready to pay for all their Supplies in furs and as the present is the Time for their bringg the same in I think that this matter deserves immediate attention you will therefore be kind enough to mention it to the House

I am Sir with the greatest Respect your Most Hble Servt

Ja Sullivan

Hon James Warren Esqr

*Letter from Committees of Newbury, Haverhill, Bath, &c.
June, 1776.*

To the Honourable the Council, and general Assembly of the Province of the Massachusetts Bay,

From the Committees of the Towns of Newbury, Haverhill, Bath and Mooretown met at Newbury June 25, 1776. On Account of some very alarming News from St Johns, received the Evening before by two Men, from Onion River, of public Veracity.

That they saw a Letter from General Sullivan to Lieu^t Allen, to have all the Inhabitants of the Towns on Onion River to Remove with all possible Dispatch, not knowing but the Enemy would be upon them soon, this they received last Thursday Evening, and they removed the next Day. That it was feared the Enemy would get the upper hand, the sick of our Army were all sent to Crown Point. In the Generals Letter it was said the Regular Army consisted of about thirty thousand, and fifteen hundred Canadians and five hundred Indians

The Continental Army was retreated to St John's, And last Fryday a very heavy fire of Cañon was heard all the day.

The Committee voted to send Major Jonathan Hale and Capt. Robert Johnston with the Above said Information to Head Quarters at Massachusetts Bay and New Hampshire, and to inform them of the dangerous situation these Parts were in, and that except we are immediately supported we shall be obliged to quit these Parts. In our extreem Danger, as exposed every day to the Enemy, the Committees beg the Favor of two hundred fire Arms and Ammunition equal, As so much is necessary for our selves. And if the above Information be true, which we do not dispute, this fertile part of the Country must be soon abandoned to the Enemy except timely Aid can be had of a sufficient Number of Men as well as Arms and Ammunition, the Damage of which to the Continental Cause is needless for us to represent. We would only further add, that if it be judged best to make a stand here a few Small Cannon will be necessary. We are Gentlemen your humble Servants

James Bayly   } Chairmen for
Jacob Bayley   } Newb^y & Haverhill

In the House of Representatives June 28, 1776

Read and committed to Coll Orne Coll. Bagley Mr Wright with such as the Hon^{bl} Board shall join

 Sent up for Concurrence

Tim^o Danielson Sp^r pro Tem

Council June 28th 1776

Read & concurred & Jerem^h Powel & Jos. Cushing Esqr are joined

John Lowell Dp^y Sec^y P T

The Committee of both Houses appointed to take into Consideration the Letter from Newbury & Haverhill, requesting a Supply of Arms and Ammunition, in their exposed situation have attended that service, and beg leave to report that considering the Arms and Ammunition Supplyed the Men in the Continental Army, and the destitute Circumstances of the Colony upon the Eastern frontiers, & upon the Sea Costs, are of opinion that it is not at present in the Power of this Court to Comply with the Request made in said Letter —

Jer Powell p Order

In Council June 29th 1776   Read & Accepted
Sent down for Concurrence   John Lowell Dp^y Sec^y P T

In the House of Representatives June 29th 1776

 Read & concurrd   Tim^o Danielson Sp^r p Tem

Report. 1776.

The Committee of both Houses appointed to confer together Upon the Subject of the last requisition from the Continental Congress beg leave to report—

that two Regiments on the Continental Establishment be forthwith raised within the Several Counties in this Province Excepting the Counties of Cumberland & Lincol_ Dukes County & Nantucket and the Towns of Cape Ann, Marblehead, & Boston by a draft Imeadiatly to be Made of Every twentieth man in the Alarm, & training band Lists exclusive of those already raised or ordered to be raised — And that some effective Measures be taken to Inforce the raising the five thousand men Already granted by this Court for Canada & New York.

Jer: Powell p Order

In Council July 8th 1776   Read & sent down

Jn° Avery Dpy Secrt

Letter from the Committee of Machias. July 9, 1776.

To the Honble Council & The Honble The House of Representatives of the Colony of the Massachusetts Bay

We the Committee of Safety for Machias, beg Leave to Acquaint your Honours that on Satturday Last came into our Harbour the Viper Sloop of War, & She has taken five fishing Vessels, Two of which had about one hundred Quintals of fish Each, all which Vessels were taken as they were passing by our Harbour bound home. & said Man of War after Tarrying here Two days sailed for Annapolis Royal with her prizes where the Ship Marlin of Eighteen Guns Lyes. there to fix out one or two of the schooners for Tenders to Cruize upon the Shore for three Months to pick up Every

Vessel that passes. her station is as we are Informed by Mr Ralph Hacock from Mount Desert to Granmenan. Mr Hacock was Master of one of the Vessels Taken. owned in this place and the Capt of the Viper gave him Leave to Come on shore by his pleading the great necessity of his family. and Mr Hacock gives further Information that the Viper mounts Ten guns six pounders. and Twenty swivels. & has one hundred & Thirty Men. but have been at Two thirds allowance all their Cruize. We would Inform your Honours that had the Machias privateers been here we should have Tryed to have taken the Viper but being destitute of any such assistance we Lye Almost at the Mercy of our Enemies. if we cannot pass with our Vessels we cannot maintain our families but a short time in this place. Therefore we beg that your Honours would take our Difficult Circumstances into your Consideration and Grant us such Relief as you in your Wisdom shall think proper and we the Committee as in duty bound will Ever pray

By order of the Committee   Benj^a Foster Char^n

Letter from Benj. Austin. July 19, 1776.

Boston 19 July 1776

S^r I have lookt over the Court & Council Files for Octr last & can find nothing of the order of Court for presents to the Penobscot Indians, am therefore at a loss what to do in procuring the Presents for the St Johns & Mickmacs, I beg the fav^r you would desire the Secret^y to Examine the Files preceeding Oct^r & those that follow, I was told they were all in Boston, but its not so — if these Articles are not to be found, I beg the favor the Honble Board would let me know what Articles I am to procure as I shall wait in Town this day for the Same — The <u>Gorget & Heart</u> I have two Men at Work upon, & hope to have them by Tuesday.

I am S^r your Most Obed^t Servt

B Austin

The Honble Thomas Cushing Esqr

Letter from Wm Loud.   July 20, 1776.

Muscongus Island near Bristol July 20th 1776

S^r I saw a Letter from Colo^{ll} Wm Jones of Bristol to Capt Jam^s Hilton of s^d place Informing him of the Capture of Generall Thompson & many officers, as also the Retreat of Generall Sulivan to St Johns and the Doubt of his ability to Support that post as also that 1500 Canadians and 500 Indians were Employ'd by Gen^{ll} Burgoine to Attack our back Settlements also orders for s^d Hilton to have his Company of Militia in order of Defence — Capt Hilton sent Inteligence Eastward to the Settlements — But S^r in my oppinion Inteligence without Amunition will be of little service, and I do not think that one tenth part of the Inhabitants have any, Neither do I think it possible for them to be Supply'd Except by the Congress and therefore at present in a Wooful condition if attack'd   I Doubt not S^r but that you Remember Mr Waterman Thomas of Waldoborough who was up to the Congress the Year past on Acc^t of Supply for many Settlements but could not obtain it, now if no Speedy Supply, and the Enemy approach you may Expect Dismall news from this quarter —

As the Inhabitants have been Drove to great Straits on Acc^t of not having market for their Lumber the Year past and the Supports of life having been so dear to them I cannot see how it is possible at present for them to Raise cash for Amunition and if Some way cannot be propos'd as to furnish for a hereafter pay then farewell to Defence — I Imagine it will be some time before the many Settlements will be notify'd of the Danger and be Abe to Meet & Consult measures for Safety, and as there are Many Settlements and Islands that have no Representatives or acquaintances in the Congress I Desire y^t you would be so good as to use y^r Endeavours to have a Supply for them on Such Terms as You may think propper Which will be ever Esteem'd as a favour done to y^r Hum^{bl} Servt

Wm Loud

N. B. I beleive Islands & non Incorporated places are not omitted in the province tax and as for my part I am and have been ever Ready & willing to pay such & have done it many Years.

S^r the favour of a line from You to Inform me w^t Dependance may be had on Acc^t of Amunition Directed to my Self or Waterman Thomas Esqr of Waldoborough will greatly oblidge Y^{rs} &^{c} W. L——

N. B. I have four that bear Arms

Superscribed:

To John Taylor Esqr one of the Provincial Congress to be left at the Most propper place in Watertown as you may think

p̱ favour of Capt Martindale

Letter from Hon. James Bowdoin.   July 25, 1776.

Boston July 25. 1776

Honble Gent^n

The enclosed Petition from Winslow came to hand ye last Evening. The most effectual means of Securing the Eastern Parts of the Colony from an inland-Attack, and quieting the minds of the people setled there, I humbly apprehend is to engage the St Johns, Mickmac Penobscot and other Eastern Indians to engage heartily in the war, agreable to Genl Washington's Request.

For this Purpose I beg to suggest to your Honours, whether it would not be proper, that three or four or more Suitable Persons be engaged to go imediately into the Indian Country, along with the Indians that are now here, and inlist them into the Service without delay. I cannot but apprehend such a measure would be attended with Success, and that General Washington in that Case would in a short time have a considerable body of them: which would answer the double purpose of assisting him, and securing our Eastern Frontiers, which otherwise may be in great danger of being broken up by these same Indians.—

I am most respectfully Yr Hon^{rs} most obed^t hble Servt

James Bowdoin

To ye hon^{ble} Council of Massach^{ts} Bay

In Council July 25 1776

Read & Order'd that John Winthrop Saml Holten & John Taylor Esqr be a Comittee to take this Letter with ye Petition accompanying the same under Consideration & Report—

Jno Avery Dp^y Sec^y

Letter from Hon. James Bowdoin. July 30, 1776.

Boston July 30, 1776

To his Exc^y Genl Washington

Sir

At ye time your Excy's Letter was rec^d requesting the aid of this Governm^t in procuring a body of ye Eastern Indians for the Service of the United States, it happend very fortunately, that a number of them were here as delegates from ye St John's and Mickmac Tribes in Nova Scotia.

They came on a visit to you in consequence of y^r Letter to them, which they produced: And soon after a couple of Chiefs arrived here from the Penobscot Tribe. At the Conference held with the former there appeared in them a very good disposition in favour of the united States, and the Genl Court having resolved that a Regiment should be raised for the Service of ye States to consist of 500 Indians & 250 English, it was strongly urged upon them to join with us in the war: And accordingly they have engaged to do it, and have signed a Treaty for that purpose. By what they said at ye Conference it appeared the six villages they represented could furnish about 120 men: but as those villages are at a great distance from each other, their Men dispersed in hunting, and they proposed to call the whole to consult together, they said they should not be able, and they could not engage to come till the next Spring. The St John's Delegates however, on being told they lived near, and could be soon here again, promised to return early in ye Fall with about 30 of their Tribe.

There are six other villages of Mickmacs, who had not been informed of your letter, and had not therefore sent Delegates, but are equally well disposed, and have about ye same number of men belonging to them. These therefore can probably furnish for the Service a like number with ye other.

With regard to the Penobscots, They appeared well disposed. They said that when G^l Washington sent his Army to Canada, five of their People went with them, & were at ye Siege of Quebec: two of whom were wounded, and three taken Prisoners who had Since returned; that they had been promised, an allowance sh^d be made to those who went with Col^o Arnold; the Support of whose families in their absence had been a great burthen to them: and that they had no recompence for these services. They were told this matter would be represented to Gen¹ Washington, and that what is right & just he would order to be done. They said further they looked on themselves to be one people with us, and that whatever Governm^t we were under, they were willing to subject themselves to; that they had no doubt that their tribe would be willing to join Gen¹ Washington and that when they got home they w^d call ye tribe together and consult them for that purpose

This good dispositions appearing in all ye Indians, the Council thought it best, in consequence of your letter, to send with the Indians into their own Country, the most suitable persons that could be had in order to procure wth ye utmost expedition the number of Indians you desire may be engaged in ye Service of the States, or as many as can be procured. An armed Vessel is accordingly engaged to carry these Indians to Penobscot and St Johns where those tribes will be respectively assembled, and all that can be persuaded, inlisted into the Service imediately. Mr Fletcher, who came with the Penobscots, is employed in this Business with regard to that Tribe, and Major Shaw employed with regard to ye St John's and their neighbours at Passamaquoddy. It being expected a considerable number might be had from these tribes in a short time, the said Vessel was engaged in order to bring them up hither as soon as may be. One Mr Gilman is also employed, to go to the St Francois Indians, and engage as many as he can of them.

On the Conference with St John & Mickmacs (a copy of which is enclosed, together with a Copy of the Treaty) three of them offered themselves to join ye army at New York immediately, and their offer was accepted: as it might not only Secure ye fidelity of the Tribes they belonged to but induce many others of them to engage in ye Service. Another has since joined them. Accordingly these four, one of whom can speak French, will immediately set off for New

York, under ye conduct of Mr Wm Shaw: who is ordered to wait upon you with them.

The Council hope these measures will be effectual for the Purpose they were ordered. In their name & behalf I have the honour to be with every Sentiment of respect

Yr Excy'^s most obed^t hble ser^t

James Bowdoin

The names of the four Indians above-mentioned viz Joseph Denaquara of Winsor who Speaks English & French } Mickmacs
Peter Andrè of La Hève
Sabattis Hetoscobuit of Gaspee
Francis of St John's

Georgetown August 3^d 1776

Whereas, Application has been made to the several Towns in this Coloney, to procure a Sum of hard Money to carry on the Canada Expedition with Success, to be exchanged for continental Bills; we the Subscribers, do hereby promise that we will pay to the Committee of Georgetown aforesaid, the Sum set to our Names, on the Conditions above in hard Money:

Witness our Hands.

Ja^s McCobb two hundred Dolors	£60	00	00
Hannah McCobb fifty Dolors	15	00	00
Jordan Parker 20 Dollars	6	0	0
Thomas Capron 20 Dollars	6	0	0
Saml MCobb 50 Doll^s	15	0	0
Willm Rogers 30 Dolars	9	0	0
John Parker one hundred Dollars	30	0	0
Nath^ll Wyman Nine Dolors	2	14	
David Mors Aight Dolers	2	8	
William Walles fore Dollers	1	4	

Sarah McKentier Nine Dolers	2	14	
William Sprague Ten Dolors	3	0	0
George Rogers 20 Dolors	6	0	0
Daniel King 16 Dolors	4	16	0
James Butler 16 Dollars	4:	16	0
John Hinson Sixtey Dollers	18	00	0
William Butler 16 Dollors	4	16	0
James Juett 40 Dollars	12	0	0
Benj^a Lemont 20 Doluers	6	0	0
James Lemont 20 Doluers	6	0	0
David King 13 Dollers	3	18	0
Jn° Wood Fifteen Dollars	4	10	
Hony Sewall Twenty Dolers	6	0	0

Letter from Timothy Langdon. Aug. 9, 1776.

Pownalboro' 9th August 1776

Sir

I should take it as a favour if you wou'd look over the records of Council for August & September 1775 & inform me if Lieu^t Nathan Smith deliverd any papers relating to the Schooner Gammon or Phillips Master if there are any such papers if you will send me a pass from Admiral Graves that is amongst them, or copy of it you shall be satisfied for your trouble

I am Sir Your humble Servant

Tim° Langdon

Mr John Avery

Letter from Col. Jon: Mitchell. Aug. 9, 1776.

To the Honorable, the Council of the State of the Massachusetts Bay

May it Please your Honors

As I have some particular Business, of a private Nature which renders my being personally at Boston about the middle of September, of very great importance to me; I therefore take the Liberty to ask your Honors Permission for Leave of Absence to go thither at that Time, which, (should you think proper to grant) I shall esteem a particular favour:

I can with the greater freedom sollicit your Indulgence herein, as we shall soon be in a tolerable state of defence at this Place, and I hope as well prepared for the Reception of the Enemy as our Number of Men and Cannon will permit — I wish to tarry no longer Time, than what is absolutely necessary for the Accomplishing my Business

I am with profound Respect your Honours Hb^l Servt

Jona^t Mitchell

Falm^o 9th Augt 1776

In Comittee of Council Augt 14th 1776

Ordered that the Prayer of the within Petition be granted and that he the said Col^o Mitchell have a Parole of Absence to go to Boston and attend his own private Business about the Middle Sepr next agreeable to his Request and to return to his Duty as soon as he can

Jno Avery Dp^y Sec^y

Letter from Thomas Fletcher. Aug. 16, 1776.

To the Honble the Councill of the State of Massachusetts Bay —

May it please your Honours Agreeble to your Instructions Deliverd me in Councill Dated 27th July 1776 To proceed to ye residence of the Penobscot Indians to Endeavour to Enlist as many of them as I could to serve in the War under his Excellency General Washington — Agreeable to my Instructions Immediatly on my Arrival at Penobscot, I Proceeded up the river accompany'd with Col^l Lowder to

Mr Jere : Colburns near Penobscot Village where I meet with some Indians, & sent to the Tribe to acquaint them of my Business and in Answere to it they appointed Tuesday 13th August to meet me at Colo Lowders at ye Falls Accordingly they meet with Eighteen Cannoes amounting to about thirty besides Woemen & Children. I read to them my Instructions & also his Excellency Gen¹ Washingtons request to Inlist Indians, & the Establishment for ye Pay of the Army. Their Answer is as follows. That they don't think that any of their young men can be spar'd, for that they don't know how soon they may be wanted to Defend themselves against the English Army.

They hear by the Eastern Indians that their is a great many English Ships gone up Cannada River with Troops— and that their is a Large Fort Built on Point Levy Oppisite Quebeck & by whom they don't know and their is now a strong guard of English kept at Soceconick a french settlement on Shodier River, which is the reason that their young men don't Choose to Engage at Present for fear that the English party may induce French & bad Indians to come amongst them & Destroy them and us — otherwise they would Emediately join General Washington in his Army at the Southward — They say they shall keep men to make Discoveries & from time to time will Inform us of their proceedings, for their safty and ours, as we are all of one familly — They were ask'd If the Colony should raize a Number of men as Rangers to reconnotoier the Country, to watch the Motion of the Enemy — wether any of their young men would join the Party they reply'd they would willingly —

They desired me to inform you that all the Settlers on their, were present at this Interview, and that they agreed that the English shall remain as far up the River as ye Tide flows & no farther, & those that were settled above should be remov'd, and the Boundary Line should be at the head of the

Tide, & Gave the settlers leave to Tarry on their Lands untill they got in their Harvest —

There was a Number of their young men that was desireous to go up to the Court I told them unless they Inlisted for one or two years that it would not Answere the Intention of the Colony & therefore I would not Consent to their going — I beg leave to Subscribe my self

Your Honors most Obedient Humble Servt to Command

Thos Fletcher

Penobscot River Augt 16th 1776

In the House of Representatives Sept. 2^d 1776

Read and committed to Coll Coffin Capt Batchelder & Mr Sergeant with such as the Honble Board may join — Sent up for Concurrence

J Warren Spk^r

In Council Sepr 3. 1776

Read & Concurr'd Jabez Fisher and John Tay

John Av—

Letter from Major Danl Ilsley. Aug. 20, 1776.

Falmouth August 20th 1776

Gentlemen

I am Sorrey to troubel you with an Acc^t of the Deseegreable Situation of our Troops under the Command of Coll Mitchell — the Coll has all along Shown Himself More unlike a Soldier or a Gentleman then any thing Els- the task is Deseegreable to Shew to the Publick the Defects of a Superior — I am Censable of the Desadvanteg I am under when Speeking of such was it only the Personal ill treatment Rec^d my Self (Knowing my obligation to my Superior) I might have Boarn With Such Usage When the Coll took the Command it was my Gratest Ambition (Knowing how

intierly unacquainted with the Buisness he had engaged in)
to Inform him as far as my Small Abillityes w^d admit of —
it was by the Coll^s Desier I keept the orderly Book in the
Same manner as whilst I Commanded — tho Never in the
Least Controul^d me all he had to Do with the matter was to
Sign his name to the orders — yet I was often abused in
other matters — as to his Giveing aney Instructions Con-
searning the Loins Foorts Batteries or Prepareing tools timber Plank wood or Iron for Gun Carreges he Did not Chues
to Consarn himself with — the Reason I Suppose is their was
a Posability of marking the Caller — Provided the General
Court Shuld Disaprove Such Proceedings — By this time the
New arrangment Coms to falmouth for Ranking the Captn^s
at which time I Request the Coll to give General orders to
the Regiment in his own name that they might no their
alarm Post and their Duty in case of an alarm — and the
Duty of Guards and to Establish the Rank of Captains —
the Coll Refused Giveing any orders of the kind to any
Body Except Capt Morten and Lowell — which the Coll
asked me to Rate — I Declind telling him I Culd not think
it Proper to give orders to two Captn^s only when the whol
Regiment was neglected — I then Desiered the Coll to Call
the Regiment together and Let them no their Ranks — the
Coll Ripled he Shuld not meddel with the matter — I told
him I was Inform^d the Counsel had Ranked the Regement —
He Said it was the first he Ever [heard] of^t — I told him I was
well inform^d their was an order Counsel in falmouth for Ranking Capttains he Replid it was the first he Ever heard of it
the matter was Intierly New to him — I Replid the third time
in Near those words Coll I am well Inform^d that an order of
Counsell has bin Deliverd into your hand for that Purpes
and I am Surpriesd to hear You Say You Never heard of it
— the Coll in a pasion Said if the Counsell had Dun any
Such thing it was the most astonishing Proceeding he Ever

heard of — the Counsell had taken that upon them that Did not Belong to them that he Did not Beleve the Counsel Consarnd with it — for he had no Letter with it and talked with Coll Powell and Coll Powell Said he Never heard a word of it and Did not Beleve the Counsell Ever Consarnd with Ranking the Captn^s — and if he Coll Mitchel Executed that order Captn^s Hooper and Lithgow wd Leav the Service — that the Rank was only By the falmouth Representetives without his Desier that he only asked them to get Capt Morton Rank^t — I told the Coll that was not the Case for I was Present that he wd be glad to have them Rank^t and made no Destention who Shuld be first or last in Rank and the Coll well New that the Regiment was at that time without Rank from the Day that he first mustered them which was on the 19th of May — as to the two Compy^s Leaving the Service I am Sorrey Such thing Shuld be mentioned — We have Six Companies five of them is agreed to a man if I am not Deceived — I am Sorrey it Shuld be Said by the Coll that Capt Lithgow w^d Leav the Service for Such Reasons — it is far from it — he is a gentleman well attached to the Caus of his Countrey Studies for the Peace of the Regiment and is willing to Continue in falmouth or march into any Part of Amarica if Cald upon — Coll Mitchel has not Reviewed the Regiment Since the 19th of May or ordered them togather Since the 29th — I have often Pled with the Coll and Urged the Necesity of the Reg^t Being well Disceplnd I have attempted to Call the Regiment togather for Exercise and Review and the Col^o has forbid any Such thing more than once or twice to my Self — and he has forbid Captn^s Crocker Lithgow Lord and Lowell of meeting togather at the Parrade or Exerciseing togather and told them it was Contrary to his orders for any Regimental Perrade whatever and he w^d allow of no Such thing the Capt^s farther Urged that they Vallew^d Nothing about the Rank if he w^d Permit as many Companies as have a Desire of Exerciseing togather they Should take it as a favour But the Col° Refused them as they Informᵈ me — Saying it might be Considered as a Regimental Perrade which he Did not allow of — the 4 Captnˢ have been Repremanded for marching to the meeting hous with 4 Compyˢ togather on the Sabath tho agreable to his own orders of Agᵗ 11ᵗʰ & 18ᵗʰ yet so Contrary to his mind that he Sent a New order for all the Captains to march Seperate Dated at 12 oClock the Inclosed is a Coppey is it Posable for officers and Soldiers who are well attached to the Caus of their Countrey to Baer this from a man who has not the Least Idea of a Soldier or his Dutey — Neither will he be advised by his officers — But Compels his Regiment to Live in the Neglect of their Dutey — I Se no Part of his Conduct as a Soldier But what is arbitrary and Depending Intirely upon his own will that want the name of a Soldier — You will find by the Collˢ orders of Agᵗ 11ᵗʰ and 18ᵗʰ that I was ordred to Se them Complid with — that the Regᵗ go to meeting in order — the Drums Give the time of Day as they Marchd I no of no order but the Drums and Companys Going togather the Coll was so Displeased to Se 4 Companies March agreable to his own orders tho not to his mind that he Sent out the New order Dated agᵗ 18th 12 o Clock which you have Inclosed — the officers ware Supprised Sum of which appliᵈ to me to no my mind Consarning the orders I told them it was the Sabath I was Loth to advise. But as I had the Colls order for the Dutey of the Day. I Shuld Be on the Perrade at the Usual time & if the Companies ware their I Shuld Lead them to the Meeting hous which was accordingly Dun — the Coll it Sems was Very angry to Se that the Regiment ware Like to be united the officers ware Repremanded for Disobeying orders — the Colonel will not talk with me on the Subject. But agreat Deal about me —

it is true they the Soldiers have Dun agrate Deal of work in fortifying and with Chearfullness which is not Common amongst Soldiers and Culd we be Permitted to Quallify our Selves for their Defence: it might be the means under God of Saveing Part of the Countrey from the Raveges of our Enemies — I w^d not be understod that I am Clear of all Blame Neither Do I Contend on my own account it Cost me maney a weresom hour when I might be at Rest Culd I be Content to Lie in the Night of my Dutey —

the Post we hold is of the gratest importence to this State and Shu^d the Enemy attack us whilst Coll Mitchel will Not Suffer the Regiment to be Reviewed Regulated or Examined or give aney order for that Purpus, the Consequence must be Shocking — the Millitia that w^d Probably Com to our assistence Might Expect to Se us in Sum order I wish it might Prove So —

I Shall take it as Doing me a favour if You will Lay my Letter Before the Honourabel Court or Before the Honourable Counsell for this State as Soon as it Can Conveniently be Dun I think it a Duty which has to Long ben Neglected —

I am Gentlemen with Respect Your Deutful Servt at Com^d

Daniel Ilsley

To the Gentlemen Representetives for the town of Falmouth —

Letter from Thos Rice. Aug. 22, 1776.

We whose Names are hereunto subscribed not only in Obedience to the Recommendation of the General Court, but from an earnest & sincere Desire to promote the Liberty & Happiness of America, do voluntarily offer to exchange hard Money for Continental Bills when called upon therefor; to the amount of the Number of Dollars affixed to our respective Names to be applied in carrying on the War in Canada —

Mens Names	No	Dols	Mens Names	No	Dols
Ebenezer Whittier		40			
Jn° Langdon jun		35			
John Barber		30			
Tho⁸ Rice		4			

Sir

In Obedience to the Recommendation of the General Court I have obtained what Subscription I could in the East Precinct in said Town, for the exchanging hard Money for Continental Bills & herewith transmit the same, I found in general a ready mind amongst the People, but they had not ability; Our means of getting money not only in this Town but County is at an End and what little the People had they are now oblidged to part with for the Necessaries of Life. Every thing the People have in their Power to do for the publick Weal they in general are ready to perform, and hope impossibilities are not expected.—

I am in behalf of the Committee of Correspondence your Honors most Obedient humble Servt

Thos Rice

Honble James Warren Esqr

Letter from Francis Shaw. Aug. 28, 1776.

Machias 28th August 1776

Honble Gentlemen,

(Copy by Mr Gardner)

After Removeing many Difficultys started by the Crew of the Diligent, and laying wind bound several Days We sail'd from Piscataqua the 14th Instant and arrived here the 25th after being Confined in Gouldsborough six Days by the Viper Man of War, who took two Sloops from this place within about six Miles of us, as we run into Gouldsborough and lay off and on that Harbour most of the Time, as We had not more than half our Compliment of Men, and them but very Indifferent. Capt Lambert tho^t proper to let the Ship Remove before We should proceed, by Persons that have been taken and Released, We find she has but ten Carriage Guns, Eighteen Swivels and about 100 Men, one half of them Diseffected and only want an oppertunity of being properly Engaged to rise on their officers. Her present Station is between Grand Manan and Seguin, should she Fall in with two of your Honors Sloops of War, I dare say they would Clear this Coast of the greatest Scourge they have had since the Commencement of the present War,—

Should I succeed in gitting a Number of Indians it would be Imposible to git them to the Westward, unless the Viper is removed from her Station, add to that the Distress this Country must be in as they can get no provisions from the Westward past Her, and the advantage our Enemy has, by supplying the English W. Islands with Lumber and Fish they take

I would further add, one or more Ships are loading at Annopalass that the Inhabitants of Nova Scotia come to Passamaquodia for Lumber for them, and as several have been taken and afterwards Clear'd by your Honors our Armed vessels are Intirely Discouraged from taking them, and unless some Stop is put to that Trade, and the Viper removed, the acts of the Honble Continental Congress against the English Islands being supplyed will be Frustrated, and this Country ruined —

Capt Smith informs me that the Indians that have been in lately are very desierous of going to Cumberland, that some have offer'd to bring the Field Officers of that Regiment away, and from Letters lately Receiv'd from there, the Gentlemen agree in oppinion that the Conquest of that Fort may be easily Effected, by our Friends there and a few

Indians, however as your Honours would not give me Liberty to go there I shall not presume to do it, unless the prospect be so Clear that I should think it a Neglect of Duty not to attempt it.

Augt 30th Since I wrote the foregoing Mr Gardner and several others taken in the Sloops from this place have arrived here as Mr Gardner takes passage in the Diligent, he can Informe you that they have Rec^d acc^{ts} of Coming down, and both Ships being Sent to St Johns after us Concluding it would not be prudent for the Diligent to proceed to St John's. We have tho't best for her to Return to your Honors —

I shall just Mention that the Schooners people Complained of not being paid for past services I am affraid it might be the same for this Trip therefore I was oblig'd to promise them that this Muster Roll would be paid Immediatly on their Return, and they now expect your Honors will make my promise good — several Bales of Goods by accident broak open on board the Schooner & 1 p^s Linnen & several small articles are missing — no doubt the Capt must be accountable as I Often caution'd him against leaving the Cabbin Door open when absent.—

if the Diligent should be sold Capt Lambert has Express'd a Desire to serve your Honors in any other Vessel that may be Sent this way, as I cant pretend to be a Sutable judge of the Qualifications necessary for a Commander I shant pretend to say any more than he has bro't us thus far safe and I suppose would have gone further if I had tho't it prudent —

I meet Mr Preble at Piscataqua and Engaged him as Interpreter which was very Luckey as the Person I expected to git here is absent — The Reason I did not let the Diligent lay here it was so uncertain when I should Return, & the Expence would have been much greater than proceeding in two Boats with our provisions — I have two Days waiting a fair Wind I shall Embrace the first, and Make all possible Dispatch Informing you of my proceedings by every favourable oppertunity —

I Remain with much Esteem Gent^n Your most Hum^l Servt
Fra: Shaw

P. S. If I dont meet any Vessel to take the Indians, I shall be moveing Westward in Boats & Canneaus as far as Gouldsborough there and at this place they may hear from Me —

To the Honble the Council & Honble Hou-- of the State of Massachuse--

Letter from James McCobb. Sept. 3, 1776.

Georgetown Sept. 3, 1776

Honoured Sir

I Send Inclosed the Subscription of a few of the Inhabitants of this Poor Town. I Believe we are all to a man hearty in the Common Cause. but our Poverty Restrains us. the Resolve of the Honourable Court Never Came to hand. untill the first of August. which was the Reason of our being so far behind hand. our not having a Post Established any farther than Falmouth which is fifty miles from here is a very great damage to us. we han^t an opertunity to know our Dutey. the money will be Ready as soon as the Bills is sent Down. and I suppose mostly in Dolors the Honourable Court will be Pleased to order how it will be transported.

I am Honour^d Sir with the Greatest Respect Your most
Humble Servant
in behalf of ye Committee   James McCobb Chairman
Henry Gardner Esqr

N° 16.

In the House of Representatives Septem' 7th, 1776.

John Taylor Esq' brought down the following form of a Letter reported by the Committee of both Houses to whom was committed a Letter from M' Thomas Fletcher as an answer to the same.

Watertown Sept' 7th, 1776.

Sir

The Council have receivd your favor of the 27th of July informing us that the Indians of the Penobscot tribe, for Good reasons by them suggested, conclude not to engage in the Continental Army at present.

Therefore the Thirty Pounds put into your hands to enable You to enlist and bring up a number of the said Tribe can not be improv'd for that purpose, therefore the General Court direct that You return said Thirty Pounds to Henry Gardner Esq' Receiver General for this State, and take his receipt therefor the first safe Opportunity.

In Council Sept. 7th 1776
Read & Accepted   Sent down for Concurrence
Read & Concurr'd.

Report. 1776.

The Committee appointed to Consider what Towns Shall be abated, of their Proportion of the Taxes that might be laid on them, agreeable to the last Valuation, and what part of Such Tax Shall be Abated them, have considerd the matter, and beg leave to Report, the folling abatement to the Towns hereafter named (Viz)

Boston   1/3   Sep' 7th 1776

Roxbury	1/5		Tho⁸ Crane pʳ order
Charlstown	8/9	9/10	
Marblehead	1/2		
Glocester	1/3		
Falmouth	1/2		
Plymouth	1/8		
the County of Lincoln	1/3		
Wellfleet	1/10		
Manchester	1/8		

Letter from James Lyon. Sept. 1776.

Honorable Gentlemen

I have often troubled the Court with my scribling, & once with my presence, but was neither known nor regarded, because I did not approach in a <u>parliamentary way</u>, tho' supported, or rather sent, by the most respectable men in this place — Do your Honors expect all the formalities of a Court from <u>loggers</u> & <u>millmen</u>?

I once more beg leave to approach, with due respect, & to speak with freedom, without offence. My subject is the Country, which lies between Penobscot & Nova Scotia; & should I appear to express myself with too much energy & pathos, I hope it will be imputed solely to my exquisite sensibility of my subject. I feel what I say, & mean, if possible, that your Honors shall feel it likewise.

It has often been asserted, if we may credit human testimony, by members of this Honᵇˡᵉ Court, that the Eastern Country is a <u>moth</u>, that it has cost more than it is worth, & that it would be wisdom in the Government to neglect it utterly, & suffer it to sink — I suppose that part of the Country East of Penobscot is meant, for the other part is in some measure represented, better known, & surely worth saving. I shall, therefore, take it for granted that the part only, in which I live is the moth to Government.

I readily grant that your Honors are competent Judges of the qualifications of your own members, but since you never yet pretended to infallibility, it is possible, that in some instances, ignorant & illiterate have by some means or other, crept in among you. And whenever this happens, I blame not this Honble Court, but those, who sent them. Were I permitted even to name what I think the necessary qualifications in a good Statesman, I should say, He ought to be a gentleman of an enlarged mind, well furnished with historical facts & an extensive acquaintance with men & things, & with the constitution of his own Country, in particular, & with every part of his dominions; he ought also to be a gentleman of established integrity & extensive benevolence, who esteems the happiness of every part of the State his own highest happiness & glory. Such a person will do honor to a public station & diffuse peace & joy thro' the State; while the person destitute of these qualifications is really a nuisance & a curse to the public in any exalted sphere. Have these gentlemen, therefore, who think & speak so lightly of this Eastern Country, all these necessary qualifications? Have they any of them? Not to mention their profound acquaintance with history, ancient & modern, & the grand & interesting occasions of the rise & fall of states, kingdoms & empires, do they know any more of a valuable part of their own dominions, than they know of the extent of Country, & the nature of the soil, in the moon? And are not their integrity & benevolence strongly to be respected, when they openly oppose every thing that is motioned for the benefit of this infant Country, if attended with a trifling expense? & publickly declare their willingness, that thousands of wholesome inhabitants, & as brave a people, as any on the face of the earth, should perish in all the horrors of famine & war? But they are my superiors—

Our situation is far more deplorable, than the situation of the Boston people ever was, till the town was shut up. And perhaps we are as useful members of the State. Yet donations were generously heaped upon them from almost every quarter. But did we ever ask for charity? Some of the principal inhabitants of this place, petitioned for a scanty pittance for their minister, & the ostensible reason assigned for not granting it was, " The petition does not come before us in a parliamentary way. The sums asked for, with this single exception, have always been requested as a loan, which, we think, we shall be able to pay, with interest, when the times are settled—I suspect, however, that this Honble Court, in general, have too contemptible an opinion of this part of the Eastern Country. I beg leave, therefore, to speak a few words in its commendation. I have travelled over a great part of Pennsylvania, New Jersey, New York, Connecticut, Rhode Island, Boston Government, & Nova Scotia, & been an inhabitant of all these States, except Connecticut & Rhode Island: & call myself something of a judge of lands. And I must say, That the Eastern Country, in my opinion, is equal to any I ever saw. The climate, if not so pleasant as some others, is more healthy, & the natural increase of inhabitants is greater. The soil is exceedingly natural to grass, & when properly subdued, will produce immense quantities of beef, butter, cheese &c—

It produces excellent wheat, rye, barley, oats, peas, beans, hemp, & some indian corn in the internal parts, & almost all kinds of roots. The proportion of barren land is probably less than in most other Countries.— To these things I must add the fishery on the Coasts, which will in time support an incredible number of people & furnish our navy with able seamen.—

However meanly, therefore, some persons may think of this Eastern & extensive part of the Continent, I assert, without claiming the spirit of prophecy, that it will one day vie with the other States of America in greatness & glory, if not give them law. Your Settlements here are promising children, in their minority who must be tenderly nursed, & when grown to manhood, will become the support and consolation of their aged parents.

Should your Honors, notwithstanding, think them a moth, & not worth keeping, I beg of you to dispose of the country, together with the right of dominion, & give us, the inhabitants the offer. We will engage to procure purchasers, who will give you 15 times as much as it will cost you. We shall then soon become a free and <u>independant State</u> ourselves. And I assure you, we shall think Nova Scotia <u>worth</u> annexing to our dominions.

And if your Honors think us worth keeping, I beseech you, by all the tender emotions of the human heart, & by every thing sacred — to take some care of us. The coast would be worthy of a guard, were there not an inhabitant upon it, but the inhabitants amount to thousands, who are a hardy brave people, & acquainted with the climate & the nature of the soil, & therefore are better than twice the number, that could be sent here, for such would have every thing to learn. But — Pardon my freedom! Instead of encouraging & supporting us hitherto, as we ought to have been, this Hon[ble] Court has neglected us, & taken our privateers, our principal strength, which cost us our blood, from us. And in consequence of this, a number of industrious fishermen, & all the vessels, on which we depended for present subsistence, have been taken by brittish robbers, & a number of our respectable people, men, women, & children, carried into captivity. If any of our people have represented these two privateers as useless, while here, they certainly mistook our true interest. They were a terror to our enemies, & under God, if I mistake not, our salvation last summer. Now they are gone, our enemies barges infest our harbours & take our vessels —

Should your Honors now ask, what I mean by all this? I reply. I earnestly request you to send one of your frigates, or two or three of your ablest privateers to take the ship that infests our coasts, & clear the way for fishermen & coasters; & then perhaps some generous persons may be disposed to send us bread & take some of our lumber. I ask for a small army to subdue Nova Scotia, or at least that some person or persons, may have leave to raise men, & go against that Province, at their own risque. I believe men enough might be found in this county, who would chearfully undertake it, without any assistance from Government. The people this way are so very anxious about this matter, that they would go in whale boats rather than not go. Provided they might call what they took their own in common with the good people of that Province. I confess, I am so avaricious, that I would go with the utmost chearfulness. I hope, however, I should have some nobler view, for I think it our duty to relieve our distressed brethren, & bestow upon them the same glorious priviledges, which we enjoy, if possible, & to deprive our enemies, especially those on this Continent, of their power to hurt us. With these views the Committee of this place were petitioned for leave to go against that Province. And had our request been granted, in all probability, that Country had now been intirely ours, & vast quantities of provision would have been cut off from our enemies. Mess[rs] Shaw, Foster & Smith would now do the business. But were our General Court, at their own expense to take Nova Scotia, the other States of America would have no pretentions to any part of it. And the acquisition would be unspeakably great. That Province is invaluable, & would make ample amends for the expense, & we must have it, or our fishery is lost. Now it is almost defenceless, & nearly nine tenths of its inhabitants would bid us a hearty welcome, & now it may be taken without much loss of blood, if any, but hereafter it may cost us very dear.—

I highly approve of the noble spirit & resolution of Capt. Eddy, & heartily wish him success, & all the honor of reducing Nova Scotia, provided our General Court do see fit, that any of their own subjects should share it with him. The reduction of that Province is a matter of the utmost consequence to this place, & would relieve us of many of our distresses.—

Should it be thought that I meddle with matters which do not belong to me, & that the Committee of Mechias ought to have written. I acknowledge, that their writing would have been the parliamentary way, but at present, this is almost impracticable, for they are much dispersed & broken to pieces, two of them are taken by the enemy, & one at the westward. Indeed we are all in a poor broken situation. If, therefore, the Committee cannot write, why may not I? especially when I write nearly the sense of all the members of the Com^{tee} whom I have seen, & the sense of almost every inhabitant? The meanest Subject of a _free_ State may complain, when agrieved, to the highest Court, & draw near to the supreme authority, with filial confidence & freedom. I mean to do no more. This is my _birthright_: & should I neglect to improve it, when conscience, & the distresses of all around me command, your Honors yourselves would blame me. But I forget myself & intrude too far.

I am, with great deference & respect, Your Honors most faithful but distressed servant & subject

Ja^s Lyon

The Honble The Council & House of Commons of the State
of the Massachusetts Bay —

P. S. I am heartily sorry that the officer I recommended to the Honble Court, has not acted with all that dignity & honor, that could be wished. When I wrote in his favor, I had no knowledge of his inclinations to impose on the public

The vessels lately taken going out of this place were a brig from St Croix, John Coulson Master, the Sloop Unity formerly belonging to Capt. Ichabod Jones, & a sloop belonging to Mr Jonathan Pierson of Newbury —

In Council Sepr 10th 1776

Read & comitted to Richard Derby Ju^r Esq with the Letters from Major Francis Shaw and Mr Stephen Smith accompaning the same with such as the Honble House shall join to take the same under Consideration & Report —

Sent down for Concurrence   Samuel Adams Secr^y

In the House of Representatives Sept. 10th 1776

Read and concurred & Brigad^r Preble & Mr Palfry are joined —

J Warren Spk^r

In Council Sepr 12th 1776   Ordered that Eldad Taylor Esqr be a Comittee to take s^d Letters under Consideration in the Room of Richd Derby Ju^r Esq excused

John Avery Dp^y Sec^y

Certificate.   Oct. 4. 1776.

We the Subscribers Commission'd Officers of five Companies station'd at Falm°, do hereby certify to all whom it may concern, That Major Daniel Ilsley, second in Command at this place, has invariably discovered a disposition to support the order and promote the discipline of the Corps in this Regiment, a laudable Zeal in planning and forwarding the Fortifications carrying on here, and we believe always aimed at preserving Union and establishing Harmony among the Troops, and in our Opinion deserves the Approbation of the Officers, as a Gentleman & a Soldier

Falm° 4th October 1776

Nath¹ Cousens	Rich⁴ Harnden	William Crocker
Josiah Davis	Ebenezer Most	William Lithgow Ju^r
John Skillin	George White	Tobias Lord
Amos Andrews	John Goodwin	Briant Morren
Abner Lowell	Isaac Battle.	

Petition of Maj^r Danl Ilsley.   Oct. 11, 1776.

Watertown Octob^r 11th 1776

To the Honourable Counsel for the State of the Massachusetts Bay the Petition of Daniel Ilsley Humbly Sheweth that your Petitioner Being appointed By your honours Commission — Second in Com^d at falmouth — which office he has Indeavoured to honour by a faithfull Discharge of the obligation I was under for the honour Dun me in my appoint — But Being Prevented by Colonel Mitchel my Superior in Com^d — whos Conduct as an officer has Bin Laid Before Your honours by a Letter or Petition from the Committees of the Several towns for the County of Cumberland — who must be Better acquainted with the Col^s Carrector as a Privet gentleman — the princaple officers in the Reg^t Being Present at the time the Colonel was with the County Committee — their Proceedings must be Impartial and their acc^t of the Colonels Neglect is undouptedly true — But the Colonel on his Return from watertown — Shew to my Self and the Cap^{ns} an order from your Honours Laying aside all Regimental Perrads — and Rank of the Reg^t unknown — which has alarmd the officers of five Companies with a Suspicion that we have been Represented to your Honours as being Disloyal

— that our meeting togather for Exercise was attended with Evils Such as Indangered the State — Your Petitioner is of opinion that Shuld the Enemy attack the Seacost men whilst in Such an unsetled State Many good Soldiers must fall a Sacrifice or abandon their Post with Shame therefore Pray Your Honours w^d appoint a Committee from the Honourable Bord to Examin papers which have Com to your honours Knowledg — Conserning the Neglect of Colonel Jonathan Mitchel —

And your Petitioner as in Duty Bound Shall Ever Pray
Daniel Ilsley

In Council Octr 11th 1776

Read & Comitted to John Whetcomb Esq to take the said Petition into Consideration & Report —
John Avery Dp^y Sec^y

Extract of a Letter.   Oct. 15, 1776.

Extract of a Letter from a Gentleman at Falmouth Casco Bay —
dated Oct. 15, 1776.

It is surprising Sugar continues so dear, when such immense Quantities are brought in; but I am informd that the Rich Merchants are bringing it all up to ship to Spain: Surely they cant be Friends to the Country to suffer the Common People, the Support of the Country to give such exorbitant Prices for necessaries, that they may make themselves exorbitantly rich — They may pretend what they will, but it is plain they have little or no regard to the good of the People — therefore no Friends to the Country — and I hope the Government will interpose to prevent oppression from our own Grandees as well as those of England —

Order 1776.

In Council Oct.* 19, 1776

Ordered That William Phillips Esq.* with such as may be join'd by the Hon.* House be a Committee to treat with the Owners, of a Prize Ship lately arrivd at Falmouth laden with Woolen & other dry Goods — respecting the purchase of such part of the s^d Goods as may be wanted to cloath the Troops raisd by this State to serve in the Continental Army.

    Sent down for Concurrence

                              John Avery Dp^y Sec^y

In the House of Representatives Octr 19, 1776

    Read & concurrd & Mr Otis & Mr Appleton are join'd

                                        J Warren Spk

Report.

The Committee of both Houses have attended the within service & find upon enquiry that there is a considerable quantity of Woolens Lead &c on board the within mentioned Prize Ship and also on board another Prize in Salem Harbour, which the Owners are of opinion that they cannot dispose of at private Sale, nor any other than Public Vendue, to give satisfaction to the Captors.

Therefore beg leave to report as their opinion that it is necessary to take some effectual measures for the purchasing those articles immediately

                              Wm Phillips p Order

    In Council Oct. 23^d 1776.

        read and sent down

                                John Avery Dp^y Sec^y

Copy of record. Rev. Jacob Bailey's Case. Oct. 28, 1776.

At a Meeting of the Committee of Correspondence &c for the Town of Pownalborough Octr 28$''$ 1776 —

The Committee having received Information That the Revd Jacob Bailey had refused to read the Declaration of the Right Honble the Continental Congress for Independency; and also that he the said Jacob still continues upon every Lord's Day to pray in Publick for George the Third King of Great Britain, as our King and Governor, according to the Liturgy of the Church of England. They accordingly summoned the said Mr Bailey to appear before them, and after a full hearing & Consideration of the Evidence, as also of the Defence of the said Bailey They resolv'd

1   That the said Jacob Bailey did refuse to read the said Declaration in Contempt of an Order of Council for this State requiring him to read the same —
2   Resolv'd That the Reasons assigned by the said Jacob Bailey for not reading the said Declaration, and which he has fil'd with the Committee, have a direct Tendency to undermine the Foundation of the United States of America —
3   Resolv'd, That it appears to this Committee That the said Jacob Bailey still persists in praying for the King of Great Britain, on every Lords day in publick, as the King and Governor of these united States; thereby approving of his Tyrannical Measures, against these States and of the Bloodshed in which they are involved
4   Resolv'd That the said Jacob Bailey is in Principle and Practice, a most inveterate and dangerous Enemy to the Rights and Liberties of these United States —
5   Resolv'd That the said Jacob Bailey appear before the General Court of this State, on or before the second Tuesday of the next Session of the said Court, to

answer for his Conduct relating to the Crimes aforementioned, & to any other Matters that may then and
there appear against him

        Chaˢ Cushing Chairman
A True Copy Att. Chaˢ Cushing Chairman

Rev. Mr. Bailey's Reasons for not reading the Declaration of Independence.

Gentⁿ

I was very unwilling to give any Offence by refusing to read the Declaration for Independency, neither was I desirous of bringing myself into any further Trouble — But when I came seriously to examine the solemn Oaths I had taken and the Nature of my Subscriptions, I found I could not comply without offering great Violence to my Conscience and incurring, as I apprehend, the Guilt of Perjury —

I concluded that nothing more could be expected in the Affair than passive Obedience and Non-Resistance; and if an Active Compliance was required, I must persist in my Neglect, and patiently submit to the Penalty, resolving with the Apostle, That it is my Duty to obey God rather than Man.—

I would further observe, That my Conduct has been agreable to that of my Brother Clergy Men of the Church, who have all (except Mʳ Parker) neglected to read the Paper for Independency and I may add if rightly informed, several Congregational Ministers have done the same, notwithstanding they were not under the like Obligations —

I have consulted the most eminent Writers, & find that both Divines and Civilians agree with the Psalmist, That an Oath ought to be observed as sacred (except the Matter of it is unlawful) tho a Man swear to his Hurt, and that rather than break it he should be ready to abide by any Consequences which may attend his stedfast Adherence to it.—

I had the Oaths administred to me in the Time of Divine Service on a Sunday, at the Church of St James, in the presence of a Multitude of Spectators, where I was requir'd to repeat every Word, laying my Hand at the same Time on the Holy Gospels; after which I signed a declaration to the same Purpose ex Animo, and then was order'd to St Martins the King's Parish Church, where I took the Sacrament as a Confirmation of my Oath—

Gent, A Church or Place of Religious Worship ought to be sacred to Truth, and no Minister ought to publish any Thing but what he really believes agreable to the Truth. And if he declares any Thing against the Conviction of his own Mind, let who will be the Author or Director, he must, I think be highly dishonest, and disregard every Dictate of Honor, Conscience and Integrity — Now if I firmly believe as I have solemnly sworn, That no Authority has Power to absolve me from my Oath, and I find the Declaration contains such an Absolution, I cannot read it without the grossest dissimulation. I both act directly against my Oath, and deal deceitfully with the present Government — If after swearing expressly as I have done, that the Pope, for Instance, has no Authority to absolve me from my Oaths, I should in a place of sacred Worship, against my Belief, in Obedience to any other Authority declare that the Pope has absolved me from my Oath of Allegiance, would not every body conclude That I had broken my Oath. Again, supposing I had taken an Oath of Fidelity to the Congress and had solemnly renounced all other Power that should attempt to subvert their Authority, and afterwards, the Army, for Instance, was to set up in Opposition to the Congress and to proclaim their General King of America, and should order me to publish such a proclamation in a place of publick Worship, could I honestly comply?

[Gent.

I have lived a considerable Time in the World, and have passed thro' a Variety of Scenes, without being consider'd heretofore as a Seditious, injurious, revengeful or malicious Person —

There are several People in this Neighbourhood, and in this very Town who knew my Life and Conversation when very young, and I presume if called to give Testimony would declare that my general Conduct was sober, peaceable and inoffensive —

At College I was known to two of the Gent^n present, and defy them to charge me with any Crime and I appeal to the College Records, from which it will appear that I was never punished during my Residence there in the space of 4 years. I afterwards kept a publick school in several places from each of which I carried ample Testimonials of my good Behaviour to England, when I went there for Ordination — and besides was fully recommended by a large Number of principal Gentlemen and near 30 Clergymen of different Denominations — And since my Residence in the Eastern Country, I think none can justly charge me with being treacherous, turbulent, designing or factious — Who have I knowingly defrauded? have I studied to injure any one in his lawful Business? have I endeavour'd to foment or encourage private Quarrels, or officiously intermeddled with the religious, civil or domestic Concerns of my Neighbours — have I labour'd to create Discord in Families, or contended with any one in the Law, even to recover a just debt. have I taken any thing from the poor and necessitous, or sought to enrich myself at the Expence of others.— I can lay my hand upon my heart and declare I never attempted to render a human Being miserable, or took Pleasure in afflicting an unfortunate fellow Creature —

And pray, Gentlemen, what have I done to injure the American Cause? have I taken up Arms in favor of Britain? have I gone into any publick Meetings to defend or establish the Pretensions of either the King or Parliament? have I prevented any one from enlisting into the Service? have I by Word or Writing conveyed any Intelligence to the Enemy? have I ever attempted to escape out of the Country, even when I had an Opportunity, or have I aided abetted or assisted the Invaders of America? why then am I charged with being an Enemy to my Country: what is my Crime. Is it these Connections I cannot dissolve! I am criminal only for acting as every honest Man ought to act in same Circumstances in rather choosing to suffer the Penalty (if any such is annexed) to an Order of Council, than to feel the Eternal Reproaches of a Guilty Conscience.— I would observe further, that supposing I was really in my heart unfriendly to the Country (which I absolutely deny) it is not in my Power to injure it. Can any Person without Money, without Influence, without Authority, without opportunity, in such a remote Corner, do any thing to obstruct the wheels of Government, or to determine the Operations of the War?— Is it not therefore ungenerous & a little inhuman to render any uneasy, who has neither power nor Inclination to hurt you —

Gent^n I sincerely wish to see the Prosperity of my Country and am willing to submit to the Authority of the present Government in all lawful and indifferent Matters; but to declare my self absolved from my former Oath of Allegiance I am convinced is neither lawful nor indifferent —

I acknowledge that I have not complied with the Order of Council, and have neglected to read the Paper for Independency; but I assure you that Refusal proceeded not from any Contempt of Authority, but from a Principle of Conscience, and I am willing to throw myself upon the Mercy of those

Hon[l] Gentlemen, and to submit to whatever Punishment they shall be pleased to inflict.

Octob[r] 28th 1776. The foregoing are submitted to the Committee of Correspondence for the Town of Pownalborough as my Reasons why I did not read the Declaration for Independency —

Jacob Bailey

A True Copy   Att. Ca[s] Cushing Chairman

Report of Selectmen of Town of Falmouth concerning claims for losses caused by destruction of town by Capt. Mowat.

Persuant to an Order of the great and General Court, we the Select Men of the Town of Falmouth do hereby Certify that the foregoing Acc[t] of the Losses sustained by the Inhabitants of s[d] Town by the Enemys burning the same in October 1775 is a Just & true Acco[t], which account was by the several sufferers rendered in (generally upon Oath) to a respectable Committee chosen by the Town in Nov[r] 1776, who did then Examine & Liquidate the same; which Committee did consist of the following Persons, viz[t]

Peter Noyes Esq[r]	Nathaniel Wilson
John Waite Esq[r]	Richard Codman Esq[r]
Enoch Moody	John Johnson Jun[r]
Daniel Ilsley	Joseph Noyes Esq[r]

Shepperday

County of Cumberland Nov 3[d], 1776

To the Committee of the Township of Machias.—

Gentlemen!

We have sent to your care Cap[t] Lieu[t] John Walker and twelve other persons taken by us at Shepperday which please to send to the Westward as soon as possible   we would have you take particular care of cap[t] Walker as he is a Countryman of yours and wou'd be very glad of an opportunity of Joining the Regulars again.—

We are all in high spirits and our party encreases daily, we are in hopes of being strengthned further by Col° Shaw if Possible — beg that you would inform the Honorable Council of our proceedings — if you have any News from the Westward beg that you wou'd send it to us by the Bearers.

we are Gentlemen Y.r Humble Serv^{ts}

Jon^a Eddy

Shepperday Novr 3^d 1776—

Capⁿ Stephen Smith,

Sir/

You being in the service of the United States must beg your assistance in conveying the prisoners taken by us to Head Quarters as soon as possible

I am Sir y^r Hb Serv^{ts}

Jon^a Eddy

Cumberland Novr 12th 1776

Pursuant to Instructions We proceeded from Boston raised a few Men and arived at Cumberland in High Spirits where Some of the Inhabitants Joyned us and we Seized a Vessel in the Harbour with a Great Quantity of Stores &c for the Garrison and besides an Officer and twelve Men that we Sent back from Shepody we have taken above Thirty Prissoners and have attempted the Garrison but Cannot take it without Some Canon and Mortars nor Can we git off what we have taken without Some help as there is a Man of War in the Bay we have Therefore to Intreat of the Province of the Massachusetts for our Selves and for the Inhabitants of Nova Scotia to send some Privatiers into the Bay and Some Troops and Military Stores That we May be able to Promote the General Cause and add another Provence to the United Colonies.

I Must refer you for further Intiligence to Mr Throop the Bearer and Subscribe in the Utmost hast
   Your Most Obliged Obed^t Humbl Servt
           Jonathan Eddy
To the Hon^bl Council & Assel^y at Boston

Petition of the Committee for the County of Cumberland.
Nov. 13, 1776.

To the Hon^d Court of the Massachusetts Bay

Whereas Capt Eddy with a Small Party Has Invaded Cumberland and Taken a Guard of 12 Men Also a Provision Vessel with her Guard and a Vessel from Anopolis with Produce for this Place and has Attempted to Storm the Garrison but finds it Impractible with all the Assistance he can Raise here and as Inteligence is Already Gone to Hallifax We are in the utmost Distress Therefore beg for the Preservation of our Lives and the Lives of our Families For Immediate Help of 500 or a Regiment of men if it may be with 2 Mortars Ammunition and Provision and we your Humble Petitioners as in Duty Bound Shall Every Pray

 Cumberland November 13th 1776

    Simeon Chester
    Elijah Ayer
    Wm How
    Ebenezer Gardner   Committee
    Robert Foster   of Safety
    Petter Campbell   for the County
    John Bent   of Cumberland
    William Maxwall
    Michell Burk
    Obadiah Ayers

For particulars we must refer you to Mr Throop on whom you may depend.

Letter from Charles Cushing. Nov. 16, 1776.

Pownalborough Novr 16th 1776

Sir/

I here enclose you Copys of the Records of the Committee of Correspondence of this Town relating to the Revd Jacob Bailey the Episcopal Itinerant Missionary here, who is declared an enemy to the rights of America by said Committee, in order that the Genl Court may take the matter into Consideration & take such effectual Measures thereon as the Court in their Wisdom shall think proper for discountenancing such dangerous principles & practices as he has been Adjudged guilty of by said Committee — The reason he gave why he would not read the Declaration was because that he had taken the oath of Allegiance in the year 1760 to King George the Second — & he said that the same Oath was still binding upon him to Pay the same Allegiance to George the Third — And he further said that if the King should break his oath by which he was bound to Govern his subjects agreeable to Law, yet his Subjects who were under the oath of allegiance were still bound by the same to pay him the same allegiance as though the King had governed his Subjects strictly agreeable to Law & his oath & nothing could Absolve the Subject from their Allegiance let the King Conduct as bad as possible — If this Doctrine be Just what becomes of all the old officers in the United States that have taken the Oaths of Allegiance! Have they all incured the guilt of Perjury! If they have: It would have been better to have worn fetters & Chain & endured the greatest Tirañy that George the Third his Ministry & the Devil could impose — but those Sentiments are erroneous & False & have no foundation in truth & righteousness and I dare Say the Genl Court will take care that such Doctrines should not prevail — If they are Connived at the States will be Saped in their Foundation — Amongst the enclosed are a

Copy of his reasons, which he sign'd for not reading the Declaration — but he was not so particular as to say that the oath he was Under was made to King George the 2^d for which reason, I thought proper to Observe the same to You as aforesaid (the oath of Allegiance is not to the King & his successor) together with what he said upon his examination — You will se_ by the resolves that he was charged with Praying for the King — the evidence in support of that was his own Confession — further he did not duly observe the Days of Fasting — he had a Proclamation last May two Sabbaths before the Fast — but never read it to his People — He met with his People on the Day — but what they Fasted for they could not tell & he did not inform them & it is Certain he did not Observe the Contents of the Proclamation — he never Prayed for the Success of our Arms as therein directed — It was on Acc^t of those Clauses in the Proclamation in favor of our Land that he did not read it I conclude — He never failed of reading Proclamations from the Governor when they came in Season, and Proclamations before that from the Congress he treated with contempt — he would not even Observe the day — He gave Bond agreeable to the 3^d resolve which Bond I here enclose you Should be glad you would deliver it to the Treasurer & in case he should not appear agreeable to the last resolve that then he may be cited to appear agreeable to the Condition of the Bond if the Court should think proper to Send for him — Also you have enclosed an Acc^t of the Committe's leasing out an Estate — The mast that Col Lithgow & you & I were to take care of Some of them want to be piled up anew Should be glad you would consult Col. Lithgow & write down orders to Luke Lambard who lives near to them to do it —

     I am Sir Your most H^{ble} Servt

         Chas Cushing

To Samuel Freeman Esqr

Letter from Wm Tupper. Nov. 27, 1776.

Machias Novem^r 27. 1776

Hon^rd Gent^men

The Committee of Safety for the County of Cumberland In Nova Scotia have Represented to us the extreem difficulties they labour under by means of their Joining with Capt Eddys party and have very importunately requested all possible aid from us & every body able to afford them the least Assistance. And tho we do not altogether approve of Capt Eddys going there in so loose a manner. & with so small a party. yet we are Disposed to help them as far as we are able and shall encourage all the men we can Spare. to go. the inhabitants of that unhappy County, upon the appearance of Capt Eddy ware reduced to the Shocking dilemay of Being Either plundred and butchered by their friends. or of incuring the highest displeasure of their own Government the latter alternative they preferred and now lie Exposed to the rage of an abandoned administration and their wicked instruments —

They also in form us that they have high Expectations from our Court & that Colo^l Shaw will soon arive to their assistance, with a sufficient armement. We earnestly request your Honors therefore in your great compassion to send them Speedey Relief.

We are your Honers Very Humble Servants
By order of the Committee   Wm Tupper Clerk

To the Hono^l Council and House of Assembly of the State of the Massachusetts-Bay

Letter from Roland Cushing. Dec. 4, 1776.

To the Honourable the Councill of the State of the Massachusetts Bay

Having received the honour of an appointment, to the Second Majority, in the second Regiment of Millitia in the County of Lincoln; the duties of which office, from the weakness of a declining State of health; I am unable to execute; and which a due regard to the welfare of my Country forbids me longer to retain — Your Honours therefore, will please to accept my resignation of said office with my most respectful acknowledgments for the same — Any service which may be in my power to render my Country will be done with the greatest chearfulness —

I have the Honour to be with the profoundest Respect your Honours most obedient & very Humble Servt

Roland Cushing

Pownalborough December 4th 1776

Letter from Noah Mo^{ton} Littlefield. Dec. 4, 1776

Wells Decr 4th 1776

To the Honble Board

I have Received a Letter from the Secr^y by your honours Direction which Shoes the Honour Confered On Me In the Apointment of Lieut^t Colon^l In A batalion Now Raising Whareof Ebenezer francis Esqr Is Colon^l —

I thank your Honours for the Undeserved favour Confired On Me and Am Ready & Chearful to Serve In the American Army for the Defence of the united Estates of America and Hope My Conduct Will Do honour to the Apointment

from your Humble Servt

Noah Mo^{ton} Littlefield

Letter from Col. Jon^a Mitchell.

To the Honorable the Council and House of Representatives of the Colony of the Massachusetts Bay

May it Please your Honors In Obedience to the Establishment I have ordered a Serjeants Guard consisting of a Serjeant & Nine Men to Saco River — A Serjeant and 10 Men to Kennebec River, and the like Number to Harpswell, who proceeded for their several Stations Eight days since — I should have sent out Guards before, but apprehended the necessity of the Works carrying on here, which are now considerably forward, demanded the presence of all the Troops stationed at this Place — larger Numbers I thought could not be spared, consistent with the Public Service, but if I have erred herein your Honors Orders will determine my future Conduct — I take the Liberty to represent to your Honors that Cannon are much wanting, without which our Fortifications must be rendered useless, except to the Enemy — I need urge no further to your Honours the necessity of having a supply of Cannon, as you are not unacquainted with the Importance of this Post not only to the Province of Main but to the preservation of all the United Collonies

I am with profound Respect your Honors very
  Humble Servant
         Jonathan Michell

Letter from Wm Lithgow Junr

To the Secretary of the Honorable Council of the State of Massachusetts Bay —

Sir, Being informed that you wrote me some time since, on the Subject of my appointment to a Majority, in one of the new Regiments now raising in this State on the Continental Establishment, under the command of Col° Ebenezer Francis, which I had not the honor to receive; and as it is my Opinion that no private or interested views are a sufficient Apology, at this critical and important day to decline the service of our oppressed, insulted Country, I take this Method to express my Gratitude for the honor done me, and also to signify to the Honorable Board (tho' not without the most humiliating Sense of my own inexperience & want of military knowledge) my chearful Acceptance of the Appointment; however repugnant to my private Advantage or Emolument.

 I have the honor to be with the most Profound Respect
  Your Honor's very humb^{le} Servant
           Wm Lithgow Junr
Boston 9th Decr 1776

Letter from Joseph Dimuck. Dec. 23, 1776

To the Honorabel the Counsel of the State of the Massachetts Bay Gentelmen —

you may Remembr that you gave ordors for Raising Two Companys To Be Stashond on Nashone the Cap^{tns} have Borth Ben With me Sence & Returnd and Say thay Cannot Inlist any men By Reson of the Wages Being So Loo I have Ben Indavoring to foraw^d the mater But find that To Be the younavarcel Compaint — if your Honers Are pleas^d To Give any farther ordors About the Mater I Shall Indaver To Conduct Agreabel thair to
     I am yours To Sarve
Dated att falmouth   Joseph Dimuck
Desembr ye 23 1776

 Iu Council Decr 27' 1776
Read and thereupon Resolved, That Walter Spooner Esqr with such as the Hon'ble House shall appoint be a Comittee

to consider the above & Report what is necessary to be done thereon —

 Sent down for Concurrence   Jn° Avery Dp^y Sec^y

In the House of Represent^s Decr 27, 1776

 Read and Concurred and Mr Holten & Mr Ellis are joined
      Sam^ll Freeman Speak^r P T

Letter from Col. Eben^r Francis   Jan. 3^d 1777.

        Ticonderoga June ye 3^d 1777

Hon^d Sir

 Presuming you belong to the Gen^r Assembly this year Shall just Mention a few Among the many dificulties we labour under I Have now in my Reg^t More than 100 good men that have not had a blanket to Cover them. the Greater part of them have been here Upwards of two months I need not Represent to you the hardships they must have undergone & still do on that account not more than one half of their Arms are fit for Service, many of them no Shoes nor Hose to their feet Some few of them would be glad to have drawed their money for their Cloathing but it Cannot be obtained What can we Expect from Soldiers uncloathed by day & no Blankets to Sheild them from this Cold Clay Soil by night & Miserable Arms at a time when we Hourly Expect to be Attacked I leave you to Answer. Miserable poor Rum from 30/ to 42/ £m^y* & other things in proportion no Sort of Cloathing to be had at any Rate their duty very hard. Notwithstanding all those dificulties before mentioned. to admiration the soldiers are in good spirits in hopes of being

* Sterling money.

Supplied by & by. is it possible to be as we are informed that Cloathing & arms for two full Reg^ts are deposited at Boston while we in this Northern department are Suffering for want I have 490 men Arrived. I Expect Some more on the Road & they are very fine men it is a pity to let them suffer & die it will Cost a Great Sum of money to get more. we have on the Ground Militia & Artificers Included between 4 & 5000 I should be glad if it is possible we might have a Uniform & pay for what Cloathing the Soldiers have had. if there is any Scarlet Cloth in the State Store you will very much Oblige me if you would procure 50 yards for my Officers & triming for the Same & I will see you paid. you may depend on it that there is not any of our States Cloathing arrived Here yet Should any Come it will go in the Continental Store & be promiscuously dealt out to all & what prise they please to Set on it Could it be directed to major Smith y^r Commissary here it would be much better for he is a worthy man although he has no Stores to deal out Sir I trust you will Enquire into this affair & Remedy the dificulties we now labour under if in your power & let our men suffer no longer for what is their right as for News I Have but very Little the Enemy the last we heard from them was about 20 miles below Crown point.

Several Officers have Lately been taken up for Innoculating in Camp & are now on trial

my Regards to all friends

   I am with Respect y^r Humble Sr^t in Health
            Eben^r Francis

Superscribed
Beverly A member of the House of the State of the Massachusetts Bay

In Council June 21: 1777
 Read & Sent down   Jn° Avery Dp^y Secr^y

Letter from the Council to Gov. Nicholas Cook. Jan. 23, 1777.

Council Chamber Jany 23^d 1777.—

S^r We have Receiv'd yours of the 15th Instant and have Observ'd the Contents   General Spencer has Informed us he soon expected the Arrival of One to Act in the Character of Continental Commissary when Arrived will provide for Victualling the Troops   finding it difficult Calling on ye Militia at this time in order to furnish our Proportion of the Men to be station'd at Rhode Island as it would be Detrimental & Impede Raising men for the Continenal Service the General Court In lieu thereof have Ordered One Quarter part of the Militia from the County of Lincoln Consisting of   now on their March for New-York Col Joseph North Commander immediately to March to Providence in the State of Rhode Island there to be Subject to & Under the Command of General Spencer —

Measures have also been taken to Prevent Mr Mumford the Post Rider from Detentions by the Ferrymen in this State.

In the Name & in Behalf of the Council I am your
    Most Humble Servt

Letter from John Preble.   Jan. 27, 1777.

MajorVeel Jany 27th 1777

Hon^d Gentlemen

I sail'd from Boston the 18th of December and did not Reach the mouth of this River till the 13th Jan^y & then have to transport my Goods on the Ice 60 miles which will Cost me at least 70 Dollars.   this makes the Goods with the Boston price come deare to the Indians.   they Complain much

of the prises & say if they cant have Goods cheaper they
must Trade with the Enemy, then they want to be trusted
in the Winter, which I shant do without orders from your
Honours no further than take plate at What it Weighs —

Sixteen Indians has been with Capt Eddy Serving as Soldiers at Cumberland they have behav[d] Brave & acquitted
their selves well their familys are Redus[d] by it, must Recommend them to your Honours Consideration as Cap[t] Eddy
perswaded them to go with him.

they have prise money due which I hope Cap[t] Eddy will
see them paid Am Brose is come up in Consequence of it, &
to see your Honours, I must beg the favour your Honours
will send me directions what prises to give for furs &
Wheather I may trust them at your Honours Risque of Bad
depts made —

I have Convers[d] with the Chiefs of this Tribe and they to
a man are harty in our Cause — have likewise seen one of the
Micmack Chiefs who told me their Tribe is determin[d] to Rest
easey & Remain Nutrals during the Contest between the Old
England people & Boston men —

I must Observe to your Honours with Submission, that as
Am Brose Bear is a Sober Sensible man & has behav[d] so Well
at Cumberland think him deserving a Commission among the
Indians he is much fitter to take Care of the Tribe than
Peer Tomer

I Shall Gitt a list of the Indians Names As Soon as possible & Send your Honours. I think their may be a Company
of Smart Indians imbodyed one half English & the other half
indian officers for the protection of the Eastern department)
Am Brose has desired me to Recommend to your Honours
Consideration a french priest for them the Committy here
has Supply[d] those indian familys that went to Cumberland
with provitions while their husbands was Absent which they
want me to Refund saying it was Major Shaws promise to

pay the men monthly Wages as Soldiers. I shall do nothing without your Honours Orders.

I am may it please your Honours Your Honours Most Obedient Humble Ser^t
John Preble

Superscribed:

On the Service of the State of the Massachusetts To The Hona^{ble} the Council & House of Representatives of the States of the Massachusetts Bay —

In Council March 18 1777   Read & Comitted to the Comittee on the Petition of John Allen Esq & the Memorial from the Counties of Cumberland & Sunbury in Nova Scotia
Sent down for Concurrence

John Avery Dp^y Sec^y

In the House of Representatives March 18' 1777 —
Read & concurred
J Warren Spkr

Letter from Selectmen & Comm^{ee} of Safety for Winslow. Feb. 14, 1777.

Winslow February 14, 1777

Sir,

Sollicitude for the Publick Welfare, and a Desire of discharging the several Trusts reposed in us with faithfulness to our Constituents, is the only Apology we can make for thus addressing you, and we trust that a Gentleman of your known Patriotism will require no other.—

In the Spring of the Year 1775 one Ephraim Ballard from Oxford in this Colony took Possession of a Fortress in this Town known by the name of Fort Halifax, with about four Hundred Acres of land adjoining the same, claimed by Doctor Sylvester Gardner late of Boston.

Our Committee of Safety having received the Resolve of the General Court of the twenty third of April last, and being credibly informed that the Doctor, fearing the just Resentment of his injured Country-men had fled from Boston with the Kings Troops in March last, and that the said Ballard was of Principles inimical to the glorious Cause in which we are engaged, apprehended themselves warranted to take the said Fort and Land into Possession and lease them out. Accordingly they waited on Mr Ballard and requested him to deliver them up — He told them that he had hired them of the Doctor, (For Proof of which he produced the Original of which we have taken the Liberty to inclose you a Copy) and could not deliver them up to them or any Persons whomsoever; but desired that if they took Possession he might have the Refusal of a Lease.

The Committee, being dissatisfied with this Answer, advised with the Committees of three of the neighouring Towns and several private Gentlemen, who informed them that the Fort and ten Acres of the Land were the Property of the State, and therefore, that they thought the Committee had no Right by said Resolve to dispossess the Occupier. Under these Circumstances the Matter rested till about three Weeks ago, when a Number of the Inhabitants complained to the Committee that Mr Ballard with a Number of People (supposed to be unfriendly to the grand American Cause) from the next Town were cutting and haling Mill Logs on the Premises, upon which one of the Committee waited on him and remonstrated against this Conduct, to which he replied, That he had lawfully purchased the Trees and that the Committee had no Right to interfere in the Business; And the People above-mentioned, being examined, answered that they were no otherwise concerned in the Business than as they were hired by Mr Ballard.—

This Affair's being so peculiarly circumstanced makes it very difficult for us to act so as to quiet the Minds of the good People of this and the neighouring Towns, who are very uneasy — We therefore most earnestly request, that you would employ your Influence in the General Court to obtain particular Instructions to the Selectmen and Committee of this Town for their Conduct in this intricate piece of Business, and that they may be sent as soon as may be; and that you will afford us all the other Assistance in your Power.

We have the Honor to be, with the greatest Respect, Sir Your most obedient humble Servants

    Ezekiel Pattee   } Select Men of
    Jonah Crosby } Winslow

    Zimri Heywood } Committee of
    John Tozer   } Safety for Winslow

Honble James Bowdoin Esqr

Letter from Ezekiel Pattee.   Feb. 16, 1777.

         Winslow February 16, 1777
Sir

The Anxiety of Mind which I am under for the publick Safety will I hope plead my Excuse for addressing a gentleman in your exalted Station without having the Honor of a personal Acquaintance with you.—

The Spring before Last one Ephraim Ballard from the Western parts of this Colony came into this Town and took Possession of Fort Halifax and four Hundred Acres of Land adjoining there, having hired them as he said of Doctor Gardiner late of Boston.

Our Committee after receiving the Resolve of the General Court of the 23^d of April last, and being informed that the Doct^r had fled from Boston with the Kings Troops, and that Ballard was of Tory Principles, applied to him and requested that he would deliver the Premises into their Possession

He replied that he had hired them of the Doctor and could not deliver them up.

The Committee desirous of proceeding with all possible Caution, advised with the Committees of the neighbouring Towns, who informed them that the Fort and ten Acres of Land were the Property of the Colony, for which Reason it was their Opinion they had no Right to dispossess Ballard. They therefore let the Matter rest till a few Weeks ago when some of the Inhabitants complained that Ballard with a Number of Persons from the next Town, who were unfriendly to the Cause of Liberty, were logging on the Fort Farm — This induced one of the Committee to go to Ballard and remonstrate against his Conduct, who answered that he had lawfully purchased the Trees, and no person had a Right to forbid him the Use of them. And the People at Work with him as abovementioned, upon being interrogated, replied that they had no other Business wth the Logs than to cut and hale them for Mr Ballard, they being hired by him for that Purpose.— The peculiar Circumstances of this Affair seeming to require special Instructions from Authority, the Select Men & Committee have, by my Advice, wrote you by this Opportunity requesting you to exert your Powers in the General Court in order to obtain them, to which I beg leave to subjoin my earnest Sollicitation, as the People here are very much exasperated and may possibly proceed to Extremities if the Matter is not soon settled,—

I am with great Respect Sir, Your most obed^t hble Servt

Honble James Bowdoin Esq   Ezekiel Pattee

Letter from Tristram Jordan. April 25, 1777.

Pepperrellbor^o April 25th 1777

Dear Sir

By Order of Council 136 men is to be Draughted out of ye Militia in ye County of York: out of that number Brigadier Moulton has assign^d 43 out of my Regiment now Sir, you are Sensible how freely the men has inlisted out of my Regiment for ye American Army as I gave you an Account of them Some Time Since: Nine men besides the Acc^t you had have gone from Capt Fryes Company: and what men has inlisted Since ye Returns Made by ye Several Militia officers to me: I cannot tell but I Believe there has been Several: Which has Thinn^d our men much and I Really Think it is not prudent to Take any more men from this Quarter for you are Sensible we are Expos^d to ye Enemy and if any Naval or Land forces Shou^d come to make an Attack on falmouth were is their Succour to come from and I verily Think that the Enemy^s Ships will go to Falmouth: for we have Such Good Friends as I make not ye Least Doubt will Inform them that no Soldiers are Station^d at Falmouth Sufficient to Defend the Place and I think the men from the Regiment Ought not to march to the Southward. from ye Circumstances I have Mention^d and many more that might be Offer^d — the men are Principally Draughted and I Suppose will be Ready to March Soon: and I shall order them to March As Soon as they are Ready unless they are Prevented by an order from Council: which Sir I hope you will Try to obtain: I have Inform^d ye Brigadier that my Regiment have furnish^d their Quota of Troops to ye Continental army: but have had no answer from him, therefore I Tho^t it Expedient to Write you on ye Subject —

 I am Sir with Esteem & Respect your Sincere Friend
   & Humb^l Servt Tristram Jordan
To James Sullivan Esqr

Letter from Jon^a Lowder. May 21, 1777.

Penobscutt 21st May 1777

Sir yesterday Lieut^t Gillman was at Penobscutt Old Town with the Indians on Business that they sent to him for — before his arrival, he was met by Esq' Ausing an Indian, who told him they had Certain Intelligence of a great Number of Indians & Regulars coming across the Country in order to Distress & Destroy the several Rivers of Penobscutt, Kennebeck & St Johns, they are Commanded by Lonear a French Colonel in the Regular service, and I belive it may be Depended upon as a Fact, and I desire you would Communicate this to the several Committees below, that the people may be warned to be in readiness when called for.

N B   The Indians here will keep a good look out, and promise to Inform us with any thing that Effects us.

  I am — your Hum^l Servt

            Jon^a Lowder

To Col^l Jon^a Buck —

  a true Copy   Signed Jon^a Buck

Letter from Jonas Mason.   May 22, 1777.

To the Honourable the Council of the State of Massachusetts Bay —

May it please Your Honors. With thankfullness I acknowledge the Honor confer'd on me by a late Council of this State in Appointing me a Justice of the Peace for the County of Cumberland & also a Justice of the Infer^r Court of Common Pleas for said County. Conscious not only of my incapacity for the proper discharge of the Duties of Said Offices, but now fully Sensible of my decays by reason of old Age and that I Stand in the way of Gentlemen of Superiour Abilities for the discharge of said Trusts, humbly beg leave to resign my Commission for the said respective Offices.

That Your Honors & the Great Council of the United States of America may be under the Divine direction & Blessing in all their & Your Councils & Determinations, in this day of difficulty & Distress, is the earnest desire of Your Honors much oblidged, humble Servant

Jonas Mason

North Yarmouth May 22, 1770.

Letter from Col. Josiah Brewer. May 27, 1777.

Penobscott May 27th — 1777

Sir I thought it Necessary to acquaint Y^r Honour, That Lieu^t Andrew Gillman who comãnds the Guard stationed here, was on a scout at the Frontier Settlements: was met with by one of the Indian Chiefs of the Penobscotts, who was coming down the River to acquaint the Inhabitants; That Three Indians arriv'd from Canada ye 25 Ins^t, (who were sent by ye Tribe to get intelligence): they bring ye following intelligence viz: That there was a Large party of Canada Indians, amounting to about 80ty in Number: together with a number of Regulars & Canadians, Commanded by one Lonier a Frenchman, now a Col^l in the British service: and by ye information they could gather they were Designed to come across the Country to ye Heads of ye several Rivers, to use their Influence with all the Tribes of Indians they meet with in their journey, to engage them in ye British Service, in order to Destroy ye Inhabitants on ye several rivers Viz St Johns, Penobscot & Kenebeck.— I shall take necessary methods to Secure ye Inhabitants with ye Reg^t of Militia under my Command; wch is very small; occasion'd by a Number being Inlisted in ye Continental Service —

Lieu^t Gillman will keep Scouting parties but to Waylay their Carrying Places.

The Britains give ye Indians great Presents of Money, to gain them to, & secure them in their service.

In Case of any special Emergency from the Enemy: I shall apply to Col¹ Jonathan Buck for Necessary Reinforcements to assist us: who I have served wth a Coppy of this in order to obtain it.

I am, Honoured, Sir, With Great respect, Your most obedient, and, Most Humble Servant,

Josiah Brewer

To the Honble Artemas Ward Esqr

In Council June 18, 1777   Read & sent down

Jn° Avery Dp^y Sec^y

In the House of Representatives June 19, 1777

Read & committed to Coll Prescott & Mr Dix with such as the Hon Board shall join

Sent up for Concurrence   J Warren Spkr

In Council June 19, 1777

Read & Concurred and Timothy Danielson Esq is joined

Jn° Avery Dp^y Sec^y

Letter from J. Allan. May 30th 1777.

Mechias May 30th 1777

May it Please Your Honours — I write you in great haste the 26th Ins^t giving an Acc^t that the British Armed Sloop Gage had gone up the River St John, & of the Arrival of Capt Jn° Preble with Capt West, whom I had sent to the mouth of the River, and brought the melancholy Acc^t that the Inhabitants were forc'd to submit. This Step has given me great Uneasiness; I could not fall upon any Plan wherein I could be assur'd of the least Success; Nothing appear'd so Eligible as my taking a birch Canoe, but Pierre Jommo the Chief with some others having been on board, & Mr Gould hearing of my Commissions & Business, had offer'd a Considerable Premium for me. This detain'd me. I collected the Indians to whom I could get Intelligence, & have had some Conference, to outward appearance satisfactory, & have been oblig'd to deviate from my original Plan of Æconomy, & be very lavish: Necessity Commands it if we keep them in our Interest.

On the 28th the Revd Mr Noble & Doctr Nevers arriv'd here, after going through a series of Difficulty & Troubles during their Journey through the Woods, who Confirm the above Acct & that Mr Israel Perley was taken Prisoner to Halifax.

Yesterday about three °Clock, Capt Howes (the Bearer of this) arriv'd, by whom I Recd the agreeable News, of the Britons having Evacuated the River, but with an Intent to Return with all Expedition to Erect two Fortifications; On hearing this I concluded it absolutely necessary to Endeavour to secure that Part with what Strength I could raise till your Honors' Determination.

For fear of a second Eddy's Affair, I thought it expedient to act upon this Plan that the Inhabitants might not suffer, should your Honors not think proper to pursue any Measures that Way.

As the Indians at their own Option went to Head Quarters & made a solemn Treaty with the Massachusetts State & the latter being under a strong Obligation to fulfill certain Promises, it was highly requisite for the Honor & Dignity of the State, to have it fulfilld and Executed; and as some of the Enemy had been upon the said River to persuade the Indians to turn against the States, & force the English & French Inhabitants to swear allegiance; some of whom had been overcome, it must appear highly reasonable that a force should go to act upon the Defensive, to prevent the Enemy from getting further Possession till the Business is done with the Indians. I mean by this to secure the different Passes as well as possible with what goes & not to have any thing to do with Inhabitants, nor Even to go amongst them, otherwise than what may be necessary for our Defence. I consulted with the Machias Committee, Mr Lyon, & the Gent^n from St John's, who much approv'd of it. I accordingly set off this Morning with about 40 Men including Indians & two of the small Guns belonging to the Minsheat, where I shall Endeavour to take such Precautions in acting on the Defensive till I know your Honors Determination.

I Rely & trust that your Honors will consider the deplorable State of this Country & should not be so pressing, was I not Convinc'd of the great Importance of this Part, & the Advantage the Enemy will reap therefrom

I have Rec^d several Informations, That Col. Gould has sent into Canada for one Bailey a French Priest who was formerly in Nova Scotia & a great Jacobite. Gould also gives Information that a Number of Gentlemen in Boston had frequently solicited for a number of Troops to be sent there which would certainly be done in a short Time — That he had a Letter from Jno Anderson giving a State of Matters, particularly the diff^t Speculations about the River St Johns.

News from Halifax that the Hessians were order'd home — That 16000 Men was the Number coming abroad. That a Number of Transports which came some time ago to Halifax from New York were sent up the Bay of Fundy for Provisions; I fear this is intended for some secret Expedition near your Honors plann'd by these Villains who lurk within the Bowels of your Country & who I fear (if not speedily done something with,) will bring things to an unhappy Crisis: I hope that Justice which is so requisite & what I think a Commanded Duty in time of War will take Place.

The Bearer Capt Howes, can inform you of many Particulars, which may prove satisfactory.

I shall leave Orders for my little Schooner on her Return to proceed immediately up St Johns River: I must earnestly Request of your Honors that you will as Expeditiously as possible inform me what is your Determination, for at present I am at a great Expence, which as it is a thing Contrary to what was expected when at Boston, & which may be call'd an Usurpation in me, that I shall be liable to pay it myself which I am not at present altogether so Capable of; & indeed if admitted to the publick Expense, I shall be as much Concern'd if it is not approv'd of.

I must Recommend that John Anderson of Newburn may be secur'd, as also his Wife, she is an Intriguing Person & has been always remarkable for Intelligence, & I am thoroughly Convinc'd he has given as much information as any Person. I trust sour Speeches & friendly Gestures will not overcome or prevent Justice.

Time not permitting to wait I must pray your Honors to indulge me so far as to Communicate to the Honble the Continental Congress my Proceedings with such other Matters as you please, respecting me,

I am with the utmost Respect Your Honors most
    Obed^t Most devoted humble Servt
                              J Allan

P. S. Should any thing be done this Way I Recommend the Bearer Capt Howes, who appears to be a Man of an Universal good Character; a good Pilot & well acquainted with the Affairs of that Country.

He has lost a Vessel there. I must beg /if Consistent with the Service/ he may be Employ'd.

Just Intercepted a Letter from John Long to John Anderson which is D^d the Committee who will Inform you therewith.

In Council June 6th 1777

Read & Comitted to the Comittee appointed to consider Honble John Hancocks Esq Letter of the 13th Ulti^o inclosing a Resolve of Congress of the same Date and the Petition of the Comittee of Machias and the Papers accompanying the same.

Sent down for Concurrence   Jn° Avery Dp[y] Sec[y]

Letter from J. Allan. June 4, 1777.

Boston Town June 4th 1777

Gentlemen

This will be del[d] You by M[r] John Preble Truckmaster for the Indians of S[t] Johns river By the late Movements here he was forced to Leave that Imployment which was Occation'd By the part the Inhabitants had taken in the Cause now Contend'd for in America, & Notwithstanding the Obligations Enter'd into, they have thought proper to Return back & Seek Shelter under that Government, which is now become the most Contemptable of Any upon Earth & Voluntarily Submit to the Mandates of those who is Endeavouring to bring Great Britain as well as America into the Most abject Slavery —

There being at present some Property belonging to the Massachusetts State and M[r] Preble having Some business to Settle I expect he will be Permited to Persue those Necessary Measures to Secure his Effects & Settle Such Matters as he has Contracted —

The Indians is still Acting the Vertious part to whome the United States are Under some Obligations to fulfill Certain promises, I have now Come for that End & fully Rely that me nor any of my people be Molested my business being solely with the Indians. I shall Not have Any Connection watever with the Inhabitants nor TransAct Any business with them that may Expose them to the Resentment of thiere New friends who wou'd have had no Mercy on them was it not fear but this I Leave to Your Own reflection You are possessed of Moral Agency & know best for your Own Safety —

I further Expect there will be no Obstruction on your part in procureing some Necessary refreshments for my Men for which ample Satisfaction shall be Made —

I shall take every Precaution to Prevent Any damages to Any Person dureing my Stay

      I am yours &c —

a true Coppy   J Allan

 To the Inhabitants of Manciville

Report. 1777.

State of Massachusetts-Bay

       In Council June 5th 1777

 The Com^{tee} of both Houses upon Mr Hancock's Letter of the 13th ult^o inclosing a resolve of Congress of the same date; & the Petition of the Com^{tee} of Mechias & the papers accompanying it report as their opinion —

That an expedition to the River St Johns in Nova Scotia, is not only necessary in order to secure the Inhabitants of the Counties of Cumberland & Sunbury (who have applied to Congress for protection) in that State, from the cruel oppression & violence of our common enemy; but also, for the preservation of all our Settlements lying to the Eastward of Casco-Bay; & for preventing that Short & easy communication between our enemies in Canada with those in Nova Scotia, through said River, which they are now fortifying for that purpose.

That in order to carry this expedition into effect, there be one Regiment raised, as soon as possible in the Counties of Lincoln & Cumberland within this State, to consist of 728 men Officers included, & to be upon the continental establishment, be raised by enlistment for a term not exceeding Six Months.

That there be a sufficient naval force provided, to Convey all the necessary stores to said River, or such other place as may be ordered; not only sufficient for said Regiment, but also for such volunteers & Indians as may join them in this expedition for Securing that part of the Country against the depredations of the Independency of the united States of America.

That a general Officer be appointed by the whole Court, to command & direct this whole affair, under such orders as may from time to time be given him by the Council, to whom he frequently make return of the State & circumstances of the forces, & all proceedings in this expedition

That the whole force, by Land & Water, shall rendezvous at Mechias as soon as possible & there receive the orders of said general Officer, to which, there shall be paid the Strictest obedience, by all inferior Officers, & others, who may be employed in this affair.

That four Field-pieces, with two 12 pounders & two Small Mortars be Sent with the Stores, to be used for the defence of the same, when at Mechias, or for such other purposes as the Commander may order.

That the Court appoint the Warrant & Field-Officers, & the Commissary, with such other Officers as they may see fit, exclusive of Captains & Subalterns, & non-commission-Officers: Blank Commissions for Cap[ts] & Subalterns to be delivered to the Commander who, with the Field Officers, shall appoint them, & deliver their Commissions, when they have raised their Companies: And the Captains & Subalterns shall appoint the noncommission Officers for their respective Companies, to be approved or disapproved of by the Field-Officers.

That the Com^tee of Mechias be repaid in kind, all the Stores which they have supplied, agreeable to their Petition.

That there be delivered to said general Officer, a compleat set of blank Commissions & Warrants for a whole Regiment Consisting of eight Companies to be raised from the Inhabitants of the State of Nova-Scotia or the Eastern parts of this State or the observing a Similar rule of conduct in all the appointm^ts, with that held up in the above paragraph. **A.** Said Regim^t to be continued in Service One Year, unless sooner discharged.

That the Commander be vested with power to dismiss the first Regiment if he may judge it necessary, when the Second is compleated; or, to employ both in any service for the united States which he may judge prudent to put them upon, in this or the State of Nova-Scotia.—

That a Com^tee be appointed to make application to the Commander of the Alfred Man of War, & to the Owners of such private Ships of War as are likely to be obtained, & which may be needed for this, & to agree as the Court may order. And, that they also be Cloathed with Ample power to furnish every necessary Article for this expedition.

That, if the measure is adopted, not a moment is to be lost; for the enemy ought to be disrested before they have planted themselves strong; & their present naval Strength being small, may probably be taken.

The Com^tee are further of opinion, That tho' the expence of this expedition will vastly exceed what the Congress had in contemplation when they passed said Resolve; yet as the object is much greater than is therein pointed out; & as the Congress had, some Months since, directed our views to still greater Objects, which this State did not then think proper to attempt; they judge it highly probable, that the whole expence will be continental.

All which is humbly submitted by the Com^{tee} who ask leave to Sit again as soon as the Papers are returned into their hands

          J. Palmer p ord^r

In Council June 5, 1777
 Read & sent down   Jn° Avery Dp^y Sec^y
In the House of Representatives June 6th 1777
 Read & accepted — as amended & thereupon — Order'd — That it be recommitted to be drawn into a Resolve —
  Sent up for Concurrence   J Warren Spk^r
In Council June 6 1777
 Read & Concurred   Jn° Avery Dp^y Sec^y

Report.

The Committe appointed to consider the papers relative to David Thatcher Esqr of Yarmoth and report what is proper to be done, have attended that Service, and are of oppinion that s^d Thatcher ought to be esteemed a friend to these States and that that matter Subside.

Report

The Committee appointed to consider the Acco^{ts} of John Allen Esqr and his Letter of the 10th March have attended that Service and beg leave to Report — a State of Facts as followeth —

That on Examining said Acco^{ts} they find due to Col° John Allen as Commanding Officer of the Troops rais'd by this State for the Defence of Mechias — the Sum of £237..7..9½ which sum ought to be paid him out of the Publick Treasury of this State —

That Col° Allen hath drawn out of the Truck House and Commisary's Store at Mechias Provisions and other Articles for the Suply of the Indians there to a considerable amount which he hath pass'd to the C^r of the United States —

That on Inspection of his Acco^{ts} as Agent of the Indians as he hath adjusted them, there is a Ball^{ce} due to him of the Sum of £622.7.11¾ to be paid by the United States —

Your Committee beg leave to report as their Opinion — that it is necessary that Col° Allen be supply'd from the Publick Treasury of this State with the sum of £1200 — to enable him to discharge the Debts already contracted; and to carry on the Business of Agency with the Indians —

That Col° Allen be supply'd with 4 Whale Boats — and an Oyl Cloth Marque —

That Lieu^t Albee with thirty Men now under his Command & whose time of service expires in June, next, be continued in Service untill the 1st of Decr next — and that Provisions be sent for the same —

That a Surgeon be appointed for the Troops —

That a Letter be wrote to Congress by the President of the Council inclosing all Col° Allen's Letter which he hath wrote to this Court — with his Acco^{ts} as Agent for the Indians — acquainting them with what they have Advanced Col° Allen — and desiring that they would take some proper Order respecting his further supply.

That it is unprofitable and cannot tend to the Benifit of this State to continue a Truck House at Machias. And that the same ought to be continued only by the United States under the Direction of Col. Allen as Continental Agent for the Indians and that Congress be inform'd thereof —

That a Bill be bro't in — to prevent Person's trading with the Indians at Mechias or any way supplying them with strong Drink — under severe Penalties

Letter from Francis Shaw. June 6, 1777.

Machias 6th 1777 —

May it Please your Honors

Undoubtedly before this you have been Informed by Capt Smith of the Movements of the Enemy at St John's River, by advice of the Different Committees I have Inlisted into the Continental Service during the Terme of two Months, a Captain a Lieutt & forty two Men, and hope this day to sett off to the Assistance John Allan Esqr who left this Eight days since — Relying on your know_ Candor and Generosity, I have obligated myself to the Party for their wages, the Committee of this place have done the same with Regard to this Provissions.

I have not the least doubt of keeping the Indians Freindly to the American cause, they must be dearly bought, and the Truck-houses well Supplyed. I doubt not you will give us every Assistance, as the preservation of so Valuable part of this state Intirely Depends thereon,—

Inclos'd you have Copy of a Letter from Col Lowder to Coll Buck which I Receiv'd a few hours before I left Home, to which I Refer your Honors —

and am with all Respect, your Honor's
Most Humle Servt
Fra. Shaw

To the Honble Council & Honble House of Representatives of the State of Massachusetts Bay

In Council June 28, 1777 Read & Comitted to the Comittee to whom was referred the Letter from Benjn Foster

Sent down for Concurrence

Jno Avery Dpy Secy

In the House of Representatives June 28, 1777

Read and concurrd

R T Paine Spkr pr. temp

Letter from Saml Jordan Esq.   June 7, 1777.

Union River June 7th 1777

Gentlemen

I think it Incumbent on me to acquaint you of the proceedings of some of the Inhabitants of this place.

Last week we had an account sent us from Penobscot that their was an army of Indians with Regulars a Coming Down upon the Rivers Kennebeck Penobscot and St Johns which made us very uneasy, and a number of the Inhabitants of this Place met, and as I am Informed some of which proposed to send some Person or Persons to meet the army up Penobscot River in order to Capitulate and come under their protection and give up their arms   I think such proceedings is contrary to the Liberties of this and the other States and I make no Doubt in my own mind from many things I have observed in maney Persons that if such an army should come they would gladly embrace the oppertunity and I think my self and some here is in danger of our Lives if such a thing should happen one of these set of People said a few Days ago that he was told the Regulars had sent to Machias to submit and if they came it was the determination of the Inhabitants to submit.   I write the above that your Honours may act as you think Best   I should be glad for maney Reasons not to have my Name made Publick in this matter unless you should think it Best.   Mr Thos Milliken the Bearer of this Letter can Inform your Honours as to the above.

I am your Honours most obedient and most Humble serv^t

Samuel Jordan

To the Honble the Councel of the Massachusetts State

Letter from Charles Chauncy Esq. June 12, 1777.

Kittery 12th June 1777

Sir

I had the Honour a few days ago to receive a Letter from the Honble Board acquainting me, of my Election as a Member of the Council. The receipt of which gave me much concern, when I reflected upon the State of my Health, & the undeserved favour done me.—

I am heartily desirous of doing everything within the Limits of my capacity, for the Publick service, in this difficult day; but the Indisposition, I am now labouring under, and have for six months past been confined with, Obliges me to resign the Honble appointment; which at this Juncture I would not have done, notwithstanding my unfitness for the station, was there any possibility of my acting therein, and giving that attendance which would be incumbent upon me.—

I am with great respect to the Honble Assembly your most obedient & humble Servant,

Cha Chauncy

In Council June 18, 1777
 Read & Sent down

Jno Avery Dpy Secy

Honble the President of the Council of the State of Massachusetts Bay

Letter from Col. J. Allan. June 18, 1777.

Autpaque River St Johns, June 18, 1777

May it Please Your Honors

I Wrote to you of the 18th 26th & 30th Ultom Giveing Your honours an Account of the Various movements of the Enemy at St Johns & thiere Leaveing it. According to

What I Mentioned in my Last the same day (30th) I proceeded with 4 Whale Boats & 4 Birch Cannos Leaving Cap^n West & Twenty Men Under his Command, which with the Indians & my own Men Amountd to forty three I arived at Passamaquody By 6 O clock next Morning & that Evening reach'd the Chief of Passamaquody's Wigwam were I found three Birch Cannoes from St Johns who had Come thro the Lakes for me, on my Landing I was Saluted By all the Indians who ranged themselves in a Single file (about thirty and fired several Rounds in thiere fashion. I had a Conference the same Evening with much satisfaction — After Refreshing the Men I dispatch'd Cap^n West with his Boats for St Johns to Prevent Inteligence of Our Movements. the Next Morning (Sunday) I set off with Thirteen Canoes, overtook Cap^n West Same Evening Arriv'd at Musquash Cove about 9 Miles from St Johns, there I formed our Position to Go, on, after geting Some Refreshment I sent off (about 10 O clock at Night) Cap^n John Preble with Two Indians in a Birch Canoe to the Hearbour for discovery, in aboute an hour after I sat off With Two Boats & 6 Birch Canoes Leaving the Other Two Boats. Provisions &c with Other Canoes which had familys. to Come Next day, but Notwithstanding our dispatch'd it was Clear day light before we Arriv'd. finding the Coast Clear & being determind to Seize Hazen & White who where the promoters of bringing the Man of War there, I immediately sent of— Cap^n West with 16 Men to Cross above the falls. distant three Miles, & an Indian with a Birch Canoe. all which was Executed so well; that about 6 Oclock both these Gentlemen were Secured — About 9 O Clock I Arrived at the old Fort (Frederick) when Cap^n West Came accross with his Prisoners. on Confereing with them. they Uterly denied haveing any thing to do in the matter. but said it was Premediated design of the Government sence Eddys affair that Col^l Gould told them it was determind to Erect a fort at the Mouth of the River, & one About 40 Miles up, that Gould returnd with the Utmost dispach with a draft of Matters in Order to Return with all Expedition after Conversing some time with These Men I thought it Expedient from My Own Setuation & Circumstances of thing on the River, which by this time I became More Acquaintd with, to Leave these Gentlemen on their Parole with thiere Famelies till the determination of Cort was Known; or more Strength. I Accordingly sent them Home, and that Afternoon Pass'd the Falls with all the Boats & Canoes the Whole haveing Arrivd by 4 O Clock P M. I Encampd About one Mile above the Falls: were I receivd a more Certain Account of the diffrient movements, And I am sorry to say that the People has not Acted with that Spirit as becoms the Subjects of Liberty, Much Division has been Among them, those Who were Sperietd in the Cause follow'd too Much the Method of the Continent by letting the disaffected go aboute & Insenuate Diffrient Tales, & haveing no Encouragment of Succour from the Westward and being Surprizd so Suddenly the Whole Gave up & are now become the Subjects of Britain, the Greatest Part is I Believe as Zealous as ever & it is there Earnest request that a Sufficient Force May be sent from the Continent. are also Conscious of What will be the Consequence shoud the Bitians Get a Hold here, as it will Command the Eastern Country and Open a Communicati[n] into Canada, all that I can say for the Inhabitants is this, that they Might have very Easyly deffended the Mouth of the River by Secureing the Falls Against 1000 men, but they Neglected this from Various Obstructions in their Consultations, they Admitted the Britiners about 100. Men to surprize them suddenly and Passively Submited & took the Oath of Allegience, Many of them were Robd of thier all Many were those who had taken the Oath, they Appeard by What I can

learn dejected & forlorn & Sorry for what is done. but how
to Manage the affair they Appear at a Loss. Stupid &
fluctuating from this Your Honours may form a Jugment of
the Setuation of this River —

theres Some that are Great Zealots for Britain among
them is one Lewis Mitchel, who is well Acquaintd with the
diffrient parts of the Country and Often Goes to Halifax, is
of an Insinuateing Turn Perticularly Among the French and
Indians. he was one of the two who went last March to Git
Troops. I was ditermind to Secure him if Posible —

On the 3^d Instant I Gave Cap^n West his Instructions
which was to Range the Woods from Hazen Across the
River above the falls Round to the Old Fort, to Keep himself Secriet not to be any where but in the Woods &
Endeavour to Annoy & disturb the Enemy in thier Lodgment (shoud they Come) till further Orders —

I Proceedd my self with Two Boats & 6 Birch Cannoes
up the River on the 4th about 10 OClock Mr Preble and me
with three Indians went to Mitchels house & took him. Hes
now a Prisoner with me, in the Afternoon I Got up to Mangerville & went a Shore Opposite the Town & Wrote a Letter to the Inhabitants (a Copy of Wich is here for your
Honors Peruseal) I woud Observe to Your Honours that
upon hearing of the Inhabitants submiting to Brittain I was
determind not to Go in Any of the Houses, nor go to Any
Settlement nor have Any Conection or Intercourse with
them Otherwise then Procureing some Refreshments & every
Night I Encamp in the Woods distant from Any House —

On the 5th at day light Proceeded on, & when Within one
Mile of the Indian Settlements. a Centery Haild & desired
us to Stop till he Acquainted the Rest of Our Coming —
after a Signal was Given We Proceeded. When in Sight
the Indians formd in a Single Line between Fourty & fifty in
there Shirts Painted fired a fieu dejoy which we Answerd,

upon my Going ashore one Piere Toma. Ambroise & the Other Chiefs Reciev⁴ me in form — I walk'd towards the Wigwams When Pasing the Line of Indians before mentiond, they began a fireing & Continued some Minutes — after them all the Squas ranged along Curtsying as I pass'd, Went to Ambroises Wigwam where all the Captains attended & the Young Men Came in one by one & seluted me & then went of. we Pas'd the Evening in telling News, I Lodg'd in the Wigwaum. I am Reather More Perticular in Mentioning these Triffeling Matters, It is only to Give Your Honours an Idea of Thiere ways. & the Friendship which some of them Retains for America who were the Occation of this Method of Complimenting.

I shall very Likely, be very Perticular in Communicateing our Diffrient Proceedings & Conferences, till Your Honours desire me to Desist from Troubling you — The next day I Conversed with several Indians privately & found that I had a very hard task to Go Through with Little hopes of Success. I found that several were Vastly fond Colo¹ Gould and Seemd Undetermind what to do. when some of the Chiefs were on Board the Bible was Presented for them to Swear Allegience which they Comply'd with. Piere Toma in Perticular appear'd Enraged at his Treatment when in Boston. Said he was not Treated as he Ought to be & what was Promised him therefore he was determind to Go to Halifax — I used every Argument I was Master of to Dissuad him from his Design & to Convince him of the Good Disposition & Intention of the States towards the Tribes & that I had Come to do them Justice: with the Same Authority as Monsieur Besuébair in the French time. this Pleased them Much & upon the Whole I Gaind such an Assendency over the other Indians that they Interpos'd. for the Present Appeared somwat Satisfyd till another Conference among themselves — On the 7ᵗʰ about 11 O Clock I was sent for to Piere Tomas Wigwams where I found all the Chiefs & Young Men. after I was Seated. Ambroise Rose and in a Solome Attitude Address'd the Chiefs Giving An Accou^t of his Embasy and dil^d him a String of Wampum Then Addressd the Young Men in the Same Manner delivering them Another String of Wampum, they all Answerd him Agreeing with what he had done, & that they were still United in friendship one with Another they then dispersed — About an hour after I was Again sent for to Ambroises Wigwams were I found the Whole Present. One of the Chiefs then Rose & Addressd me in the Same Manner as Monsieur Beauébear was in the French time, as thiere Contryman in behalf of the Congress & Gene^l Washinton after taulking Much upon Matters Concerning themselves & Welcoming me. I was present^d With a String of Wampum from the Chief. then Another String was Given from the Chiefs & Young men. Piere Tomma then Rose & takeing the two Strings from me, Addressing me in behalf of the Whole Jointly & then Returnd them to me. we then Parted after I had Invited them to My House on Monday to Give them an Answer, on Which day they all Attended. When I deliverd them three Strings of Wampum —- after Introduceing the Conversation I stated to them As Clearly as Posible the Nature of the dispute & what Occationd the War between America & Brittain all which Appearently Gave Much satisfaction, we Parted Great friends. I have ever Since attended the Visiting the diffrient Wegwams & Conversing privately with them — Giveing them a Minute Detail of Matters which they Gave Great Attention to. On the 8th I Rec^d a Letter from Cap^n West Giveing me an Account of his takeing a Schooner from Halifax with Sundrys On board Amoung Which was some English Goods which I shoud have been Extreemly Glad of had they Been sent up here but for Fear of Being Block'd up he sent to Mechias 2 days after Colo[l] Shaw Arriv'd at the Mouth of the River with 45 Men.

On the 9th I Recievd Intelligence in 9 days from Quebeck that Gener[l] Burgoyn Arrived there About the 16th of May, with About three Hundred men he Stay'd there but Eight & forty hours & Sett off for the Lakes. the Canadians were very much distress'd that every 6th Man was Drafted, & were daily deserting that they were very much discouragd and Appeard Certain that they Cou'd not Penetrate farr, As they heard of the Great Strength of Ticonderogo that those that were Advocates for America suffer'd much, Gov[r] Carleton is to Continue at Quebec.

on the 11th Mess[rs] Hazen & White haveing been Made Prisoners on Seeing the Brittish Ship Coming into the River; which prov'd to be the Vulture Sloop of Warr. with her Came a Sloop with Supplys Cap[n] West Board[d] the Sloop, but such Numbers Coming from the Ship, & no Prospect of Success he thought best to Quit her. the Brittinors being somewat Intemidated Thought proper to Set Sail the Next day, but I fear their Return with Superior Force —

I have sent a Canoe for Other Indians on the Head of the River whome I Expect this Week — I have sent Another to Merameekee with a String of Wampum, to Let them Know of my Business and Intention of Being Amoung them, which I Intend doing when I Can Get the St Johns Indians a little more Secure & Settled, a Number of them I Expect will Go with me I have also sent off after an English Officer who is Amoung them up the River who Calls himself a Deserter but I presume is a spy —

Since my Arrival I have Imploy'd several of the Indians in Sending them about with Express to the Other Tribes By wich I Keep up their Spieriets I am Compeld at Present to Stay here for I Fear on my Leaving this Place the Indians woud be Immediatly down the River the Impression Colo[l]

Gould has Made on their Minds seems to Occation an Unsteady Conduct so much (that Notwithstanding) thier Fair Speeches & friendly behaviour at Times I after all think they Will Leave us — I Can hardly Write Any thing Certain about them And I doubt Not but my Own Letters may Conterdict one Another for thiere Beheavour is so Changeable, And When Any thing is on the Carpet on Either Side they Appear So Assiduas & Sanguine. that I am often Led to Suppose they are Come to A final Determination which brings on an Unsteadyness in my own Conduct with them & my Letters often Dictated as the Situation of my mind is, After a Conference —

But upon the Whole I must say there is none acted more Vertuous Even Those that are more Refind. they Are naked & in Great want of Provisions Notwithstanding they Persevear, and only in Distress will Purchais from the Adhearents of Great Brittain. Many of them sence the Treaty & Promises Made them have Quitted Hunting their familys I find in Great Distress, with Many Complaints on the Arrival of Coll° Shaw I call'd a Meeting of Chiefs Sachems & Young Men to Lay in their Complaints and upon the whole was that they had not the Treatment they Expected. this Expectation was found'd on the French Custom. which was when they went to War their Famelys were Supplyd and Whatever was Lost in War or drunkeness was made up to them. for they say the Evil which arrises to them is in Consequence of thier being in the Service there is no Convinceing them to the Contrary they say they were also Promised hard Money & Many Other things —

Their Councels have often Met sence my Arrival here: And have always been Called to Consalt; thier Maner of Beheaviour is both Solemn & Orderly — I have somewat Elated their Spiriet & Ambition By Convinceing them of thier Cosequence Among Other Matters Agreed upon was the Prices of Furrs with Some Staple Commodities Your Honours may think the furrs are Placed high But this I Presum'd a Piece of Policy from this Reason that it was no Likely hood Any American wou'd purchais'd furrs with hard Money. that Furrs sent to the Continent bears a Great Advance Equevilant to the Goods purchais'd that this Method woud Naturly Occation a Jealousy & Dispute between the Indians and the Adhearents of Brittain, as the Latter woud Refuse to pay the Price, & very Likely Supplys might not arrive time enough from the Continent all which I thought wou'd Tend to the Service of the States, this Arrangement is to the 1st of January —

I have Only to add in Respect to the Indians. that there must be timely Supplys, it will now take 15 or 20 pieces of Strouds for this Tribe, besides Other Matters in proportion & a Considerable Quantity of Corn & other Provisions, it Cannot be Supposed that these Persons will Keep Always so Quiet without Assisting them (I mean for their furrs in payment) if they are Forced to Deal with the Brittains the Consequence is Obvious & Sure & it must soon take place if not Speedly prevented I woud Try at Meramechee for some Cut Money is Wanting —

Mr John Preble, has been very Assiduous and Active he was Forced to flee & Secure his Effects in the Woods, Quantitys of which were found & Embezzell'd by Tories & Soldiers. some things has been got. I have Orderd them to be Remov'd from Masigerville to this Place. the Indians have taken most of them — I have sent Mr Preble to Mechias for what Things I brought to Procure what Else he Can, Before the Brittains Get to the River, But after all this Preparation if a Force Does not Come; it will be Imposible to Keep their Interest — I am at Present at a very Great Expence haveing been forced to be very Lavish & Likely to be far more then I Expected. I must therefore Earnestly request Your Honours to Give me Speedy Information what is your Intention that I may Order things Accordingly —

I have Recieved no Perticular News from Cumberland Nor do we Know Any thing of the State of the Famelys Sence Decem^r Any more then In General. The Property of persons absconding. & those who Refuse the Oath is mostly Sized and Sold Several Famelys turnd out of their Homes — I am reather afraid to send to Know for fear of Exasperateing to more Cruelty. & Little Expect to see my family this Year if Ever —

The River is Now Quiet, 60 Men at the mouth of the river & my Keeping the Indians at Home & now & then Raising a Small Allarm, to put the Indians in a little Motion Staggers the whole Inhabitants & Keeps any Inclination from Attempt any thing — Many has been Here Makeing the Greatest profession of Friendship — I desire them to Keep away. I was determind to have no Connection watever with any Others but the Indians & declind Any of thier Company this way. as I shoud not Trouble Aney of thier Houses. And as Yet I have not been in Any House sence I am on the River —

The bearrer Doct^r Nevers who is a Person who has Sufferd the Greatest hardships, the most part of his Interest Carried off by Mr Gould & himself Lyable every day to be made a Prisoner, his Charector in Private Life as well as his Zeal for his Country — Being a Great Instrument in Keeping the Indians Quiet in Furnishing them with Provisions &c Merrits the friendship of every person Concernd. Must therefore recommend him to your Honours favour —

The Schooner which West took & Sent to Mechias belongs to the States. Except so Much as the State pleases to allow to the Captures your Honours will please to Authorize Cap^n Smith or some Other trusty Person to Secure the Property.

I am with much duty & Respect Your Honours
  Most Ob^t very hbl S^t J Allan

P. S.   I must pray a parcel of Wampum may be spared from the States, As I am much in want.

June 20th 1777

This afternoon 3 Birch Canoes Arrived from the head of the River with seven very respectable men Chiefs, they sent for me, & precented me with a string of Wampum, Declaring the utmost friendship, signifying their Acknowledgment & Obligation in sending to them in such a friendly Manner, I Expect a Conference to-morrow — about an hour After the Canoe returned from Marimishe from the Micmacs, sending me a Long string of Wampum Declaring the most fervent Zeal for America — with there Good wishes & Love towards me — that an Express was immediately sent of to Collect the whole Chiefs at Marimishe where I shall meet them — By this Last Canoe, I heard of a Boat from Cumberland with 16 Unhappy persons being Down the river on there way to me — I woud mention that the paper Money will not pass at present.   Let me beseech your Honours to Consider the Distress Country —

Letter from George Stillman.   June 18, 1777.

Boston June 18th 1777

To the Honorable the Council of the State of Massachusetts Bay

May it Please your Honors   Being acquainted by the Dep^y Sec^y in /consequence of your Honors direction/ of my Appointment as Major of a Regiment to be Raised in ye Counties of Cumberland & Lincoln for an Expedition to ye River St John in Nova Scotia &c with due acknowledgement of the Honor done me by ye General Court in this Appointment, tho I wish a person more competent to ye Business had been appointed Yet from A desire of Serving my Country at her call, especially in a Struggle which is at once ye cause of

Liberty & yᵉ rights of Human nature relying on yᵉ Candor of the General Court and my Countrymen I do accept of sᵈ appointment and Shall endeavour to Serve them to the extant of the poor abilities of yʳ Honors most

Obedient Humble Seᵗ

George Stillman

Letter from Col. Moses Little   June 1777.

Boston June 1777

Sir I this Morning recᵈ your favʳ acquainting me with the Honor done me by the General Assembly of this State in appointing me to the Command of the Forces destined for Nova Scotia — I feel myself very sensibly affected by this Mark of their Esteem & am extremely sorry that the broken State of my own Health occasioned by the severe Services of the last Campaign & the peculiar Situation of my Family at this Time oblige me to decline this honorable Appointment —

With my best Wishes for the Success of this Expedition & my warmesᵗ acknoledgmᵗˢ to the honorable Court I am

Sir Yr mo. Hum Sᵗ

Moses Little

To Mʳ J Avery

  In Council June 19, 1777 Read & sent down

Jnº Avery Dpʸ Secʸ

Letter to John Allan Esq   June 20, 1777

Council Chamber June 20ᵗʰ 1777

Sir/ We have received yours of the 18ᵗʰ & 26ᵗʰ ultº, & attended to their Contents;

Agreeable to the last Recommendation of Congress, this State have taken into consideration the circumstances of the

Inhabitants of St John's River & other Eastern parts, & have ordered one Regim^t to be raised in this State, & 1 Company of Matrosses, to serve 6 Months; & also that another Regim^t be raised in the Province of Nova Scotia to serve 12 months; & the Field officers for the 1st Regim^t are already appointed — We tho't it prudent to give you this early notice of our designs, in order to enable you to form your measures with the Indians & other Inhabitants of those parts: And you may depend upon our pushing this expedition into effect with all possible dispatch — Your prudence will direct you to keep this matter as secret as circumstances will permit, lest the Enemy should endeavor to intercept us.

In the Name, & by Order of Council
John Allen Esqr

Letter from Jon^a Warner. June 25, 1777.

May it please your Honors

By the Direction of your Honors the Secretary has Acquainted me of my appointment as Brigadier General to Command the Forces Destined to St Johns in Nova Scotia and requires my immediate answer —

I could wish a Person of more Experience had been made choice of as your Honors Must be Sensible that Military knowledge and Experience is highly necessary in an undertaking of this importance and the little opportunity I have had to Qualify myself for so important an affair, but since it has pleas^d your Honors to appoint me to Command in this Expedition I will exert my poor Abilities and endeavour to Deserve the Honor Confer^d on your Honors most obedient
Humble Servt

Jon^a Warner

Boston June 25th 1777
To the Honourable Board

Letter from Francis Shaw. July 4, 1777.

Machias 4th July 1777 —
May it Please your Honors

The following is a short Narrative of our proceedings since I wrote your Honors from this Place —

After a passage of three days we reach'd Musquash Cove ab^t three Leagues West of St John River, during the Night We heard several Cannon, on which We Concluded Immeadiatly to send off a Boat of observation, which Returned in the Morning; and Inform'd that a Ship & Sloop were under sail coming out of the Harbour — as soon as they were well Clear of the Land, we push'd into the River & joined Capt Wests party — after taking such steps as we thought Necessary to secure our Boats & provisions &^{c} &^{c} I proceeded up the River to Aukepague, after settleing my Bussiness with Mr Allan & the Indians, I sett off for the Mouth of the river, intending immeadiatly for this place, leaving the Command (with the advice of Mr Allan) with Capt Dyar, on my arrival I found the Ship Vulture had been in the Harbour 2 Days, that on Monday the 23^d June upwards of 40 Men Attempted to Land in two Boats, near where we had a party of 21 Men Stationed, who gave them so warm a Reception that after 20 Minuits they were glad to drift off to the Ship, the side of one of the Boats that was next to our fire was so shattered, they were obliged to heel her Gunnel too, to prevent her sinking — it is uncertain how many Men they lost, but it was generally supposed by the Spectators they had 16 or 18 Killed & Wounded, one through a Glass saw 8 hoisted on board the Ship — our party did not suffer the least Damage —

I tarried there several days untill two Ships more and one Sloop had arrived, and Concluding they did not Incline to attempt landing again, I left them on the Evening of ye 29th June in high spirets, the Boats & provisions well secured, and they posted in such a possition as to Defey the Enemy to defeat them, unless assisted by the Inhabitants, who I think will generally join our party as soon as they are Inform'd of your Honors Determination to defend the River, notwithstanding the oath lately Extorted from them — here with you have two Letters from John Allan Esqr which were intended to be delivered by Doc^r Nevers, as his Vessel could not pass the ships, he is prevented proceeding for the present

I am with much Respect & Esteem Your Honor's
Most Humble Servt

Fra: Shaw

To the Honble Council & Hon^{le} House of Representitives at Boston.

Letter from Col. Alex^r Campbell. July 13, 1777.

Number Four July 13th 1777
yesterday Received Letters from the Committee & Major George Stillman of Machias, wherein I have the Following Acc^t Viz^t that the Captains Dyer & West, had made an Honorable Retreet from St Johns, /they Commanding a Recruiteing Partey: to Watch the Enemys motions/ there was at that time, in St John three men of War two Tenders And a Sloop belonging to the British King, the number of men on bord these Vessels is unCertain, but we are Certain they Landed 120 men, at one Peabodys, at Mahogany Bay So Called. They March^d through the woods two miles & a half, our Troops having timely Notice, thought Best to call in their Gards and Secure a Retreet — they Accordingly Detach^d their main Body, to a place Called great Bay Above the Falls to Secure their Boats. Leaving Cap^n Dyer With twelve men to Observe the Enemys Motions — Captain Dyer let the Main Body Come within good muskett Shot, then

fired and Retreeted. on his Retreat fell in with the Enemys Flanque Gaurd, who fired on them at ten or twelve yards Distance killed three and two Slightly Wounded, who got off with Captain Dyer, our Party imedeatly Retreated up River, at one oClock was Seen 25 miles up, Next Day the Enemy follow^d up River.— this intilegence Comes Straight from St Johns, By one Mr Bromfield, a Gentleman of undoubted Credit and Veracity, who Supposes our troops intirely Safe, as the Enemy proceeded but only 20 or 30 miles up River, he was also Eye Wittness to the scurmish: by the same Authority, we find the Enemy well inform^d of the Eastren Campaign, two Ships from New york was Despacth^d Imediatly who was into St Johns. The Maremaid of 36 guns the Ambuscaid of 32 D^o with another Ship, With Orders to Cruise Between Machias Harbour and Mount Desert to intercept our fleets on their way Eastward — this from Machias at the Same Time Desireing me to Communicate the Same Westward — and as it is become the Duty and intrest of Every Well Efected Person to Exert and Streech Every Nearve in Oposition to Ministerial Tirany and Oppission — precaution and Prevention being the Best of Action ; I would Earnestly Recommend to all Officers of the Continental or States Troops, Commanders of forts, or Millitia, Commanders of Privatteers, Committees, and others who may have it in their Power, that they use Every Means that the Commanders of Troops or Ships Engag^d on the Present Expedition Eastward: may have Timely Notice of this matter So as to Govern them-selves Accordingly — A mistake of this Kind, may Prove Extreemly Fattal, to the Eastren Countrey and a Damage to the Publick Cause in Generall — the Contrary of which is the Sincere Desire of a friend to his Countrey

    Alex : Campbell Lieu^t Coll
     Eastren Rege^t County Lincoln

NB   its carefully to be observ ᵈ that Mʳ Bramfield informs that the Ships have left Sᵗ Johns and now on their Cruise: and often Seen on the Coasts between Mount Desert and Machias how many more may be Collected is uncertain.

Superscribed:
On the Publick Service Express
To Aney Officer Commanding in State or Continental Service, Committees and others friends to America

pʳ Capᵗ Davis

Letter from Meshech Weare.   July 14, 1777.

In Committee of Safety Exeter July 14ᵗʰ 1777

Sir/   By a Currier Just Come in from N° 4 we have receiv'd a Confirmation of the unhappy affair at Ticonderoga and that the party under Col° Warner (mentioned in Genˡ Sᵗ Clair's Letter Suffered very much, no particulers are Come to Hand but by reports of the Soldiers who have Stragled in to N° 4 many of them wounded — that Several Field officers are among the Slain — the Army we hear are gone to Bennington, tho many of the Soldiers, are on their way home some officers from this State, who were on their way to Join the Army have Stop't at N° 4 and are Collecting all the Continental Soldiers, who Come in there, to march them back to Join their Regiments — all our Militia who marched on the alarm have returned Home and we have had no opportunity to give any new orders on this occasion —

As the Enemy without Doubt will Endeavour to make all the Advantage the‿ Can by their late Success, we think of the highest Importance, that Some Spirited measures Should be Immediatly Taken — and Desire you will Communicate to us as Soon as possible your Sentiments on the Occasion, and what method your State may adopt.

By order of the Committee —

I am with Due regard your most Obed[t] Hum[l] Serv[t]

Meshech Weare Chairman

Hon[ble] Presiden_ of Council of the State
of Massachusetts Bay —

Letter from Francis Shaw

Gouldsborough 15th July 1777

May it please your Honor's,

on my arrival at Machias the 14th Instant I wrote your Honor's, and gave you the particular situation of our party on the River S[t] John's.

By M[r] Broomfield of Newbury just arrived, I have the disagreeable News that the Enemy had Landed 120 Men against our party and after a Short Engagement obliged Cap[ts] Dyer & West to retreat up the River, leaving two killed & one Mortally wounded, since dead, he further Informs our people were seen 20 Miles up the River with their boats the same day, I doubt not they will be able to Join M[r] Allan & his party, & hope soon to have more favourable Accounts from them — I am with much Respect & Esteem

Your Honor's Most Hum[l] Serv[t]

Fra: Shaw

To The Hon[ble] the Council & House of Representatives of the Massachusetts State

Letter from Meshech Weare. July 16, 1777.

State of New Hampshire

In Committee of Safety July 16th 1777

Sir, The Accounts we are continually receiving make it more than probable that our Northern Army have suffered very much on their retreat — and that these who escaped are much scattered — We have sent Officers to N° 4. to stop all the Soldiers on their way home, as well those of the other States as our own — and we understand a considerable number are collected there.—

We have received no Letters from the Army, and know not the Rout they have taken, & are greatly at a loss what Measures are necessary to be adopted at this important Crisis — We therefore desire a Communication of your Sentiments on this Subject — Our General Court will meet Tomorrow, and we are sure will readily coincide with our Sister States in using the most spirited means to retrieve the Losses and save our Country from threatened destruction —

By order of the Com[tee]

I am Sir Your Obed[t] Hum[ble] Serv[t]

Meshech Weare Chairman

Hon[ble] President of the Council of
Massachusetts Bay

P. S. The Inhabitants of our Frontier Towns on Connecticut River are sending their Committees in the most pathetic manner, begging to be supplied with fire Arms as half of them (they say) are destitute, and other parts of the State not much better stocked — We must again repeat our solicitation in the most urgent manner to our Sister State to sell us some of the large Quantity of Guns they have lately imported, or a considerable part of our Militia must remain unwilling spectators of the War in which they would gladly assist their Country.— We are also in the greatest want of Lead, and pray to be supplied with what you can spare of that Article —

M Weare

INDEX.

A

A, —— J., letter of, 294.
Abbot, Asa, signed Andover petition, 20.
    Darius, ditto, 20.
    David, signed Suncook petition, 205.
    Ephraim, signed Andover petition, 20.
    Francis, asked to furnish powder, 337.
    George Jr., signed Andover petition, 20.
    Isaac Jr., ditto, 20.
    John 5th, ditto, 20,
    Jonathan, ditto, 20.
    Nehemiah Jr., ditto, 20.
    Samuel, signed Suncook petition, 205.
    Stephen, signed Andover petition, 20.
Acts of Incorporation, of Belfast, 199; Broad Bay, 200; Freetown, 226; Lebanon, 32, 33; Narragansett No. One, 135; Pondstown, 122, 124, 126.
Acts relating to Preaching, 185; York Bridge, 119.
Adams, Abigail, 294.
    Henry, signed Narragansett petition, 160.
    Jacob, his losses at Falmouth, 301.
    John, 294, 331.
    Joseph, signed Narragansett petition, 159.
    Samuel, signed Boothbay petition, 170; one of the Committee of Correspondence, 241; defamed, 275; as secretary, 385.
    Thomas, ensign, 333.
Address to Continental Congress, 296, 297.
Adkinson, Humphry, signed Narragansett petition, 181.
Advertisement of the Earl of Stirling, 85.

Albany, 238.
Aldswood, Robert, grant to, 189.
Alexander, Sir William, first Earl of Stirling, 85, 89, 90, 91.
Alexandria, name of a proposed town, 86.
Allbee, Benjamin, signed Freetown petition, 17, 217.
    Jonathan, ditto, 217.
    William, signed Machias memorial, 115; justified the conduct of Stephen Jones, 292.
Allen, ——, signed Freetown petition, 17.
    Lieut. ——, 356.
    James, signed Freetown petition, 217.
    John, member of the General Court, 407.
    Col. John, reported the success of the enemy, 414; his plan, 414; a premium offered for, 414, 415; deviated from his plan, 415; started on an expedition, 416; intercepted Anderson's letter, 417; amount due him, 422; drew from truckhouse, 422; should be supplied from the treasury, 423; to be continued in the service, 423; an Indian agent, 423; Shaw to go to, 424; went to Passamaquoddy Bay, 427; at Musquash and Fort Frederick, 427; arrested Mitchell, 429; at Mangerville, 429; wrote a letter to the people, 429; met Indians, 429, 430, 431, 433, 434, 436; sent for other Indians, 432; keeps up the Indians' spirits, 432; seized property, 435; keeps the Indians at home, 435; letter to, 438; met Col. Shaw, 439; sent letter by Col. Shaw, 440; troops to join, 443; letters of, 414, 417, 418, 426; report on his accounts, 422,

Alley, John, signed Boothbay petition, 171.
Jonathan Jr., ditto, 171.
Joshua, ditto, 171.
Samuel, ditto, 171.
Amaroscoggin, *see* Androscoggin.
Ambroise, an Indian, 406, 430, 431.
Ammunition, sent to forts, 54; needed at Falmouth, 242, 338; needed in the Eastern parts, 244, 356, 357, 360, 361; needed at Brunswick, 244, 245; taken from fort, 245; Congress should supply Indians with powder, 245; the colonists expect to manufacture their own powder, 255; more needed at Winslow, 265; sent to Annapolis but carried to Arundel, 266, 274; needed at Belfast and Penobscot, 268, 269; captured at Machias; but more needed, 282, 314; Goldthwait to deliver arms to the committee, 285; powder arrived at Philadelphia, 294; the enemy sent powder and balls to the Indians for the latter to attack the provincials, 323; armament at Quebec, 328; powder for the privateers, 337; Salem purchased a supply of Abbot, 337; the amount at Kennebec, 340; powder for the colony, 346; can not be supplied, 357; needed to be used with intelligence, 360; needed in Cumberland, 395, 396; expected at Machias, 399; needed by Col. Mitchell, 401; armament for St. Johns River expedition, 420; needed in the Connecticut Valley, 444.
Anderson, Abraham, signed Windham petition, 73.
James, part owner of the Loyal Legion, 310.
John, of Newburn, taken prisoner and released, 311; he and his wife intriguing, 416, 417; letter of intercepted, 417.
Andover, 19, 20, 196.
Andre, Peter, a Micmac of La Heve, joined the provincial army, 365.
Andrews, Amos, signed the certificate for Ilsley, 386.
Ephraim, signed the Machias memorial, 115.
Joseph, alias Saunders, supposed to have committed murder, 14.
Androscoggin, Indians, 279.
River, 161, 162, 163, 214, 215, 279.
Annapolis, 262, 263, 266, 302, 303, 323, 325, 358, 375, 396.
Answer to Lyon, the Rev. James, 174; Memorial of Ministers of York, 183; petition of Machias, 284.
Appleton, Mr.——, member of the General Court, 388.
Archer, John, his losses at the destruction of Falmouth, 306.
Armament, *see* under Ammunition.
Armstrong, Jonathan, a rioter at Falmouth, 147, 148.
Army, Congress to establish an, 256; *see* also under soldiers.
Continental, 356, 357, 378, 411.
Royal, 356, 360.
Arnold, Gen. Benedict, Indians with him in Quebec expedition, 363.
Arundel, a vessel seized which belonged at, 266, 273; mate obliged to enter the king's service, 266, 273; vessel brought to the home port, 266, 273; Committee of Correspondence of, 267; representatives in Congress, 247; examination of papers of Jones and Hicks at, 275, 276.
Assembly, the, Goldthwait a member of, 271; the home government desired to hinder the usefulness of, 271, 272; at Watertown, 291; *see* Congress Provincial.
Atkinson, Theodore, 47.
Aubens, Phillip, signed Sebascodegin petition, 76.
Aukepague, 426, 439.
Auld, James, signed Boothbay petition, 171.
Austin, Abiel, signed Suncook petition, 205.
Benjamin, desired information about presents for Indians, 359; gorget and heart being made for, 360; letter of, 359.
Zebediah, signed Suncook petition, 205.
Autpaque River, 426, 439.
Averell, Joseph, 302.
Avery, John, deputy-secretary, 358, 362, 366, 367, 385, 387, 388,

INDEX

Avery, *continued.*
403, 404, 407, 414, 418, 422, 424, 426, 437.
Robert, of Norwich, captured, 282; killed, 282.
Ayer, Elijah, signed Cumberland petition, 396.
Moses, signed Pondstown petition, 119.
Simon, deposition of, 60; oath, 61; a proprietor, 61.
William, signed Suncook petition, 205.
Ayers, Mr. ——, of Portsmouth, 249.
Obadiah, signed Cumberland petition, 396.

B

BABBIDG, COURTNEY, signed receipt for Deer Island, 285.
Babcock, George, his land claimed by New Hampshire, 109, 110; desired another grant, 109, 110; land granted to, 111, 112.
Backet, Thomas, signed Machias letter, 292.
Bacon, Capt. Edward, of Barnstable, 344.
Bagley, Col. Jonathan, member of the General Court, 20, 50, 51, 357; grant to, 33.
Moses, his losses at the destruction of Falmouth, 308.
Bailey, } Rev. ——, 416.
Bayley, }
David, home in Pownalborough, 352; signed a bond, 354.
Jacob, selectman of Haverhill, 357.
Rev. Jacob, complaint against, 349; unduly attached to Great Britain, 349, 353; did not read pnblicly the proclamations of Congress, 349, 353, 389, 393, 397; to give bond and appear at court, 349, 353, 354; his home in Pownalborough, 352; prayed for George III, 389, 397, 398; result of his reasons, 389; an enemy to the country, 389; summoned to court, 389, 390, 398; his reasons for not reading the Declaration of Independence, 390, 391, 397, 398; his previous life, 392; not an enemy to the country, 393; will suffer for his principles, 393, 394; the records concerning to be sent to the general

Bailey, *continued.*
court, 397; why he prayed for the king, 397; his sentiments erroneous and false, 397, 398; did not observe fast-days, 398; did not pray for the success of our army, 398; read only the proclamations of the royal governors, 398; his contempt for Congress, 398; gave a bond, 398; bond of, 352.
James, selectman of Haverhill, 357.
John, his losses at the destruction of Falmouth, 310.
Joseph, ditto, 305.
Josiah, ditto, 306.
Baker, Caleb, as a witness, 354.
John, his losses at the destruction of Falmouth, 307.
Joseph, signed Suncook petition, 205; deposition of, 208.
Josiah, his losses at the destruction of Falmouth, 307.
Solomon, signed Falmouth petition, 217.
Bakerstown, meeting of the proprietors of, 60; agent to be paid, 60, 61; to be laid out, 61.
Ballard, Ephraim, of Oxford, took possession of fort and land belonging to Dr. Gardiner, 242, 407, 408, 409; inimical to the cause, 408, 409; would not deliver the property, 408, 409, 410; illegal proceedings of, 408, 410.
Baptists, exempt from ecclesiastical tax, 185.
Barber, John, will exchange coin for paper money, 374.
Barley, 381.
Barnard, Mr. ——, 243, 248.
Rev. ——, of Andover, 205.
Edward, signed the Suncook petition, 205.
Thomas, ditto, 205.
Barnet, John, signed Belfast petition, 198, 232.
Mos., ditto, 198.
Barnstable, 344.
Barnum, Job, justified the conduct of Stephen Jones, 295,
Barry, Jeremiah, his losses at the destruction of Falmouth, 307.
Barter, Benjn., signed Boothbay petition, 171.
John, ditto, 171.
Joseph, ditto, 171.
Nichs., ditto, 171.

Barter, *continued.*
  Saml., ditto, 171.
  Saml., Terts, ditto, 171.
Bartlett, Cutting, signed Narragansett petition, 160.
  Enoch, signed Narragansett memorial, 176.
Baskinridge, Somerset County, England, 86, 87.
Batchelder, Capt. ——, member of the General Court, 369.
Bates, Benjamin, 218.
Bath, letter from, 356.
Batteries being erected near North Yarmouth, 319; *see* also Forts.
Battle, Isaac, signed certificate for Ilsley, 386.
Bay of Fundy, 264, 282, 314, 345, 347, 355.
Bayley, *see* Bailey.
Beach, 271.
Beal, Ebenezer, justified the conduct of Stephen Jones, 292; in needy circumstances, 314;
Bean, David and others, desired more time, 83; more time granted to, 84.
Beans, 381.
Beath, Jeremiah, signed Boothbay petition, 171.
  John, ditto, 171, 234; a selectman, 234; one of the Committee of Correspondence, 260.
Beauébear, ⎫
Besuébair, ⎬ Mons. ——, 430, 431.
Beef, 381.
Belcher, Andrew, councilman, 10.
  Gov. Jonathan, 44, 45, 46, 47, 49.
Belfast, bounds of, 197, 199; no school at, 137; the people of desired to be incorporated, 197; right to levy taxes and sell lands, 198; incorporated, 199, 231; town meeting to be called in, 199, 200; Waldo's heirs sold land in, 231; incorporation proved to be a hinderance, 231, 232; desired permission to tax or sell unsettled lands, 232; proprietors to be notified, 232, 233; the people poor, 268; ammunition needed at, 268, 269; the people will support the cause of liberty, 269; corn to be sent to, 283; arms for, 283; powder for, 283.
Benjamin's River, 268, 285.
Bennington, Vermont, 442.

Bent, Elijah, signed Machias petition, 41.
  John, signed Cumberland petition, 396.
Bernard, Gov. Francis, letters of, 49, 52, 54; messages of, 2, 30, 31, 38, 61, 66; speeches of, 59; mentioned, 6, 7, 10, 11, 14, 16, 17, 18, 20, 21, 23, 25, 26, 28, 29, 32, 39, 47, 48, 56, 59, 62, 64, 65, 68, 70, 74, 77, 78, 83, 84, 87, 88.
  John, in custody of Col. Thompson, 300; his bondsmen, 300; not to remove his vessel, 300; nor correspond with the enemy, 300.
Barre, John, signed Machias petition, 41.
  Wesbruk, ditto, 41.
Berreck, William, signed Fort Pownall petition, 57.
Berry, Ambrose, signed Narragansett petition, 160.
  John, in need, 302, 314.
  Tomas, signed Narragansett petition, 160.
Berwick, a boundary, 25, 26, 32, 33, 68; home of Capt. Gerrish, 274; the representative in Congress, 274, 374.
Beverly, ——, member of the General Court, 404.
Bevveys, John, signed Machias memorial, 115
Bible, the, translated, 35.
Biddeford, a boundary, 29, 159, 175, 181; Committee of Inspection, 289; Sullivan's letter dated at, 355; representative in Congress, 374; letter of, 288.
Bigmore, George, signed Muscongus petition, 18.
  John, ditto, 18.
Bills, Continental, *see* under Currency.
Birch, 271.
Bishop, James, signed Pondstown petition, 118.
Black, David, part owner of the Loyal Legion, 310.
Blake, Mr. ——, of Montreal, 239.
Blancher, Joseph, his loss at the destruction of Falmouth, 306.
Bliss, Col. ——, member of the Provincial Congress, 327.
Blue Hill Bay, 153.
Blunt, Ephraim, signed Suncook petition, 205.
  Isaac, signed Andover petition, 20.

INDEX 449

Blunt, *continued.*
  John, signed Pondstown petition, 118.
Boards, 239.
Boats, 154.
Bollan, William, agent for Province of Massachusetts Bay, 89, 156, 272.
Booker, Jacob, signed the Boothbay petition, 171.
  John Jr., ditto, 171.
Booms, 237.
Booney, Joel, signed Machias petition, 41.
Boothbay, formerly called Townsend, 166; Dunbar induced people to settle at, 166; poverty of the settlers, 167, 168; depredations of Indians at, 167, 168; furnished men for the army, 167, 168; harrassed by pretended proprietors, 168, 169; some settlers paid three times for their lands, 169, 170; incorporated, 169; has a meeting house, 169; people of carried firewood to Boston, 169; ever loyal to the king, 169, 170; a boundary, 216, 226; town meeting held in, 233; proceedings of the same, 233; the same illegal, 234; new town meeting to be called, 234, 235; obscure and insignificant, 259; passed patriotic resolutions, 259; people would not use tea, and adopted the non-importation covenant, 259; appointed a Committee of Correspondence, 259, 260; officers of the militia resigned, 260; people elected officers, 260; company of minute men formed, 260; chose delegates to Congress, 260; paid tax directly to Congress, 260; will indemnify the constable, 260; will part with liberty only with life, 260; petitions of, 166, 233.
  Meeting House, 169, 233.
Boston, 11, 13, 14, 21, 27, 37, 49, 54, 83, 134, 143, 146, 147, 148, 151, 152, 153, 158, 169, 170, 186, 213, 220, 225, 233, 235, 236, 239, 240, 241, 242, 256, 262, 263, 264, 266, 273, 276, 277, 279, 280, 281, 288, 293, 304, 310, 315, 317, 319, 320, 323, 325, 338, 342, 343, 348, 358, 359, 361, 362, 366, 367, 381, 395,

Boston, *continued.*
  396, 402, 404, 405, 407, 408, 409, 416, 417, 418, 430, 436, 437, 438, 440.
  Committee of Correspondence, 235, 241, 242.
  Council Chamber, 1, 3, 10, 39, 59, 62, 66, 88, 91, 106, 131, 147, 403, 437.
  Gazette, 220.
  Harbor, 235, 320.
  Hospital, Military, 315.
  Men, a name for the Provincial soldiers, 406.
  Newspapers, 32.
  Capt. Winthrop, 333.
Bouden, John, signed Fort Pownall petition, 57.
  Paul, ditto, 57.
Boundaries, dispute with New Hampshire, 4, 5, 6, 12, 13, 25, 43, 45, 46, 47, 48, 49, 50, 51, 52, 59, 64, 100, 102, 109, 132, 165, 187, 188, 204, 214, 215, 218, 219, 221, 228, 229; fixed, 108; the true eastern, 142; not settled for Narragansett, 180; the line between the English and Indians, at tide water, 368, 369.
Bourn, Melatiah, 342.
Bow, the proprietors of claimed land in Suncook, 199, 204, 206.
Bowdoin, James, 10, 42, 81, 90, 134, 143, 151, 344, 348, 409, 410; letters of, 361, 362, 365.
  William, 151.
Bowdoinham, to send a representative to the Assembly, 290; resolution not to do so, as town is too distant, 291; has been visited by fire, 291; in sympathy with the cause, 291; letter of, 290.
  Meeting House, 291.
Bowen, Nathan, presented the petition for Windham, 71.
Boyd, Thomas, signed letter for Machias, 292.
Boynton, Amos, signed Machias petitions, 41, 115; bill of, 302.
  John Jr., signed Narragansett petition, 181.
Brackett, John, signed letter for Falmouth, 242.
Bradbury, Mr. ——, justice of the peace, 147, 148.
  Benjamin, signed Narragansett petition, 181.
  Jabez, his loss at the destruction of Falmouth, 306.

Bradbury, *continued.*
   Jacob, signed the Narragansett petition, 181; his losses at the destruction of Falmouth, 309.
   John, councilor, 1, 24; his losses at the destruction of Falmouth, 307.
   Joseph, signed the Narragansett petition, 181.
   Mary, her losses at the destruction of Falmouth, 309.
   Merrill, bill for cabins, 302.
   Roland, his losses at the destruction of Falmouth, 309.
   Samuel, ditto, 306.
   Thomas, signed the Narragansett petition, 181; his losses at the destruction of Falmouth, 307.
   William, signed the Narragansett petition, 181.
Bradford, Cornelius, signed Muscongus petition, 18.
   Gamaliel, 1.
   Joshua, 18.
Braintree, 322.
Brattle, William, 1, 88, 90, 134, 143, 147, 174, 193.
Brazer, John, signed Muscongus petition, 18.
Brazier, Harrison, his losses at the destruction of Falmouth, 309.
Breda, Treaty of, 207.
Breed, Nathaniel, signed the Freetown petition, 17.
Brewer, Col. Josiah, letter of, 413, 414.
Bridge over York River, built, 19; passengers to pay toll, 119; rates, 119, 120; rules, 120, 121; those who can pass free, 120, 121.
Bridges, Josiah, died, 92.
   Moody, agent, desired change of land in township, 28, 29, 98; people can't sell land, 28; people in arrears of taxes, 28; land grants changed, 94; the new not equivalent for old lands, 95, 98; desired to be quieted in peaceable possession, 95; desired to hold township as originally granted, 98; petitions of, 28, 29, 94, 98.
Bridge's Town, a boundary, 165.
Brier, Samuel, signed Boothbay petition, 170.
Brigantine, a, 345.
Briggs, *see* under Vessels.

Briggs, *continued.*
   Cornelius, his losses at the destruction of Falmouth, 308.
Brimhall, Cornelius, ditto, 308.
Bristol, England, 139.
   Maine, home of Eggleston, 107; Richard Fullford settled in, 107, 108; a boundary, 200, 202; letters from, 292, 360; in distress, 226, 297; Congress asked to send supplies to, 296, 297; why Congress can't comply with the request, 297, 298.
   Round Pond, 107.
Broad Bay, situation of, 14; desired the removal of the shire town, 15; desired to be set off, 15; incorporated, 200; bounds of, 200, 201, 202; town meeting to be called in, 202; petition of, 14, 15.
   Back Cove, 201.
   Havanna Point, 201.
   Jones Neck, 201.
   Passage Point, 201.
   River, 201.
Broad, Ephraim, his losses at Falmouth, 309.
Bromfield, Mr. ——, of Newbury, 441, 442, 443.
Brooks, Isaiah, signed Narragansett petition, 181.
Brown, Capt. Henry Young, purchased land and laid out a town, 4, 222; the same claimed by New Hampshire, 4, 24, 63, 223; sued, 4; to be sustained by Massachusetts, 4, 5, 6, 7, 24, 63, 223; more land granted to, 5, 6, 24, 63, 101; conditions of the new grant, 5; threatened the grantees of New Hampshire, 13; his precipitation presumed to be unknown by Massachusetts, 13; sum advanced to, 25; sum due from, 25; not to prosecute, 63; at great expense and trouble to reap advantages from his land, 63, 64; desired boundary should be settled, 64; conditions of further grants, 102; to settle his claims upon the government, 102; further allowance in money from the government, 103; has been sued by those to whom he sold land, 116; desired further relief, 116, 117; complied with the conditions, 222; to keep

Brown, *continued.*
    possession of the land, 223; to prosecute claimants, 223; paid, 223, 224; new grant to, 222; subject to damages, 224; paid damages, 224; not reimbursed by the government, 224; Maj. Phillips claimed the land, 224; can produce evidence to support facts, 224; money which he received was paid out by the order of the General Court, 225; conditions on which he will settle, 230, 231; his losses at the destruction of Falmouth, 308; petitions of, 62, 64, 116, 222, 224.
    J., letter of, 238.
    John, surveyor, 29, 39; letter of, 39.
    John, of Belfast, 198, 231, 232.
    Joseph, signed Freetown petitions, 17, 217; signed Pondstown petition, 119; signed Suncook petition, 205.
    Joshua, his losses at the destruction of Falmouth, 307.
    Silvanus, ditto, 308.
    William, member of the General Court, 82; bill of, 302; his losses at the destruction of Falmouth, 306.
    Wright, signed the Pondstown petition, 119.
Brownstown, 19.
Brunswick, people of staunch for the country, 243, 244; Parry's papers signed at, 248; home of Samuel Thompson, 249, 269, 274; prisoners to be sent to, 287; men enlisted in, 333; representative in Congress, 274; molasses sold at high prices at, 339; exportation of the same stopped, 340; Committee of Safety, 340; letters from, 244, 339.
Bryant, } Mr. ——, his land a
Bryent, } boundary, 102, 116; one of the committee to examine Parry, 299.
    Bartholomew, bill of, 302.
    Eleazer, signed Machias petition, 41.
    James, signed Pleasant River petition, 94.
    Capt. Jonathan, justice of the peace, 208; his losses at the destruction of Falmouth, 307.

Bryant, *continued.*
    Samuel Davis, signed the Machias petition, 41.
    Walter, his deposition referred to, 12, 48, 49; lines run by him, 24, 25, 45, 47, 50, 51; his survey doubted, 45, 46, 49, 50, 52; objections to his line, 46; interrogated, 47, 49, 51, 52.
Buck, Capt. and Col. Jonathan, signed the Penobscot letter, 269; settled eight miles from Fort Pownall, 271; letters by, 273, 277; corn to be sent to, 285; Lowder's letters to, 412, 424; to be asked for reenforcements, 414.
    Jonathan Jr., signed Fort Pownall petition, 57.
    Nathaniel, signed Pleasant River petition, 93.
    Thomas, signed Machias petition, 41.
    Thomas Jr., ditto, 41.
Buckminster, Col. ——, 111.
    Joseph, 70.
Bullock, William, and others to remain possessors of the land, 136; conditions of the grant, 136, 137.
Buncker, Gerard, 86.
Bunten, Andrew, signed Suncook petition, 205.
Burgoyne, Gen. John, 329, 330, 360, 432.
Burk, Michell, signed Cumberland petition, 396.
Burnam, }
Burnem, } Job, signed Machias petition, 41.
Burnum, }
    John, his losses at the destruction of Falmouth, 307.
    Samuel, signed the Machias petition, 41.
    Solomon, signed Boothbay petition, 170.
Burnham, James, of Arundel, 267.
    Job, his bill, 302.
Burns, Geo., his loss at the destruction of Falmouth, 307.
Burrill, John, speaker, 34.
Butler, James, his subscription for the St. John's expedition, 366.
    John, his losses at the destruction of Falmouth, 306.
    William, his subscription to the St. John's expedition, 366.
Butter, 311, 381.
Buxton, England, 135.

Buxton, *continued.*
  Maine, Narragansett No. One, 135; incorporated, 135; bounds of, 135; named, 135; origin of name, 135*n*; town meeting in, 135, 136, 235; to concur with Committee of Correspondence, 235; resolutions relating to American liberty, 235, 236.
B——, Daniel, justified the conduct of Stephen Jones, 292.

C

CALEF, DR. ——, member of the General Court, 79.
Call, John, signed Boothbay petition, 171.
  Obediah Jr., as a witness, 354.
Cambridge, Mass., 131, 228, 256, 333.
Cammet, Dudley, his losses at the destruction of Falmouth, 309.
Campbell, Lieut. Col. Alex., gave report of British vessels, 441; letter of, 440.
  Petter, signed Cumberland petition, 396.
Canada, 26, 56, 168, 238, 240, 255, 328, 329, 342, 358, 363, 413, 416, 419, 428.
  Expeditions to, 22, 27, 59, 77, 99, 100, 365.
  River, 368.
  Rowley, 5, 6, 28, 29.
Canadians, 246, 356, 360, 432; also called the French.
Canady, Nicolus, signed Freetown petition, 16.
Cannon, *see* under Ammunition.
Cape Ann, Mowat found it expedient to attack, 342; exempt from the draft, 358.
Cape Elizabeth, Second Parish of Falmouth, 71, 79, 99; representative from in Congress, 274, 355; number of soldiers at, 338.
  Fear, 329.
  Forschue, alias Yarmouth, 345, 347, 351.
  Porpois, 263.
Capepersue, same as Cape Forschue.
Capron, Thomas, subscribed for Canada expedition, 365.
Cargill, Col. Thomas, 322.
Carlton, Dudley, letter, 84.
  Maj. Gen. Sir Guy, 239, 241, 328, 329, 432.

Carrying Place, 413.
Cartel, for exchanging prisoners, 331.
Carter, Caleb, his loss at the destruction of Falmouth, 306.
  Joseph, one of the Committee of Correspondence, 265.
Casco Bay, 270, 288, 319, 387, 419.
Castine River, 90.
Cate, Edward, signed Pleasant River petition, 94.
Cates, Joseph, selectman of Gorham, 78.
Catharine II, to send infantry to assist the British, 304.
Cattle, 310, 311, 345, 347.
Caughnawaga Indians, 240.
Cedar, 271.
Chace, Caleb, represented Gorham in Congress, 355.
Chadbourn, } Benjamin, petitioned
Chadburne, } in behalf of Lebanon, 25, 26; to issue warrants for town meetings, 33, 68; member of the Provincial Congress, 301, 319.
Chadwick, Mr. ——, member of the General Court, 174.
Chaloner, John, justified the conduct of Stephen Jones, 292; his bill as a surgeon, 303.
  Dr. William, justified the conduct of Stephen Jones, 292; accompanied Stillman, 314.
Chamberlain, John, signed Suncook petition, 205.
Champlain, Samuel de, named Mount Desert, 141; the first European on the eastern shores, 142.
Champney, Morrice, member of the General Court, 111.
Chandler, David, signed Andover petition, 20; signed Suncook petition, 205.
  Isaac, signed Andover petition, 20.
  John, signed Pondstown petition, 118.
  John Jr., ditto, 119.
  Joshua, signed Andover petition, 20.
  Nathan, ditto, 20.
  Nathaniel Jr., ditto, 20.
Chaplain, *see* under Ministers.
Chapman, Anthony, signed Damariscotta resolutions, 238.
  Nathan, ditto, 238.
Charlestown, Mass., 379.

INDEX 453

Chase, Amos, signed Narragansett petitions, 159, 175.
Ephraim, second lieutenant Eastern River Company, 314.
James, signed Freetown petitions, 17, 217; signed Narragansett petition, 159.
John, signed Freetown petition, 217.
Chaudiere (Shodier) River, settlements guarded by the English on, 368.
Chauncey, Charles, of the Provincial Congress, 274, 299, 301, 319; declined reelection, 352; letters of, 352, 426.
Cheese, 381.
Chester, proprietors claimed land in Suncook, 206.
Simeon, signed Cumberland petion, 396.
Child, Thomas, signed St. Paul's parish petition, 192; his losses at the destruction of Falmouth, 309.
Churchmen, exempt from ecclesiastical tax, 185.
Clams, sometimes the only food for people at Boothbay, 167.
Clark, Abraham, justified the conduct of Stephen Jones, 292.
Alexander, signed Belfast petition, 232.
Clay, Daniel, signed Narragansett petition, 181.
Richard, ditto, 181.
Clayford, Jaco., signed Fort Pownall petition, 57.
Clements, James, ditto, 58.
Timothy, ditto, 58.
Clemons, Ezekiel, signed Sebascodegin petition, 77.
Clewly, Isaac, signed Fort Pownall petition, 58.
Clifford, Isaac, signed Freetown petition, 217.
William, ditto, 16, 217.
William 2nd, ditto, 217.
Clinton, Maj. Gen. Sir Henry, 328, 329, 330.
Club Law in Machias, 113; also called Mob Law, which see.
Coal, Ebenezer, signed Pleasant River petition, 93.
see also Cole.
Cobb, Chipman, his loss at Falmouth, 307.
James, ditto, 309.
Samuel M. Jr., signed Boothbay petition, 171.

Cobb, *continued*.
Thomas, his loss at Falmouth, 306.
see also McCobb and MttCobb.
Cobbiseconta, timber at, inspected, 152.
Great Pond, 118, 127.
Cobham, Abigail, her losses at the destruction of Falmouth, 309.
Cochran, John, signed petition of Belfast, 198.
Codman, Richard, submitted list of Falmouth losses, 310, 894.
Cofferin, William, assessor at Windham, 210; to oath to the valuation illegally, 211.
Coffin, Col.——, member of the General Court, 369.
Nath'l, his losses at the destruction of Falmouth, 309.
Samuel, signed Pleasant River petition, 94.
Coin, *see* under Currency.
Colburn, Jere, 368.
Colby, Abel, signed Freetown petition, 17.
Lot, ditto, 16.
Noar, ditto, 217.
Colby, Rogles, ditto, 217.
Cole, Jabesh, one of Waldoborough Committee of Correspondence, 267.
James, justified the conduct of Stephen Jones, 292; in needy circumstances, 314.
Joseph, wounded at Machias, 303.
see also Coal.
Collson, Hatr., signed Fort Pownall petition, 58.
Ichabod, ditto, 58.
Josiah, ditto, 58.
Colwell, Sebaen, ditto, 57.
Combs, Anthony, signed Sebascodegin petition, 77.
Anthony Jr., ditto, 76.
Joseph, ditto, 76.
Committees of Correspondence and Safety, 235, 239, 241, 246, 247, 250, 251, 253, 259, 260, 265, 267, 278, 270, 283, 285, 287, 288, 293, 294, 314, 316, 318, 320, 326, 328, 331, 334, 340, 349, 353, 357, 358, 384, 389, 394, 396, 397, 399, 407, 409, 410, 412, 416, 418, 421, 442, 443.
Conaticut, people of Frenchman's Bay to purchase provisions at, 290.

Concord, Mass., 250, 261, 274.
  Goal, 276, 277.
Condeskeeg Stream, 153.
Condon, Lucy, her losses at the destruction of Falmouth, 307.
  Samuel, signed Muscongus petition, 18.
Confirmations to, Fuller, Capt. Joshua, 161; Otis, James, 164; Phips, David, 162.
Congregational Churches, 185.
Congress, Continental, 239, 240, 244, 258, 259, 265, 267, 272, 275, 296, 297, 298, 331, 339, 349, 354, 358, 360, 375, 389, 391, 417, 423, 431.
  General, 237.
  Provincial, 236, 237, 238, 244, 245, 246, 247, 248, 250, 254, 256, 259, 260, 261, 265, 266, 267, 268, 269, 270, 272, 273, 275, 276, 277, 278, 279, 280, 283, 284, 285, 286, 287, 288, 291, 293, 302, 310, 316, 330, 347, 349, 361, 374, 398, 418, 419, 421, 437; representatives from the District of Maine, 274, 354.
Connecticut, 86, 240, 273, 275, 282, 381.
  River, 227, 229, 444.
Conway, 42, 43.
Cook, Elijah, signed the Muscongus petition, 18.
  Gov. Nicholas, 405.
Coolbroth, James, bill of, 302.
Cooper, Thomas, signed the Fort Pownall petition, 57.
  William, member of the Provincial Congress, 318, 327.
Corbet, Benjamin, signed the Machias petition, 41.
Cord wood, *see* Fire wood.
Corliss, William, signed the Machias memorial, 115.
Corn, Indian, 345, 347, 381.
Cornwallis, Maine, 303.
  Gen. Charles, Earl, 329, 330.
Corsair, Mary, her loss at the destruction of Falmouth, 307.
Cortew, Samuel Jr., signed the Boothbay petition, 171.
Cotton, John, deputy-secretary, 6, 7, 9, 23, 32, 74, 82, 84, 97, 98, 102, 110, 111, 112, 117, 135, 137, 149, 160, 161, 166, 174, 177, 182, 186, 193, 202, 212, 215, 218, 220, 226, 227, 228, 230, 233, 235; letter of, 11.
Coulson, Capt. John, master of the Unity, 385.

Coulson, *continued*.
  Capt. Samuel, his goods seized by Thompson, 253.
Courts, the place for holding not easily attended, 14, 15, 16, 17; people of Boothbay desired the removal of, 15; people of Freetown desired the removal of 16; people of Muscongus and Medumcook desired the removal of, 17, 18.
Cousens, Nathaniel, of Falmouth, signed certificate for Ilsley, 386.
  Samuel, signed the Fort Pownall petition, 57.
Coverly, Mary, her losses at the destruction of Falmouth, 307.
Cox, John, of Falmouth, his sloop impressed, 64; attacked, 64; desired remuneration, 64, 65; to be paid, 65; captured by the enemy, 269; his loss at the destruction of Falmouth, 305; petition of, 63.
  Lemuel, his losses at the destruction of Falmouth, 309.
Crags, Moses, signed the Fort Pownall petition, 57.
Craigg, James, signed the Pondstown petition, 119.
Crane, Thomas, member of the General Court, 379.
Crarge, Samuel, signed Fort Pownall petition, 57.
Crary, Oliver, signed Penobscot letter, 269.
Craven, Joseph, signed Boothbay petition, 171.
Crawford, Rev. William, chaplain and surgeon at Fort Pownall, 58.
Crocker, Capt. ——, of Falmouth, 371.
  John, signed petition for Machias, 41.
  William, signed certificate for Ilsley, 386.
Crockett, Josiah, signed receipt for Deer Island, 285.
Crosby, Abigail, her loss at the destruction of Falmouth, 306.
  Jonah, one of the Committee of Correspondence of Winslow, 265, 409.
Cross, Mr. ——, member of the Provincial Congress, 318.
  Caleb, signed Freetown petition, 217.
  Joshua, ditto, 17, 217.

Cross, *continued*.
  Noah, ditto, 217.
  River, 216.
  William, signed Freetown petition, 217.
Crown Point, 356, 404.
Cumberland County, 10, 11, 22, 64, 71, 74, 84, 146, 148, 177, 208, 210, 212, 253, 257, 309, 315, 321, 333, 339, 355, 358, 379, 386, 394, 395, 396, 399, 406, 407, 412, 419, 420, 435, 436; petitions of, 339, 396.
Cumming, Thomas, his losses at the destruction of Falmouth, 309.
Cunhill, Joseph, signed Boothbay petition, 171.
Cunningham, Archibald, of Boston, 315.
  James, signed Suncook petition, 205.
  John, signed Freetown petition, 17, 217.
  Mary, her loss at the destruction of Falmouth, 307.
  William, signed Freetown petition, 17, 217; signed Narragansett petition, 160.
Currency, continental bills, 58, 373, 374, 436; coin, 58, 365, 373, 374; cut money, 434; hard money, 434; sterling money, 403.
Curtis, Charles, signed Fort Pownall petition, 57.
  James, signed Brunswick letter, 245; member of the Committee of Correspondence, 340.
Cushing, Caleb, member of the General Court, 20, 301.
  Charles, one of the Committee of Correspondence, 350; member of the General Court, 390, 394; sent report concerning Rev. Jacob Bailey, 397, 398; report concerning masts, 398; member of the Council, 426; his health, 426; letters of, 397, 426.
  Joseph, member of the General Court, 357.
  Loring, signed Falmouth petition, 79.
  Roland, declined an appointment, 400.
  Thomas, member of the General Court, 6, 7, 23, 29, 32, 33, 65, 66, 68, 74, 82, 84, 97, 98, 99, 100, 101, 102, 110, 111, 112, 117,

Cushing, *continued*.
  121, 124, 126, 129, 130, 132, 134, 135, 136, 137, 156, 162, 163, 164, 165, 174, 177, 179, 182, 184, 186, 193, 200, 202, 212, 215, 218, 220, 222, 226, 227, 228, 230, 233, 235, 360; signed Falmouth petition, 79.
  William, to issue warrants for town meetings, 123, 125, 128.
Customs, officers of the, made seizures, 8, 10; obstructed, 9; *see also* under Trade.
Cutt, Edward, member of the Provincial Congress, 274, 374; to examine Parry, 299.
Cutter, William, to raise a regiment, 333; where he enlisted his men, 333; letter of, 333.

D

DALTON, JEREMIAH, signed Freetown petition, 17.
Damariscotta, not a township, 236; considered the distressed condition of the country, 237; revolutions of, 237, 238.
Danforth, Samuel, member of the Council, 1, 88.
Dane, John, signed Andover petition, 20.
  William, ditto, 20.
Danielson, Timothy, member of the General Court, 351, 357, 414.
Danks, Capt. Isaac, master of the Falmouth packet, 315, 320.
  to carry a cargo to Boston and there receive orders, 315; his vessel captured and brought to Gouldsborough, 320.
Darling, Eliakim, signed Andover petition, 20.
Dartmouth, Earl of, letter of 304; mentioned, 186, 206.
Davenport, Joseph, signed Pondstown petition, 119.
Davidson, John, signed Belfast petitions, 198, 232.
Davis, Capt. ——, 442.
  Col. ——, member of the General Court, 340.
  Charles, signed Boothbay petition, 171.
  Ebenezer, signed Muscongus petition, 18.
  Grafen, ditto, 18.
  Israel, signed Boothbay petition, 171.

Davis, *continued.*
Israel Jr., ditto, 171.
Jacob, signed Muscongus petition, 18.
Jno. Dresser, signed Boothbay petition, 171.
Josiah, signed Ilsley petition, 386.
Moses, signed Freetown petition, 217.
Nathaniel, signed Machias petition, 41.
Samuel, signed Muscongus petition, 18.
Capt. Solomon, of Barnstable, 344.
William, signed Muscongus petition, 18.
Zachariah, ditto, 18.
Daws, Jonathan, signed Boothbay petition, 171.
Dawse, John, ditto, 171.
Day, Abner, signed Freetown petition, 16.
Day & Scott, consignees, 263, 265, 315.
De ——, Stephen, signed Sebascodegin petition, 76.
DeBerdt, Dennis, to get a settlement of a boundary, 24; letter of, 58.
Decker, David, signed Boothbay petition, 171.
Declaration of Independence, 389, 390, 393, 397.
Deering, Nathaniel, his loss at the destruction of Falmouth, 307.
Deer Island, people of, in distress, 279; wants supplied, 285; people of, seize a vessel, 332.
Delano, Seth, signed Pondstown petition, 119.
Denaquara, Joseph, a Micmac of Winsor, spoke three languages, 365; joined the army, 365.
Depositions of Ayer, Simeon, 60, 61; Baker, Lovejoy and King, 208; Holt, Benjamin, 205; Holt, Stephen, 195; Richardson, Josiah, 70; Smith, Samuel, 273; Wardwell, Jeremiah, 335; Whittier, Ebenezer, 274.
Derby, Richard, to purchase powder, 337; a member of the General Court, 385.
Deserters from the British vessels, 314, 319, 320.
Dexter, Samuel, 88.

Devens, Richard, commissary-general, 337.
Dey, James, signed Boothbay petition, 171.
Moses, ditto, 171.
Dilbeney, James, signed Machias memorial, 115.
Dillany, James, justified the conduct of Stephen Jones, 292.
Dillaway, James, his bill for attending the wounded, 303.
Dimuck, Joseph, letter of, 402.
Dinsmore, David, of New Gloucester, sent on a tour of discovery, 246.
Disko, Samuel, signed Pleasant River petition, 93.
Dix, Jonas, member of the General Court, 20, 103, 414.
Doane, Col.——, of Wellfleet, 344.
Doddings, Capt.——, master of Senegal, 288.
Dodge, Zachariah, signed Freetown petition, 217.
Dole, John, his loss at the destruction of Falmouth, 307.
Domett, Jos., signed petition of St. Paul's Parish, 192.
Donnel, Benjamin, signed Narragansett petition, 181.
Joseph, ditto, 181.
Thomas, 290.
Doring, Edward, 194.
Dorria, Capt.——, 14.
Dow, Ebenezer, signed Falmouth petition, 17.
Nathan, signed receipt for Deer Island, 285.
Downe, Samuel, desired more time, 20, 21.
Doyne, Francis, signed Suncook petition, 205; compensated for his loss, 206.
Drisko, John, signed Pleasant River petition, 93.
Joseph Jr., ditto, 93.
Dryburg, Robert, his loss at the destruction of Falmouth, 306.
Dubuisont, Joseph, signed Machias petition, 41.
Duck Puddle Brook, 200.
Puddle Pond, 200.
Due, Margaret, her losses at the destruction of Falmouth, 306.
Duke's County, 358.
Dummer, Gov. William, 37.
Dun, Arthur, signed Pondstown petition, 119.
Dunbar, Col. David, led settlers to Townsend, 166; failed to give

Dunbar, *continued*.
the promised deeds, 166; his authority superceded, 167.
Dunham, Capt. ——, of the Vineyard, 345.
Dunn, Samuel, signed the Falmouth petition, 79.
Dunning, Andrew, 340.
Lieutenant, Robert, 333.
Durham, John, signed Belfast petition, 198.
John Jr., ditto, 198.
Tolford, ditto, 232.
Durrell, Benjamin, one of the Arundel Committee of Correspondence, 267; represented Arundel in Congress, 374.
Dutch, 207.
Duties prevent harmony, 157.
Dwight, Nathaniel, surveyor, his plan of Bullock's land accepted, 136.
Dyer, Capt. ——, 439, 440, 441, 443.
James, signed Machias petition, 41; his bill for guarding prisoners, 302.
Samuel, signed Falmouth petition, 79.

E

EAST RIVER, 345.
Eastern, Bay, 80.
Country, a moth, 379, 380, 382; not worth protecting, 379, 381; equal to the other provinces, 381, 382; Rev. James Lyon's prophecy concerning, 382.
River, 138, 153.
River Company, officers of, 313, 314.
Eastman, Richard, signed Suncook petition, 205.
Eaton, Jacob, his land a boundary, 201.
John, signed Narragansett petition, 181.
Rev. Samuel, settled at Sebascodegin Island, 75; infirm, 76.
Eayr, Joshua, signed Fort Pownall petition, 57.
Eddy, Capt. Jonathan, sent prisoners to Machias, 394, 395; raised recruits, 395, 396, 399; captured a vessel, 395, 396; not successful in taking a garrison, 395, 396, 427; his expedition not altogether approved, 399; Indians served under, 406; has money for In-

Eddy, *continued*.
dians, 406; letters of, 394, 395, 396.
Eddy's affair, 427.
Egamogging Reach, 140.
Eggleston, Hezekiah, his home at Bristol, 107; descended from Richard Fullford, 107; his land title lost, 108; desired confirmation of land title, 108; testimonies to be taken to settle title, 110, 111; petition of, 107.
Elbridge, Giles, grant to, 189.
Elden, Nathan, signed Narragansett petition,, 181.
Elder, William, assessor of Windham, 210, 211, 212; took an oath on valuation of the town, 211; Grasham brought an action against, 211; desired the General Court to release him, 211; forfeiture remitted, 212; petition of, 210.
Eliott, ⎫ James, signed Machias
Elliot, ⎭ petition, 41; to levy taxes at Machias, 185, 186; justified the conduct of Stephen Jones, 292.
John, deserted the British fleet, 320.
Ellis, Mr. ——, member of the General Court, 403.
Elvins, Richard, signed Narragansett petition, 160.
Elwell, Benjamin, ditto, 160.
Jonathan, his losses at the destruction of Falmouth, 309.
William, signed Muscongus petition, 18.
William Jr., ditto, 18.
Emerson, Edward, signed Boothbay petition, 171.
Emery, ⎫ Jonathan, signed Ponds-
Emry, ⎭ town petition, 118.
Joseph, his loss at the destruction of Falmouth, 307.
Nathaniel, signed Pondstown petition, 119.
England, 55, 104, 130, 139, 147, 148, 187, 195, 207, 255, 263, 272, 288, 341, 387, 392.
Church of, members of exempt from tax to support the Congregational churches, 185; petition St. Paul's Church, 191; Bailey adhered to the liturgy, 389; all the clergy of, except one, refused to read publicly

England, *continued.*
    the Declaration of Independence, 390.
English, the, trade with Indians restricted, 30; purchased land settled on, 37; always held the country west of Penobscot, 207; the Indians will join with those in New England, 240; the French will gain by non-importation acts, 240; the home government sent vessel against, 255; the colonists in favor of opposition, 255; ships gone up Canada River, 368; guard at Soceconick, 368; not to settle above tide-water, 368; regiment to be raised to include Indians, 363; blockaded the provincials, 375; gave great presents to the Indians. 413; to erect forts on St. Johns River, 415; must be forced back, 415; had a spy among the Indians, 432.
Erving, John, councilor, 1, 147.
Essex County, 61, 196.
Gazette, *see* under Salem.
Exeter, N. H., 442.

F

FABYAN, JOSHUA, to raise a company, 333; represented Scarborough in Congress, 355.
Fairbanks, Benjamin, signed Pondstown petition, 119.
Falmouth, a larger part interested in preventing the seizure of Ilsley's goods, 8, 9, 10; home of John Cox, 64; part of the First Parish desired to be set back to the Second Parish, 78, 79, 99; rioters released men from the goal, 84; reward offered, 84; proceedings stayed in setting back the Second Parish, 99; Arthur Savage, comptroller of customs at, 143, 148; mob law in, 143, 144, 145, 147, 148; Savage's family left, 146, 147; Savage gave the names of the rioters, 147; why the oath was not administered, 147; proceedings of the Council in regard to the riot, 147; two of the rioters apprehended, 155; other names reported, 156; taken members of the Church of England,

Falmouth, *continued.*
191, 192; to omit taxing the same, 193; home of Samuel Freeman, 209; in need of ammunition, 242, 335; Capt. Mowat at, 243, 250, 252, 253, 317; sent Matthews and Dinsmore on a tour of discovery, 246; an Indian ambassador at, 270; representatives of in Congress, 274, 355; home of Enoch Freeman, 274; Lane arrived at with Indian chiefs, 288; Neat and the Senegal at, 288; Neat left without a pass, 289; people of uneasy, 289; losses sustained by the people by the destruction of, 305, 306, 307, 308, 309, 310; list of losses altered and submitted to Congress, 310, 394; the destruction of alarmed the adjacent country, 317; Mowat to winter at, 317; British fleet reported at, 319; report of the burning of, 319, 320; fires were set by hand, 320; Gen. Frye to take command of troops at, 321; Ilsley in command of sea coast at, 338, 386; Frye's plan of defense of, 338; number of soldiers at, 338; soldiers ill at, 339; Mowat followed the orders of Gage at, 342; Howe's account of the destruction of, 342, 343; will soon be in a tolerable state of defense, 367; Mitchell's letter dated at, 367; Ilsley's letter dated at, 369; new orders for the military at, 370; limits of the post, 377; abatement of taxes in, 379; Col. Mitchell in command at, 386; high price of sugar at, 387; order relating to a prize ship at, 388; forts underway at, 401; Dumick's letter dated at, 402; defense weakened, 411; letter of the selectmen, 242; mentioned 6, 14, 29, 208, 212, 245, 250, 253, 283, 318, 370, 373, 386.
Falmouth, Committee of Correspondence, 250, 345, 350, 351.
Goal, 84.
Harbor, 317.
Meeting House, 372.
Neck, 251, 317, 318.
St. Paul's Church, 191, 309.

INDEX 459

Farley, M., member of the General Court, 301.
Farnam, Joseph, signed Boothbay petition, 171.
Farnsworth, James, his bill for going to Annapolis, 303.
William, signed Boothbay petitition, 15; one of the Waldoborough Committee of Correspondence, 267.
Fast Days, 398.
Fellows, Cornelius, signed Narragansett petition, 160.
Gustavus, ditto, 160.
Nathaniel, ditto, 160.
Samuel, ditto, 160.
Fernald, Pelatiah, his losses at the destruction of Falmouth, 307.
Fickett, Thomas, signed Falmouth petition, 79.
Fields, Samuel, signed Andover petition, 20.
Fire wood and cord wood carried to Boston, 169; to Portsmouth, 187; to Piscataqua, 331, 335.
Fisher, Jabez, member of the General Court, 301, 369.
Fisheries, the, 58, 86, 265, 271, 375, 381, 384.
Fisk, Mr. ——, member of the General Court, 134.
Daniel, selectman of Sturbridge, 337.
Fitch, Timothy, of Nantucket, 344, 345, 346, 350.
Fitts, Simeon, signed Narragansett petition, 160.
Flax, 272.
Fletcher, Capt. ——, interpreter, 153, 364.
Thomas, to return money given him to enlist men, 378; letter of, 367.
Flies cause illness, 152.
Flint, Capt. John, the land granted to, was in New Hampshire, 220, 221.
Thomas, signed resolutions of Damariscotta, 238.
Flood, James, his losses at the destruction of Falmouth, 308.
Floyd, Joseph, signed Boothbay petition, 171.
Flucker, Thomas, as councilor, 1, 10, 88; as secretary, 121, 123, 126, 129, 130, 132, 134, 143, 147, 162, 163, 164, 179, 184, 186, 193, 200.
Fogg, Sarah, signed Machias petition, 41.

Forage, 263.
Formalities not with loggers and millmen, 379, 381.
Forts and garrisons, those reduced should be replaced, 1, 2, 39; message concerning the reduction of, 2, 3; the pay of the officers insufficient at, 38; not enough men at, 38; suitable provisions should be made for, 39; message of the board concerning, 41, 42; Goldthwait to augment the garrison at Fort Pownall, 52, 53, 55; at times in the hands of the Indians, 53, 62; small garrisons encourage the insults of Indians, 53, 61, 62; petitions should be sent for larger garrisons, 54; ammunition sent to, 54; to be repaired, 54; settlements encouraged by respectable, 62; the Castle to be garrisoned by the regular forces, 105; the retiring men should be paid, 105; Fort Pownall to be continued, 105; Fort Pownall dismantled, 245, 268; at St. Johns captured and destroyed, 310, 311; the enemy may build on Falmouth Neck, 317; petition to fortify the same, 317, 318; batteries erected near North Yarmouth, 319; Frye's new plan for those at Falmouth, 338; built by Congress, 342; built at Point Levi, 368; improved at Falmouth, 372, 373; Ilsley's zeal in planning and forwarding, 385; Eddy's unsuccessful attempt to capture, 395, 396, 427; underway at Falmouth, 401; to be erected on St. Johns River, 415; to be erected by Allen, 428.
Fort, at Boothbay, 167.
at Cumberland, 375, 395.
at Point Levi, 368.
at Port Royal, 34.
at St. Johns, 310.
Castle William, 1, 2, 3, 39, 41, 42, 53, 105.
Frederick, 427, 429.
Halifax, 126, 242, 407, 408, 409, 410.
Pownall, 1, 2, 3, 38, 89, 41, 42, 54, 56, 61, 65, 105, 138, 139, 140, 155, 158, 186, 255, 268, 270, 271.
Ticonderoga, 241, 433, 442.

Fossey, Capt. Thomas, 345, 346, 347.
Foster, Benjamin. signed Machias petitions, 41, 115, 174; to levy taxes at Machias, 185, 186; led the people in the capture of Jones' tender, 282; a magistrate at Machias, 314; one of the Committee of Safety, 359; could have helped the county had he had permission, 383; his letter referred to a committee, 424; letter of, 172, 173.
Ephraim, signed Suncook petition, 205.
Jacob, signed Machias petition, 41.
Capt. Jeremiah, thanked by Congress, 287; to have charge of captured vessels, 287.
Isaiah, signed Machias memorial, 115.
John Wooden, ditto, 115.
Moses, signed Suncook petition, 205.
Robert, signed Cumberland petition, 396.
Wooden, signed Machias memorial, 115.
Fowler, Philip, signed Narragansett petition, 160; his loss at the destruction of Falmouth, 306.
Fox, Mr. ——, 284.
John, his losses at the destruction of Falmouth, 310.
France, 55, 56, 168.
Francis, a Micmac of St. Johns, joined the army, 365.
Col. Ebenezer, letter of, 403; mentioned, 400, 401.
Frankfort, an inconvenient place for the courts to meet, 14, 15, 16, 17, 18; a boundary of Belfast, 197, 199.
Franklin, Benjamin, travelled for his health, 156; on business for the province, 156, 157; too troublesome to keep small accounts, 157; letter of, 156.
Freeman, Mr. ——, of Eastham, member of the General Court, 210.
Elizabeth, her losses at the destruction of Falmouth, 309.
Enoch, justice of the peace, 10, 11; refused to administer an oath, 146, 148; his reason for the same, 147, 148; signed the Falmouth letter, 242; member

Freeman, *continued.*
of the Provincial Congress, 274, 301; appointed one of the Committee of Safety, but declined, 278; desired to be appointed to care for a regiment, 279; his losses at the destruction of Falmouth, 305; letters of, 14, 245, 277, 383.
Enoch Jr., his loss at the destruction of Falmouth, 306.
Nathaniel, member of the General Court, 299.
Samuel, merchant, resided at Falmouth, 209; desired the General Court to provide a remedy whereby he could obtain his dues, 209; as secretary of the Provincial Congress, 246; an assurity for Mowat, 252; as speaker, 301; his loss at the destruction of Falmouth, 306; as agent for Horton, 306; represented Falmouth in Congress, 355, 398, 403; memorial of, 209, 210.
Freetown, desired the removal of the courts, 16; desired the division of Pownalborough, 16; number of families at, 216, 226; under difficulties because not incorporated, 216; meeting house at, 216; bounds of, 216, 226; asked to be incorporated, 216; area, 216; incorporated, 226; town meeting to be called in, 227; petition of, 216; act of incorporation of, 226.
French, the, can obtain no foothold in Canada, 55, 56; ignorant and governed by priests, 239; to be neutral, 240; the officers are, but privates are not, willing to fight, 240; would monopolize the Indian trade, 240; are court sycophants and why, 241; Dinsmore and Matthews sent to the Canadians, 246; the English will be satisfied if the Canadians have no designs, 246; may attack the back settlements, 254; officers in command of English regulars and Indians, 412, 413; they must be forced back, 415; a priest for Indians, 416; Mitchell insinuating among, 429.
French, Zethem, signed Fort Pownall petition, 58.

Frenchman's Bay, part of Gouldsborough, 139; land at is good, but has no pines fit for masts, 139; in need of provisions, 290; to purchase at Conaticut, 290.

Frevoy, John, of Yarmouth, 323.

Friswell, Capt. Benjamin, master of British gun ship, captured the Three Brothers, 316.

Frost, James, his losses at the destruction of Falmouth, 306.
Samuel, signed Pondstown petition, 119.

Frye, Capt. ——, men taken from his regiment, 411.
Maj. ——, member of the General Court, 66.
Col. and Gen. Joseph, settled Fryeburg, 5, 6, 24, 63, 106; to open a store, 106; desired a liquor license, 107; license granted to, 110; his land a boundary, 222; to take command at Falmouth, 321, 338; his new plan, 338; petition of, 106; mentioned, 47, 50.

Freystown, } settled by Joseph
Fryeburg, } Frye, 106; number of families at, 106; situation of, 106; Frye to move to, 106; not incorporated, 107; liquor license in, 107, 110; mentioned, 19, 24, 206.

Fryse, J., justice of the peace, 206.

Fuller, Capt. ——, member of the General Court, 79.
Capt. Joshua, townships granted to, 100, 161; the same claimed by New Hampshire, 100; expense of settling, 100, 101; another grant to, 101; confirmation of grant, 161.

Fuller's Town, otherwise Sudbury, Canada, 214, 215.

Fullerton, Ebenezer, signed Boothbay petition, 171.
James, ditto, 171.
John, ditto, 171.
William, ditto, 171.

Fullford, Francis, heir of Richard, settled in Bristol, 108.
Richard, ditto, 107; ancestor of H. Eggleston, 107, 108.

Fulton, Robert, selectman, signed Bowdoinham letter, 291.

Furs, 406, 434.

G

GAGE, GEN. THOMAS, 231, 233, 235, 266, 276, 342.

Galt, Andrew, signed Suncook petition, 205.
Patrick, ditto, 205.

Gardiner, } Daniel, signed Free-
Gardner, } town petition, 217.
Ebenezer, signed Cumberland petition, 396.
Henry, Receiver-General, 260, 267, 353, 374, 376, 378; chosen a representative, 260; resided, at Stow, 261; to receive taxes from Partridgefield, 261.
Capt. John, owned the tract granted to John Whitman, 227, 228; the same fell within boundary of New Hampshire, 228, 229; received no consideration, 228; new grant to, 228, 229; position and area of the same, 228; his home at Cambridge, 228; petition of, 227, 229.
Dr. Sylvester, signed Kennebec petition, 151; visited by the inspector of woods, 152; his son joined the inspector's party, 152; leased land to Ballard, 242, 407, 408, 409; fled from Boston, 408, 409; letter of, 242.

Gardnerstown, home of Jonathan Hicks, 276.

Garland, John, signed Narragansett petition, 181.

Garrisons, see under Forts.

Gaspee, 365.

George II, 398.

George III, 32, 67, 91, 114, 119, 122, 123, 126, 135, 166, 181, 185, 200, 226, 389, 397.

Georges Shoales, 316.

Georgetown, fined for not returning a representative, 129; begged that the fine be remitted, 129; the reason why there was no representative returned, 129, 130; fine remitted, 130; assistance sent to, 130; homes of Sewall and Parker, 236; Edward Perry agreed not to ship masts from, 247; Perry erroneously held in custody at, 247; Perry's letters dated at, 247, 249; Perry to be detained there, 269, 270; Parry brought from, 299; Hobby and

Georgetown, *continued.*
　Hubbs resided at, 300; raised a subscription for the Canada expedition, 365, 377; the people patriotic but poor, 377; no post to, 377; petition of, 129.
Georgetown Committee of Correspondence, 251, 260.
　Mast Dock, 237, 247.
Georgia, 255.
Gerrish, Col. Joseph, member of the General Court, 5, 215, 219.
　Maj. Samuel, agent of Bakerstown, 60; desired pay, 60.
　Capt. William, member of the General Court, 274.
Germaine, Lord George, letters of, 328, 331; letter to, 342.
Getchel, Benjamin, signed Machias memorial, 115.
　Joseph, ditto, 41, 115.
　Joseph Jr., justified the conduct of Stephen Jones, 292.
Giles, Joseph, signed Boothbay petition, 171.
Gilichet, Joseph, justified the conduct of Stephen Jones, 292.
Gill, Moses, member of the General Court, 301.
　Patrick, Thomas, of Biddeford, 289.
Gillman, Lieut. Andrew, to remain at Penobscot, 341; a deputy to the Indians, 364; on a scout, 411, 413; met Indians, 411, 413; received intelligence of the approach of the enemy, 412, 413; will keep scouts on the lookout, 414.
　John, signed Belfast petition, 198.
Gilmore, David, ditto, 198.
　James, ditto, 198, 232.
Glechlan, William, ditto, 198.
Glimor, David, ditto, 232.
Gloucester, 285, 321, 379.
Glover, Daniel, signed Freetown petition, 217.
Goals, only one in Lincoln County, 138; there could be one at Fort Pownall, 138.
Godhill, Donald, signed Fort Pownall petition, 58.
Gold, 149.
Goldthwait, Capt. Thomas, commander at Fort Pownall, to augment the garrison, 52, 53, 54, 55; to call the Indians together, 55; signed Fort Pownall petition, 58; his services

Goldthwait, *continued.*
　solicited, 84; gone to Boston, 153; letter received from, 186; to call a town meeting at Belfast, 199; the Indians exasperated with, 245; Indians will take him captive, 245; as a witness, 264; wrote a letter for Sherriff, 264; surrendered Fort Pownall, 268; signed the letter for Penobscot, 269; member of the Assembly, 271; a friend of the constitution, 272; to deliver arms to the committee, 285.
Gooch, Benjamin, justified the conduct of Stephen Jones, 292.
　Benjamin Jr., ditto, 292.
　James, ditto, 292.
　John, ditto, 292.
Gooding, James, his losses at the destruction of Falmouth, 308.
　James Jr., ditto, 308.
Goodman, Capt. Noah, to examine Parry, 299.
Goodwin, Capt. Ichabod, represented Berwick in Congress, 374.
　John, signed certificate for Ilsley, 386.
Gookin, Simon, his losses at the destruction of Falmouth, 306.
Goose River, 201.
Gordon. Tristram, signed Narragansett petition, 160.
Gore, the, dispute concerning, 180.
Gorges, Sir Ferdinando, 155, 188.
Gorget for Indian, 360.
Gorham, two-thirds of the land is owned by non-resident proprietors, 77; the expense of supporting the minister is unequally divided, 77, 78; land of non-residents should share the burden, 78; a boundary of Narragansett No. One, 135, 159, 176, 180, 182; claimed land in the same, 180; home of Solomon Lombard, 274; representatives in Congress, 274, 355; petition of, 77.
　Maj. ——, of the British army, 329.
　Nathaniel, grant to, 165.
Gould, Col. ——, sent for a French priest for the Indians, 416; heard of the different speculations about the St. Johns River, 416; reported the proposed erection of forts, 427,

Gould, *continued.*
428; the Indians fond of, 430; made the minds of the Indians unsteady, 433; carried off Dr. Nevers' interests, 435.
Mr. ——, offered a premium for J. Allen, 414.
Robert, desired further time, 21, 22; time granted, 23.
Gouldsborough, distance from Pleasant River, 93; the nearest magistrate is at Machias, 113; land poor in some sections, in others better, 139; pines inferior, 139, 140; harbor good, 139; no man from would ship with Capt. Smith, 139, 140; timber inspector at, 153; the Falmouth packet brought to, 320; home of Nathan Jones, 332, 333; Shaw at, 374, 443; the Viper captured vessels near, 374; Shaw will return to, 377; Shaw's letter dated at, 443.
Harbor, 139.
Gove, Asa, signed Freetown petition, 217.
Ebenezer, ditto, 217.
Nathan, ditto, 217.
Solomon, ditto, 217.
Gowing, James, member of the General Court, 24.
Grafon, Jacob, signed Muscongus petition, 18.
Grafton, John, ditto, 18.
Gragg, Joseph, signed Belfast petition, 198.
Capt. Samuel, his company at St. Georges, 322.
Grand Manan, 142, 359, 375.
Grashom, Caleb, of Windham, brought action against the town, 211, 212.
Grass, 271.
Graves, Admiral Samuel, 273, 330, 366.
Gray, Harrison, 1, 10, 42, 88, 147.
John, signed Freetown petition, 17.
Great Bay, 440.
Greely, Else, his loss at the destruction of Falmouth, 308.
Greenlaw, John, part owner of the Loyal Legion, 310.
Greenleaf, B., member of the General Court, 301.
Ebenezer, signed Narragansett petition, 160.
Richard, ditto, 160.

Greenleaf, *continued.*
Samuel, ditto, 160.
Greenwich hospital money, 272.
Greenwood, John, his loss at the destruction of Falmouth, 307.
Grele, Joseph, signed Pondstown petition, 119.
Moses, ditto, 119.
Grifen, Jacob, signed Muscongus petition, 18.
James, signed Andover petition, 20.
Griffiths, Henry, justified the conduct of Stephen Jones, 292.
Grindle, Joshua, signed Fort Pownall petition, 57.
Groas, Robin, signed Pleasant River petition, 94.
Groffaim, Josiah, signed Narragansett petition, 160.
Gustin, Ebenezer, his loss at the destruction of Falmouth, 307.
G——, Solomon, signed Freetown petition, 17.

H

HACOCK, CAPT. RALPH, his bill for bringing a surgeon, 302; reported depredations of the British cruiser, 359; his vessel seized, 359.
Hale, Maj. Jonathan, 356.
Nathaniel, his loss at the destruction of Falmouth, 306.
Halfway Creek Ponds, 197, 199.
Halifax, 55, 246, 263, 265, 277, 312, 314, 317, 319, 320, 329, 338, 342, 348, 350, 355, 415, 416, 429, 430, 431.
Dock Yard, 248, 250, 269.
Hall, Benjamin, signed Suncook petition, 205.
Isaac, signed Sebascodegin petition, 76.
Isaac Jr., ditto, 76.
John, ditto, 76; signed Pleasant River petition, 94.
Joseph, signed Sebascodegin petition, 77.
Nathaniel, ditto, 77.
Stephen, 147.
Hallowell, incorporated, 128n; named for the Hallowell family, 128n.
Benjamin, signed Kennebec petition, 151.
Family, 128n.
Hammond, Archelaus, signed Machias petition, 41.

Hampton, 43.
Hanasdon, Ebenezer, signed Boothbay petition, 171.
Hancock, John, of the Provincial Congress, 66, 160, 275, 417, 419.
Hanover, House of, 171.
Hans, John, his losses at the destruction of Falmouth, 306.
Harding, Jesse, ditto, 308.
  Joseph, ditto, 308.
Hardwick, 276.
Harmon, Benjamin, signed Sanford petition, 69.
  Naptali, ditto, 69.
  Nathaniel, desired more time, 83; more time granted, 84.
Harnden, Richard, signed certificate for Ilsley, 386.
Harper, William, his losses at Falmouth, 307.
Harpswell, included Sebascodegin Island, 74, 75; to be notified that Sebascodegin desired separation from, 77; men enlisted in, 333; represented in Congress, 355; guard sent to, 401.
Harriman, Asa, signed Fort Pownall petition, 57.
Harris, Nathaniel, land granted to, 109; the same claimed by New Hampshire, 109.
  Samwill, signed Boothbay petition, 171.
Harrison, Jemima, her losses at the destruction of Falmouth, 306.
Harrod, Jonathan, signed Fort Pownall petition, 57.
Harvard College, 81, 96, 101, 132, 162, 163, 164, 165, 215, 219, 221, 222, 228.
Harwood, Thomas, signed Suncook petition, 205.
Haseltine, Samuel, signed Narragansett petition, 181.
  Timothy, ditto, 181.
Hasey, William, signed Sebascodegin petition, 77.
Haskell, Francis, signed receipt for Deer Island, 285.
Hasket, Moses, his losses at the destruction of Falmouth, 305.
Hasty, James, 51.
Hatch, Ed., signed Freetown petition, 17.
  Joseph, his losses at the destruction of Falmouth, 306.

Hatch, *continued.*
  Mark, member of the Committee of Safety, 332.
Haverhill, letter of, 356; mentioned, 60, 61, 357.
Hay, 140, 141, 262, 263, 266, 276, 315, 344, 345, 347.
Hazen, Mr. ——, a prisoner, 432.
  and Jarvis of Newberry, 86.
Heart, making for Indian, 360.
Heath, William, 111.
Hemlock, 271.
Hemp, 381.
Hemphill, David, signed Belfast petition, 198, 232.
Henaker, Mr. ——, contractor, 151.
Herdy, Abel, signed Narragansett petition, 181.
Heriss, Daniel, signed Boothbay petition, 171.
Herrick, Capt. Henry, member of the General Court, 174, 210.
Hervendon, Joseph, signed Boothbay petition, 171.
  Nehemiah, ditto, 171.
Hessians, 416.
Hetoscobuit, Sabattis, a Micmac of Gaspee, joined the army, 365.
Hewes, Elihu, letters of, 271, 277.
  Joseph, member of Congress, 272.
Heywood, Zimri, one of the Committee of Correspondence, 265, 409.
Hicks, Jonathan, in the service of the king, 266; as a prisoner, 266; on Smith's sloop, 266, 274; sent to Congress, 266, 274; his papers examined, 275; uncertain which side to take, 276; at Gardnerstown, 276; inimical to the liberties of the country, 276, 277; at Plymouth, 277; admitted himself to be a tory, 277; desired to be out of the noise, 277; his reason for being on Smith's sloop unknown to Smith, 277; sent to the Concord goal, 277.
  see also Hix.
Hides, 331.
Highannas, 344.
Hill, Daniel, signed Machias memorial, 115.
  Japeth, justified the conduct of Stephen Jones, 292.
  Jeremiah, signed Narragansett

Hill, *continued.*
    petition, 176; to call a town meeting in Narragansett, 182.
    Joseph, justified the conduct of Stephen Jones, 292.
    Obediah, signed Machias petition, 41; justified the conduct of Stephen Jones, 292; bill of, for milk, 302.
    Theodore, justified the conduct of Stephen Jones, 292.
Hillsborough, Earl of, 158.
Hilton, Amy, her losses at the destruction of Falmouth, 308.
    Capt. James, of Muscongus, 360.
Hingham, troops to be stationed at, 322.
Hinkley, Aaron, signed letter of Brunswick, 245; sold molasses at a high price, 339.
Hinson, John, subscribed for the expedition to Canada, 366.
Hiron, Samuel, signed Freetown petition, 217.
Hix, William, signed Pleasant River petition, 94.
    see also Hicks.
Hobby, John, as a witness, 237; bondsman for John Bernard, 300.
Hobert, Israel, member of the General Court, 340.
Hodge, Robert & Co., 316.
Hodgkins, Philip, 390.
Hog, Capt. ——, fired cannon at Falmouth, 251.
Hog Island Road, 319.
Hogs, 311.
Holbrook, Abiezer, signed Sebascodegin petition, 76.
    John, selectman of Sturbridge, 337.
    Jonathan, signed Sebascodegin petition, 76.
Holby, Remington, to procure hunters, 246.
Holmes, Joseph, signed Machias petition, 41.
    Samuel, his house a landmark, 40, 80, 95; signed Machias petition, 41.
Holt, Benjamin, signed Suncook petition, 205; an early settler at Suncook, 205; ejected from part of the land, 206; made oath, 206; deposition of, 205.
    David, signed Andover petition, 20.
    John Jr., ditto, 20.

Holt, *continued.*
    Joseph, ditto, 20.
    Joshua, ditto, 20.
    Nathaniel, signed Suncook petition, 205.
    Stephen, early settler at Suncook, 195, 196; impoverished by law suits, 196; made oath, 196; deposition of, 195.
Holton, John, signed Boothbay petition, 171.
    Samuel, member of the General Court, 301, 362, 403.
Holway, Ladwick, justified the conduct of Stephen Jones, 292.
Hooks and lines, needed at Deer Island, 285.
Hoole, William, his losses at the destruction of Falmouth, 306.
Hooper, Capt. ——, of Falmouth, 371.
    Benjamin, of Biddeford, member of the Committee of Correspondence, 289.
    Noah, a convoy, 288.
Hopkins, John, signed Narragansett petition, 181.
    Simeon, signed Sebascodegin petition, 77.
Hopkinson, Caleb, signed Narragansett petition, 181.
    John Jr., ditto, 181.
Horn, Mary, her losses at the destruction of Falmouth, 308.
Horton, William, ditto, 308.
House of Commons of Massachusetts, 293, 384.
Houses, size of, to be erected in new townships, 81, 96, 100, 136.
Houston, Samuel, signed Belfast petitions, 198, 232.
    Samuel Jr., ditto, 198.
Hovey, John, one of the Committee of Correspondence, 267.
    Samuel, signed Narragansett petition, 181.
Howard, James, to issue warrants for town meetings, 122, 123, 125, 126, 127, 128.
How, } Ichabod, signed Ponds-
Howe, } town petition, 118; a selectman of Winthrop, 191.
    Elijah, signed Cumberland petition, 396.
    William, signed Machias memorial, 115.
    Maj. Gen. Sir William, 304, 328, 342.

Hewell, Arthur, his losses at the destruction of Falmouth, 308.
Howes, Capt. ——, as bearer of letters, 415, 416, 417; a pilot and man of good character, 417.
Hubbard, Thomas, 1, 10, 88, 143, 147, 174.
Hubbs, Obe., bondsman of John Bernard, 300.
Huff, George Canfield, signed Freetown petition, 217.
Humphrey, Richard, signed Pondstown petition, 119.
Huntley, Jabez, justified the conduct of Stephen Jones, 292.
Hurley, Pierce, signed Fort Pownall petition, 58.
Hustin, William, his loss at the destruction of Falmouth, 306.
Huston, John, released from the goal, 84.
Hutchins, Jonathan, signed Freetown petition, 217.
Hutchinson, Gov. Thomas, letters of, 155, 158, 186, 206; message of, 132; speeches of, 103, 106, 130, 131; mentioned, 91, 92, 94, 99, 102, 106, 108, 110, 112, 114, 116, 117, 126, 130, 132, 137, 143, 147, 152, 154, 159, 162, 163, 164, 166, 175, 177, 179, 182, 184, 188, 190, 208, 210, 212, 215, 216, 217, 218, 220, 222, 226, 227, 228, 229, 230.

I

ILSLEY, MAJ. DANIEL, in command of sea-coast at Falmouth, 338, 386; submitted list of Falmouth losses to Congress, 310, 394; complained of Col. Mitchell, 369, 373; became an orderly, 369, 370; certificate in favor of, 385; prevented from doing his duty, 386; letters of, 338, 369; petition of, 386.
Enoch, his store examined, 8; his goods seized, 8, 10; mob carried away his goods, 9, 11; a considerable part of the town interested in his defense, 9; his losses at the destruction of Falmouth, 308.
Isaac Jr., his losses at the destruction of Falmouth, 306.
Indians, the, acts concerning the supplies of, 7, 30, 31, 37, 38; act concerning the trade with,

Indians, *continued.*
7; retarded the settlements, 26, 107; the government to punish murderers of, 30, 34; tenderness of the government toward, 30, 35, 36, 38; those of the east not objects of domestic regulations, 30, 37; hunting and trading the cause of trouble, 30; private trade prohibited with, 30, 31, 34, 35; none murdered by the government, 34; without license, no land to be bought of, 35, 36; provisions made for the religious instruction of, 35, 37, 416; drink not to be sold to, 35, 36, 423; some laws still enforced, 36, 37; a truck-house erected for trade with, 37, 117; the English purchased their lands, 37; prevented surveys, 45; the insolent to be repressed, 52; the forts are at times in their hands, 53, 62; small garrisons encourage insults, 53, 61, 62; the leaders to be punished, 54, 55; not to be deceived by stories of war, 55; if they desire to fight, they will fight alone, 56; to pay damages, 56; plundered by priests, 56; have not made satisfaction for damages, 62; at St. Georges, 64; rooted out by settlements, 85; desired to see Thomas Scammall, 153; to be employed as guides, 153; depredations at Boothbay, 167, 168; pretended deeds used at Boothbay, 168; won the battle at Pigwacket but were terrorized, 203; urged to join the king's troops against the people of Boston, 240, 241; refused to join, 240; exasperated because a fort was dismantled, 245, 255; Congress should secure the interests of, 245, 438; to be examined in regard to their joining the the English, 246; may attack the back settlements, 254; to be supplied with powder, 255; the colonists ask what they want, 255; those of Stockbridge join the colonists, 256; Lane sent to raise a company among, 256; a chief as an ambassador, 270; hearty in the cause, 270; consulting which

Indians, *continued.*
side to take, 279; some one should negotiate with, 279, 362; arrived at Falmouth, 283; with Lane, 286; at Watertown, 286; the British sent ammunition to, 323; to be stirred up to cut off the people of Machias, 323; letter to, 341; chose Lowder for truckmaster, 341; not contented with Preble, 341; no truckmaster to trade with, 355; ready to pay for supplies, 355; in the regular army, 356, 360; no order found for presents to, 359; those at the east to be engaged by the provincials, 361, 362; delegates at Boston, 362, 363; came to meet Washington, 363; a regiment to be raised with part English soldiers, 363; a delegation which represents six villages, 363; to consider. 363, 364; St. John's promised to return, 363; some tribes not represented, 363; some joined Canadians and some the provincials, 363; those who went with Arnold not paid, 363; considered themselves as one people with the colonists, 364; an armed vessel to take them home, 364; four will join the army at once, 364; names of the same, 365; Fletcher sent to, 367; Washington's address read to, 368; can not spare their young men, 368, 378; young men fear an attack of the English, 368; will keep men to watch and report, 368; will join the rangers, 368; the tide-water the boundary of English settlers, 368, 369; some young men desired to go to the court, 369; cannot go unless they enlist, 369; if enlisted they cannot be conveyed westward, 375, 377; desire to go to Cumberland, 375; offered to capture field officers, 375; cost of transportation makes goods dear, 405, 406; either cheaper goods or trade with the enemy, 406; desire credit, 406; serving as soldiers with Eddy, 406; money raised to pay, 406; either hearty or

Indians, *continued.*
neutral, 406; one deserved a commission, 406; desired a French priest, 406, 416; Shaw promised pay to those who served as soldiers, 406, 407; gave notice of the approach of the enemy, 411, 412; approaching the rivers with the regulars, 412, 413; commanded by French officers, 412, 413; received great presents from the British, 413; we must be lavish to keep them, 415; made a treaty at their own option, 415; with Allen, 416; the United States under obligation to, 418; to be conveyed to St. John's river, 420; Allen as agent, 423; trade in strong drink prohibited, 423; Shaw expects to keep them friendly, 424; people of Union River heard of the approach of, 425; under command of Allen, 427; sent with Preble, 427; Mitchell at work among, 429; met Allen, 429; held conference with Allen, 430, 431, 433, 434, 436; their friendship for America, 430, 436; enraged with their treatment in Boston, 430; somewhat satisfied, 430; Allen sent for more to meet him, 432; an English spy among, 432; Allen keeps up their spirits, 432; cannot be trusted, 433; in want, 433; price of furs settled with, 434; must have timely supplies, 434; kept quietly at home, 435.

Indians, Canadian, 270, 413.
Eastern, 7, 30, 37, 254, 362, 368.
St. Johns, 318, 355, 359, 362, 363, 364, 432.
Infantry to be sent by Russia to assist England, 304.
see also under Soldiers.
Ingersoll, } John, his losses at the
Ingorsel, } destruction of Falmouth, 309.
Jared, of New Haven, 86.
Ingraham, John, signed Boothbay petition, 171.
Joseph, his loss at the destruction of Falmouth, 306.
Innoculating in camp, officers arrested for, 404.
Intelligence should be used with ammunition, 360.

Ireland, 156, 194, 329.
Isle of Shoales, 44.

J

JACKSON, RICHARD, provincial agent, 271, 272; reported that the home government desired to make the Assembly useless, 271, 272; faithful, yet turned out of his position, 272.
Jacobites, 416.
Jamaica, 207, 350.
  Farm, 52.
Jameson, Alexander, signed Muscongus petition, 18.
  Paul, ditto, 18.
Jeffery, George, 47.
Jeffries, Mr. ——, 241.
Jenks, Benjamin, his loss at the destruction of Falmouth, 306.
Jeremiah, signed Machias petition, 41.
Jeremi Squom Island, 216, 226.
Jewett, James, signed Narragansett petition, 160.
Johnson, Mr. ——, of Lynn, 284.
  J., signed St. Paul's parish petition, 192.
  James, his losses at the destruction of Falmouth, 310.
  John, signed Freetown petition, 217.
  John Jr., submitted Falmouth losses to Congress, 310, 394.
  Noah, signed Suncook petition, 205; grant to, 219.
  Capt. Robert, 356.
Johnston, John, his losses at the destruction of Falmouth, 308.
Jommo, Pierre, an Indian, 414; see also Toma.
Jones, Mr. ——, of Windsor, 264.
  Ephraim, his losses at the destruction of Falmouth, 309.
  Ichabod, attorney for Machias, 40; signed Machias petition, 41; report on the petition of, 80, 95; vote on the petition of, 80, 95; land granted to him and associates, 80; to levy taxes at Machias, 185.
  Capt. Ichabod, arrived at Machias with two sloops and a tender, 280; sent out a paper asking for protection, 280; moved his tender nearer, 280; people in town meeting passed a vote in his favor, 280; brought vessels to the wharf

Jones, *continued*.
  and gave out provisions, 280; part of the people determined to capture him and stop his business, 281; an attempt to capture him in church failed, 281; sloops captured but tender fled, and lashed to Capt. Toby's vessel, 281, 385; tender got off, seized and robbed a vessel, 281, 282; people gave chase, 282; tender captured, 282, 283, 284, 287; prisoners carried to Pownalborough, 283, 287; tonnage of his sloops, 284; Longfellow paid for capturing, 302.
  Josiah, as super-cargo, 264, 266, 273, 274, 276; his papers examined, 275; claimed to be only a passenger, 276; in service of Gage, 276; a refugee, 276; an enemy, 276; committed to the goal, 276.
  Nathan, desired further time, 21, 22; time granted, 23; his home at Gouldsborough, 139, 332, 333; petitioned for the return of his vessel, 333, 335; his petition considered, 333; the reason for the capture to be inquired into, 334; petition of, 332.
  Nathaniel Jr., signed Falmouth petition, 79.
  Pearson, his loss at the destruction of Falmouth, 306.
  Stephen, signed Machias petitions, 41, 174; signed Machias memorial, 115; to levy taxes in Machias, 185; concerned with Ichabod Jones, 281, 313; his conduct justified, 202; his home at Machias, 293; faithfully served his country, 293; wished success to the American arms, 293; letter of, 293.
  Col. William, of Bristol, 360.
Jordan, Rushworth, to issue a warrant for town meeting, 135; one of the Committee of Safety, 289.
  Samuel, member of the Provincial Congress, 320; letter of, 425.
  Tristram, men taken from his regiment, 410, 411; his regiment had furnished its quota, 411; letter of, 410.

Josselyn, Joseph, of Hanover Co., 216; purchased land rights of the heirs of Bates, 218; his land claimed by New Hampshire, 218; desired another grant, 218; another grant to, 218; petition of, 217.
Jost, John, signed Boothbay petition, 15.
Juett, James, subscribed for the Canada expedition, 366.

K

KELLEY, AARON, signed Boothbay petition, 171.
  Benjamin, ditto, 171.
  Christopher, his loss at the destruction of Falmouth, 307.
  Mary, ditto, 306.
  Philip, ditto, 305.
  Thomas, signed Boothbay petition, 171.
  William, signed Machias petition, 41.
Kennay, see Kenney.
Kennebec, 81, 118, 152, 340.
  Proprietors, 155.
  Purchase, 149.
  River, 90, 118, 122, 124, 126, 127, 128, 149, 154, 155, 158, 188, 191, 206, 246, 249, 269, 270, 297, 401, 412, 413, 425.
  Long Reach, 300.
Kennebunk River, 68.
Kennedy, James, signed Boothbay petition, 171.
  Thomas, ditto, 171.
  William, ditto, 171,
Kenney, } Abijah, signed Boothbay petition, 171.
Kennay, }
  Henry, ditto, 171.
  John, ditto, 171.
  Joshua, assaulted a justice of the peace, 113, 114.
  Love, bill for guarding and boarding prisoners, 802.
  Patrick, signed Freetown petition, 17.
  Samuel, signed Machias petition, 41; signed Boothbay petition, 171.
  Thomas, signed Boothbay petition, 171.
  Thomas second, ditto, 171.
Kent & Oxnard, their loss at the destruction of Falmouth, 309.
Ketley, Samuel, signed Boothbay petition, 171.

Kimball, John, signed Narragansett petition, 181.
Joshuay, ditto, 181.
Kincaid, Patrick, signed Boothbay petition, 171.
King, Daniel, subscribed for the Canada expedition, 366.
  George, 225.
King's woods, 133; see under Timber.
Kittery, home of Rev. Benj. Stevens, 184; home of Charles Chauncy, 274, 426; troops to be stationed at, 321; representatives in Congress, 274, 374.
Kneeland, Bartholomew, signed Pemaquid petition, 190.
Knight, Lieut. ——, 327, 328.
  Capt. Jonathan, justified the conduct of Stephen Jones, 292.
  Thomas, signed Machias memorial, 115.
Knights, Daniel, signed Boothbay petition, 170.
  Capt. Jonathan, 313.
  William, assessor at Windham, 210, 211, 212; contracted for masts, 210.
Knowls, Samuel, signed Pleasant River petition, 94.
Knox, John, signed Suncook petition, 205; deposition and oath of, 208.
Ksihor, Paul, signed Boothbay petition, 15.
Kubler, David, ditto, 15.

L

LA HIVE, 365.
Laighton, Benjamin, signed Freetown petition, 17.
  Solomon, ditto, 17.
Laint, Joseph, signed Narragansett petition, 181.
Lake Champlain, 238.
Lambart, } ——, bearer of Parry's letter, 248, 249.
Lambert, }
  Gideon, selectman, signed Winthrop petition, 191; signed Pondstown petition, 119.
  Jonathan, his loss at the destruction of Falmouth, 307.
  Capt. Luke, master of the Diligent, 375, 376.
Lampson, Nathaniel, signed Boothbay petition, 171.
Lancaster, Daniel, signed Fort Pownal petition, 57.

Lancton, the Rev. Samuel, 184.
Lane, Jabez, signed Narragansett petition, 181.
　John, ditto, 160.
　Capt. John, sent to raise a company of Indians, 256; brought Indians to Falmouth, 270, 283; gave a favorable report, 272; thoroughly in the service of his country, 277, 278; with four chiefs at Congress, 286; his accounts nearly correct, 286; amount paid to, 286; remuneration, 286; cannot go to the Indians, 341; letter of, 270.
Langdon, Mr. ——, 289.
　Jonathan, will exchange hard money for bills, 374.
　Samuel, his account allowed, 225.
　Timothy, as a witness, 300; letter of, 366.
Laperare, 239.
Larrabee, Isaac, signed Machias petition, 41; signed Machias memorial, 115.
　Capt. Nathaniel, to bring powder to Brunswick, 245; a member of the Committee of Safety, 340.
Lawrence, Amos, his grant in New Hampshire, 220; settled the grant, 221; desired a new grant, 221; new grant to, 221, 222; letter of, 220.
　Joshua, his loss at the destruction of Falmouth, 306.
Laythan, Bengimand, signed Freetown petition, 217.
Leach, James, represented Cape Elizabeth in Congress, 355.
Lead, 285, 444.
Leather, 332, 335.
Leavit, Daniel, signed Narragansett petition, 181.
　Samuel, ditto, 181.
Lebanon, granted (1783) 25; area of, 25; settlement of retarded, 26; minister settled at, 26; number of families at, 26; the people of, desired to be incorporated, 33; incorporated, 33; people to meet in town meeting at, 33.
Lebbee, see under Libbey.
Lee, Jeremiah, presented the petition of Windham, 71.
Leeman, signed Freetown petition, 217.
　John ditto, 17, 217.

Leeman, continued.
　Nathaniel, ditto, 217.
Leisham, John, signed Boothbay petition, 171.
Leissner, Charles, signed Broad Bay petition, 15.
Lemont, Benjamin, subscribed for the Canada expedition, 366.
　James, ditto, 366.
Leonard, Col. ——, member of the General Court, 210.
Lerote, John, signed Boothbay petition, 171.
　John Jr., ditto, 171.
Letters of,
　A. J., 293, 294.
　Allen, Col. John, 414, 417, 418, 426.
　Arundel Committee of Correspondence, 267.
　Austin, Benj., 359.
　Bernard, Gov. Francis, 49, 52, 54.
　Biddeford Committee of Inspection, 288.
　Bowdoin, James, 361, 362, 365.
　Bowdoinham Committee, 296.
　Brewer, Col. Josiah, 413.
　Brown, John, 39, 238.
　Brunswick Committee, 244, 339.
　Campbell, Col. Alex. 440.
　Carlton Dudley, 84.
　Chauncey, Charles, 352, 426.
　Cotton, John, 11.
　Council, the, 405.
　Cushing, Charles, 397, 426.
　Cushing, Roland, 399.
　Cutter, William, 333.
　Dartmouth, Lord, 304.
　De Berdt, Dennys, 58.
　Dimuck, Joseph, 402.
　Eddy, Jonathan, 395, 396.
　Falmouth selectmen, 242.
　Fletcher, Thomas, 367.
　Foster, Benj., and others, 172.
　Francis, Col. Ebenezer, 403.
　Franklin, Benjamin, 156.
　Freeman, Enoch, 14, 245, 278, 283.
　Gardiner, Dr. Sylvester, 242.
　Gentleman of Falmouth, a, 387.
　Germain, Lord George, 328.
　Hewes, Elihu, 271, 277.
　Howe, Maj. Gen. William, 342.
　Hutchinson, Gov. Thomas, 155, 158, 186, 206.
　Ilsley, Maj. Daniel, 338, 369.
　Jones, Stephen, 293.
　Jordan, Samuel, 175.
　Jordan, Tristram, 410.
　Lane, John, 270.
　Langdon, Timothy, 366.

Letters of, *continued.*
  Lithgow, William Jr., 401.
  Little, Col. Moses, 437.
  Littlefield, Noah M., 400.
  Lord, William, 360.
  Lowder, Jonathan, 411.
  Lyon, Rev. James, 174, 326, 379.
  Machias Committee of Safety, 283, 310, 350, 358.
  McCobb, James, 377.
  Mason, Jonas, 412.
  Mitchel, Col. Jonathan, 366, 400.
  Mowatt, Capt. H., 243.
  Newbury, Haverhill and Bath, 356.
  Otis, James, 321.
  Parker, Stephen, 322, 324, 346.
  Parry, Edward, 247, 249, 335.
  Partridgefield, 261.
  Pattee, Ezekiel, 409.
  Penobscot, 268.
  Pickering, Timothy Jr., 337.
  Powell, Jeremiah, 319.
  Preble, Col. Jedediah, 253.
  Preble, Capt. John, 405.
  Provincial Congress, 254.
  Rice, Thomas, 373.
  Robinson & Walton, 322.
  Ross, Alexander, 14.
  Scammell, Thomas, 152.
  Sewall, Dummer, 247.
  Shaw, Francis, 374, 424, 439, 443.
  Sherriff, Maj. William, 262, 264, 265.
  Simpson, Joseph, 305.
  Stillman, George, 436.
  Stirling, the Earl of, 87.
  Sturbridge, 336.
  Sullivan, Gen. James, 355.
  Thompson, Samuel, 243.
  Tupper, William, 399.
  Tyng, William, 84.
  Waldo, Francis, 8.
  Waldoborough Committee of Correspondence, 367.
  Warner, John, 438.
  Warren, Joseph, 293.
  Weare, Meshech, 442, 443.
  Wentworth, Gov. J., 11, 47, 48.
  Winslow Committee of Correspondence, 265 407.
  Wood, Abiel, 258.
Lewis, George, signed Boothbay petition, 171.
  John, represented North Yarmouth in Congress, 274, 355.
  William, signed Boothbay petition, 171.
Lexington, battle of, 276, 277.
Libbee, ⎱ David, signed Machias
Libby, ⎰ petition, 41.
  Ebenezer, ditto, 41.
  Ezekiel, signed Machias memorial, 115.
  George, signed Machias petition, 41.
  George Jr., ditto, 41.
  Jacob, ditto, 41.
  Joseph, signed Machias memorial, 115; a justice of the peace, 314.
  Reuben, signed Machias petition, 41; signed Machias memorial, 115.
  Samuel, signed Machias petition, 41.
  Sarah, ditto, 41.
  Timothy, ditto, 41.
License to sell liquor at Fryeburg, 107, 110.
Lime, 158.
Limestone, 158.
Lincoln, Mr. ——, one of the committee to examine Parry, 299.
  Benjamin, 1, 50, 223, 299, 301, 327.
  County, 14, 16, 17, 107, 112, 114, 122, 123, 124, 125, 127, 134, 149, 199, 200, 216, 226, 227, 233, 236, 237, 247, 258, 259, 265, 275, 295, 296, 300, 315, 352, 358, 379, 405, 420, 436, 441.
  County Goal, 138.
  Joseph, signed Sebascodegin petition, 76.
  Lithgow, Capt. and Col. William Jr., at Falmouth, to leave the service, 371; signed the certificate for Ilsley, 386; had the care of the masts, 398; his commission not received, 401; accepted the honor, 402; letter of, 401.
  Little, Col. Moses, desired pay for his services, 60; to command the forces sent to Nova Scotia, 437; declined the appointment, 437; letter of, 437.
  Moses, letter of, 437.
  Paul, his losses at the destruction of Falmouth, 305.
  Pond, 201.
  River, 197, 199.
  Samuel, signed Belfast petition, 198.
Littlefield, Noah Morton, appointed lieutenant-colonel, 400; letter of, 400.

Littlefield, *continued.*
  Samuel, signed Fort Pownall petition, 57.
Livermore, Samuel, on the boundary commission, 50; his land claimed by New Hampshire, 109, 110; desired another grant, 109, 110; grant to, 111, 112, 131, 132, 163, 164; conditions of the grant, 132; his grant a boundary, 162; plan of his township, 163.
Livingston, Philip J., of New York, 86.
Livius, Peter, 47.
Logs, *see* Lumber.
Loggers not given to formalities, 379.
Lombard, Solomon, represented Gorham in Congress, 274.
London, 58, 134, 156.
  St. James' Church, 391.
  St. Martin's Church, 391.
  Whitehall, 304, 328.
Lonear, Col. ——, a French officer in command of Indians and regulars, 412, 413.
Longfellow, Daniel, signed Machias petition, 41.
  David, signed Machias memorial, 115; as a second-lieutenant, 313.
  Jonathan, signed Machias petition, 41; justice of the peace, 112, 114; assaulted, 113, 115; must have assistants to perform his duty, 113, 115; to levy taxes in Machias, 185; memorial of, 112.
  Nathan, signed Machias petition, 41; signed Machias memorial, 115; bills of, 302, 303.
  Stephen, justice of the peace, 10, 11; his loss at the destruction of Falmouth, 305.
Long Pond, 28, 31, 94.
Look, Benjamin, signed Pleasant River petition, 93.
  Daniel, ditto, 93.
  Capt. Tobias, at Falmouth, 371; signed certificate for Ilsley, 386.
  William, letter of, 360.
Lothrop, Mr. ——, member of Machias Committee of Safety, 284.
Loveitt, Isaac, signed Falmouth petition, 79.
  Jonathan, ditto, 79.

Lovejoy, Caleb, signed Suncook petition, 205.
  David, ditto, 205; deposition and oath of, 208.
  Joshua, signed Andover petition, 20.
Lovel, Col. ——, member of the Provincial Congress, 327.
  Shubael, of Barnstable, 344.
Lovewell, John, signed Suncook petition, 205.
  Col. John, his heirs were grantees of Suncook, 195, 203, 205, 208, 219; killed at Pigwacket, 203.
  Solomon, inn-holder and selectman, bill of, for caring for Edward Doring, 194; signed North Yarmouth petition, 194.
Low, Cornelius, of New Brunswick, 86.
  Nathaniel, signed Narragansett petition, 160; agent for the Provincial Congress, 285.
  Samuel, signed Fort Pownall petition, 57.
Lowder, Col. Jonathan, preferred by the Indians as truckmaster, 341, 355; accompanied Fletcher on an embassy, 367, 368; letter of, 411; his letter forwarded, 424.
  Jonathan Jr., signed Fort Pownall petition, 57.
Lowell, Capt. Abner, in the army at Falmouth, 370, 371; signed the certificate for Ilsley, 386.
  John, deputy-secretary, 351, 357.
  Joseph, signed Fort Pownall petition, 57.
  Samuel, his losses at the destruction of Falmouth, 309.
Lowther, Mrs. ——, ditto, 309.
Ludwig, J., signed Broad Bay petition, 15.
  Jacob, ditto, 15.
Lumber, 191, 280, 285, 312, 317, 324, 344, 350, 360, 375, 408, 410.
Lunt, Moses, his loss at the destruction of Falmouth, 307.
Lyde, G., signed St. Paul's parish petition, 192.
Lyman, Rev. Isaac, 183, 184, 225.
Lyon, the Rev. James, invited to settle at Machias, 172, 173; will settle at same, 174, 175; one of the Committee of Correspondence, 283, 284, 314; what he found in Sprey's luggage, 326; his letter reached

Lyon, *continued.*
the House of Representatives, 334; furnished Parker with the means to purchase provisions, 343; not regarded at court, 379; sharp words to the court, 379, 383, 384; had travelled in other provinces which he compared to the eastern parts, 380; his prophecy of the greatness of the eastern parts, 382; consulted with John Allen, 416; letters of, 326, 379.

M

MABERY, MARGARET, her losses at the destruction of Falmouth, 307.
McCobb, Capt. ——, motioned that measures be taken to preserve masts, 246; on a committee for the same, 246.
   Hannah, subscribed for the Canada expedition, 365.
   James, petitioned for Georgetown, 129, 130; signed Boothbay petition, 171; subscribed for the Canada expedition, 365; letter of, 377.
   Samuel, signed Boothbay petition, 171; subscribed for the Canada expedition, 365.
   William, signed Boothbay petitions, 171, 234.
   see also Cobb and Mtt Cobb.
McConnell, Samuel, signed Suncook petition, 205.
McDonald, Lachor, signed Fort Pownall petition, 57
   Owen, signed Pleasant River petition, 94.
   Robert, signed Narragansett petition, 160.
McFarland, Andrew, signed Boothbay petition, 171.
   Andrew Jr., ditto, 171.
   John Murray, ditto, 171.
   Robert, signed Fort Pownall petition, 57.
   see also Mtt Farland.
Macgregor, James Jr., signed Belfast petition, 198.
McKentier, Sarah, subscribed for the Canada expedition, 366.
McKenzie, Kenneth, signed Fort Pownall petition, 57.
McKown, Patrick, signed Boothbay petitions, 171, 234.

Mclalen, Hugh, signed Gorham petition, 78.
McLean, Lunchlan, signed Fort Pownall petition, 57.
McLeeline, Dr. John, at Fort Halifax, 242.
McLellan, Capt. Joseph, bearer of a letter, 242; his losses at the destruction of Falmouth, 309.
McNiel, ——, widow, her bill for sundries, 303; with her children in poor circumstances, 314.
Machias, taken possession of, 39; bounds of, 40, 41, 80, 95, 96; area of, 40; number of people at, 40; have no minister, 40, 139; have no schoolmaster, 40; desired a grant of land, 40; desired to be incorporated, 40; granted to Ichabod Jones and associates, 80, 95; plan to be returned, 80, 96; conditions of the grant, 80, 81, 82, 96, 97; the distance from Gouldsboro, 93, 113; home of J. Longfellow, 112, 114; people of, enemies to law and government, 113 and 114; distance of, from a magistrate, 113, 115; club law in, 113, 114; the law abiding desired assistance, 114, 115; the land is of good quality, 137; trees in, not suitable for masts, 137, 140; has a good harbor and river, 138; salmon abundant at, 138; authority should be strengthened at, 138; deputy sheriff sworn in, 138; not incorporated, therefore has no constable, 138; distance from Fort Pownall, 189; desired to maintain preaching, 139; number of residents at, 139; the Rev. James Lyon invited to settle at, 172, 173; desired permission to levy taxes to support the gospel, 173, 174; committee appointed to consider the same, 174; Lyon will settle at, 174, 175; the people cannot support the gospel at, 185; a committee appointed to levy a tax to support the gospel, 185, 186; Capt. Jones with two sloops and a tender arrive at, 280; papers asking for protection of Jones handed about, 280; tender moved nearer the town, 280;

Machias, *continued.*
town meeting held, 280; the people through fear passed a vote favorable to the business of Jones, 280; the vessel brought to the wharf and part of the people given provisions, 281; a part of the people determined to stop the business of Jones, 281; first attempt failed, 281; threat to burn the town, 281; sloop captured but tender moved and lashed to Toby's vessel, 281; tender made off and seized a sloop, 281, 282; the people gave chase, 282; tender surrendered, 282, 283, 284, 287; where battle was fought and how long it lasted, 282; ammunition obtained but more needed, 282; prisoners to be taken to Pownalborough, 283, 287; tonnage of the sloops, 284; one sloop to be armed for defense, 284; Congress to send officers for the sloop, 284; prisoners to be taken to Congress, 287; the people justified the conduct of Stephen Jones, 292; home of Stephen Jones, 293; captured vessels brought to, 310; people in need and fear the enemy, 311, 312, 313, 314; vessels at, 312; sent a list of those who fell in battle to Congress, 313; the people spent their time in the public service, 313; officers in command at Eastern River, 313; men wounded and in need, 314; British deserters at, 314; vessels preparing to attack, 314; powder needed at, 314; attempts to stir the Indians to attack, 323; powder sent privateers of, 337; Parker went to, to obtain provisions, 343, 344, 345, 346, 347, 348, 350; opposite the Bay of Fundy, 345; Parker's petition dated at, 346; Parker's notes held at, 351; an exposed position, 355; the Viper seized vessels at, 358; privateers being absent there is no coast defense, 359; petitioned for relief, 359; Shaw at, 374, 424, 443; the Committee of Safety dispersed, 384; Capt. Walker sent to, 394; Tupper's letter

Machias, *continued.*
from, 399; help expected from Col. Shaw, 395, 399; the people of, reduced to being butchered or plundered, 399; Allen's letter from, 414; Allen held a council at, 416; the petition of, to be considered, 418; the St. Johns River expedition to rendezvous at, 420; the people to be paid for fitting out the same, 421; Allen's dues for defending, 422; Allen drew from the truckhouse at, 423; truckhouse to be continued, 424; strong drink not to be sold to the Indians, 423; report that the enemy had been sent against, 425; captured goods sent to, 431, 435; Preble sent to, for supplies, 434; Shaw's letter dated from, 439; Stillman at, 440; vessels to cruise off, 441, 442; Committee of Safety, 326, 327, 359; letters of, 293, 310, 350, 358; memorial of, 114; petition of, 173; report of commissioners, 137; mentioned, 115, 320, 326, 334, 419.

Account of the capture of the king's cutter, 280.

Eastern River, 313.

Harbor, 441.

Western Falls, 313.

Mahogany Bay, 440.

Maine, representatives of in Congress, 274, 354; mentioned, 6, 43, 59, 111, 132, 188, 253, 381, 382, 383, 384.

Majabigwaduce, 268, 284, 331; Committee of Correspondence, 332.

Major Veel, 405.

Manchester, 379.
John, signed Machias petition, 41.

Manciville, }
Mangeville, } 419, 429, 434.
Mansigerville, }

Mansfield, Isaac, presented Windham petition, 71.

Manufactures, home, 272.

Maples, 271.

Marblehead, 72, 74, 321, 323, 358, 379.

March, *see* Marsh.

Marimishe, 436.

Marines to be posted at Halifax, 329.

INDEX 475

Marks of, Berre, John, 41; Bouden, John, 54; Bryant, Eleazer, 41; Clay, Daniel, 181; Drisk, John, 93; Garland, John, 181; Getchell, Joseph, 41; Godhill, Donald, 58; Grindle, Joshua, 57; Kelley, William, 41; Kubler, David, 15; Libby, Sarah, 41; P——, John Henry, 15; Page, Joseph, 58; Pratt, Tim., 57; Smith, John Morton, 58; Toben, Mathew, 57; Warren, Daniel, 57; ——, John, 15; ——, Joseph, 94.
Marque of Oil Cloth, 423.
Marsh, ⎱ Col. ——, to raise a regiMarch, ⎰ ment in Maine, 254, 257; no disrespect meant for, 257.
  David, township granted to, 21.
  Samuel, petitioned for Scarborough, 177, 179; remitted fines to be paid to, 179; signed Belfast petition, 198; represented Scarborough in Congress, 274.
Marshfield, 277.
Marston, Brackett, his losses at Falmouth, 310.
Martha's Vineyard, 93.
Martin, James, signed Fort Pownall petition, 57.
  John, his losses at the destruction of Falmouth, 308.
  Maj. ——, 315.
  Oberlach, signed Broad Bay petition, 15.
  Samuel, married the daughter of Richard Fullford, 107.
Martindale, Capt. ——, 361.
Mary II, 36.
Mason, Jonas, declined to be a justice of the peace, 412; letter of, 412.
Man, John, signed Suncook petition, 205.
Massachusetts Bay, Province of, 12, 20, 25, 26, 27, 28, 39, 42, 43, 44, 45, 46, 47, 51, 56, 59, 64, 70, 74, 77, 78, 83, 86, 89, 91, 92, 94, 106, 112, 114, 116, 128, 129, 143, 149, 159, 166, 172, 173, 175, 177, 179, 182, 188, 190, 194, 195, 196, 204, 205, 206, 207, 208, 210, 212, 216, 217, 220, 229, 231, 233, 236, 247, 250, 254, 266, 269, 273, 280, 283, 291, 293, 296, 302, 310, 315, 316, 332, 335, 339, 343, 350, 356, 358, 362, 366, 367, 377, 384, 395, 396, 399, 400, 401, 402, 407, 412,

Massachusetts, *continued.*
415, 418, 424, 425, 426, 436, 443, 444.
House of Commons, 293, 384.
Masts, 137, 139, 141, 149, 150, 151, 153, 154, 155, 210, 237, 242, 246, 247, 248, 249, 250, 269, 287, 295, 296, 317, 398.
Matthews, Jabez, sent on a tour of discovery, 246.
  John, signed Sebascodegin petition, 76; signed Boothbay petition, 171.
Maxwell, William, signed Cumberland petition, 396.
Maycook, William Jr., signed Fort Pownall petition, 57.
Maynard, Stephen, signed No. Six petition, 229.
Mayo, Ebenezer, his loss at the destruction of Falmouth, 307.
  Simeon, ditto, 305.
Medumcook, people of desired the removal of the shire town, 17, 18.
Meeting Houses, must be erected in every township, 81, 96, 100, 101, 112, 132, 136, 161, 163, 164, 165, 219, 220, 222, 228; none at Belfast, 231; none at Pondstown, 118; none at Sanford, 69; none at Winthrop, 191; at Boothbay, 169; at Bowdoinham, 291; at Freetown, 216; at Narragansett, 159, 160; at Scarborough, 179; at Sebascodegin Island, 75.
Memorials of, Freeman, Samuel, 209; Longfellow, Stephen, 112; ministers of York, 182; North Yarmouth and New Gloucester, 316; people of Machias, 114; Savage, Arthur, 143; Small, Samuel, 78; Wyman, Joshua, 175.
Merameekee, 432, 433.
Merrill, Abel, signed Narragansett petition, 181.
  Lieut Nathan, 333.
  Peter, his loss at the destruction of Falmouth, 307.
  Samuel, signed Narragansett petition, 181.
  Stephen, signed Freetown petition, 217.
Merrimac River, 187, 213, 217, 227, 229.
Merryconeag Neck, 75.
Mery, Joseph, signed Freetown petition, 217.

Meserve, Daniel, justified the conduct of Stephen Jones 292.
Solomon, signed Machias petition, 41.
Messages, of Bernard, Gov. Francis, 2, 30, 31, 38, 61, 66; Council, the, 41, 42; General Court, the, 34; House of Representatives, 66; Hutchinson, Gov. Thomas, 132.
Michell, *see* Mitchell.
Micmacs, the, 359, 362, 364, 365, 406, 436.
Middleboro, 348.
Middlesex County, 27, 70, 276, 277, 353.
Milberry, Samuel, 292, 302.
Militia, *see* Soldiers.
Miller, James, signed Belfast petitions, 196, 198, 232.
Stephen, signed Pemaquid petition, 190.
William, pilot of the Loyal Legion, 311.
Milliken, Martha, widow, signed Narragansett petition, 160.
Thomas, bearer of a letter, 425.
Millmen not formal, 379.
Mills, 22, 109, 138, 141, 153.
Mines, 149.
Ministers, } settled and supported
Ministry, } in every township, 26, 81, 96, 100, 101, 112, 132, 136, 161, 215; provided for Indians, 35; none at Machias, 40, 139; at Fort Pownall, 57, 62; pay for one at Fort Pownall, 65; none at Sanford, 69; taxes to support, 71, 72, 73, 74, 77, 78; Sebascodegin desired a new one, 76; none at Pondstown, 118; had free passage over York bridge, 121; none at Machias, 139; an itinerary at Machias, 139; No. Four, 140; remuneration of, 172; desired information in regard to settling in new places, 183; to be paid out of the provincial treasury, 184; petition not granted for the support of, 381; reason why, 381; should keep their oaths, 390, 391, 397; should publish no untruths, 391.
Minot, John, his losses at the destruction of Falmouth, 309.
Stephen, signed Pemaquid petition, 190.
Minute men, 249, 260.

Miservey, Daniel, first lieutenant at Western Falls, 313.
Mispecka, or Moosepeck, 281.
Missionaries for the Eastern parts, 225.
Mitchell, } John, signed Belfast
Michell, } petition, 198.
Capt. Jonathan, signed Falmouth petition, 79; signed North Yarmouth petition, 194; desired leave of absence, 367; the same granted, 367; complaints against, 369; ignorant of his business, 369, 370, 371, 372, 373; had no reviews, 371; as the commander at Falmouth, he prevented Ilsley from doing his duty, 386; neglectful, 387; sent guards to Saco, Kennebec and Harpswell, 401; why he sent no more, 401; needed cannon, 401; letters of, 366, 400.
Joseph, signed Pleasant River petition, 93.
Lewis, a zealous tory, arrested 429.
Noah, signed Pleasant River petition, 93.
William, ditto, 93.
Mob law, 9, 10, 11, 84, 113, 143, 144, 145, 147, 148, 149, 155, 156; called also Club Law; and *see* Riots.
Molasses sold at high prices, 339; the exportation of prohibited, 340.
Money, *see* Currency.
Montgomery, Samuel, signed Boothbay petition, 171.
Montreal, 238, 239, 330.
Moody, Cutting, signed Narragansett petition, 160.
Enoch, his losses at the destruction of Falmouth, 308; submitted list of losses to Congress, 310, 394.
Joshua, his losses at the destruction of Falmouth, 309.
Nathaniel G., ditto, 308.
Moon, William, signed Boothbay petition, 171.
Moore, James, signed Freetown petition, 217.
John, signed Belfast petition, 198.
Jonathan, signed Freetown petition, 217.
Robert, signed Suncook petition, 205.

Morretown, letter of, 356.
Moosepeck, or Mispecka, 281.
Mores, Edward, signed Penobscot letter, 269.
  Samuel, signed Sebascodegin petition, 77.
Morren, Briant, signed certificate for Ilsley, 386.
Morrill, Simeon, signed Freetown petition, 217.
Morrison, Joseph, signed Belfast petition, 198.
  Samuel, ditto, 198.
Morrson, John, justified the conduct of Stephen Jones, 292.
Morse, David, subscribed for the Canada expedition, 365.
  Jonathan, his losses at the destruction of Falmouth, 307.
  Jonathan Jr., ditto, 305.
  Stephen, ditto, 305.
Morton, Capt. Bryant, in command at Falmouth, 338, 370.
  Ebenezer, signed Muscongus petition, 18.
  Ebenezer Jr., ditto, 18.
  Perez, deputy-secretary, 296, 298, 299, 301, 314, 318, 320, 322, 327, 336, 339.
Mosely, Sarah, her losses at the burning of Falmouth, 308.
Most, Ebenezer, signed certificate for Ilsley, 386.
Motley, Thomas, his losses at the burning of Falmouth, 308.
Moulton, Brigadier ——, took men from Jordan's regiment, 410, 411.
  Daniel, selectman of York, 92.
Mount Desert, 92, 140, 141, 209, 359, 441, 442.
Mount Sweag, 226.
  Bay, 216.
Mountfort, Edmund, his losses at the burning of Falmouth, 307.
  Samuel, signed petition of St. Paul's parish, 192; his loss at the destruction of Falmouth, 307.
Mowatt, Capt. Henry, Parry's letter to, 248; Tyng to convey his letter, 249; commander of the Canceau, 250; good conduct of, 250, 251; taken prisoner, 251; his threat, 251; paroled, 252; his excuse for breaking his parole, 252; his boat seized, 253; destroyed Falmouth, 317; to winter at Falmouth, 317; at North Yarmouth, 319; followed

Mowatt, *continued*.
  the orders of Gage in burning Falmouth, 342; Howe's account of, 342, 343; letter of, 243.
Mtt Cobb, John, signed Boothbay petition, 171; *see also* Cobb and McCobb.
Mtt Farland, Ephraim, signed Boothbay petition, 171; *see also* McFarland.
Mugrige, Peter, oath of, 332.
Mulliken, Benjamin, laid out a township, 19; his township granted to others, 28, 94; ousted from Rowley, Canada, 28; desired permission to sell delinquent rights, 28, 29; new lands granted to, 31, 32; the land not equivalent, 95, 98; desired the proprietors to be quieted, 95; to receive back his land, 98; and hold the same, 98; his land a boundary, 205, 219; petition of, 28.
Mumford, Mr. ——, a post rider, 405.
Munson, Joseph, signed Machias petition, 41; justified the conduct of Stephen Jones, 292.
  Stephen, signed Machias petition, 41.
Murray, Col. ——, member of the General Court, 193.
  James, signed Belfast petition, 232.
  John, signed Boothbay petition, 171.
  Jonathan, ditto, 171.
  Robert, ditto, 170.
Muscongus, the people of desired the removal of the shire town, 17, 18; Richard Fullford lived near, 107; Loud's letter dated at, 360.
Musquash Cove, 427, 439.
Mussey, Benjamin, selectman, signed letter for Falmouth, 242.
Muster roll, 376.
M——, Joseph, signed Fort Pownall petition, 57.

N

NAILS, 332, 335.
Nantucket, 324, 344, 345, 350.
  County, 358.
Narragansett No. One, plan of taken, 29; incorporated, 135; bounds of, 159, 175, 180, 181,

Narragansett, *continued.*
182; number of families in, 159; meeting house and minister, 159; desired to be incorporated, 159, 175, 176; proprietors to be given notice of petition, 160, 176, 177; the act of incorporation not assented to, 176; new resolution passed, 176; petition dismissed, 177; new petition presented, 177; petition against incorporation, 179: reasons of the objectors, 179, 180; number of rights in, 180; proportions of the two parties, 180; boundaries not entirely settled, 180; the larger proprietors object to, 180; Scarborough people at the Gore, 180; claims of Gorham, 180; act of incorporation, 181; town meeting to be called, 182; *see* Buxton.
Gore, the, 180.
Meeting House, 159, 160, 176.
Narragansetts, the, 217.
Nash, Isaiah, signed Pleasant River petition, 94
James, ditto, 94.
Joseph Jr., ditto, 94.
Samuel, ditto, 93.
Nashome, 402.
Naskeeg Point, 140.
Nason, Edgecomb, as convoy, 288.
John, signed Narragansett petition, 181; town clerk of Buxton, 236.
Robert, signed receipt for Deer Island, 285.
Nathan, Webster, signed Freetown petition, 217.
Neat, Thomas, sent to Congress for examination, 288; supposed to be a spy, 288; born in Britain, 288; lived and travelled in America, 288; a steward, 288; at Boston and Falmouth, 288; left the ship to go to Philadelphia, 289; the captain of the sloop demanded his return, 289; hired a horse to enter Falmouth, 289; examined and discharged, 290; to go south, 290.
Nesmith, Benjamin, signed Belfast petition, 232.
Nevers, Dr. ——, a suffering patriot, 415, 435, 440.
New Boston, a boundary, 22, 23; men enlisted in, 333.

New Brunswick, 86.
New Castle, a boundary, 216, 226.
New England, 27, 28, 70, 77, 78, 85, 92, 94, 151, 179, 194, 196, 210, 216, 231, 233, 240, 266, 347, 350, 352, 353.
New Gloucester, home of David Dinsmore, 246; alarmed by the destruction of Falmouth, 317; desired assistance for defense, 318; men enlisted in, 333; memorial, 316.
New Hampshire, 4, 5, 6, 24, 25, 44, 46, 47, 48, 50, 51, 155, 165, 187, 195, 196, 204, 206, 208, 213, 214, 215, 218, 220, 223, 224, 228, 229, 335, 336, 443.
Grants, 240, 241.
New Haven, 86.
New Jersey, 43, 86, 381.
New York City, 279, 290, 304, 416, 441.
Bayard Street, 86.
Exchange, the, 86.
New York, Province of, 43, 207, 275, 358, 381, 405, 464, 465.
Newark, 86.
Newbury, letter of, 356; mentioned, 39, 60, 86, 357, 385, 443.
Newburyport, 285.
Newfoundland, 329, 330.
Newichwannock River, 43, 45, 50, 51, 52.
Head, 50.
Newman, Thomas, his loss at the destruction of Falmouth, 306.
Newton, 225.
Nichols, Alexander, to call a town-meeting, 202.
John, his loss at the burning of Falmouth, 307.
William, signed Belfast petition, 232.
Noble, Rev. ——, 415.
Rachel, signed Pemaquid, petition, 190.
North, Col. Joseph, 405.
North Yarmouth, desired pay for caring for Edward Doring, 194; home of John Lewis, 274; alarmed by the burning of Falmouth, 317; desired assistance, 318; British vessels arrived at, 319; deserters came to, 319; battery erected near, 319; men enlisted in, 333; representative from, in Congress, 274, 355; home of Jonas

INDEX 479

North Yarmouth, *continued.*
  Mason, 413; memorial of, 316; petition of, 194.
Northampton, 334.
Norton, Seth, signed Pleasant River petition, 94.
Norwich, 282.
Nova Scotia, 43, 142, 206, 250, 255, 263, 264, 269, 273, 310, 320, 322, 323, 324, 325, 329, 344, 345, 347, 348, 350, 354, 362, 375, 379, 381, 382, 383, 395, 407, 416, 419, 421, 436, 437, 438.
Nowell, Zachariah, his losses at the burning of Falmouth, 309.
Noyes, Col. ——, member of the General Court, 66.
  David, his loss at the burning of Falmouth, 309.
  Isaiah, ditto, 308.
  Capt. Joseph, bearer of the Falmouth letter, 242; his loss at the burning of Falmouth, 308; submitted the list of losses to Congress, 310, 394; represented Falmouth in Congress, 355.
  Moses, his loss at the burning of Falmouth, 309.
  Noah, ditto, 307.
  Peter, submitted the list of losses to Congress, 310, 394.
  Samuel, signed Narragansett petition, 160.
  Timothy, his losses at the destruction of Falmouth, 309.
  Zebulun, signed petition of St. Paul's parish, 192; his loss at the destruction of Falmouth, 308.
Nye, Mr. ——, member of the General Court, 79.

O

OAKS, 152, 187, 271.
Oates, Samuel, signed Machias letter, 292.
Oath, Freeman would not administer one, 146; his reason for refusing, 147, 148.
Oats, 381.
O'Brian, ⎫ Dennis, justified the
O'Brion, ⎭ conduct of Stephen Jones, 292.
  Fannater, signed Machias petition, 41.
  Gideon, ditto, 41; justified the conduct of Stephen Jones, 292.

O'Brian, *continued.*
  Capt. Jeremiah, assaulted a justice of the peace, 113, 114; led the people to capture Jones's tender, 282; thanked by Congress, 287; with Foster, to have charge of the captured vessels, 287; one of the Committee of Safety, 310.
  John, his bill as messenger, 302; powder delivered to, 337.
  Morris, signed Machias petition, 41; justified the conduct of Stephen Jones, 292.
  William, justified the conduct of Stephen Jones, 292.
Ogden, Isaac, of Newark, 86.
Old Town, Penobscot, 411.
Oliver, A., secretary, 2, 8, 29, 32, 33, 39, 65, 68, 74, 77, 99.
  William, signed Fort Pownall petition, 57.
Onion River, 356.
Orders to Danks, Capt. Isaac, 315; regarding a prize ship, 388.
Orne, Col. Azor, member of the General Court, 357.
Osgood, Abram, signed petition of St. Paul's parish, 192; his loss at the burning of Falmouth, 307.
  Samuel, appeller, 225; signed Andover petition, 20.
Ossipee, Great, River, 19, 20.
  Little, River, 19, 20.
Otis, Mr. ——, member of the General Court, 134, 388.
  James, letters of, 321; mentioned, 134, 147, 164, 165, 301, 327.
  Col. Joseph, of Barnstable, 344.
Oulton, Anne & Comp., losses of, at Falmouth, 309.
Owen, Ebenezer, his losses at the destruction of Falmouth, 309.
  John, signed Narragansett petition, 181.
  William, selectman, signed letter of Falmouth, 242.
Oxen, 315.
Oxnard, Edward, signed petition of St. Paul's parish, 192.
  Thomas, ditto, 192.

P

PAGE, JOSEPH, signed Fort Pownall petition, 58.
  Simon, signed Sebascodegin petition, 76.
Paine, R. T., speaker, 424.

Palfry, Mr. ——, member of the General Court, 385.
Palmer, Joseph, ditto, 301, 316, 334, 422.
Paper money, 436; *see* also Currency.
Parker, Rev. ——, the only Episcopalian who read the Declaration of Independence in public, 390.
  Abijah, his loss at the burning of Falmouth, 306.
  John, subscribed for the Canada expedition, 365.
  Jordan, of Georgetown, gave bond for keeping Parry, 237, 247; should be released, 247; bond void, 287; subscribed for the Canada expedition, 365.
  Stephen, signed Machias petition, 41, 174; signed Machias memorial, 115; signed Machias letter, 173; to levy taxes at Machias, 185; reported the operations of the British at Annapolis, 323; a patriot detained in another province, 323, 324, 325; delay in sending letter, 323; took passage for Philadelphia, 324, 343, 345, 346, 347, 348, 350; at Yarmouth, 325; furnished with a letter by Lyon, 343; unable to purchase supplies at Philadelphia, 344; arrived at Barnstable, 344; still unsuccessful, 344; encouraged by Lovell, 344; not successful with Congress, 344, 346, 347, 350; to embark in trade, 344, 345, 347; hindered in Nantucket, 345, 350; applied to Falmouth, 345, 350, 351; arrived at Nova Scotia, 345, 347, 350; trade in the same, 345; arrived at Machias, 345, 346, 347, 351; espoused the cause of liberty, 345, 346, 347, 348; his notes held at Machias, 351; his letter referred to a committee, 351; letters of, 322, 324, 346; petition of, 343.
  Mrs. Stephen, 325.
Parry, } Edward, interviewed in
Perry, } regard to masts, 150; an enemy to American rights, 237, 287; in custody, 237, 247, 249, 269, 336; interrupted by the people, 243; will not ship masts, 247, 248; the Committee of Safety agreed not to disturb him, 247; erroneously arrested and obliged to give bond, 247, 248; should be released, 247; his papers seized, 248, 249; his papers copied, changed and circulated, 248; cannot supply masts for Halifax, 248; how arrested and compelled to give bond, 249; only to be released by an act of Congress, 249, 250; why arrested, 250; expects Congress to order the bond cancelled, 250; a contractor for masts, 269, 287, 300; hindered from performing his contract, 269, 270; his home in New Hampshire, 270; desired to be released, 270, 336; to be brought to Congress, 287; Sewall and Parker his bondsmen and the bond is void, 287, 295; committee appointed to examine, 299; to be sent to some inland town, 301; his affairs at home need his attention, 335; held no office and injured no one, 336; paroled for three months, 336; selectmen can't grant his release, 336; letters of, 247, 249, 335; petition of, 269, 287.
Parsons, Isaac, member of the Committee of Safety, 318.
Partridgefield, Congress demanded speedy payment of money from, 261; not able to pay the required tax, 261; why poor, 261; has sent required quota, 261; begged to be excused, 262; letter of, 261.
Passageesewokey Harbor, a boundary, 197, 199.
Passamaquoddy, 117, 364, 375.
  Bay, 427.
  Bay Islands, 142.
  Indians, 427.
  River, 142.
Passidoukeag, the, 55.
Patrick, John, signed Freetown petition, 217.
Pattee, Ezekiel, selectman, and one of the Windham Committee of Safety, 265, 409; letter of, 409.
Patten, John, signed Andover petition, 20.

Patterson, James, signed Belfast petition, 198, 232.
  Nathaniel, ditto, 198, 232.
  Robert, ditto, 198.
  William, ditto, 232.
  William Jr., ditto, 198.
Peabody's, 440.
Pearce, John, member of the General Court, 111.
  Richard, ditto, 111.
  see also Peirce and Pierce.
Pearl, Simeon, signed Freetown petitions, 17, 217.
Pearson, Moses, his loss at the burning of Falmouth, 309.
  Will., ditto, 309.
Pearsontown, plan made of, 29; a boundary, 159, 175, 182.
Peas, 381.
Peaslee, Nathaniel, a justice of the peace, 61.
Peirce family, 107, 108.
  John, signed Fort Pownall petition, 57.
  see also Pearce and Pierce.
Peircentown, 135.
Pemaquid, 89, 90, 230.
  Company, 189, 190, 230.
Pennicook, 195, 208, 213, 215; later Rumford, 213.
Pennsylvania, 381.
Penobscot, 57, 153, 207, 268, 269, 279, 286, 320, 334, 341, 355, 367, 368, 379, 411, 413.
  Bay, 86, 197, 199, 231.
  Indians, 245, 283, 286, 341, 359, 362, 363, 364, 367, 378, 411, 413.
  River, 57, 62, 84, 85, 86, 90, 131, 134, 156, 188, 268, 271, 272, 273, 284, 341, 367, 369, 412, 413, 425.
Pepperellborough, 135.
Pequakett, } 5, 6, 19, 203, 219, 223.
Pigwacket,
  Battle of, Lovewell killed at, 203; the Indians terrorized at, 203.
Percy, Lord Hugh, 329, 330.
Perkins, Ephraim, his sloop hired as a transport, 263; price to be paid him, 264; directions to, 264.
  Joseph, signed Boothbay petition, 170; member of the Committee of Safety, 332.
Perley, Israel, a prisoner, 415.
Perth, Amboy, 86.
Petcher, Reuben, signed Fort Pownall petition, 57.
Petersburg, 304.

Petitions of, Anderson, Abraham, 71, 73; Andover, 18, 19; Bean, David, 83; Boothbay, 166, 233; Broad Bay, 14; Brown, Henry Y., 62, 64, 116, 222, 224; Brown John, 231; Bridges, Moody, 28, 29, 94, 95; Church of England, 191; Cox, John, 64; Cumberland, 396; Downe, Samuel, 20; Eggleston, Hezekiah, 107; Elder, William, 210; Fort Pownall, 56; Freetown, 16, 216; Frye, Joseph, 106; Gardner, John, 227, 229; Georgetown, 129; Gorham, 77; Ilsley, Daniel, 386; Johnson, Noah, 202; Jones, Nathan, 21, 332; Josselyn, Joseph, 217, 218; Lawrence, Amos, 220; Livermore, Samuel, 108; Machias, 173; March, Samuel, 177; Medumcook, 17; Miller, James, 196; Mulliken and Bridges, 28, 29, 94, 95; Muscongus, 17; Narragansett, 159; North Yarmouth, 194; Parker, Stephen, 343; Parry, Edward, 269; Pondstown, 117; Richardson, Joseph, 26; Sanford, 68; Sebascodegin, 74; Thornton, Matthew, 20; Township No. Five, 92; Walker, Timothy, 212, 214; Whittemore, Samuel, 229; Winthrop, 190; York, 91.
Petterson, William, signed Belfast petition, 232.
Pettingall, Benjamin, his loss at the burning of Falmouth, 306.
  Daniel, ditto, 306.
Philadelphia, 293, 294, 312, 343, 344, 348, 350.
Phillips, Capt. ——, of the Gammon, 366.
  Maj., claimed the land granted to Henry Y. Brown, 224.
  Samuel, justice of the peace, 196; member of the General Court, 215, 220.
  William, member of the General Court, 388.
Phillipstown, a boundary, 19; incorporated, 67, 68; bounds of, 68; warrant to be issued for a town meeting in, 68.
Phinney, Col. Edmund, a selectman, signed Gorham petition, 78; to enlist a regiment, 253, 257, 283; papers returned to, 254; no disrespect meant for, 257.

Phips, David, petitioned for land, 99, 100; township granted to, 100, 162; title confirmed, 162; petition of, 99.
Physician, *see* Surgeon.
Pickering, Timothy Jr., 337.
Pierce, Daniel, 47.
  see also Pearce and Peirce.
Pierre Jommo, an Indian, 414.
  see also Toma.
Pierson, Jonathan, of Newbury, his sloop captured, 385.
Pike, James, signed Narragansett petition, 159.
  Timothy, his losses at the burning of Falmouth, 308.
Pine Trees, 137, 139, 140, 141, 149, 150, 153, 154, 271.
Pineo, Jonathan, justified the conduct of Stephen Jones, 292.
Pinkham, Solomon, signed Boothbay petition, 171.
Pirates, 244.
Piscataqua, 331, 335, 374, 376.
  Harbor, 43, 44.
  River, 43.
Pitcher, Ezra Jr., signed Broad Bay petition, 15.
Pitts, Mr. ——, of the Provincial Congress, 318.
  James, councilor, 1, 10, 42, 88, 147; signed Kennebec petition, 151; signed report concerning Pemaquid, 230.
  William, traded with Parker, 345.
Planks, 246, 248, 249, 250, 269, 301.
Pleasant River, same as Township No. Five, 92; situation of, 92; number of families at, 92; not orderly, 92, 93; people desired that Wilmot Woss be appointed a justice of the peace, 93; united to Machias, 281; prisoners at, 303; petition of, 92.
Plumer,
Plummer, } Moses, 93, 309.
Plymouth Council, 90, 189.
  Mass., 266, 273, 277, 379.
  Patent, 155.
  Purchase, 118.
Plympton, Daniel, selectman of Sturbridge, 337.
Point Levi, 368.
Pondstown, situation of, 118, 122, 124; desired to be incorporated, 118; no minister or school at, 118; proposed bounds of, 118, 126, 127; de-

Pondstown, *continued*.
  sired exemption from taxes, 118; roads to be built at, 118; incorporated, 126, 127; warrant to be issued for town meeting at, 127; named, 127; officers to be voted for, 128; petition of, 117.
Pool, Abijah, his losses at the burning of Falmouth, 308.
Porterfield, Patrick, member of the Provincial Congress, 316.
Portland, Willis' History of, cited, 310; *see* Falmouth.
Portsmouth, 48, 152, 155, 187, 215, 336.
Pomfret, 240.
Port Bill, the, 235, 236.
  Royal, 34.
  Royal Expedition, 109.
Post, none further than Falmouth, 377.
  Rider, a, 405.
Potatoes, 285, 315.
Pote, Capt. ——, obliged to furnish Thompson with cash and provisions, 253.
  Jeremiah, his losses at the burning of Falmouth, 309.
Powder, 245, 255, 283, 285, 294, 314, 323, 337, 346; *see* also Ammunition.
Powell, Jeremiah, councilor, 1, 88; a member of the Committee of Safety, 318, 320; his letter to be considered, 318; his letter, 319.
  Col. Jeremiah, justice of the peace, 10, 11, 147, 148, 371; member of the General Court, 357, 358.
Pownalborough, a boundary, 14, 15, 16, 17, 18; should be separated from Frankfort, 15, 16, 18; the returns of the town meeting to be sent to the General Court, 123, 125, 128; home of Thomas Rice, 227; Wood's letter dated from, 258; question about Dr. Rice being a representative for, 298, 299; home of David Silvester, 316; Committee of Safety, 349, 353; homes of David and the Rev. Jacob Bailey, 352; Langdon's letter dated at, 366; care of the Rev. Jacob Bailey, 389; Bailey's reply submitted to, 392, 394; Charles Cushing's letter dated at, 397; Roland

Pownalborough, *continued.*
    Cushing's letter dated at, 400;
    Jordan's letter dated at, 410;
      exposed situation of, 411.
    Goal, 283, 287.
Pratt, Tim., signed Fort Pownall
    petition, 57.
  William, ditto, 57.
Preble, Mr. ——, interpreter, 376.
  Abraham, selectman, signed letter of Bowdoinham, 291.
  Col. and Brigadier, signed petition of St. Paul's parish, 192;
    an assurity for Mowatt, 252;
    chairman of the Committee of
    Correspondence, 253, 254, 256;
    knew nothing about the deserter, 289; his loss at the
    burning of Falmouth, 305;
    represented Falmouth in Congress, 355, 385; letters of, 253,
    283.
  Jedediah Jr., signed petition of
    Fort Pownall, 57.
  Capt. John, Indians to tell their
    wants, 256; not a satisfactory
    truckmaster, 341; did not accept the office, 355; arrived at
    Machias, 414; bearer of a letter, 418; obliged to leave his
    position, 418, 434; on a voyage
    of discovery, 427; arrested
    Mitchell, 429; active, 434; sent
    to Machias for supplies, 434;
    letters of, 405, 407.
Prescott, Col. James, member of
    the Provincial Congress, 301,
    322, 414.
Press, the liberty of the, suppressed, 239.
Priests, 56, 239, 406, 416.
Prince, Capt. ——, 262.
  Christopher, 324.
  Paul & Co., 306.
  Silvanus, 194.
Prisoners, military, returned, 330;
    to be exchanged, 330, 331.
Privateers, 310, 311, 320, 359; *see*
    also under Vessels.
Providence, 405.
Pullen, James, signed Pondstown
    petition, 118.
  Stephen, ditto, 119.
Purenton, Nathaniel, signed Sebascodegin petition, 77.
Purrinton, James, his loss at the
    burning of Falmouth, 305.
Putnam, Gen. Israel, 240.
P——, John Henry, 15.

Q

QUAKERS, 185.
Quebec, 239, 241, 246, 304, 328, 329,
    368, 432.
  Bill, the, 239.
  Siege of, 363.
Queen's Birthday, the, 157.
Quinby, Joseph, his loss at the
    burning of Falmouth, 308.
  Joseph Jr., ditto, 308.

R

RAND, BENJAMIN, his loss at the
    destruction of Falmouth, 308.
Randell, Isaac, ditto, 307.
Rangers, *see* Soldiers.
Rankins, Constant, signed Sebascodegin petition, 77.
  James, ditto, 77.
  John, ditto, 76.
Raymon, Paul, ditto, 76.
Raymond, Capt. William, township granted to, 22, 27; bounds
    of same, 22, 23.
Raymond's Town, 165.
Recruits, *see* under Soldiers, 395.
Reed, Andrew Jr., signed Boothbay petition, 171.
  Audrey 3d, ditto, 171.
  David, ditto, 171.
  John, ditto, 171.
  Joseph, ditto, 171.
  Samuel, justified the conduct of
    Stephen Jones, 292.
  William, signed Boothbay petition, 171.
Regiments to be raised in Maine,
    253, 254; impracticable to
    raise one in Cumberland, 257;
    more to come from England,
    263; reinforced, 340; to be
    raised by a draft, 358; one to
    include both English and
    Indians, 363; needed in Cumberland, 396; to be raised in
    Cumberland and Lincoln counties, 420, 438; *see* also under
    Soldiers.
Regulars, the, *see* under Soldiers.
Remuneration of ministers, 172.
Rent, Bicomian, signed Boothbay
    petition, 171.
Reply of the Council to Stirling,
    88.
Reports of, abatement of taxes,
    378; Allen's, John, accounts,
    422; Brown's, Henry Y., petition, 4, 5, 24, 82, 103; Damaris-

Reports, *continued.*
cotta petition, 237; Sewell's, Dummer, petition, 395; examination of Parry, Edward, 300; Fuller's, Joshua, petition, 100; Hancock's letter, 419; Johnson's, Noah, petition, 219; Jones and Hicks, 275; Jones, Ichabod, 80; Jones', Nathan, petition, 333; powder, 340; Lane's, John, accounts, 286; Livermore's, Samuel, petition, 131; Machias commission, 137; Phips', David, petition, 99; Scott's, D., petition, 298; seaport defenses, 321; Sweetser's, Seth, petition, 230; Thatcher's, David, papers, 422.

Resolves on and of, Anderson's, Abraham, petition, 73; Belfast's petitions, 232, 235, 236; Brown, Henry Y., 5, 6; Bullock's, William, land, 136; Eggleston's, H., petition, 110; Falmouth, First Parish's petition, 99; Frye, Joseph, 110; Machias, 286; Mulliken's, B., petition, 98.

Rhode Island, 43, 381, 405.

Rice, ——, a name in Adams' intercepted letter, 295.
Seth, signed Township No. Six petition, 229.
Dr. Thomas, of Pownalborough, to call a town meeting, 227; justice of the peace, 275; his seat in the Assembly questioned, 298, 299; will exchange coin for bills, 374; letter of, 373.

Rich, Samuel, signed Machias petition, 41; signed Machias memorial, 115.

Richards, Humphrey, signed Falmouth petition, 79.
James, signed Freetown petition, 17.
Joseph, ditto, 17, 217.

Richardson, Josiah, an agent, 26, 28, 59, 60; land granted to, 215; deposition and oath of, 70.

Richmond, Col. ——, member of the General Court, 66, 289.
Ezra, ditto, 290.

Ridley, James, signed Sebascodegin petition, 76.
James Jr., ditto, 77.

Riggs, Daniel, his loss at the burning of Falmouth, 306.

Riggs, *continued.*
Joseph Jr., ditto, 307.
Josiah, ditto, 308.
Wheeler, ditto, 306.

Ringe, Thomas, signed Freetown petition, 217.
Riots, 10, 11, 84, 113, 114, 145; see also Mob Law.
River of Canada, 368.
Roads in Sanford, 69; in Windham, 71; needed at Pondstown, 118.
Robbins, Jonathan, signed Broad Bay petition, 15.
Roberds, George, signed Falmouth petition, 79.
Roberts, Job, signed Narragansett petition, 181.
Robinson, Haunce, overpaid, 322; letter of, 322.
John, signed Muscongus petition, 18; signed Falmouth petition, 79.
Rockingham County, 208.
Rogers, George, subscribed for the Canada expedition, 366.
William, ditto, 365.
Ropes, Nathaniel, councilor, 1.
Ross, Alex., justice of the peace, 10, 11; as a witness, 8; letter of, 14.
David, mate of the Loyal Legion, taken a prisoner, 310.
Elizabeth, widow of Capt. Alexander, 249.
John, signed Sebascodegin petition, 76.
Joseph, ditto, 76.
Thomas, ditto, 77; signed Freetown petition, 217.
Round Pond, Bristol, 107.
Rowley, Canada, 5, 6, 28, 29.
Roxbury, 276, 379.
Royal Artillery, the, 315.
Isaac, councilor, 1.
Ruggles, John, of Hardwich, 276.
Rum, 316, 403.
Rumford, formerly Pennicook, 213; Timothy Walker purchased land at, 213, 214; incorporated, 213; in New Hampshire, 213, 214.
Russell, Dr. ——, bearer of memorial, 318.
James, councilor, 1, 10, 42, 88.
Thomas, signed Andover petition, 20.
Ruynels, Samuel, signed receipt for Deer Island, 285.
Rye, 381.

Ryswick, 207.
R——, Matthias, signed Narragansett petition, 181.
Matthias Jr., ditto, 181.

S

SACO RIVER, 24, 28, 29, 63, 94, 100, 101, 111, 132, 135, 159, 175, 181, 182, 205, 218, 219, 221, 222, 228, 401.
Sagadahoc, grantees of a township in, desired further time, 21, 22, 83, 84; illegal settlers at the east of, 104.
St. Christopher's, 207, 316.
St. Clair, Gen. Arthur, 442.
St. Croix, 80, 89, 90, 142, 385.
River, 95, 142, 143.
St. Eustatia, 14.
St. François Indians, 240, 364.
St. Georges, 64, 322.
River, 316.
Shoals, 316.
St. Johns, 238, 340, 356, 360, 365, 376, 416, 427, 440, 441, 442.
River, 310, 412, 413, 414, 416, 417, 418, 419, 424, 425, 426, 438, 443.
River expedition, 419, 420, 421, 436.
St. Vincents, 14.
Salem, 244, 337.
Essex Gazette, 215, 220.
Harbor, 388.
Salmon, 86, 138, 311.
Falls River, 4, 25, 26, 32, 33, 43, 50, 51, 52.
Falls River, head, 50.
Falls River, north-easterly branch, 51.
Falls River, south-westerly branch, 51, 52.
Trouts, 139.
Sanborn, John, released, 84.
Sands, Ephraim, signed Narragansett petition, 181.
Samuel, ditto, 181.
Sanford, incorporated, 69; people from New Hampshire settled in, 69; no minister at, 69; no meeting-house or schoolmaster at, 69; area of, 69; desired exemption from taxes, 69; petition of, 68.
Capt. Thomas, a rioter, 147, 148; his loss at the burning of Falmouth, 308; as administrator, 308.

Saunders, alias Andrew, Joseph, 14.
Savage, ——, of Pownalborough, voted illegally, 299.
Arthur, comptroller of customs, 9, 143, 145; assaulted, 143, 144, 145, 148; his life in danger, 146; will go to Boston, 146; gave names of the rioters, 147; memorial of, 143.
Habijah, signed Pemaquid petition, 190.
John, ditto, 190.
Capt. William, of Falmouth, 143, 144, 145, 146, 147, 148, 296, 298.
Savages, see Indians.
Saw mills, see Mills.
Sawyer, Joseph, signed Falmouth petition, 79.
Sayer, Ebenezer, represented Wells in Congress, 274.
Sayward, Jonathan, member of the General Court, 20, 24, 26.
Scammell, Thomas, returned from his survey, 155; letter of, 152.
Scarborough, plan of, taken, 29; a boundary, 135, 159, 175, 180, 181, 182; always willing to support the government, 177, 178; fined for not sending a representative to Congress, 178; extra expense of settling a minister, 178; errors of tax collector, 178; expense of repairing the meeting house, 178; destructive fire in, 178; petitioned for remission of fines, 178, 179; fines remitted, 179; families at the Gore, 180; home of Samuel March, 274; representatives in Congress, 274, 355; deserters sent to, 320.
Gore, the, 180.
Schemle, Andrew, one of the Committee of Safety, 267.
Schoeffer, John Martin, signed Broad Bay petition, 15.
Schools, } none at Machias,
Schoolmasters, } 40; none at Sanford, 69; must be in every township, 81, 96, 100, 132, 136, 162, 163, 164, 165, 215, 219, 220, 222, 228; none at Pondstown, 118; none at Belfast, 197.
Schooner, see Vessels.
Scotland, 156.
Scott, Mr. ——, of Halifax, 263, 265.

Scott, *continued*.
  Daniel, report on the petition of, 298.
  James, first-lieutenant at Eastern River, 314.
  John, signed Machias memorial, 115.
  Samuel, ditto, 115; signed Machias letter, 173; signed Machias petition, 174.
Scouts, *see* Soldiers.
Sea coast men, in the army at Falmouth, 338.
Seamen impressed, 320.
Seaports, report on the defense of the, 321.
Searl, Capt. Isaac, member of the General Court, 174.
Sebago Pond, the Great, 22, 23.
Sebascodegin Island, called Shapleigh's Island, 74; in Harpswell, 74; number of families at, 74; had meeting house and minister, 75; desired to be a seperate parish, 75, 76; had a minister only part of the time, 75, 76; Harpswell to be notified of the petition, 77; petition of, 74.
Semple, John, part owner of the Loyal Legion, 310; taken prisoner, 310.
Seguin, 375.
Sergeant, Mr. ——, member of the General Court, 369.
Settlements, encouraged by respectable forts, 62; land granted and not granted, 104; land on the Kennebec began to attract attention, 128; made without authority, 131, 133, 155, 158, 168, 187; the charter concerning, 133; trespasses to be removed, 133, 134; committee appointed to attend to, 134; prosperous, 155, 158, 382; report of the committee, 134; *see* Townships.
Sevey, George, signed Machias petition, 41.
  Capt. Joseph, ditto, 41; signed Machias memorial, 115; in command at Eastern River, 313.
Sewall, Dummer, of Georgetown, bondsman for Parry, 236, 237, 247; should be released, 247; bond void, 287; willing to remain on part of the bond, 295;

Sewall, *continued*.
  in public service, 260; letter of, 247.
  Henry, as a witness, 300.
  Hony, subscribed for the Canada expedition, 366.
  Samuel, selectman of York, 92.
Shapleigh's Island, 74.
Shattuck, Moses, his losses at the burning of Falmouth, 308.
  Summers, ditto, 307.
  Zebadiah, signed Andover petition, 20.
Shaw, Col. Francis, desired further time, 21, 22; time granted, 22; a deputy to the Indians, 364; blockaded, 373, 374; arrived at Machias, 374, 424, 443; reported the condition of affairs in Maine, 375; promised pay to the sailors, 376; spoke well of Capt. Lambert, 376; engaged an interpreter, 376; why he did not retain the Delight, 376; to go to Gouldsborough, 377; can give information, 383; Machias expects help from, 395, 399; promised wages to Indian soldiers, 406, 407; enlisted men, 424; to go to the assistance of Col. Allen, 424; expects to keep the Indians friendly, 424; arrived with men, 432, 433, 443; at Musquash Cove, 439; met Col. Allen, 439; sent letter for Col. Allen, 440; his letter before Congress, 385; letters of, 374, 424, 439, 443.
  James, signed Machias memorial, 115.
  Josiah, his loss at the destruction of Falmouth, 306.
  Samuel, justified the conduct of Stephen Jones, 292.
  William, to accompany an Indian to Washington, 365.
Shearman, Eleazer, signed Boothbay petition, 171.
  Mary, her loss at the destruction of Falmouth, 309.
Sheepscot River, 216, 226.
Shelburn, Earl of, 30, 34, 66, 67.
Shepard, Alexander, a rejected township granted to, 225.
Shepperday, 394, 395.
Shey, William, a bill drawn on, 312.
Shirriff, Maj. William, deputy-quartermaster-general, 262,

Shirriff, *continued*.
315; contract with Ephraim Perkins, 262, 264; supplies consigned to, 315; letters of, 262, 264, 265.
Shithen, Japeth, signed Machias memorial, 115.
Shodier, 368; *see* Chaudier.
Shute, Benjamin, signed Penobscot letter, 269.
Shuttuck, Moses, signed St. Paul's parish petition, 192.
Silver, 149.
Silvester, *see* Sylvester.
Simmons, W., signed St. Paul's parish petition, 192.
Simpson, Joseph, represented York in Congress, 374; letter of, 305.
Josiah, desired more time, 83; more time granted, 84.
Jos. Jr., selectman of York, 92.
Sinclare, ⎫ ——, sworn in deputy
Sinkler, ⎭ sheriff, 138.
John, signed Machias memorial, 115.
Nathaniel, rent for his sloop, 302; justice of the peace, 314.
Six Nations, the, 240.
Skillin, John, signed certificate for Ilsley, 386.
Capt. Samuel, signed Falmouth petitions, 79, 99.
Sloops, *see* Vessels.
Small, ——, signed Sebascodegin petition, 77.
James, signed Falmouth petition, 78, 79.
T. Jr., signed Sebascodegin petition, 76.
Smith, ——, furnished supplies for Machias, 303.
Capt. ——, of Bristol, Eng., 139.
Maj. ——, commissary at Ticonderoga, 404.
Benjamin, township granted to, 217.
Elihu, signed Pondstown petition, 119.
Capt. George, 375, 383.
Isaac, signed Pleasant River petition, 94; owned molasses at Brunswick, 339.
John, of Perth Amboy, 86.
John Morton, signed Fort Pownall petition, 58.
Jonathan, of Philadelphia, 343.
Lucy, her loss at the burning of Falmouth, 310.
Lieut. Nathan, 366.

Smith, *continued*.
Samuel, of Arundel, his sloop seized by Graves, 266, 273; induced to join the king's service, 266, 273; sailed with arms to Nova Scotia, 266, 274; had Jones and Hicks on board, 266, 273, 274, 276, 277; took the vessel to Arundel, 266, 274; knew not why Hicks was on board, 277; deposition of, 273.
Capt. Stephen, justified the conduct of Stephen Jones, 292; in charge of privateer, 310; seized the Loyal Briton, and destroyed fort at St. Johns, 310, 311; his letter before the General Court, 385; asked to assist in conveying prisoners, 395.
Rev. Thomas, represented the First parish, 99; his loss at the burning of Falmouth, 309.
Snow, ——, represented Harpswell in Congress, 355.
Ebenezer, his loss at the destruction of Falmouth, 307.
Elisha, of St. Georges, his losses, 315, 316; signed Sebascodegin petition, 76.
Isaac, signed Sebascodegin petition, 76.
John, ditto, 76.
Snow shoes for the troops, 239.
Socenomick or Chaudier River, 368.
Soldiers, enlisted men to be clothed as, 53; more can be sent higher up the river, 55; desired that Crawford be retained as minister at Fort Pownall, 57; sent to relieve St. Georges, 64; eight to be sent to Fort Pownall, 65; wages for the same, 65; furnished by Boothbay, 167, 168; commanded by Goldthwait, 186; the British, to be ready to go to Boston, 239; snow shoes for, 239; in disguise to explore, 239; only French officers willing to fight, 240; Phinney to enlist a regiment, 253; Maine cannot spare, 253; March to raise a regiment, 254; Stockbridge Indians enlist, 256; Lane sent to raise a regiment among Indians, 256; Congress to establish an army,

Soldiers, *continued.*
256; enlisting progresses slowly, 257; impracticable to raise two regiments in Cumberland, 257; Boothbay officers resign, 260; people elected officers, 260; more regiments arrive from England, 263; coasters to carry timber to, 274, 275; at Marshfield, 277; officers of regiments raised in Maine, 279; no provision made for those Phinney is to enlist, 283; an army to be raised and equipped, 295; army to continue at Boston, 304; hopes of having a large army in America, 304; Russia to send infantry to assist England, 304; captured at St. Johns, 310, 311; expensive lumber, 311; officers at Eastern River, 313; Frye to assume command, 321; where troops should be stationed on the sea coast, 321; billeted in St. Georges, 322; re-enforcements to be sent to Howe, 328, 340; to sail from Ireland, 329; marines at Halifax, 329; regiments reincorporated, 330; Cutter and Fabyan to raise companies, 332; where men were enlisted, 333; marched from Cambridge, 333; Ilsley in command, 338; number at Falmouth and Cape Elizabeth, 338; lack ammunition, 338; sickly, 339; regiments to be raised by a draft, 358; Hilton's to be placed in order of defense, 360; a regiment of English and Indians to be raised, 363; four Indians join the army, 364, 365; the English sailed up the Canada River, 368; Indians will join the rangers, 368; trouble with Col. Mitchell at Falmouth, 369, 370, 371, 372; regiments not reviewed, 371, 373; trouble about the service on Sunday, 372; would, if permitted, qualify themselves, 373; parades discontinued, 386; suspicion of disloyalty, 386, 387; poor discipline will cause disorder, 387; a countryman who joined the regulars, 395; recruited in Cumberland, 395; with the aid of the inhabitants seized a

Soldiers, *continued.*
vessel from Annapolis, 395, 396; unsuccessful in an attempt to take a garrison, 395, 396; needed in Cumberland, 396; cannot be recruited at Nashone, 402; in need at Ticonderoga, 403, 404; for Rhode Island, 405; Indians under Eddy, 406; Boston men, 406; pay promised to Indians who served, 406, 407; drafted in York county, 410; taken from Jordan's regiment, 410, 411; regulars and Indians approaching, 412, 413; commanded by French officers, 413; Hessians ordered home, 416; regiments to be raised in Cumberland and Lincoln counties, 420, 438; armament of the St. Johns expedition, 420; officers, 420, 421; to be continued by Allen, 423; surgeon for, 423; Canadians drafted, 432; for Ticonderoga, 442, 444; to join Col. Allen, 443.
Somerby, Abraham, signed Narragansett petition, 160.
Somerset county, England, 86.
Southerland, James, assaulted a justice of the peace, 113, 114.
Spain, 387.
Spaniards, the, 207.
Spars, 249, 269, 279.
Speeches of, Bernard, Gov. Francis, 59; Hutchinson, Gov. Thomas, 103, 106, 130.
Spencer, Gen. Joseph, 405.
Spooner, Walter, member of the General Court, 402.
Sprague, Abiel, signed Machias petition, 41; bill as messenger, 302.
 Abiel, 2d, ditto, 41.
 Abier, signed Machias memorial, 115.
 William, subscribed for the Canada expedition, 366.
Spruce, 271.
Spry, Lieut, Thomas, papers found in his baggage, 326, 327, 328.
Stackpole, James, signed Sebascodegin petition, 76.
 William, ditto, 76.
Standwood, Samuel, 245, 340.
Stanford, Joseph, signed Falmouth petition, 79.
 Josiah, ditto, 79.
 Robert, ditto, 79.

Stanley, Mr. ——, his schooner had Frevoy on board, 323.
Stanyan, John, signed Sanford petition, 69.
States, the, 435, 436; *see* also United States.
Statesman, what constitutes a, 380.
Stel, John, signed Belfast petition, 198.
Stevens, Abraham, his loss at the destruction of Falmouth, 307.
Amos, signed Pondstown petition, 118.
Asa, signed Narragansett petition, 181.
Rev. Benjamin, as trustee, 183, 184; his account allowed, 225.
Benjamin Jr., signed Suncook petition, 205.
Chare, signed Pleasant River petition, 94.
Edmund, ditto, 94.
Hubbard, signed Freetown petition, 217.
Joseph, signed Pondstown petition, 119.
Stevenson, John, his loss at the burning of Falmouth, 305.
Stickney, Mr. ——, member of the General Court, 193.
Capt. David, 14.
Esther, her loss at the burning of Falmouth, 306.
Mary, ditto, 309.
Stillman, ——, his bill for supplies, 303.
Maj. George, member of the Committee of Safety, 283; sent to Congress with an account of Machias, 313; accompanied by Dr. Chalnor, 314; to have command of a regiment, 436, 437; at Machias, 440; letter of, 436.
Stimson, Ephraim, signed Fort Pownall petition, 58; signed Belfast petition, 198.
Richard, signed Belfast petition, 198.
Stirling, Capt. Frederick, master of the Loyal Legion, 311; sent to the General Court, 311.
William Alexander, Earl of, to sell his land, 85, 86, 87, 89, 90; office of, 86; agents of, 86; sent title of the land to Bernard, 87; his letter before the Council, 88; his right to the land denied, 89, 91; founda-

Stirling, *continued.*
tion of his claim, 90, 91; a proclamation issued, 90, 91; advertisement of, 85; letter of, 87.
Stockbridge Indians, 256.
Stoddard, Col. ——, 66.
David, his loss at the burning of Falmouth, 310.
Stone, Capt. ——, a rioter, 147, 148; member of the General Court, 289.
Benjamin, signed Brunswick letter, 245.
Daniel, signed Machias petition, 41; as attorney, 41; justified the conduct of Stephen Jones, 292.
John, signed Machias petition, 41.
John 2d, ditto, 41.
Jonathan, one of the Committee of Correspondence, 267.
Solomon, signed Machias petition, 41.
Storer, George, signed Broad Bay petition, 15.
Joseph, represented Wells in Congress, 374.
M., signed Broad Bay petition, 15.
Storey, William, member of the Provincial Congress, 318.
Stover, Walton, his loss at the burning of Falmouth, 307.
Stowe, 353.
Stowell, Nathaniel, town clerk of Partridgefield, 262.
Streetland, Daniel, deserter from the British fleet, 320.
Strout, Anthony, signed Falmouth petition, 79.
Daniel, ditto, 79.
Joshua, ditto, 79.
Stuart, Charles, quartermaster, deserted the British fleet, 320.
Sturbridge, 336.
Sudbury, 27.
Canada, otherwise Fuller's Town, 215.
Sugar, 316, 387.
Sullivan, Gen. James, represented Biddeford in Congress, 374, 411; ordered removal of people, 356; retreat of, 360; letter of, 355.
Sunbury county, 407, 419.
Suncook, Stephen Holt settled at, 195; granted to Capt. Lovewell and others, 195, 203, 205,

Suncook, *continued.*
208, 219; claimed by New Hampshire, 195, 204, 206; purchased by blood, 195; proprietors worried, 195, 204; people of received no consideration, 196, 206, 208; people of impoverished by law suits, 196, 204, 208; granted to those who were in the Pigwacket fight, 203; the people of desired a grant of land on the Saco River, 204, 205; Benj. Holt settled at, 205; claimed under the Mason grant, 206; claimed by Chester, 206; several of the proprietors were reimbursed, 206, 208.
Proprietors, 195.
Surgeon, at Fort Pownall, 57; at Machias, 302.
Swain, James, his loss at the destruction of Falmouth, 306.
Swan, Gustavus, signed Fort Pownall petition, 57.
Sweetser, Jane, her loss at the burning of Falmouth, 305.
Seth, signed Pemaquid petition, 190, 230.
Sylvester, David, of Pownalborough, hired a sloop, 316; sailed for St. Christopher, 316; vessel seized on his return voyage and he made prisoner, 316.
Joseph, his loss at the burning of Falmouth, 308.
Sylvester Canada, 161, 163.

T

TAFT, ——, a prisoner at Machias, 303.
Isaac, justified the conduct of Stephen Jones, 292; in needy circumstances, 314.
Tarpaulin Cove, troops stationed at, 321.
Taxes and Taxation, in arrears, 28, 29; Sanford desired exemption from, 69; for roads, 71, 72; to be raised in Windham, 71, 72, 73; for ministerial charges, 71, 72, 73, 74; delinquent lands to be sold for, 72, 73, 74; unequal at Gorham, 78; to be deferred, 105; Pondstown desired exemption from, 118; to be levied to support ministers, 173, 174, 185, 186; levied on members

Taxes and Taxation, *continued.*
of the Church of England, 192; the church desired power to tax its members, 192; Falmouth to omit taxing members of St. Paul's church, 193; Belfast desired power to levy, 198, 232; illegal valuation oath in Windham, 211; rate to be levied, 232; Boothbay paid to the Provincial Congress, 260; Partridgefield not able to pay, 261; Waldoborough will send to Gardner, 267; York desired abatement of, 305; without representation, 235, 236; nonincorporated places to pay, 361; report on the abatement of, 378.
Taylor, Eldred, member of the General Court, 301, 385.
John, member of the Provincial Congress, 301, 322, 361, 362, 369, 378; a justice of the peace, 335.
Tea, the destruction of, 258.
Act, the, 259.
Tea vessels, the, 275.
Tebbets, Giles, signed Boothbay petition, 171.
Ichabod, ditto, 171.
James, ditto, 171.
John, ditto, 171.
Nathaniel, ditto, 171.
Nathaniel Jr., ditto, 171.
Tebbut, Joseph, signed Pleasant River petition, 94.
Tenders, *see* Vessels.
Thaiter, ——, a name in Adams' letter, 295.
Thatcher, David, of Yarmouth, a friend of the States, 422.
Thomas, Jesse, signed Muscongus petition, 18.
John, his bill for breeches, 302.
Joseph, his losses at the destruction of Falmouth, 308.
Waterman, of Waldoborough, 360, 361.
Thompson, ⎫ Jeremiah, signed
Thomson, ⎭ Fort Pownall petition, 58.
Joseph, signed Sebascodegin petition, 76.
Col. Samuel, had the custody of Parry, 237, 247, 249, 269, 270; the arrest was contrary to the will of the Committee of Safety, 247; seized Parry's papers, 248, 249; aided by the

Thompson, *continued.*
minute men, 249; why he arrested Parry, 250; fitted out a vessel to surprise the Canceau, 250; asked to desist, 251; said he had dropped the design, 251; captured a prisoner, 251; paroled one prisoner: released the other under conditions, 252; would have satisfaction, 252, 253; his high-handed operations, 253; a true friend of liberty, 253; might have caused the destruction of Falmouth, 253; his home at Brunswick, 269, 274; represented Brunswick in Congress, 274, 318; to remove the masts collected by Parry, 287; unnecessary that he remove the same, 296; had John Bernard in custody, 300; letter of, 243.

Thompson, Thomas, signed receipt for Deer Island, 285; signed Machias letter, 292; a member of the Committee of Safety, 340.

William, signed Fort Pownall petition, 57; signed Sebascodegin petition, 76.

Gen. William, captured, 360.

Thorndike, Ebenezer, signed Falmouth petition, 79; township granted to, 209.

Robert, signed Falmouth petition, 79.

Robert Jr., ditto, 79.

Thornton, Mathew, desired further time, 20, 21.

Thrasher, John, his losses at the destruction of Falmouth, 308.

Jonathan, ditto, 306.

Throop, Mr. ——, bearer of a letter, 396.

Thurlo, John, his loss at the destruction of Falmouth, 306.

Thurston, Benjamin, signed Narragansett Petition, 160.

John, ditto, 160.

Ticonderoga, 403.

Timber, etc., 82, 84, 104, 131, 133, 137, 139, 141, 142, 187, 274, 287.

Tinkham, Mr. ——, of Yarmouth, 345, 347.

Tinkler, Nathaniel, signed Machias petition, 115.

Tinney, George, signed Pleasant River petition, 94.

Titcomb, Benjamin, neighbor of Arthur Savage, 144, 145, 146,

Titcomb, *continued.*
147, 148; his loss at the destruction of Falmouth, 305; as agent for Kelley, 305.

Toben, Mathew, signed Fort Pownall petition, 57.

Tobey, Capt. ——, Jones' tender lashed to his vessel, 281; compelled to act as pilot, 281, 282.

Tollman at York bridge, 150.

Toma, } Piere, an Indian, 406,
Tomer, } 414, 430.
Jommo, }

Tomson, Cornelius, signed Muscongus petition, 18.

Towns, the maritime, are not destitute of informers, 142.

Townsend, former name of Boothbay, 166.

Townships, purchased and laid out by H. Y. Brown, 4; the confliction with New Hampshire, 5, 13; more land granted to H. Y. Brown, 5, 6, 222; conditions of the grants of, 5, 6, 23, 80, 81, 82, 86, 100, 101, 112, 132, 136, 137, 150, 161, 163, 164, 165, 215, 219, 220, 222, 228; three laid out near Pequakett, 19; people of Andover desired a grant, 19, 20; in Sagadahoc desired further time, 21, 83, 84; flourishing, 22; the plan of Raymond accepted, 22; one of 1733 desired to be incorporated, 25, 26; people of Sudbury petitioned for one, 27; proprietors can not sell delinquent rights, 28; permission to sell the same desired, 29; plans lost, 29; John Brown to make new plans, 29; Mulliken to change his site, 31, 32; delinquents to be notified, 32; no settlement made without proper authority, 34, 35; security desired of applicants, 60, 61; to be laid out, 61; Machias granted to Ichabod Jones and others, 80; a means of rooting out the savages, 85; laid out in a territory later claimed by the Earl of Stirling, 89, 91; proclamation, 90, 91; granted to David Phips and others, 100, 162; Fuller's claimed by New Hampshire, 100; another grant to Fuller, 101, 161; Fryeburg granted to Joseph Frye, 106;

Townships, *continued.*
Harris' grant claimed by New Hampshire, 109; another grant to Harris, 111, 112; four incorporated in 1771, 128; granted to Livermore and others, 132, 162, 163, 164; Bullock and others to retain possession, 136, 137; people well spoken of, 140; prosperous and permanent, 140, 141; number of families in thirteen, 140; granted to James Otis and others, 164, 165; Boothbay incorporated, 1764, 169; part of Narraganset opposed incorporation, 179, 180; Narraganset incorporated, 181; granted to Ebenezer Thorndike and others, 209; sold to Timothy Walker and others, 213, 214; the same claimed by New Hampshire, 213; new grant to Walker, 214, 215; grant to Benjamin Smith, 217; grant to Noah Johnson and others, 219, 220; granted to Capt. John Flint, 220, 221; granted to Whittemore and Laurence, 221, 222; Alexander Shepard Jr., rejected his grant, 225; granted to John Whitman, 227; *see* also under Narraganset.

Township No. Five, 218; petition of, 92; *see* also Pleasant River.
No. Four, 140, 440, 442, 444.
No. One, 29, 118, 135, 149; *see* also Buxton.
No. Seven, 29.
No. Six, 227, 228, 229.
No. Three, 21, 22, 149.
No. Two, 149.

Tozer, John, member of the Winslow Committee of Correspondence, 265, 409.

Trade, acts to regulate Indian trade, 7, 30, 31, 34, 35, 37, 38; Ilsley's lock seized, 8; collector of customs attacked, 9; goods spirited away, 9, 11; reward offered for offenders, 10; justices to meet, 10, 11; in the Indian country a cause of trouble, 30; a building to be hired at Passamaquoddy, 117; the French may monopolize the trade with Indians, 240; Indians exasperated because of the stoppage of trade, 245;

Trade, *continued.*
the lack of powder a hinderence, 255; the stoppage causes distress at Deer Island, 279; the losses of York in, 305; interrupted by the Viper, 375; sugar bought to be shipped abroad, 387; cheaper goods necessary, 406; the prices of furs desired, 406; prices of furs agreed upon, 434.
the Lords Commissioners of, 58, 149.

Trafton, Thaddeus, signed Machias petition, 41.
Trask, David, signed Freetown petition, 217.
Joseph, ditto, 17, 217.
Samuel, ditto, 17, 217.
Samuel Jr., ditto, 17, 217.
Solomon, ditto, 17, 217.
Thomas, ditto, 17.
Treat, Joseph, signed Fort Pownall petition, 57.
Treaties and land rights, 207; to exchange prisoners, 331.
of Breda, 207.
of Ryswick, 207.
of 1726, 37.
with Indians, 363.
Troops, see Soldiers.
Truckhouses, 37, 53, 62, 423, 424.
Truckmasters, 341, 342, 355, 418, 423.
Tucker and Newman, 306.
Tucker, Josiah, his loss at the burning of Falmouth, 305.
Tuffts, John, signed Belfast petitions, 198, 232.
John Jr., ditto, 198, 232.
Tukey, John Jr., his loss at the burning of Falmouth, 309.
Tupper, William, justified the conduct of Stephen Jones, 292; bill of, 302; clerk of Machias, 351, 399; letter of, 399.
Turner, Briggs, signed Machias letter, 292.
Cornelius, ditto, 292.
Turnips, 315.
Tyler, Moses, signed Suncook petition, 205.
Royal, councilor, 1, 10, 88.
Tyng, Mrs. Elizabeth, wife of Col. William, 249.
John, his loss at the burning of Falmouth, 309.
Col. William, sheriff, 146, 148; to convey Parry's letter, 249;

INDEX 493

Tyng, *continued.*
his goods seized by Col. Thompson, 253; letter of, 84.

U

UNDERWOOD, JOHN, signed Machias petition, 41.
Union River, township east of, 21; Samuel Jordan's letter dated from, 425; people of, alarmed by the approach of the regulars, 425; the people would surrender to the enemy, 425.
United States, so named in James Bowdoin's letter of July 30, 1776, 363; mentioned, 363, 389, 395, 397, 412, 418, 422, 435, 444.

V

VASSAL, WILLIAM, 128.
Vassalborough, incorporated, 128; named for William Vassel, 128; home of Remington Holby, 246.
Veazy, Jeremiah, signed Fort Pownall petition, 57; his loss at the destruction of Falmouth, 307.
John, his loss at the destruction of Falmouth, 407.
Vessels, arrived at and sailed from Falmouth, 14; to transport artillery, 34; sloop impressed to transport Waldo's regiment, 64; men of Machias will not ship on those belongiug to the enemy, 139, 140; masters of, concerned in the Falmouth riot, 147, 148; hired to convey the lumber inspector, 153; needed by the inspector, 154; prevented supplying the natives, 243, 244; a tender sent to dismantle a fort, 245; reports that an attempt will be made to capture the Canceaux, 248, 250; sent against the colonies, 255; Perkins' sloop hired as a transport, 263, 264; one belonging to Arundel seized, 266, 273; master obliged to enter the service of the king, 266, 273; sailed for Annapolis, 266, 273; but put in at Arundel, 266, 273; the interruption of causes a scarcity, 268; the largest can navigate the Penobscot, 271; Jones' sloop and

Vessels, *continued.*
tender at Machias, 280, 281; fight off Machias, 281, 282; tonnage of Jones' sloop, 284; one sloop to be armed, 284; Congress to commission a commander, 284; in charge of Foster and O'Brian, 287; the Senegal at Falmouth, 288, 289; should be bought to bring supplies to Bristol, 296, 298; expenses for caring for the prisoners and wounded, 302; hired to bring a surgeon, 302; the capture of, a loss to York, 305; Smith in charge of a privateer, 310; the Loyal Britain, seized by Smith, 310, 312; inventory of goods captured, 310, 311; names of those at Machias, 312; deserters from, 314, 319, 320; in the Bay of Fundy, 314; to attack Machias, 314; the Three Brothers hired and seized, 316; the British may winter at Falmouth, 317; the enemy at No. Yarmouth, 319; same at Casco Bay, 319; captured by the British in Boston harbor, 320; report of committee in Congress with regard to those captured, 320; carried ammunition to Nova Scotia for Indians, 323; at Annapolis, collecting stores for Boston, 323; Wordwell's sloop captured, 331, 335; Jones' vessel seized, 332, 334; reasons for the capture to be enquired into, 334; powder for privateers, 337; the enemy's to be driven away, 342; Mowatt to destroy, 342, 343; Perkin's sloop chased by a brigantine, 345; seized by the Viper, 358; others seized, 358, 359; equipment of the Viper, 359, 375; the Machias privateers absent, 359; Indians to be sent home on, 364; said to be in the Canada river, 368; captured near Gouldsborough, 374, 376; the Viper blockaded the coast, 375; none to convey Indian recruits, 375, 377; crews not paid, 376; Shaw's promise, 376; privateers taken from the eastern parts, 382; should be sent to protect the coast, 383; those captured going from

Vessels, *continued*.
  Machias, 385; prize at Falmouth, 388; prize at Salem, 388; seized by the recruits and people of Cumberland, 395; man-of-war off Cumberland, 395; privateers can be sent from Nova Scotia, 395; success of the British sloop Gage, 414; sailed up the St. Johns river, 414; sent to the Bay of Fundy, 416; to proceed to St. Johns river, 417; to carry forces, 420, 421; taken from Halifax, 431, 435; attempt to capture a sloop, 432; Vulture attacked, 439; at St. Johns, 440; despatched from New York to cruise off the coast of Maine, 441, 442: the armament of the same, 441.
  Alfred, the, 421.
  Ambuscaid, the, 421.
  Cauceaux, the, 243, 248, 250, 319.
  Diligent, the, 312, 326, 337, 374, 376.
  Falmouth Packet, the, 315, 320, 324.
  Gage, the, 414.
  Gammon, the, 366.
  Grayhound, the, 340.
  Halifax, the, 319.
  Infidel, 312.
  Liberty, the, 337.
  Loyal Briton, the, 310, 312.
  Machias Liberty, the, 312, 314, 337.
  Mainsheat, the, 416.
  Margaritta, the, 283, 302, 312.
  Marlin, the, 358.
  Mermaid, the, 441.
  Molly, the, 263, 264.
  Polly, the, 264, 276, 277.
  Province Galley, the, 34.
  Ranger, the, 64.
  Semitry, the, 319.
  Senegal, the, 288, 289.
  Somerset, the, 314.
  Spitfire, the, 319.
  Stanley's, 323.
  Tartar, the, 314.
  Tatamanouch, the, 312.
  Three Brothers, the, 316.
  Tythena, 331, 335.
  Unity, the, 312, 385.
  Viper, the, 358, 359, 374, 375.
  Vulture, the, 432, 439.
Viles, Joseph, signed Fort Powall petition, 57.
Vinall, David, one of the Arundel

Vinall, *continued*.
  Committee of Correspondence, 267.
Virginia, 290.
Vote on petition of Ichabod Jones, 80.

W

WADSWORTH, ——, signed Muscongus petition, 18.
Abiel, ditto, 18.
Waite, Benjamin, as a witness, 9; his losses at the burning of Falmouth, 308.
  John, his losses at the burning of Falmouth, 308.
  John 2nd., signed St. Paul's parish petition, 192; his losses at the burning of Falmouth, 308; submitted the list of Falmouth losses to Congress, 310, 394.
  Stephen, signed St. Paul's parish petition, 192; his losses at the burning of Falmouth, 309.
Waldo, Francis, collector, 146; signed St. Paul's parish petition, 192; letter of, 8.
  Brigadier Samuel, his heirs sold land, 196, 231.
  Colonel Samuel, his regiment sent to St. Georges, 64.
Waldoborough, town meeting called in, 267; Committee of Correspondence in, 267; to aid and abide by Congress, 267; to send tax to Gorham, 267; home of Thomas Waterman, 360, 361.
Walker, Benjamin, signed Andover petition, 20.
  George, his bill for guarding prisoners, 303.
  Capt. & Lieut. John, captured at Shepperday, 294, 295; a prisoner sent to Machias, 394; a countryman who joined the regulars, 395.
  Thomas, 239, 241.
  Timothy Jr., purchased a township, 213, 214; the same proved to be in New Hampshire, 213; threatened with ejectment, 213; obliged to repurchase the land, 214; petitioned for a new grant, 214; new grant to, 215; petition of, 212, 214.
Wall, John, represented Falmouth in Congress, 355.

Walles, William, subscribed for the Canada expedition, 365.
Walton, William, letter of, 322.
Wampum, 431, 432, 436.
Ward, Col. ——, member of the General Court, 20.
Artemus, 228, 414.
Wardwell, Jeremiah, sailed from Majorbagwaduce, 335; captured, 335; deposition and oaths of, 332, 335.
John, signed Andover petition, 20.
Warner, Col. ——, with Gates, 442.
Gen. Jonathan, appoined a brigadier general, 438; letter of, 438.
Warren, ——, his land a boundary, 102, 106.
Daniel, signed Fort Pownall petition, 57.
George, his losses at the burning of Falmouth, 307.
Gilbert, evidence of, 51.
James, speaker of the General Court, 193, 293, 296, 297, 299, 336, 344, 346, 355, 369, 374, 388, 407, 414, 422.
James Jr., declaration of, 51.
John, signed Machias memorial, 115.
Dr. Joseph, 241, 270, 273, 283.
Peter, his losses at the burning of Falmouth, 308.
Washington, George, 317, 322, 324, 362, 363, 364, 367, 368, 431.
Waterhouse, William, his losses at the destruction of Falmouth, 309.
Watertown, 246, 254, 261, 269, 270, 274, 277, 284, 287, 291, 295, 296, 297, 298, 305, 310, 316, 320, 321, 322, 333, 337, 339, 344, 346, 350, 354, 378, 386.
Watson, Abraham, 296.
Colman, his loss at the destruction of Falmouth, 305.
William, overpaid, 322.
Watt, John, 302.
Watts, Edward, signed petition of St. Paul's parish, 192; his loss at the destruction of Falmouth, 308.
Henry, justified the conduct of Stephen Jones, 292.
Waugh, Robert, signed Pondstown petition, 119.
Weare, Joseph, selectman of York, 92.
Meshech, letters of, 442, 443, 444.

Webb, Jonathan, signed petition of St. Paul's parish, 192.
Samuel, signed Freetown petition, 17.
Webster, ——, ditto, 17.
Mr. ——, member of the General Court, 215, 219.
Daniel, signed Freetown petition, 17, 217.
Joshua, signed Machias petition, 41; assaulted a justice of the peace, 113, 114.
Welch, David, signed Sebascodegin petition, 77.
Weld, Moses, selectman of Sturbridge, 337.
Wellfleet, 344, 379.
Wells, a boundary, 67, 68; home of Ebenezer Sawyer, 274; representative of, in Congress, 274; Littlefield's letter dated at, 400.
Josiah, signed Sebascodegin petition, 76.
Wenigeburla, Jacob, a member of the Committee of Correspondence, 267.
Wentworth, Gov. Benning, 12, 13.
Ebenezer, 181.
Gov. John, 49, 50, 51, 59, 63, 151, 152; letters of, 11, 47, 48.
Wescutt, William, signed Fort Pownall petition, 57.
West, Capt. ——, 414, 427, 429, 431, 432, 435, 439, 440.
West Indies, the, 14, 344, 346.
West, Jabez, justified the conduct of Stephen Jones, 292; his bill for guard duty, 302.
Weston, 276.
Weymouth, 322.
Whale boats, 427, 433.
Wheat, 241, 381.
Wheeler, Henry, his loss at the destruction of Falmouth, 308.
James, justified the conduct of Stephen Jones, 292.
Whitcomb, John, member of the Provincial Congress, 319, 387.
White, Mr. ——, a prisoner, 432.
Benjamin, a member of the General Court, 301.
George, signed the certificate of Ilsley, 386.
Robert, signed Suncook petition, 205.
Samuel, councilor, 1, 42, 88.
Whiting, Jonathan, selectman, signed Winthrop petition, 191.

Whitman, } ——, an innholder at
Whitmore, } Newbury, 60, 61.
Col. ——, 228.
John, a township granted to, 227.
Whitney, James, signed Suncook petition, 205.
Whitridge, Capt. James, 14.
Whittemore, Rev. ——, 206.
  Abraham, signed Bowdoinham letter, 291.
  John, signed Suncook petition, 205.
  Samuel, his land claimed by New Hampshire, 220; he had begun a settlement, 221; desired a new grant, 221; received a new grant, 221, 222; petition of, 220.
Whittier, Ebenezer, deposition of, 274; oath of, 275; will change coin for bills, 374.
Wieland, John, signed Machias petition, 41.
Wieman, Vallentino, signed Falmouth petition, 79.
Wilber, Samuel, signed Freetown petition, 217.
Wiley, } Alexander, signed Booth-
Wylie, } bay petition, 171.
  John, ditto, 171.
  Neil, ditto, 171.
  Robert, ditto, 171.
  Robert Jr., ditto, 171.
  Samuel, ditto, 171.
  William, ditto, 171.
Willard, Capt. Aaron, reported on the examination of Spry's baggage, 326; advised examination, 327; letter received from, 327; letter of, 326.
William III, 36.
Williams, Leonard, land of claimed by New Hampshire, 109, 110; desired another grant, 109, 110; land granted to, 111, 112.
  Samuel, signed Sebascodegin petition, 76.
Willis, ——, his history of Portland, cited, 310.
Wilson, Alexander, signed Belfast petition, 198.
  Archibald, part owner of the Loyal Briton, 310.
  John, signed Andover petition, 20.
  Nathaniel, submitted list of Falmouth losses, 310, 394.
  Samuel, signed Fort Pownall petition, 58.

Winchenboch, Freidrich, signed Broad Bay petition, 15.
Windham, a boundary, 22, 23; taxes to be levied for roads, 71; taxes for other expenses, 71, 72, 73, 74; sale of delinquent's lands in, 73; William Elder (1771) assessor in, 210; valuation oath of assessor, not legal, 211; Grashom brought action against the assessors, 211, 212; the forfeiture of assessors remitted, 212; men enlisted in, 333.
Windsor, 263, 264, 265, 273, 365.
Wingate, Snell, signed Narragansett petition, 160.
Winslow, incorporated, 128; named for Gen. John Winslow, 128; land and fort in, leased to Ballard, 242, 407, 409; number of families in, 265; people of, largely subsisted on fish, 265; in need of ammunition, 265; town voted to adhere to the resolutions of Congress, 265; members of Committee of Correspondence, 265; Ballard took possession of Fort Halifax, 407, 409; Ballard refused to deliver the property to the civil authorities, 408, 409, 410; illegal proceedings, 408; authorities desired instructions, 408, 409, 410; Bowdoin received letters from, 361; letters of, 265, 407.
  Isaac, owned an island at the mouth of the Penobscot, 273.
  Gen. John, his land a boundary, 124; a town named for, 128.
  Nathaniel, signed Freetown petition, 217.
Winthrop, only two families at, 1767, 190; farming a dependency in, 190; desired an exemption of taxes, that a meeting house could be built, 191; named for Gov. John Winthrop, 128; incorporated, 128; petition, 190.
  Capt ——, of Boston, 333.
  Gov. John, a town named for, 128.
  John, member of the General Court, 362.
Wiswell, Rev. John, of Falmouth, taken a prisoner, 251.
  Thomas, one of the Committee of Correspondence, 267.

Wombly, Paul, signed Boothbay petition, 171.
Wood, *see* Fire wood.
 Abiel, can not wait on Congress, 258; his losses, 258; disapproved of the destruction of the tea, and some of the resolves of Congress, 258; a true patriot, 258; recommended coasters for carrying boards, 274; did not carry timber to the troops, 274; vilified Congress, 275; gave false reports, 275; letter of, 258.
 John, his loss at the burning of Falmouth, 307.
 Jonathan, as a witness, 237; his subscription for the Canada, expedition, 366.
Woodbridge, Col. ——, member of the General Court, 284, 340.
 Joseph, signed Narragansett petition, 160.
Woodbury, Peter, his loss at the burning of Falmouth, 306.
Woodman, David, ditto, 309.
 Joseph, signed Narragansett petition, 181.
 Joseph Jr., ditto, 131.
 Stephen, his loss at the burning of Falmouth, 309.
Woodrigh, Jonath., signed Machias petition, 41.
Wool, 272.
Woolens, 388.
Woodwich, 247.
Wordwell, Daniel, sailed from Majorbagwaduce, 331; his sloop captured, 331, 332; age, tonnage and value of the sloop, 332, 335.
Worthington, Col. —— member of the General Court, 134.
Woss, Capt. Wilmot, formerly of Martha's Vineyard, desired as a justice of the peace, 93.
Wright, Mr. ——, member of the General Court, 357.
Wye River, 135.
Wyer, David, signed St. Paul's parish petition, 192; his loss at the burning of Falmouth, 307.
 David Jr., signed St. Paul's parish petition, 192.
 Thomas, his loss at the burning of Falmouth, 307.
Wylie *see* Wiley.
Wyman, Joshua, signed Narragansett petition, 160, 175, 176.

Wyman, *continued.*
 Nathaniel, subscribed for the Canada expedition, 365.
 Ross, land granted to, 206, 208.
Wyth, ——, member of the Provincial Congress, 332.

X

X——, William, signed Freetown petition, 16.

Y

YARMOUTH, 322, 323, 324, 345, 347, 357; also called Cape Forschue.
Yawl, one captured, 320.
York, desired power to administer the estate of Josiah Bridges, 92; the people of to cross the bridge free at times, 120; home of the Rev. Samuel Lancton, 184; lost much by vessels belonging to, 305; desired abatement of taxes, 305; home of Ebenezer Beal, 314; representative from in Congress, 374; petition of, 91.
 Bridge, 119.
 County, 19, 25, 32, 67, 69, 98, 106, 110, 120, 135, 159, 176, 179, 181, 182, 184, 206, 263, 287, 321, 374, 410.
 Duke of, 207.
 Memorial of associated ministers of, 182.
 River, 119.
Young, Dr. Joseph, member of the Committee of Safety, 238, 332.
 Melatiah, his loss at the burning of Falmouth, 305.
 Nathaniel, signed Machias petition, 41.
 Stephen, signed Machias memorial, 115; justified the conduct of Stephen Jones, 292.
 Timothy, his bill for digging, 303.

——, ASA, signed Muscongus petition, 18.
——, Asel, signed Freetown petition, 17.
——, Carll, signed Broad Bay petition, 15.
——, D., signed Freetown petition, 17.
——, David, signed Broad Bay petition, 15; signed Freetown petition, 15.

——, Freidrich, signed Broad Bay petition, 15.
——, G., ditto, 15.
——, G. 2nd, ditto, 15.
——, Gottfried, ditto, 15.
——, Gr., ditto, 15.
——, J., ditto, 15.
——, J. 2d, ditto, 15.
——, Jacob ditto, 15.
——, Jacob 2d, ditto, 15.
——, Jacob 3d, ditto, 15.
——, Jacob 4th, ditto, 15.
——, Jacob 5th, ditto, 15.
——, James, signed Freetown petition, 17.
——, Johannes, signed Broad Bay petition, 15.
——, Johannes 2d, ditto, 15.
——, Johannes 3d, ditto, 15.
——, Johannes 4th, ditto, 15.
——, Johannes 5th, ditto, 15.
——, Johannes 6th, ditto, 15.
——, John, ditto, 15; signed Freetown petition, 16; signed Muscongus petition, 18; signed Penobscot letter, 269.
——, John 2d, signed Muscongus petition, 18.
——, Joseph, signed Freetown petition, 17; signed Pleasant River petition, 94.
——, Joshua, signed Muscongus petition, 18; signed Narragansett petition, 181.
——, Joshua 2d, signed Muscongus petition, 18.
——, M., signed Broad Bay petition, 15.
——, M. 2d, ditto, 15.
——, M. 3d, ditto, 15.
——, M. 4th, ditto, 15.
——, M. 5th, ditto, 15.
——, M. 6th, ditto, 15.
——, Martin, ditto, 15.
——, Richard, signed Muscongus petition, 18.
——, Robert, ditto, 18.
——, S., signed Broad Bay petition, 15.
——, Samuel, signed Muscongus petition, 18; signed Pleasant River petition, 94.
——, Solomon, signed Freetown petition, 17; justified the conduct of Stephen Jones, 295.
——, Solomon 2d, signed Freetown petition, 17.
——, Thomas, signed Pleasant River petition, 94.
——, Will, signed Broad Bay petition, 15.
——, William, signed Belfast petition, 198; justified the conduct of Stephen Jones, 292.

This Index was made by Mr. Edward Denham, of New Bedford, Mass.—J. P. B.

www.ingramcontent.com/pod-product-compliance
Lightning Source LLC
Chambersburg PA
CBHW071431300426
44114CB00013B/1395